The Old Bridge of Mostar and Increasing Respect for Cultural Property in Armed Conflict

International Humanitarian Law Series

VOLUME 40

The International Humanitarian Law Series is a series of monographs and edited volumes which aims to promote scholarly analysis and discussion of both the theory and practice of the international legal regulation of armed conflict.
The series explores substantive issues of International Humanitarian Law including,

- protection for victims of armed conflict and regulation of the means and methods of warfare
- questions of application of the various legal regimes for the conduct of armed conflict
- issues relating to the implementation of International Humanitarian Law obligations
- national and international approaches to the enforcement of the law and
- the interactions between International Humanitarian Law and other related areas of international law such as Human Rights, Refugee Law, Arms Control and Disarmament Law, and International Criminal Law.

The titles published in this series are listed at brill.com/ihul

The Old Bridge of Mostar and Increasing Respect for Cultural Property in Armed Conflict

by

Jadranka Petrovic

Department of Business Law and Taxation
Monash University

MARTINUS NIJHOFF PUBLISHERS

LEIDEN • BOSTON
2013

Library of Congress Cataloging-in-Publication Data

Petrovic, Jadranka.
The old bridge of Mostar and increasing respect for cultural property in armed conflict / by Jadranka Petrovic.
p. cm. -- (International humanitarian law series ; v. 40)
Includes bibliographical references and index.
ISBN 978-90-04-21028-8 (hardback : alk. paper) -- ISBN 978-90-04-23554-0 (e-book) 1. Cultural property--Protection (International law) 2. Cultural property--Protection--Law and legislation. 3. War--Bosnia and Hercegovina--Mostar. 4. Yugoslav War, 1991-1995. I. Title.
K3791.P48 2013
341.6'9--dc23

2012041628

ISSN 1389-6776
ISBN 978-90-04-21028-8 (hardback)
ISBN 978-90-04-23554-0 (e-book)

Printed on acid-free paper.

FSC www.fsc.org MIX Paper from responsible sources FSC® C109576

Printed by Printforce, the Netherlands

We note with sadness the passing of two esteemed members of our Editorial Advisory Board – Antonio Cassese (01 January 1937 - 21 October 2011) and Leslie C Green (06 November 1920 - 27 November 2011). Antonio and Leslie were outstanding scholars and enthusiastic supporters of the IHL Series and both will be sorely missed.

Table of Contents

Foreword

It is with great pleasure that I have accepted the task of writing a foreword to the present book, written by a woman whom I have met once and have ever since regarded as a friend. Let me explain. In September 2002, a lecture tour brought me to Australia. Professor Tim McCormack, my host in Melbourne, had organised for me to have interviews with a number of his students who were pursuing doctoral research in the Asia-Pacific Centre for Military Law. One of these students was Jadranka Petrovic, and her topic, 'Cultural Property as the Target: Rethinking the International Legal Protection of Cultural Property in the Event of Armed Conflict'. In our interview, she told me that this general subject actually had been inspired by an event she had witnessed: the long drawn-out attempt at destroying the Old Bridge of Mostar, in 'the former Yugoslavia'. In 1992, escaping from the internecine violence in her country, she had found refuge in Australia. Then, on 9 November 1993, the Old Bridge was finally destroyed.

As a European and a specialist in international humanitarian law, I too had been deeply affected by the events accompanying the break-up of Yugoslavia. Their impact had been enhanced when, from December 1992, I served for some months as the chairman of the Commission of Experts the UN Secretary-General had set up to investigate and collect evidence on the gross violations of humanitarian law that were being committed on all sides. And in May 1993, the establishment of the International Criminal Tribunal for the former Yugoslavia added a powerful new element to the means and methods for the enforcement of the international humanitarian law of armed conflict.

The ICTY was inaugurated in The Hague on 17 November 1993 – eight days after the final destruction of the Old Bridge. Was this a fortunate coincidence: would the Tribunal soon be dealing with this crime, as a particularly grave one on the never-ending list of gross violations we were daily hearing and reading about? For surely, was it not the case – were not people like Jadranka Petrovic and myself convinced – that an act like the wilful destruction of this irreplaceable, centuries-old monument would immediately be recognised as a major war crime deserving instant retribution?

This is where the book by Jadranka Petrovic serves as an eye-opener. In seven chapters, the author examines the innumerable blocks facing those wishing to see the perpetrators of such a criminal act brought to justice. What exactly had been happening in and around Mostar in the period leading up to the fatal event of 9 November 1993? Was there an armed conflict in the area, among which parties; who was doing what, with what plan or purpose; who could be held responsible – and criminally liable? What law was covering the event? Specifically, given the idea that the ICTY should base its judgments on customary law: had rules on the protection of cultural property against the vicissitudes of armed conflict come to belong to that body of law? What, in effect, is 'cultural property', and did the Old Bridge of Mostar fall under that heading? Again, given the difficulty of any prosecution before the Tribunal and the enormous mass of grave crimes committed against human beings, how much time and energy could reasonably be set aside for this particular crime?

At the moment of writing, the ICTY is on its way out. In the course of its relatively brief existence it dealt with innumerable cases of gross if not horrendous war crimes and crimes against humanity, committed against human beings as well as against objects such as houses, schools, churches and mosques. In two cases, mentioned in this book, the Tribunal actually focused exclusively on objects of world-class cultural property: the partial destruction of the Old Town of Dubrovnik, a UNESCO World Heritage site since 1979.

What, then, about the Old Bridge of Mostar? Its destruction has been touched upon more than once, but without being singled out as a major item. The event now still figures, again among many other items, on the long list of offences charged against the six defendants in the case of *The Prosecutor v Jadranko Prlić* et al. This case began as long ago as 2004 and at the moment of writing is still pending before the Tribunal. As Jadranka notes at the end of her book, the destruction of the Old Bridge is unlikely to figure largely in the judgment that some time soon will come to conclude the case.

The destruction of the Old Bridge of Mostar has been the shocking event that inspired the author to undertake a study into all the intricacies of fact and law involved in the case. Her research resulted, first, in a doctoral thesis which she successfully defended in 2008 at Melbourne School of Law; and then, in the present book. I am glad that I have been able to play some role in either event: on the first occasion, as external examiner; and this time, as the author of this foreword.

The subtitle of this book reads: 'Increasing respect for cultural property'. Objects falling under the heading of cultural property may occasionally be damaged or destroyed as an unintentional by-effect of an attack on a military objective (the famous notion of 'collateral damage'). They may also, as in the case of the Old Bridge, be specially selected for attack. Increased respect for the notion of cultural property will be necessary to diminish or prevent such damage. Information and education may in turn lead to such increased respect. I am convinced that the present book and, with that, the work and effort of Jadranka Petrovic will contribute to this goal.

Frits Kalshoven
Professor (em.) of
international humanitarian law

Acknowledgements

This book is the product of research conducted over a number of years in the area of international legal protection of immovable cultural property in armed conflict. The research has first resulted in a doctoral thesis carried out at The University of Melbourne and later culminated in a book manuscript completed at Monash University.

The book was made possible due to remarkable support by these two institutions, specifically, first by the Melbourne Law School and subsequently by the Department of Business Law and Taxation, Faculty of Business and Economics, Monash University (BLT), which not only provided the financial backing in the form of scholarship, grant and paid work, but also made available the excellent research support program and assistance with editing and proofreading. I would like to thank all academic and administrative staff at both institutions with whom I had the privilege to interact during both my candidature and my work on the book manuscript for their kindness, help and encouragement.

In particular, I am deeply grateful to my thesis supervisor, Professor Tim McCormack, for his outstanding guidance, unfailing understanding and incredible amount of gentle patience over the years. I was exceptionally fortunate and, indeed, greatly honoured to work under his supervision and to have such a renowned legal scholar and a remarkable person as a mentor at the Melbourne Law School.

My special thanks to Professors Rick Krever and Christopher Arup for sharing their knowledge, wisdom and inspiration, and for their continuous support relevant to my research generally and for their scholarly interest in completing this book in particular. I have been extremely privileged to work under these two distinguished legal scholars' mentorship at Monash University.

My deepest gratitude goes to Peter Mellor for his superb assistance with the book manuscript editing. I am most obliged for his linguistic input and for his efficiency and kindness. He is the best assistant one can possibly have.

I am also very grateful to Professor Dianne Otto, Dr Helen Durham, Dr Nicola Henry, Dr Anthony McCosker and Rebecca Hughes for their helpful comments on earlier draft chapters.

The stalwart integrity, intellectual force, and collegial generosity of people associated with the Asia Pacific Centre for Military Law at the Melbourne Law

School and BLT, as well as the friendly and pleasant staff at the Melbourne Law Library and the Monash Library Caulfield made my work on this research project smoother and even more memorable.

A number of scholars external to the Melbourne Law School and BLT have shown interest in this project. I am especially indebted to Professor Frits Kalshoven, Professor Patrick Boylan, Dr Esther Charlesworth, Dr András Riedlmayer, Dr Jean-Marie Henckaerts, Suzanne Schairer, Jon Calame, Jan Hladík and Hirad Abtahi for their valuable comments and most generous help with literature and with various other research-related matters. I will be appreciative of their time and effort forevermore.

My other informed and supportive colleagues and friends also deserve to be thanked here, among them, Dr Jackson Maogoto, Dr Nicole Schlesinger, Jon Cina, Dr Hayli Millar, Dr Ben Clarke, Peter Little, Heidi Bacher, Michael Foley, Barbara Goulborn, Rod McRae, Jenny McFadden and Dianne Costello for drawing my attention to various research sources, for providing me with contact details of relevant people, and generally, for always being there for me.

I owe much gratitude to my editor, Lindy Melman, at Brill, Martinus Nijhoff Publishers, The International Humanitarian Law Series, for her unmatched help with my numerous queries, and for her encouragement, patience and kindness.

Finally, I warmly thank those who lived with me and my work in closer proximity, especially my beloved Muffin whose devotion and reliable company played a significant role in reaching the conclusion of this journey, and those who despite the years of geographical distance have never stopped believing in me, above all to my parents and my wonderful sister, to whom I dedicate this book, with love, gratitude and respect.

Abbreviations

ABH	Army of Bosnia and Herzegovina
Additional Protocol I	*Protocol I Additional to the Geneva Conventions of 12 August 1949*
Additional Protocol II	*Protocol II Additional to the Geneva Conventions of 12 August 1949*
BH	Republic of Bosnia and Herzegovina
BH War Crimes Chamber	War Crimes Chamber within the State Court of Bosnia and Herzegovina
CA	Army of the Republic of Croatia
COE	Council of Europe
Croatia	Republic of Croatia
ECMM	European Community Monitoring Mission
HB	Croatian Community Herceg-Bosna / Croatian Republic Herceg-Bosna
HDZ	Croatian Democratic Union
HVO	Croatian Defence Council
ICC	International Criminal Court
ICJ	International Court of Justice
ICRC	International Committee of the Red Cross
ICTR	International Criminal Tribunal for Rwanda
ICTY	International Criminal Tribunal for the former Yugoslavia
IHL	International Humanitarian Law
IMT	International Military Tribunal (Nürnberg)
IMTFE	International Military Tribunal for the Far East
1954 Convention	*Convention for the Protection of Cultural Property in the Event of Armed Conflict*
1954 Regulations	*Regulations for the Execution of the Convention for the Protection of Cultural Property in the Event of Armed Conflict*
1954 Protocol	*First Protocol to the 1954 Convention for the Protection of Cultural Property in the Event of Armed Conflict*

1999 Protocol	*Second Protocol to the 1954 Convention for the Protection of Cultural Property in the Event of Armed Conflict*
NATO	North Atlantic Treaty Organization
OTP	Office of the Prosecutor of the ICTY
SFRY	Socialist Federal Republic of Yugoslavia (the former Yugoslavia)
UDCD	*Universal Declaration on Cultural Diversity*
UNESCO	United Nations Educational, Scientific and Cultural Organization
UN	United Nations
UNMIK	United Nations Interim Administration Mission in Kosovo
UNPROFOR	United Nations Protection Force
YA	Yugoslav Army (National Army of the former Yugoslavia)

Chapter 1

Introduction

I Area of Research

Cultural property forms part of a broader concept of cultural heritage. Whereas the latter covers both tangibles (such as monuments and artworks) and intangibles (such as folklore and story-telling), the former embodies only material aspects of the culture and comprises unique, human-made (as opposed to nature-made) objects which are of archaeological, ethnographical, historical, artistic, architectural and other special interest. This could include books, archives, paintings, statues, scientific collections and architectural structures. Each of the world's peoples makes its contribution to the culture of the world as a whole. Cultural property, as a representative of the material traits of a racial, religious, or social group, belongs not only to the cultural heritage of the people most immediately concerned with it, but also to the cultural heritage of all humankind. This dual character of cultural property – national and international – doubles the importance of its preservation.

Despite the importance of protecting cultural property, such property is always at risk. Its survival is threatened by both nature-based and human-caused disasters. While natural disasters such as earthquakes and floods take a terrible toll on cultural property,[1] it is disasters provoked by people, including theft and pillage, urban development, neglect and the depredations of armed conflict that most seriously endanger cultural property. Various peacetime activities of human origin, such as illegal excavation of archaeological sites and dismembering of monuments, put cultural property in a weak position. However, it is armed conflict – the most destructive of all human agencies – that makes such property particularly vulnerable. Material culture is among the first, yet most easily forgotten, victims of warfare.

---

1 Earthquakes that in the 1960s destroyed the historic Moroccan town of Agadir and floods which in the same decade damaged Venice and the medieval and renaissance heart of Florence in Italy are just two examples of nature-based forces that endanger the survival of cultural property.

II Focus

Throughout history, many attempts have been made to curb the losses of precious cultural treasures during times of armed conflict, including various legal endeavours made at both national and international level. This book is concerned with the legal protection of cultural property in the event of armed conflict. Given the dual character of cultural property – national-international – a comprehensive study of this legal protection at both national and international level deserves close attention. However, such a study would be far too ambitious to fall within the scope of a research project of the size of this book. This book limits itself to the study of legal protection at the international level. Whereas the fate of movable cultural property, such as artworks and important collections of books, are worthy of investigation, to make it a more manageable project, this book further limits itself to the research of the destruction of immovable cultural objects, such as architectural structures of historic interest.

By focusing on the events in the territory of the former Yugoslavia during armed conflicts that occurred in the 1990s, the book examines the legal implications of the deliberate targeting and destruction of immovable cultural property. Drawing on the relevant rules of international humanitarian law (IHL)[2] and the jurisprudence of the International Criminal Tribunal for the former Yugoslavia (ICTY),[3] the book analyses the incident of the deliberate targeting and destruction of the Old Bridge of Mostar, in Bosnia and Herzegovina (occasionally referred to as BH in this book), which occurred on 9 November 1993, during the Croat-Muslim conflict. This analysis is conducted from a normative point of view first, before enforcement efforts are examined in order to identify issues relating to international legal protection of cultural property arising from this particular incident.

But why this Bridge? As one commentator puts it, 'a bridge is, after all, not an organic being but a thing of height and distance and stress resistance, the product of someone at a table scratching out physical calculations, figuring the angles'.[4] I find bridges significant not only for their graceful arches across water or a mountain pass but also because of something deeper. A well-conceived bridge is a connection, firmly rooted, a dependable passage from yesterday to tomorrow and from one culture to another. The symbolism of connection is especially powerful in this region of the former Yugoslavia. Its multicultural

2 For discussion of IHL, see chapter four of this volume.

3 The International Tribunal for the Prosecution of Persons Responsible for Serious Violations of International Humanitarian Law Committed in the Territory of the Former Yugoslavia since 1991, Security Council Res 808, UN SCOR, 48th Sess, 3175 mtg, UN Doc S/RES/808 (1993) [ICTY].

4 James Yuenger, 'Crossing into History: War Brings Down a Bridge that Spanned Centuries and Linked Memories' *Chicago Tribune* Thursday, 25 November 1993, http://web2westlaw.com/.

milieu rests on links of this kind. Thus, the destruction of a bridge such as the Old Bridge can constitute a terrible violation of centuries of memory and leave people grieving at a level equated with the death of a loved one.[5]

III Research Gap

The destruction of the Old Bridge has been a significant issue not only for the city of Mostar but also across the Balkans and worldwide. Ever since its destruction, the Bridge has been the subject of numerous studies predominantly concerned with the process of reconstruction.[6] No research has provided a detailed analysis of the legal implications of the destruction of this Bridge from the perspective of international law.

The scale of cultural destruction in the former Yugoslavia has shocked the world and raised awareness of the importance of the protection of cultural property in times of armed conflict. While there has never before been so much popular interest in protecting cultural heritage, of which, as noted, cultural property is a constitutive part, the protection of immovable cultural treasures from the effects of warfare has not received adequate scholarly attention. An evergrowing body of literature on the subject of cultural property protection mainly concerns movable cultural property, predominantly covering its protection in peacetime

5 Ibid.

6 See, eg, Mirjana Belanov, 'The Mostar Bridge Conservation Issues' December 1995, http://www.gen-eng.florence.it/starimost/10_contr/belanov/belanov01.htm; Andrew Herscher, 'Remembering and Rebuilding in Bosnia: An architect argues that the right blend of reconstruction can help revive multiculturalism' (1998) 5 *Transitions*, http://www.haverford.edu/relg/sells/mostar/Mostartransition.html; Sarah Meharg, 'Identicide and Cultural Cannibalism: Warfare's Appetite for Symbolic Place' (2001) 33 *Peace Research Journal* 89, also available at, http://www.gen-eng.florence.it/starimost/10_contr/meharg/meharg01.htm; Amir Pašić, *The Old Bridge (Stari Most) in Mostar* (1995) [*The Old Bridge*]; Amir Pašić, 'Mostar in Bosnia and Herzegovina', Mostar 2004 Workshop, http://www.mostar2004ircica.org/files/95/95lecture2.html [2004 Workshop]. See also, Nicholas Adams, 'Architecture as the Target' (1993) 52 *Journal of the Society of Architectural Historians* 389; Bogdan Bogdanović, *Grad i smrt* (*City and Death*) (1994) [*City and Death*]; Michael Sells, *The Bridge Betrayed: Religion and Genocide in Bosnia* (1996); Martin Coward, 'Community as Heterogeneous Ensemble: Mostar and Multiculturalism', paper prepared for the ISA Annual Convention, Chicago, 21-24 February 2001, Panel SB05: Methodological Options, Political Consequences, Saturday, 24 February, 2001, 10.30), http://www.isanet.org/archive/coward.html; Carl Grodach, 'Reconstructing Identity and History in Post-War Mostar, Bosnia-Herzegovina' (2002) 6 *City* 61.

and mainly focuses on art theft and illegal excavations.[7] Where the protection of cultural property in armed conflict is considered, it is movable rather than immovable cultural property that is at the centre of scholarly attention.[8] As far as immovable cultural property is concerned, emphasis is mainly placed on religious property, which does not necessarily constitute 'cultural' property within the meaning of the relevant norms of IHL.[9] But even then the subject is dealt with mainly in general terms. In recent years, scholarly writing on the subject of international protection of cultural property in armed conflict generally (irrespective of the type of cultural property) has been extensive and detailed, but emphasis has mainly been placed on the relevant IHL instruments.[10] Legal lit-

7 See, eg, Paul Bator, 'An Essay on the International Trade in Art' (1982) 34 *Stanford Law Review* 275; John Moustakas, 'Group Rights in Cultural Property: Justifying Strict Inalienability' (1989) 74 *Cornell Law Review* 1179; Phyllis Messenger (ed), *The Ethics of Collecting Cultural Property: Whose Culture? Whose Property?* (1989); Jeanette Greenfield, *The Return of Cultural Treasures* (1989); Lyndel Prott and Patrick O'Keefe, *Law and the Cultural Heritage* Vol 3: *Movement* (1989); David Murphy, *Plunder and Preservation: Cultural Property Law and Practice in the People's Republic of China* (1995); Lisa Borodkin, 'The Economics of Antiquities Looting and a Proposed Legal Alternative' (1995) 95 *Columbia Law Review* 377; Marilyn Phelan, 'Reclamation of Cultural Property on the International Front: Is Home Where the Art Is?' (1998) 5 *Sports and Entertainment Law Journal* 31; John Merryman, *Thinking About the Elgin Marbles: Critical Essays on Cultural Property, Art and Law* (2000) [*Elgin Marbles*].

8 See, eg, Andrea Gattini, 'Restitution by Russia of Works of Art Removed from German Territory at the End of the Second World War' (1996) 7 *European Journal of International Law* 67; Elissa Myerowitz, 'Protecting Cultural Property during a Time of War: Why Russia Should Return Nazi-Looted Art' (1997) 20 *Fordham International Law Journal* 1961; Stephen Matyk, 'The Restitution of Cultural Objects and the Question of Giving Direct Effect to the Protocol to the Hague Convention for the Protection of Cultural Property in the Event of Armed Conflict 1954' (2000) 9 *International Journal of Cultural Property* 341.

9 See, eg, Sells, above n 6; András Riedlmayer, 'Killing Memory: The Targeting of Bosnia's Cultural Heritage', Testimony presented at a Hearing of the Commission on Security and Cooperation in Europe, US Congress, 4 April 1995, Community of Bosnia Foundation, http://www.haverford.edu/relg/sells/killing.html ['Killing Memory']; Gregory Mose, 'The Destruction of Churches and Mosques in Bosnia-Herzegovina: A Rights-Based Approach to the Protection of Religious Cultural Property' (1996) 3 *Buffalo Journal of International Law* 180.

10 See, eg, Patrick Boylan, *Review of the Convention for the Protection of Cultural Property in the Event of Armed Conflict* (1993) [*Review*]; David Meyer, 'The 1954 Hague Cultural Property Convention and its Emergence into Customary International Law' (1993) 11 *Boston University International Law Journal* 349; Jean-Marie Henckaerts, 'New Rules for the Protection of Cultural Property in Armed Conflict' (1999) No. 835 *International Review of the Red Cross* 593 ['New Rules']; Jan Hladík, 'The 1954 Hague Convention for the Protection of Cultural Property in the Event of Armed Conflict and the Notion of Military Necessity' (1999) No.

erature on the subject of justice for cultural property-related war crimes is also limited,[11] although there is a very rich body of scholarly writing on the subject of international justice for war crimes generally.[12]

IV Aims and Scope

The general objective of this book is to highlight the importance of respect for immovable cultural property in times of armed conflict. The central research question of this study is whether the IHL regime on cultural property adequately responds to the deliberate targeting and destruction of cultural property in armed conflict. In considering the adequacy of the normative (IHL) regime

---

835 *International Review of the Red Cross* 621 ['Military Necessity']; Thomas Desch, 'The Second Protocol to the 1954 Hague Convention for the Protection of Cultural Property in the Event of Armed Conflict' (1999) 2 *Yearbook of International Humanitarian Law* 63; Roger O'Keefe, 'The Meaning of "Cultural Property" under the 1954 Hague Convention' (1999) XLVI *Netherlands International Law Review* 26; A. P. V. Rogers, *Law on the Battlefield* (1996), 84-106; Jan Hladík, 'Reporting System under the 1954 Convention for the Protection of Cultural Property in the Event of Armed Conflict' (2000) No. 840 *International Review of the Red Cross* 1001 ['Reporting System'].

11 See, eg, James Nafziger, 'International Penal Aspects of Protecting Cultural Property' (1985) 19 *International Lawyer* 835 ['Penal Aspects']; Cherif Bassiouni, 'Reflections on Criminal Jurisdiction in International Protection of Cultural Property' (1983) 10 *Syracuse Journal of International Law and Commerce* 281 ['Reflections']; Matthew Lippman, 'Art and Ideology in the Third Reich: The Protection of Cultural Property and the Humanitarian Law of War' (1998) 17 *Dickinson Journal of International Law* 1; Hirad Abtahi, 'The Protection of Cultural Property in Times of Armed Conflict: The Practice of the International Criminal Tribunal for the Former Yugoslavia' (2001) 14 *Harvard Human Rights Journal* 1; Sanja Zgonjanin, 'Destruction of Libraries and Archives as a War Crime' (2005) 40 *Libraries and Culture* 128.

12 See, eg, Gunnar Theissen, 'Supporting Justice, Co-existence and Reconciliation after Armed Conflict: Strategies for Dealing with the Past' Berghof Research Centre for Constructive Conflict Management, http://www.berghof-handbook.net/articles/theissen_handbook.pdf (Copy on file with author); Kenneth Gallant, 'Jurisdiction to Adjudicate and Jurisdiction to Prescribe in International Criminal Courts' (2003) 4 *Villanova Law Review* 763; Ruti Teitel, 'Transitional Justice Genealogy' (2003) 16 *Harvard Human Rights Journal* 69; Raquel Aldana-Pindell, 'In Vindication of Justiciable Victims' Rights to Truth and Justice for State-Sponsored Crimes' (2002) 35 *Vanderbilt Journal of Transnational Law* 1399; Cherif Bassiouni, 'Former Yugoslavia: Investigating Violations of International Humanitarian Law and Establishing an International Criminal Tribunal' (1995) 18 *Fordham International Law Journal* 1191 ['Former Yugoslavia']; Diane Amann, 'Assessing International Criminal Adjudication of Human Rights Atrocities' in *Third World Legal Studies–2000-2003: Into the 21st Century: Reconstruction and Reparations in International Law* (2003) 169-181.

and the adequacy of the enforcement regime (specifically, the ICTY's response), based on the incident of the destruction of the Old Bridge, this book aims to highlight the importance of cultural property, including its universal value and its special character that distinguishes it from other types of property. The book draws attention to the importance of clarity in the relevant IHL rules protecting cultural property in armed conflict and highlights the significance of justice for cultural property-related war crimes.

Despite the proliferation of IHL norms on cultural property, these norms lack clarity. At the enforcement level, preference has been given to instruments that deal with cultural property only tangentially rather than to the more up-to-date specialist treaty on wartime protection of cultural property, namely, the *Hague Convention for the Protection of Cultural Property in the Event of Armed Conflict of 14 May 1954* (*1954 Convention*). This convention, together with the *Regulations* for its execution annexed to it (*1954 Regulations*) and its two protocols, *Protocol for the Protection of Cultural Property in the Event of Armed Conflict adopted on 14 May 1954* (*1954 Protocol*), and *Protocol for the Protection of Cultural Property in the Event of Armed Conflict adopted on 26 March 1999* (*1999 Protocol*), provides for the comprehensive protection of cultural property in times of armed conflict.[13] It is important to highlight this marginal approach to the specialist treaty particularly in light of the adoption of its *1999 Protocol*, which is designed to enhance wartime protection of cultural property. This *Protocol* significantly clarifies the relevant provisions of the specialist treaty, including those relating to respect for cultural property and to individual criminal responsibility.

The ICTY has already held accountable some individuals responsible for crimes involving cultural property. However, the Tribunal is expected to complete its work by 2014. With the establishment of both the permanent International Criminal Court (ICC)[14] and the mixed international/national

---

13 *Convention for the Protection of Cultural Property in the Event of Armed Conflict*, 14 May 1954, 249 UNTS 240 (entered into force 7 August 1956) [*1954 Convention*]. As at 4 February 2012, there were 123 State parties. *Regulations for the Execution of the Convention for the Protection of Cultural Property in the Event of Armed Conflict* [*1954 Regulations*] are annexed to the *Convention* and considered an integral part thereof. The *1954 Convention* is supplemented by two protocols. The first of these is the *Protocol for the Protection of Cultural Property in the Event of Armed Conflict*, 14 May 1954, 249 UNTS 358-64 (entered into force 7 August 1956) [*1954 Protocol*]. As at 4 February 2012, there were 100 State parties. The second is the *Protocol for the Protection of Cultural Property in the Event of Armed Conflict*, 26 March 1999, 38 ILM 769-82 (entered into force 9 March 2004) [*1999 Protocol*]. As at 4 February 2012, there were 61 State parties. For an updated list of State parties to the Convention and its Protocols, see, http://www.unesco.org/culture/laws/hague/html and http://www.icrc.org/ihl.nsf.

14 The ICC is a treaty-based court. It was established by its Statute, adopted in Rome, Italy, on 17 July 1998 at the UN Diplomatic Conference of Plenipotentiaries on the Establishment of an International Criminal Court. See, *Rome Statute of the*

War Crimes Chamber of the State Court of Bosnia and Herzegovina, it remains as important as ever to examine the treatment of cultural property by the ICTY and to draw attention to the lessons learnt. While the significance of the inclusion of cultural property in the jurisdiction of the ICTY is observed, the book discusses the obstacles to effective prosecution of crimes concerning cultural property in more detail.

The book also aims to provide an informative reference on the legal implications of failure to respect cultural property in armed conflict. While the book aims to draw attention to this subject generally, the several ICTY prosecutions and convictions of military commanders for crimes which, *inter alia*, concern cultural property make it particularly relevant to the military sector.

V Methodology

Initially, field research in Mostar was envisaged, during which in-depth interviews with selected officials and other interviewees were to be conducted and relevant documents of the Croatian Defence Council (HVO) and the Army of Bosnia and Herzegovina (ABH) reviewed. However, predominantly due to an inability to gain access to the necessary persons and documents and to secure and maintain cooperation from individuals, it was necessary for this research mode to be abandoned. Instead, a combination of case study and documentary analysis has been employed.

The research relies on various sources of data collection, including documentary analysis, records and reports. The book analyses a range of data, including various UN reports and documents, reports and documents of other international bodies and of regional organisations, notably, the *Information Reports of the Committee on Culture and Education, Parliamentary Assembly of the Council of Europe on war damage to the cultural heritage in Croatia and Bosnia and Herzegovina* (*COE Reports*),[15] and ICTY indictments, judgments and other decisions, and transcripts. While ICTY transcripts in several cases have been

---

International Criminal Court, UN Diplomatic Conference of Plenipotentiaries on the Establishment of an International Criminal Court, UN Doc A/CONF 183/9 (17 July 1998) 2187 UNTS 3 (entered into force 1 July 2002), [*ICC Statute*], http://www.igc.org/icc/Rome/html.

15 In the summer of 1992, expert rapporteurs of the Committee on Culture and Education of Parliamentary Assembly of Council of Europe (COE) began to prepare reports on the wartime destruction of cultural property in Croatia and Bosnia and Herzegovina. Eleven of these reports have been published. Of particular interest here are the following reports: *First Information Report*, doc 6756, 2 February 1993; *Second Information Report*, doc 6869, 17 July 1993; *Third Information Report*, doc 6904, 20 September 1993; *Fourth Information Report*, doc 6999, 19 January 1994; *Fifth Information Report*, doc 7070, 12 April 1994; *Seventh Information Report*, doc 7308, 15 May 1995; and *Eighth Information Report*, doc 7341, 28 June 1995 [*COE Reports*].

considered, the transcripts in the case *Prosecutor v Jadranko Prlić et al*[16] (*Prlić* or *Prlić* case) have been analysed in depth because this case, *inter alia*, concerns the destruction of the Old Bridge.

Whereas the jurisprudence, as well as statutory provisions, of other international criminal tribunals, such as that of the Nürnberg International Military Tribunal (IMT), is also considered, albeit only tangentially, it is the ICTY jurisprudence with which this book is predominantly concerned and on which the book relies throughout. The reliance on the ICTY jurisprudence is primarily due to the fact that the book considers the enforcement of IHL through this particular Tribunal, specifically its response to the destruction of the Old Bridge. The case which, among other charges, involves the charge covering the destruction of the Old Bridge (the *Prlić* case) is already being dealt with by this Tribunal. Thus, the focus of the book (i.e., the ICTY's response to the destruction of the Old Bridge) makes the jurisprudence of the ICTY very relevant and explains the reliance on such jurisprudence. Although the ICTY sets precedent only for its own use its jurisprudence has been considered by other tribunals as well. Additionally, this Tribunal is the only international criminal adjudication body that in recent times has had the opportunity, and abundant occasion, to deal with serious violations of the law concerning the protection of cultural (and religious) property. While extensive research into various sources has been conducted, space constraints also determined the concentration on the ICTY jurisprudence throughout the book.[17]

Some information derives from scholarly writing and an extensive archive of media reports. The latter, among other information, sheds light on the motives behind the destruction of the Old Bridge and on the effects, domestically and internationally, of the destruction of this particular object of cultural property. An additional insight has been made into the matters under consideration through following closely (via the Internet) proceedings in the *Prlić* trial.

Throughout the research, informal contact with a number of scholars and others, whose work relates to cultural property, including Professor Frits

16 *The Prosecutor v Jadranko Prlić, Bruno Stojić, Slobodan Praljak, Milivoj Petković, Valentin Ćorić and Berislav Pušić*, Case No. IT-04-74-T [*Prlić* or *Prlić* case]. See also *Prosecutor v Jadranko Prlić, Bruno Stojić, Slobodan Praljak, Milivoj Petković, Valentin Ćorić and Berislav Pušić*, Amended Indictment, 16 November 2005, Case No. IT-04-74-AU (Initial Indictment, 4 March 2004 (kept confidential until its unsealing on 2 April 2004)) [*Prlić* Indictment]. Note that, although the ICTY sets precedents only for its own use, its jurisprudence has also been considered by other tribunals. See, eg, *Application of the Convention on the Prevention and Punishment of the Crime of Genocide (Bosnia and Herzegovina v Yugoslavia (Serbia and Montenegro))*, Merits, Judgement of 26 February 2007, ICJ Reports [2007], para 344 [*Application of the Genocide Convention*].

17 Note that earlier drafts contained a very detailed discussion on matters with which the book is concerned but due to word limitations they had to be restructured and cut back.

Kalshoven, Professor Patrick Boylan and Dr András Riedlmayer, has also provided important information and clarified certain matters of relevance to this study. Contact with Dr Esther Charlesworth (Architects without Borders) and Mr Jon Calame (World Monuments Fund), who have made a number of visits to Mostar and the area of the Old Bridge after the conflict, has been of particular interest as it provided information on the overall atmosphere of the post-war divided city of Mostar.

Since this book focuses only on one particular instance of the destruction of cultural property in armed conflict, it is difficult to assess in more general terms the adequacy of the IHL response to the deliberate destruction of cultural property in armed conflict in the Balkans during the 1990s. Notwithstanding this, the destruction of the Old Bridge is emblematic of the tragedies wrought on priceless cultural objects across the Balkans. Consequently, as the book provides an in-depth analysis of this incident, some general conclusions with respect to the deliberate destruction of cultural treasures can be drawn.

The book draws attention to a number of issues arising from the Mostar Bridge incident. However, due to space constraints, it is not possible to examine them all as closely as necessary. However, it is hoped that the bibliographical references will encourage the reader to conduct further research.

VI Structure

In addition to the introduction and conclusion, this book comprises five major sections: preliminary matters; study of the Old Bridge; relevant IHL; application of the law to the destruction of the Old Bridge; and enforcement of IHL by the ICTY. The book is structured to provide an essential background to the nature of cultural property, as well as motives behind the deliberate targeting and destruction of such property and the major enforcement efforts made in the international domain, while also providing a detailed analysis of the legal implications of the deliberate destruction of cultural property in armed conflict, with an emphasis on the question of targeting and on the question of justice.

Chapter two first addresses the major difficulties involved in defining the term 'cultural property'. The chapter then highlights the importance of cultural property. After observing the benefits of cultural property, the chapter examines the underlying principles explaining why cultural property is considered sufficiently significant to warrant international protection. This examination is followed by a brief historic overview of the impact of armed conflict on cultural property. In its final section, the chapter considers the question of the importance of international justice in relation to wilful destruction of cultural property.

Chapter three provides factual background for the legal analysis in the subsequent chapters. This chapter first considers circumstances surrounding the building of the Old Bridge and highlights the value of the Bridge from the architectural and historical point of view. Thereafter, the chapter outlines the major motives behind the destruction of the Bridge. In its final section, the chapter examines the social impact of the destruction of the Bridge.

Chapter four outlines and discusses applicable IHL. The chapter first briefly surveys the development of rules protecting cultural property in armed conflict, focusing only on major internationally binding instruments. Then, in order to identify the relevant rules in the case of the Old Bridge, the chapter examines the nature of the Bosnia and Herzegovina Croat-Muslim conflict in Mostar. This examination is followed by a brief outline of the law applicable to the destruction of the Old Bridge.

Chapter five applies the relevant law to the destruction of the Old Bridge. This chapter provides a detailed analysis of the legal nature of the destruction of the Old Bridge, with an emphasis on the question of targeting. The chapter comprises two major parts. The first part concerns the application of the relevant law to the Old Bridge and the second part discusses issues arising from such application. The first part of this chapter examines whether the destruction of the Old Bridge was lawful. The examination focuses on two major questions: first, whether the Bridge was a protected object and second, whether the Bridge was a legitimate military target. The first question considers three major areas: the subject matter of protection under the relevant IHL instruments, measures of safeguarding and distinctive marking. The second question concerns the obligation to respect cultural property in armed conflict, in particular, the prohibition on use of cultural property for military purposes, prohibition on attacking cultural property and the exception of military necessity. The second part of this chapter identifies and discusses several major issues arising from the application of IHL to the destruction of the Old Bridge, including the problems pertaining to the definition of a military objective, difficulties surrounding the principle of distinction, guarding cultural property and the impact of state sovereignty on cultural property matters.

Chapter six concerns the question of justice for the destruction of the Old Bridge. It looks at how the law protecting cultural property in armed conflict is enforced through international criminal law mechanisms, specifically the ICTY. The chapter first surveys the relevant provisions of the applicable law relating to the question of sanctions. The chapter then outlines venues for prosecution relevant to the destruction of the Old Bridge. Thereafter, the chapter discusses the approach of the ICTY to cultural property. The discussion first focuses on the relevant provisions of the *ICTY Statute* and then applies those provisions to the case of the Old Bridge. In its final part, the chapter identifies and discusses the major issues arising from the enforcement of law relevant to the destruction of the Old Bridge.

Chapter seven evaluates whether international law at its normative and enforcement level responds adequately to the deliberate targeting and destruction of cultural property in armed conflict. The evaluation is centred on the Mostar Bridge incident.

Chapter 2

Setting the Context

I An Overview

When discussing the international legal protection of cultural property in armed conflict, the following subjects warrant immediate attention: the meaning of the term 'cultural property', the importance of cultural property, the impact of armed conflict on cultural property and the necessity of justice for wilful attacks directed against cultural property. With respect to the first subject, as the effectiveness of international legal instruments granting protection to cultural property is heavily dependent on a clear understanding of exactly what property they apply to and to what extent, it is essential to define unambiguously the term 'cultural property'. However, answering the threshold question of what property qualifies as 'cultural property' and how wide a spectrum of such property is eligible for international legal protection, is a priority challenge for international law purportedly designed to protect cultural property.[1] The

1 For discussion of the definition of cultural property see, eg, Sharon Williams, *The International and National Protection of Movable Cultural Property: A Comparative Study* (1978) 1; Karen Detling, 'Eternal Silence: The Destruction of Cultural Property in Yugoslavia' (1993) 17 *Maryland Journal of International Law and Trade* 41, 45-49; Stephanie Forbes, 'Securing the Future of Our Past: Current Efforts to Protect Cultural Property' (1996) 9 *Transnational Lawyer* 235, 238; Elissa Myerowitz, 'Protecting Cultural Property during a Time of War: Why Russia Should Return Nazi-Looted Art' (1997) 20 *Fordham International Law Journal* 1961, 1966; Claudia Caruthers, 'International Cultural Property: Another Tragedy of the Commons' (1998) 7 *Pacific Rim Law and Policy Journal* 143, 146-147; Frank Fechner, 'The Fundamental Aims of Cultural Property Law' (1998) 7 *International Journal of Cultural Property* 376, 377; Markus Müller, 'Cultural Heritage Protection: Legitimacy, Property, and Functionalism' (1998) 7 *International Journal of Cultural Property* 395, 398-402; Roger O'Keefe, 'The Meaning of "Cultural Property" under the 1954 Hague Convention' (1999) XLVI *Netherlands International Law Review* 26; Janet Blake, 'On Defining the Cultural Heritage' (2000) 49 *International and Comparative Law Quarterly* 61; Manlio Frigo, 'Cultural Property v Cultural Heritage: A "Battle of Concepts" in International Law?' (2004) 86 *International Review of the Red Cross* 367, 367, 375-76.

need to seek a working definition of cultural property has been one of the major pitfalls in implementing multilateral treaties covering the protection of cultural property.[2] For instance, the *1954 Convention*, the principal international legal instrument on the protection of cultural property in times of armed conflict, together with the *Regulations* for its execution and the two *Protocols* that supplement it (the *1954 Protocol* and the *1999 Protocol*), form a true code on the subject. Yet the Convention has been an almost forgotten instrument of IHL, partly because of a 'widespread though rarely confessed confusion over the nature and extent of the "cultural property" to which it applies'.[3] The confusion is amplified by the parallel existence of the imprecise and differing definitions of cultural property given in other international instruments governing the protection of cultural property.

Just as defining what is meant by the term 'cultural property' is fraught with difficulties, explaining why cultural property is considered important – that is, what significance is attached to it so as to distinguish it from other property and to legitimise its special international legal protection – is also a hurdle which must be overcome. Notwithstanding this, there is no disagreement about the necessity for preservation of cultural property. It is widely recognised that cultural property is property of a unique kind, the value of which transcends space and time. Because of the global and intergenerational interest in cultural property, and the various dangers to which cultural property is continuously exposed, protection of cultural property does not end at national borders but requires the concerted efforts of the entire international community. While everyone should be entitled to enjoy cultural property, each person should also have responsibility to protect it for his or her own benefit and for the benefit of future generations. This responsibility should firmly stand in peacetime and should not stop in times of armed conflict when cultural property is especially vulnerable.

As it is inherently destructive in nature, armed conflict always poses a danger to the survival of cultural property. Immovable cultural property is particularly at risk. While some of the damage is collateral, at times cultural property is targeted wilfully. Throughout history cultural property has been targeted in armed conflict for various reasons, such as the marking of victory, demoralisation of the enemy and enforcement of ethnic cleansing. Yet despite the international rules proscribing the deliberate targeting of cultural property which is not justified by military necessity, blatant attacks on cultural property go largely unpunished. They are accompanied by a centuries-long impunity at both national and international level. Save for a few exceptions, States have been perennially reluctant to prosecute war crimes involving cultural property. Cultural destruction has also been enveloped in silence at the international level. It was not until recently that the rules protecting immovable cultural property in armed conflict have been enforced by international criminal courts.

---

2 See Williams, ibid.

3 O'Keefe, above n 1, 27.

This chapter sets the context for the discussion in the remainder of this book. The chapter first discusses the major difficulties involved in defining the term 'cultural property'. The discussion focuses on questions of the differing terminology, the impact of the notion of sovereignty and the indeterminacy of the concept of culture. It then explores the underlying principles explaining why cultural property is considered sufficiently significant to warrant international protection. After observing the benefits of cultural property, the chapter looks at three major grounds for international protection of such property: a universal value of cultural property and the common concern for its survival; nationalist inclination; and the duty to respect cultural property and to transfer it to future generations. Thereafter, the chapter considers the impact of armed conflict on cultural property. A brief historical overview of the destruction of cultural property highlights the reasons why cultural property is targeted in armed conflict and points to the shift in attitude to deliberate attacks on cultural property. This is followed by examination of the question of justice for the wilful destruction of cultural property. The examination concentrates on the benefits of international justice and on the international efforts to prosecute crimes involving cultural property.

II The Meaning of the Term 'Cultural Property'

A The Differing Terminology

1 International Legal Instruments

The term 'cultural property' does not have a long history in international law. The term appears for the first time in the *1954 Convention* applying to tangible, human-made material objects, both movable and immovable, such as monuments, archaeological sites, works of art, archives and museums.[4] However, the term 'cultural property' is not widely used in international law. It occurs in some other international instruments, but rather inconsistently. A range of other terms, such as 'cultural objects', 'cultural heritage', 'the cultural heritage of peoples', 'cultural heritage of every people' and 'cultural heritage of all humankind', are also used in international instruments protecting cultural property often without being defined. The varied terminology, among as well as 'within' international legal instruments, may create confusion at the implementation level.

Knowing what objects are protected by international law is of the utmost importance, particularly in times of armed conflict. Deciding what does and does not constitute a legitimate military target, thereby facilitating appropriate decisions at the operational level by the military commanders, greatly depends on a clear definition of cultural property. Thus, a more consistent approach to

4 *Convention for the Protection of Cultural Property in the Event of Armed Conflict*, 14 May 1954, 249 UNTS 240 (entered into force 7 August 1956), art 1 [*1954 Convention*].

definitions, including terminology, is desirable.[5] As one legal scholar observes, '[t]his lack of a shared definition leads to misunderstandings and makes it possible to abuse the term for political aims'.[6]

2 Scholarly Writing

Given the lack of consistency to the definitional approach in international instruments, it is hardly surprising that scholarly writing on the subject also varies. While all agree that international law cannot protect everything, especially in times of armed conflict,[7] some scholars prefer a clear and narrow definition of cultural property, encompassing only the most important cultural objects,[8] whereas others take a more expansive approach allowing as many objects as are deemed worthy of preservation by each individual State.[9] Some also suggest that any object of importance to the cultural identity of a people or group should be afforded international legal protection.[10]

Views are also divided on the question of the nature of cultural property. While a majority of commentators consider that only physical human-made

---

5 See, eg, Patrick Boylan, *Review of the Convention for the Protection of Cultural Property in the Event of Armed Conflict* (1993), para G2 [*Review*]; Fechner, above n 1, 377-78.

6 Fechner, ibid 377.

7 See, eg, Lyndel Prott, 'Problems of Private International Law for the Protection of the Cultural Heritage' (1989) 217 *Recueil des cours* 215, 266 ['Problems']; John Moustakas, 'Group Rights in Cultural Property: Justifying Strict Inalienability' (1989) 74 *Cornell Law Review* 1179, 1225-26; Müller, above n 1, 400-402.

8 See Fechner, above n 1, 377-78 (arguing that an overly inclusive definition of cultural property weakens the very notion of cultural property as well as its legal protection, and suggesting that one should distinguish cultural objects of 'a small local' or national importance from those of truly global importance). See also A. P. V. Rogers, *Law on the Battlefield* (1996), 90; Williams, above n 1, 2.

9 See generally, O'Keefe, above n 1. See also, Maja Seršić, 'Protection of Cultural Property in Time of Armed Conflict' (1996) 27 *Netherlands Yearbook of International Law* 3, 9; Boylan, *Review*, above n 5, paras B3, B6; John Merryman, 'Two Ways of Thinking about Cultural Property' (1986) 80 *American Journal of International Law* 831, 837, fn 21 ['Two Ways'].

10 On this view, cultural property should not be designated by the nation-state but by a people or group because the state-centric approach to the designation does not necessarily take into account the importance of the cultural object, for instance, to the cultural identity of indigenous peoples or national minorities. See, Roger Mastalir, 'A Proposal for Protecting the "Cultural" and "Property" Aspects of Cultural Property under International Law' (1993) 16 *Fordham International Law Journal*, 1033, 1042. See also, Andrew Herscher and András Riedlmayer, *The Destruction of Cultural Heritage in Kosovo, 1998-1999: A Post-War Survey* (2001) fn 3 [*Kosovo Report*].

objects constitute cultural property,[11] there are some who see cultural property as also encompassing objects created by nature, such as natural landscapes, ecological areas and panoramas, and even intangibles like music, dance, handicrafts and religious rites.[12] This disagreement as to the nature of cultural property has produced different views on the appropriate terminology.

Some scholars use the term 'cultural property' in academic discussions.[13] Attempting to define this term, scholars refer, for instance, to a sub-group within the notion of cultural heritage,[14] to the concept comprising both property and cultural components,[15] or to cultural objects that nourish a sense of community.[16] Professor John Merryman defines cultural property as 'objects that embody the culture – principally archaeological, ethnographical and historical objects, works of art, and architecture', but allows that 'the category can be expanded to include almost anything made or changed by man'.[17] In his attempt to define cultural property, Geoffrey Lewis refers to the concept which

---

11 See, eg, John Merryman, 'The Public Interest in Cultural Property' (1989) 77 *California Law Review* 339, 341-42 ['Public Interest']; Müller, above n 1, 398; Fechner, above n 1, 378; Mastalir, ibid 1037; Detling, above n 1, 45; Prott, 'Problems', above n 7, 1207. See also Williams, above n 1, 2; Stanislav Nahlik, 'Protection of Cultural Property' in UNESCO, *International Dimensions of Humanitarian Law* (1988) 203, 206 ['Protection']; Geoffrey Lewis, 'The Return of Cultural Property' *The Royal Society of Arts Proceedings* (1981) 435, 436. Alexander Frid, 'The Common Heritage Doctrine and the Treatment of Cultural Property: History, Theory, and Practice' (1998) *University of California Undergraduate Research Journal* 2 http://www.urop.uci.edu/Journal98/AlexFrid/Body2.html [2].

12 See, eg, Douglas Thomason, 'Rolling Back History: The United Nations General Assembly and the Right to Cultural Property' (1990) 22 *Case Western Reserve Journal of International Law* 47; Forbes, above n 1, 239-40; Myerowitz, above n 1, 1967. For discussion of the tendency to include intangibles and environmental treasures in cultural property, see, eg, Fechner, ibid; Merryman, ibid; Boylan, *Review*, above n 5, paras G6, G9.

13 See, eg, Sarah Harding, 'Value, Obligation and Cultural Heritage' (1999) 31 *Arizona State Law Journal* 291, 297 (observing that most legal instruments and scholars utilise and define the term 'cultural property').

14 See Frigo, above n 1, 369. See also, Mary O'Connell, 'Occupation Failures and the Legality of Armed Conflict: The Case of Iraqi Cultural Property' Ohio State University Moritz College of Law Working Paper Series, Year 2004, Paper 6, hosted by The Berkeley Electronic Press (bepress), http://law.bepress.com/osulwps/moritzlaw/art6.

15 See Mastalir, above n 10, 1037-38.

16 See Moustakas, above n 7, 1184.

17 Merryman, 'Public Interest', above n 11, 341. Similarly, Ana Šljivić, 'Why Do You Think It's Yours? An Exposition of the Jurisprudence Underlying the Debate between Cultural Nationalism and Cultural Internationalism' (1998) 31 *George Washington Journal of International Law and Economics* 393, 398.

> represents in tangible form some of the evidence of man's origins and developments, his traditions, artistic and scientific achievements and generally the milieu of which he is part. The fact that this material has the ability to communicate, either directly or by association, an aspect of reality which transcends time or space gives it special significance and is therefore something to be sought after and protected.[18]

Other scholars prefer the term 'cultural heritage' as a broader concept that covers both tangibles and intangibles, namely,

> all that evidence of human life that we are trying to preserve: those things and traditions which express the way of life and thought of a particular society; which are evidence of its intellectual and spiritual achievements [and] which also embodies the notion of inheritance and handing on.[19]

There are also scholars who are more restrictive in their reading of the concept of cultural heritage. For instance, Markus Müller limits the meaning of cultural heritage to objects made by men and women and defined by them in terms of the meanings and functions that are assigned to objects.[20] Müller, however, utilises the term 'cultural property' without making the distinction between this term and the term 'cultural heritage'. Finally, there are those who challenge the exclusive use of the term 'cultural property' or that of 'cultural heritage',[21] by arguing that it might be more appropriate to use both terms in a strictly complementary way.[22]

Yet, 'cultural property' and 'cultural heritage' are not equivalent concepts in international law. Whereas cultural property encompasses only material cultural objects,[23] cultural heritage is a broader concept. To be precise, the concept

18 Lewis, above n 11, 436.

19 Lyndel Prott and Patrick O'Keefe, '"Cultural Heritage" or "Cultural Property"?' (1992) 1 *International Journal of Cultural Property* 307, 307. This view is consistent with the current discussion which focuses on the need for integrated management of tangible and intangible heritage and of information related to them, where 'cultural property' is seen as inadequate to encompass these necessarily closely related items. See, eg, Lyndel Prott, 'The International Movement of Cultural Objects' (2005) 12 *International Journal of Cultural Property* 225, 226 ['International Movement'].

20 See Müller, above n 1, 398.

21 See Frigo, above n 1, 377.

22 Ibid.

23 See, eg, *1954 Convention*, art 1; *Convention on the Means of Prohibiting and Preventing the Illicit Import, Export and Transfer of Ownership of Cultural Property*, 14 November 1970, 832 UNTS 231, art 1 (entered into force 24 April 1972) [*1970 Convention*].

of cultural heritage comprises two categories or sub-concepts: tangible cultural heritage and intangible cultural heritage. The two categories are interdependent[24] but also distinctive in character.[25] As Manlio Frigo correctly observes, cultural property is only 'a sub-group within the notion of cultural heritage'.[26]

In principle, the choice of terminology does not impact upon the substantive legal protection of cultural property in armed conflict. It should not be problematic if cultural property is also termed cultural heritage since cultural property forms part of cultural heritage in any event. Since the *1954 Convention*, the specialist and principal treaty on the protection of cultural property in armed conflict, uses the term 'cultural property' to determine exactly which portion of cultural heritage is to be accorded an enhanced means of international legal protection in armed conflict, and because this *Convention* is referred to throughout this book, the term 'cultural property' is preferred for the purposes of this book. Whenever it is used in this book, and unless indicated otherwise, the term 'cultural property' refers to tangible cultural heritage, and includes human-made objects of cultural significance.

But even if the problem of terminology is settled, there are still other questions that warrant close attention such as the question of who determines which objects constitute cultural property and what number of such objects should be protected by international law?

B The State-Based Regulation of Cultural Property

A nation state, through its sovereign right to designate its own cultural treasures, plays a strong role in determining the scope of application of international instruments. International law protects those objects that States deem 'cultural' and deserving of protection under their national laws relating to cultural property, a fact which consequently makes international law in this field heavily reliant on national laws.[27]

---

24 See *Prosecutor v Miodrag Jokić*, Case No. IT-01-42/1-S, Sentencing Judgement, Trial Chamber I, 18 March 2004, Case No. IT-01-42/1-S, para 51 [*Jokić* Sentencing Judgement].

25 See, eg, *Convention concerning the Protection of the World Cultural and Natural Heritage*, 16 November 1972, 1037 UNTS 151 (entered into force 17 December 1975), art 1 [*World Heritage Convention*]; *Convention for the Safeguarding of the Intangible Cultural Heritage*, 17 October 2003, Preamble para 4, http://www.unesco.org/culture/laws/2003/html.

26 Frigo, above n 1, 369.

27 See, eg, Fechner, above n 1, 379; Catherine Vernon, 'Common Cultural Property: The Search for Rights of Protective Intervention' (1994) 26 *Case Western Reserve Journal of International Law* 435; Müller, above n 1, 400; O'Keefe, above n 1, 51.

States' central role in the protection of cultural property is not in conflict with international law.[28] It is based on the sovereign equality of States, which is the primary principle in international law.[29] By assigning States the most important role in the protection of cultural property, including the definition of that property, international law recognises the unique contribution of each State to the cultural heritage of humankind. Through the recognition of a State's contribution, the law ultimately acknowledges the contribution to the world's cultural heritage of each people existing within a State. The assumption is that in determining the nature, 'quality' and quantity of objects that are to be protected, a State takes into account cultural diversity within its national borders. However, national legislation concerning cultural property is diverse in its measures of protection. Because the definition of cultural property is heavily reliant upon national legislation, such diversity poses a problem in determining a precise definition of cultural property in international law.

The freedom of States with respect to cultural property may create problems *vis-à-vis* the very preservation of such property. Under existing international law, no State or international organisation is authorised to intervene in domestic matters in order to guarantee the protection of cultural property without the authorisation of a given State.[30] As a result, a State can do whatever it pleases with cultural property to which it is territorially linked. Even if cultural property of exceptional value to humanity is deliberately destroyed, no party outside the State in question can do anything about it. The deliberate destruction of the world's two largest Buddha statues in Bamiyan, Afghanistan, by the Taliban in March 2001, is a clear example of this problem.[31] International law could neither force Afghanistan to spare these two particular objects of cultural property from destruction nor compel it to consider them cultural objects any longer (that is, to have them designated as cultural property under domestic law).

The only exception to the prohibition on intervention in internal matters of any State is the application of enforcement measures under Chapter VII of the *Charter of the United Nations* (*UN Charter*).[32] Although it can be argued that destruction of cultural property may under certain circumstances pose a threat to international peace and security, the enforcement measures under Chapter

28 See Müller, ibid.

29 See *Charter of the United Nations*, 26 June 1945, 59 Stat 1031, TS 993, 3 Bevans 1153, art 2(1) (entered into force 24 October 1945) [*UN Charter*].

30 See Williams, above n 1, 55. But see, Vernon, above n 27 (arguing for the need to change the *status quo*, and for the right of intervention in the territorial sovereignty of individual states under limited and controlled circumstances).

31 See 'UN Seeks Laws to Halt Cultural Vandalism', 13 March 2001, posted to CNN.com/WORLD (quoting Koichiro Matsuura, Director-General of UNESCO: 'We did everything possible to prevent this happening but we have failed miserably'), http://www.cnn.com/2001/WORLD/asiapcf/03/13/afghanistan.buddhas/.

32 *UN Charter* art 2(7).

VII have never been applied exclusively for the purpose of cultural property protection.

It has been argued that because of the power of a nation-state, international legal regimes, including those concerned with cultural property, are largely powerless 'paper tigers',[33] 'only guides',[34] or 'mere legal fiction, recognized in name only, without incidents or rights that provide adequate *de facto* protection'.[35] In the view of some scholars, unless the current status of cultural property law is 'eliminated',[36] the concept of common heritage is meaningless.[37] A proposal has been put forward to allow a right of protective intervention in the territorial sovereignty of individual States by other States or international organisations to protect cultural property situated in a host-State.[38] In view of the dual appeal of cultural property – as the cultural heritage of both a particular State and of humankind – there is a 'dual accountability'[39] of a State. Given that cultural property belonging to any people ultimately belongs to all humankind, it can be argued that the international community should be entitled to intervene in situations where a State is unwilling or unable to protect cultural property situated within its borders, on the basis that such an intervention would be the only way to prevent the impoverishment of humanity's cultural heritage. Intervention for cultural protection purposes should not be optional but, in fact, should be the responsibility of the international community, especially in situations involving massive destruction of irreplaceable cultural treasures and those where the survival of cultural property of exceptional importance to humanity's cultural heritage is threatened.

The issue of intervention in the territorial sovereignty of a State has been the subject of the recent *Report of the International Commission on Intervention and State Sovereignty* (*ICISS Report*).[40] The *Report* focuses on intervention for human protection purposes. However, the principle which is espoused, that the

---

33 See Müller, above n 1, 404. See also, John Yarwood, 'Cultural Warfare' (2003) 8 (2) *Art Antiquity and Law* 191, 198.

34 See James Nafziger, 'Comments on the Relevance of Law and Culture to Cultural Property Law' (1983) 10 *Syracuse Journal of International Law and Commerce* 323, 323 ['Comments'].

35 Vernon, above n 27, 440.

36 Ibid.

37 Ibid 437; Yarwood, above n 33.

38 Vernon, ibid 437-39.

39 Ibid 453.

40 *The Responsibility to Protect*, Report of the International Commission on Intervention and State Sovereignty, December 2001 [*ICISS Report*], http://www.dfait-maeci.gc.ca/iciss/report2-en.asp. See also, *A More Secure World: Our Shared Responsibility*, Report of the High Panel on Threats, Challenges and Change, submitted to the Secretary-General, Kofi Annan 2 December 2004, http://www.un.org/secureworld.

international community has a responsibility to provide such protection, could and should extend to cultural property as well. An attack on cultural treasures is also an attack on people. Cultural property is inseparable from human dignity. Its destruction represents a violation of the human right to culture. While means of intervention for cultural property purposes should differ to some extent from those pertinent to intervention for human protection purposes, the necessity of re-characterising state sovereignty is relevant to both contexts.

Another aspect of the dependency of the definition of cultural property in international law on a nation-state's discretion concerns the volume and type of designated property. States tend to designate whatever cultural objects are situated within their borders.[41] However, in order to make international protection more manageable, some limits to States' freedom with respect to the national definition of cultural property is necessary. Notwithstanding their imprecision, international instruments do specify categories of objects and demand that certain criteria be met before an object may qualify for international protection as 'cultural' property. Consequently, in order to reflect cross-national interests *vis-à-vis* preservation of cultural property and make preservation of this property feasible in times of armed conflict, some harmonisation between national laws concerning cultural property and international law on the subject is needed. Yet harmonisation may prove challenging due to the differing understanding of what makes property 'cultural'.

C The Differing Understanding of What Makes Property 'Cultural'

The terminology makes it apparent that cultural property is property of cultural significance. The cultural significance of the property distinguishes it from other property and makes it property of a unique kind. If stripped of cultural significance, cultural objects would be merely property – commodities or consumer goods.[42] Cultural significance is based on culture. It is precisely this that raises a series of questions: how are tangible movable and immovable objects related to culture? With whose culture do such objects enter into this relationship? Is culture individual, group, community or nation-specific? What is culture after all?

The primary problem here lies with the indeterminacy of the notion of culture. In recent decades the definition of culture itself has been the subject of serious academic dispute.[43] This is not surprising because culture is not a static concept but is evolving all the time.[44] Because it is a forward-looking phenome-

---

41 See Müller, above n 1, 400.

42 Mastalir, above n 10, 1039.

43 See Thomason, above n 12, 47.

44 See Lyndel Prott, 'Understanding One Another on Cultural Rights' in UNESCO, *Cultural Rights and Wrongs* (1998) 161, 164-65 ['Understanding'].

non, culture is constantly elusive.[45] Since culture is an ever-changing concept, it might be difficult, if not impossible, to determine with precision which objects should qualify for legal protection under the rubric of cultural property. As Professor Lyndel Prott observes, 'the variety of objects regarded as important cultural property is intriguing'.[46] Nevertheless, 'every culture should be able to protect what is essential cultural heritage for them'.[47]

Notwithstanding the lack of a uniform and precise definition of culture, it is widely accepted that in general terms culture includes 'material and non-material products of human thought that are shared by a particular group or society'.[48] Cultural property, as noted, is generally considered to represent tangible objects that embody the material expression of a culture or civilisation.[49] This material expression is seen as providing a context essential to individual human well-being,[50] communal nourishing and continuity into the future,[51] as well as intercultural communication and understanding.[52]

Along these lines, two major arguments on the question of what makes a given object 'cultural' – that is, what assigns cultural significance to it so as to distinguish it from other property and to legitimise its legal protection – have been espoused: functionalism and object-centrism. Functionalism makes reference to cultural property's function in society, putting the 'user' of cultural property at the centre.[53] According to this view, the meaning of cultural property is assigned by people and cultural property thus does not exist independently of humans. It is argued that functions of cultural property, particularly identity-generation and communication, have the primary role in determining cultural significance.

---

45 See Harding, above n 13, 334.

46 Prott, 'International Movement', above n 19, 227.

47 Ibid.

48 See Detling, above n 1, 45 (accepting the definition of culture as given in Webster's Ninth *New Collegiae Dictionary* (1986) 314).

49 See, eg, Patty Gersenblith, 'Identity and Cultural Property' (1995) 75 *Boston University Law Review* 559, 562 (defining cultural property as the 'physical embodiment of culture in tangible objects'); Lewis, above n 11, 435-36; Detling, above n 1, 45.

50 See Harding, above n 13, 334.

51 See Moustakas, above n 7, 1184, 1199-2000.

52 See, eg, Müller, above n 1, 399; John Merryman, *Thinking About the Elgin Marbles: Critical Essays on Cultural Property, Art and Law* (2000), 109 [*Elgin Marbles*].

53 See Müller, ibid 399. See also Tolina Loulanski, 'Revising the Concept for Cultural Heritage: The Argument for a Functional Approach' (2006) 13 *International Journal of Cultural Property* 207-233; Brian Graham and Peter Howard (eds), *The Ashgate Research Companion to Heritage and Identity* (2008); Robert Bevan, *The Destruction of Memory: Architecture at War* (2006); Yarwood, above n 33.

The other argument focuses on the primacy of the cultural object itself.[54] Cultural objects have value in their own right independent of people. Determining the cultural significance of the object by relying exclusively on the meaning of cultural property for society assigned to it by the people concerned is seen as too dependent on emotions. The object-centrism position emphasises the fact that even if a group deems a given object 'cultural', and that object becomes cultural property, no one can force the group to protect the cultural object. Yet, this lack of regard, as noted, would result in the loss of cultural property for humankind. Consequently, under the object-centrism approach, the cultural significance of the object derives from the object's scientific, artistic, or historic importance.

The debate about the cultural significance of the object is recognisable in the so-called 'cultural internationalism v cultural nationalism' debate about the question of the legitimate guardian of cultural property. Here, the debate revolves around the question of disposition of movable cultural property. However, the arguments put forward are also relevant to an overall understanding of factors taken into account in defining cultural property in international law. The 'cultural internationalists'[55] argue that cultural property belongs to all humankind whereas the 'cultural nationalists'[56] contend that cultural property

---

54 See John Merryman, 'The Nation and the Object' (1994) 3 *International Journal of Cultural Property* 61, 74. See also Fechner, above n 1.

55 The *1954 Convention* is widely considered to take an 'internationalist' approach to cultural property. For discussion of the internationalist approach to cultural property see generally, John Merryman, 'International Art Law: From Cultural Nationalism to a Common Cultural Heritage' (1983) 15 *New York University Journal of International Law and Politics* 757 ['International Art Law']; Merryman, 'Two Ways', above n 9; Merryman, 'Public Interest', above n 11; Merryman, *Elgin Marbles*, above n 52. See also Vernon, above n 27; Fechner, above n 1.

56 The *1970 Convention* is considered to take a 'nationalist' approach to cultural property. For discussion of the nationalist approach to cultural property see generally, Richard Handler, 'Who Owns the Past?: History, Cultural Property, and the Logic of Possessive Individualism' in Brett Williams (ed), *The Politics of Culture* (1991) 63. See also, Moustakas, above n 7. The dichotomy between 'cultural internationalism' and 'cultural nationalism' has been very seriously challenged. See, eg, Prott, 'The International Movement', above n 19, 225-248 (challenging the view that 'cultural property internationalism' (Merryman) is represented by the 1954 Convention and that it has been departed from in later UNESCO instruments, and arguing that UNESCO's later instruments, such as the *1970 Convention*, do not represent an aversion to the art market but that the art trade at present is based on the secrecy of transactions, and that this has led to a number of scandals). See also, Derek Gillman, *Art Law* (2006) (reviewing the competing claims that works of art belong either to a particular people and place, or, from a cosmopolitan perspective, to all humankind, and offering an approach to moral claims and to governmental regulation and support that draws on liberal writings).

is exclusively the property of nations of origin.[57] While the preservation of cultural property is the principal concern for both schools, they differ in their approach as to whether the cultural object is a value in itself or whether the object's meaning in the nation-state should take prevalence. Like the proponents of the object-centrism approach, the cultural internationalists give preference to the cultural object as a value in itself.[58] The cultural nationalists, on the other hand, focus on the meaning of cultural property and put the culturally affiliated – an identifiable group, people, or nation – into the centre. Like the cultural functionalists, this school of thought emphasises the role of cultural property in identity-generation.[59]

The meaning of the cultural object in society is undoubtedly an important factor in defining cultural property. Cultural objects are made by humans, either individually or collectively, and their meaning in society is also constructed by humans. But cultural objects are also important markers of humanity's development and ultimately have an 'identificatory' function in the context of all humanity. In this sense, cultural property may have an identity-generation function for a group or nation most immediately concerned, but, at the same time, it may also be a value in its own right through its significance for a wider audience as a source of information, or because of its aesthetic contents or its age.[60] Accordingly, cultural property is both 'national' and 'international'.

This dual nature of cultural property is expressly recognised in the *1954 Convention* which spells out that the loss of or damage to any cultural object, irrespective of its origin, ultimately impoverishes the heritage of the entire international community:

---

57 For a review of the competing claims that works of art belong either to a particular people and place, or, from a cosmopolitan perspective, to all humankind, see eg, Derek Gillman, *The Idea of Cultural Heritage* (2006).

58 See Merryman, *Elgin Marbles*, above n 52, 43-45 (explaining that Byronism supports the claims of nations of origin, but rejecting it as a romantic misrepresentation and distortion of values that Byron perpetrated). But see P. B. Shelley, *A Defence of Poetry* (1904) 90 (claiming that '[p]oets are the unacknowledged legislators of the world).

59 See Moustakas, above n 7, 1199. For discussion on the role of cultural property in generating identity, see also Albert Elsen, 'Introduction: Why Do We Care about Art?' (1976) 27 *Hastings Law Journal* 951, 952. The International Council of Museums is of the view that the 'community of nations now considers as an element of *jus cogens* the right of all people to recover property which forms an integral part of their cultural identity'. Quoted in John Merryman and Albert Elsen, *Law, Ethics and the Visual Arts* 1-2 (4th ed, 2003) 267, quoting 'Study of the Principles, Conditions, and Means for the Restitution or Return of Cultural Property in View of Restitution of Dispersed Heritage' (1979) 31 *Museum* 62.

60 See Fechner, above n 1, 381.

> Being convinced that *damage to cultural property belonging to any people* whatsoever *means damage to the cultural heritage of all [hu]mankind*, since each people makes its contribution to the culture of the world....[61]

Consequently, all cultural property as defined in Article 1 of the *Convention* is considered part of the world's cultural heritage in whose preservation every State of the world thus has an interest, that is:

> (a) movable or immovable property of great importance to the cultural heritage of every people...(b) buildings whose main and effective purpose is to preserve or exhibit the movable cultural property...[and] (c) centres containing a large amount of cultural property as defined in subparagraphs (a) and (b).[62]

For that reason, States Parties to the *Convention* have agreed to 'take all possible steps to protect cultural property'.[63]

Similar sentiment is expressed in the *Convention concerning the Protection of the World Cultural and Natural Heritage* (*World Heritage Convention*), which highlights 'the importance, for all the peoples of the world, of safeguarding this unique and irreplaceable property, to whatever people it may belong',[64] and stresses that 'deterioration or disappearance of any item of the cultural...heritage constitutes a harmful impoverishment of the heritage of all nations of the world'.[65] The *Convention on the Means of Prohibiting and Preventing the Illicit Import, Export and Transfer of Ownership of Cultural Property* (*1970 Convention*), too, albeit in somewhat softer language, points to the 'moral obligations [of every State] to respect its own cultural heritage and that of all nations'.[66]

Because of its internationalist element, under which cultural property belonging to any people forms part of the cultural heritage of all humankind, including the generations that are yet to come, all people are only the custodians of cultural property and, thus, such property 'belongs' to everyone and to no person in particular.

---

61 *1954 Convention*, Preamble para 2 (emphasis added). Under the general rule of treaty interpretation, as spelt out in Article 31(2) of the 1969 *Vienna Convention on the Law of Treaties*, provisions of the preamble to a treaty are considered an integral part of the text of a treaty. See *Vienna Convention on the Law of Treaties*, 23 May 1969, 1155 UNTS 331, art 31(2).

62 *1954 Convention* art 1.

63 *1954 Convention*, Preamble para 6.

64 *World Heritage Convention*, Preamble para 5.

65 Ibid para 2.

66 *1970 Convention*, Preamble para 5.

Irrespective of peoples' divergent practices, which should remain diverse to some extent,[67] there are some shared values with respect to cultural property that transcend national and cultural boundaries. As both object-centrism and functionalism, or the internationalist and nationalist approach to cultural property demonstrate, everyone depends upon cultural property and everyone should respond with a sense of duty and responsibility to protect it.[68] But exactly why do people care about cultural property and what are the underlying principles for its international protection?

III Importance of Cultural Property

A The Benefits of Cultural Property

Cultural objects are objects of a special kind. Their loss is always tragic because people care about cultural property.[69] This care has a long history and is verifiable in many ways cross-culturally. As Merryman observes, from time immemorial people have made, preserved and displayed cultural objects.[70] Today, the existence of numerous museums around the world, countless museum visitors, an impressively large number of dealers, collectors, university departments of art, archaeology and ethnology, national arts ministries, and national[71] and international laws protecting cultural property, is testimony to the various ways in which present generations care about cultural objects inherited from past generations.

When international law applies, protection of cultural property is extended to both times of peace and times of armed conflict, ensuring that cultural property is always protected. For instance, the *World Heritage Convention*, applicable to time of peace, expressly states that,

> the existing international conventions, recommendations and resolutions concerning cultural…property demonstrate the importance, for all the peoples of the world, of safeguarding this unique and irreplaceable property, to whatever people it may belong.[72]

The *1970 Convention*, also applicable to peacetime, makes it clear that,

---

67 See Harding, above n 13, 304.

68 Ibid.

69 See Merryman, *Elgin Marbles*, above n 52, 98.

70 Ibid.

71 See, generally, Kifle Jote, *International Legal Protection of Cultural Heritage* (1994). See also, Halina Nieć, 'Legislative Models of Protection of Cultural Property' (1976) 27 *Hastings Law Journal* 1089, 1092 *et seq.*

72 *World Heritage Convention*, Preamble para 5.

> cultural property constitutes one of the basic elements of civilization and national culture,[73] [and that it] increases the knowledge of the civilization of [men and women], enriches the cultural life of all peoples and inspires mutual respect and appreciation among nations[74] [and that] it is incumbent upon every State to protect the cultural property existing within its territory.[75]

The *1954 Convention*, protecting cultural property in times of armed conflict, explains that,

> the preservation of the cultural heritage is of great importance for all peoples of the world and that it is important that this heritage should receive international protection.[76]

But why, one might ask, should people spend time and resources to safeguard art, monuments and other cultural property in times of armed conflict when precious human lives are at risk? When one considers deaths, loss of homes, jobs and other essentials, thinking of cultural objects might even seem inappropriate. But it would be wrong to assume that the affected people care only about their own physical survival and only need material help. Professor Patrick Boylan explains that those people are hungry, cold and frightened, but that 'their heart, their soul and their memory have also been wounded'.[77] Cultural property plays an important role in human life. In fact, the two are so interconnected that they form part of one inseparable whole.[78] Through the safeguarding of cultural property, people protect the human spirit as it manifests itself in the tangible, artistic products of culture. As one conservator of cultural property puts it:

> To the Devil's advocate who would mischievously repeat with Oscar Wilde that art is useless, I would reply that useless it is indeed—if we were to judge the matter from a purely utilitarian perspective. Art is in fact as useless to society as the spirit is to body. The human species as a biological organism *can* survive without art and culture. But the definition of what it is to be human cannot. Culture is to human civilization as trees are to the environment. That is the justification for our preoccupation with its survival.[79]

---

73 *1970 Convention*, Preamble para 3.

74 Ibid para 2.

75 Ibid para 4.

76 *1954 Convention*, Preamble para 3.

77 Patrick Boylan, 'Come Hell or High Water' *Sources* (UNESCO) No. 117, November 1999, 10.

78 Ibid 11 (quoting Herb Stovel, the President of ICOMOS Canada).

79 Miguel Corzo, 'The Hague Convention of 1954: History, Significance and Compliance' in Pamela Vandiver *et al* (eds), *Materials Issues in Art and Archaeology*

People care about cultural property for a variety of reasons. Cultural property links the present to the past.[80] While the past is often contested, cultural objects provide truth, certainty and accuracy about the past.[81] The past is appreciated because it is stable and permanent. Because of a sense of completion, '[n]othing in the past can now go wrong'.[82] Since the past is embodied and expressed in cultural objects, cultural property is the basis of the memory of humanity.[83]

People also appreciate cultural property because cultural objects are unique objects.[84] Once destroyed, they are gone forever and cannot be replaced.[85] An argument might be raised that an object of cultural property, as with any other material object, can be restored or rebuilt. However, a rebuilt object is not an adequate substitute for the original. When the original is gone, the old building techniques, authentic material and generally the old age patina – the factors that contribute to the cultural value of an object – are also gone. A rebuilt object may strikingly resemble the original, but even a perfect replica remains exactly that – a replica, or as Merryman puts it, 'a poor second best'.[86] When works of art are concerned, Merryman argues that people 'want to look at the real thing'[87] and not a reproduction. A reproduction inadequately represents the culture.[88] The same could be argued with respect to architectural structures that are considered immovable cultural property. The problem was addressed by the ICTY's Trial Chamber in *Prosecutor v Jokić* (*Jokić* or the *Jokić* case). Discussing the 6 December 1991 attack on the Old Town of Dubrovnik, Croatia, a World Heritage site, by the Yugoslav Army (YA), the Trial Chamber in its Sentencing Judgement highlighted the unique nature of cultural property by observing that:

> [r]estoration of buildings of this kind when possible, can never return the buildings to their state prior to the attack because a certain amount of origi-

---

III, Symposium held 27 April-1 May 1992, San Francisco, California, USA (1992) 5, 6 (italics in original).

80 See Moustakas, above n 7, 1195.

81 See Merryman, *Elgin Marbles*, above n 52, 102.

82 David Lowenthal, *The Past is a Foreign Country* (1985) 62.

83 See Hirad Abtahi, 'The Protection of Cultural Property in Times of Armed Conflict: The Practice of the International Criminal Tribunal for the Former Yugoslavia' (2001) 14 *Harvard Human Rights Journal* 1, 32.

84 See Moustakas, above n 7, 1223.

85 See Merryman and Elsen, above n 59, xvi (explaining that irreplaceable nature of cultural property justifies its importance and proper protection). See also, *World Heritage Convention*, Preamble para 5 (stressing that cultural property is 'unique and irreplaceable property').

86 Merryman, 'International Art Law', above n 55, 757.

87 Ibid.

88 Ibid.

> nal, historically authentic, material will have been destroyed, thus affecting the inherent value of the buildings.[89]

History and memory are stored in the old age patina and not in a rebuilt object irrespective of how remarkable the resemblance to the original may be. 'That is why modern replicas', as one commentator succinctly puts it, 'however exact, or over-restored monuments, however meticulously carried out, seem so flat, trivial, and unrevealing. Time and humanity have been scrubbed out of them'.[90] Thus, the loss of the original cultural object remains a tragedy even if such an object has been rebuilt. Nothing can lessen this tragedy.

Another reason why people care about cultural property is because cultural objects embody memory. Humanity yearns for preservation of cultural property out of its desire to remember and to be remembered, and to prevent 'the eternal silence created by the destruction of culture'.[91] As Stephen Humphreys explains, memory is essential to a human life.[92] If people do not have authentic memories of their own, they cannot know who they are, where they came from and to whom they are connected. Without memory, they are only what others tell them they are. In Humphreys' words, '[m]emory floats in the mind, but it is fixed and secured by objects'.[93] Collective memory is sheltered in cultural objects. Cultural objects visibly set a people or society apart from others. In the case of immovable cultural objects, they also noticeably indicate a certain people's or society's existence in a given geographical area. When such objects are gone, the affected people's or society's distinctiveness and boundaries disappear along with them. As a consequence, others can arbitrarily implant their own versions of the lost memory. The so-called ethnic cleansing accompanied by the destruction of cultural property in armed conflict demonstrates the problem. When people are expelled and their memory is erased through the destruction of their relics, it makes it easier for the ethnic cleansers to espouse their claim on a given territory as there is no physical evidence that the expelled people ever lived there.

Often objects of cultural property store immense amounts of their creator's love, time, energy, and many decisions as to the choice of materials, methods of work, subject matter, style, care in execution and quality of an object, which are based on a sense of obligation to those who may use the objects and on the

89 *Jokić* Sentencing Judgement, para 52.

90 Stephen Humphreys, 'The Destruction of Cultural Memory' (2001 presidential address), *Middle East Studies Association Bulletin*, Summer 2002, para 5, <http://fp.arizona.edu/mesassoc/Bulletin/Pres%20Address/humphreys.htm>.

91 Manfred Lachs, 'The Defences of Culture' (1985) 37 *Museum* 167, 168. As Jules Michelet cautions, 'Adieu le passé c'est aussi adieu la postérité'. Quoted in Lachs, ibid 168.

92 Humphreys, above n 90, para 1.

93 Ibid para 2.

creator's personal determination to make the object 'right'.[94] Consequently, such objects are 'suffused with an aura of deep moral seriousness'[95] and demand the 'user's' respect and appreciation. The widespread and systematic targeting of cultural property in the former Yugoslavia in the 1990s sorrowfully demonstrates a complete disregard on the part of the perpetrators for the creators' immense efforts – what had taken the creator in each case years to construct took mostly a matter of minutes for the destroyers to destroy.

Cultural objects are powerful symbols.[96] They bind people together, nourishing communities,[97] giving them a sense of identity,[98] and bridging the gap between cultures.[99] Their destruction or removal causes an insurmountable amount of pain[100] and is perceived as psychologically intolerable.[101] Some cultural objects, as was the case with the Old Bridge of Mostar, are so loved and treasured that they are regarded as living things.[102] Destruction of such objects is mourned by some almost as much as (sometimes even more than) the loss of human life. In some instances destruction of a cultural object can cause communities to drift apart and lead to serious violence. The destruction of the Babri mosque in Ayodhya in northern India in 1992 and the ensuing massive violence is one such example.[103]

It has been observed that people lament the destruction of cultural property because they mourn the loss of time embodied in ruins of majestic monuments or other cultural objects.[104] With that, they mourn the missed opportunity to

---

94 Merryman, *Elgin Marbles*, above n 52, 103.

95 C. Geertz, *The Interpretation of Cultures* (1973) 126.

96 See Moustakas, above n 7, 1195.

97 See, eg, Merryman, *Elgin Marbles*, above n 52, 105; Moustakas, ibid 1184.

98 See, eg, Merryman, ibid; Moustakas, ibid 1195; Paul Bator, 'An Essay on the International Trade in Art' (1982) 34 *Stanford Law Review* 275, 304.

99 See Moustakas, ibid 1223-24 and fn 186.

100 See Amy Schwartz, 'Is It Wrong to Weep for Buildings?' *Washington Post* 19 May 1994, 17.

101 See Moustakas, above n 7, 1196.

102 John Yarwood correctly observes that 'in the Balkans, the heritage…is for natives a living and highly charged environment, inviting destruction for precisely that reason'. Yarwood, above n 33, 197 and fn 13, quoting Edith Durham who in 1909 called Kosovo 'the land of the living past', Edith Durham, *High Albania* (1909) 296.

103 See, eg, Sarvepalli Gopal (ed) *Anatomy of a Confrontation* (1991) and D. Mandal, *Ayodhya: Archaeology after Demolition* (1993); Human Rights Watch Report, 'India: Communal Violence and the Denial of Justice' April 1996 vol 8 No. 2 (C), para 8, http://www.hrw.org/reports/1996/India1.htm.

104 See, generally, Humphreys, above n 90. See also Slavenka Drakulić, 'Falling Down: a Mostar Bridge' (1993) 209 *The New Republic* 14(2); Jiří Toman, *The Protection of Cultural Property in the Event of Armed Conflict: Commentary on the Convention for the Protection of Cultural Property in the Event of Armed Conflict and its Protocol,*

link the past with the future. Cultural objects are often made to outlive us.[105] Some, such as the great Pyramids of Giza, demonstrate that cultural objects can truly constitute an attempt to reach eternity. The giant Afghan Buddha statues exemplify a similar attempt. Had they not been destroyed, they would have had the potential to enrich many generations to come.

There are also a number of other reasons why people care about cultural property and why they mourn its loss. Cultural objects are admired for their exquisiteness. They are sometimes so 'painfully beautiful'[106] that they represent an inexhaustible source of inspiration to poets, musicians, painters and other artists. These objects also store information that can always be of use to someone.[107] They are an aesthetic, intellectual, educational[108] and economic resource,[109] as well as a reminder of the creativity of the past,[110] a symbol of quality,[111] pride,[112] and an inspiration for new creations.[113]

Importantly, cultural objects are a unifying force and a promoter of peace and harmony among nations. Visits to cultural sites, museums and galleries, and the study of cultural objects increase individuals' understanding about themselves and about others. The interchange of cultural property among nations for scientific, cultural and educational purposes bridges the gap of ignorance and intolerance between peoples and contributes to the promotion of intercultural dialogue. Some cultural objects have, in fact, been built or rebuilt primarily for the purpose of promoting universal peace and reconciliation. The Peace Arch, which was constructed on the border between the United States and Canada, to commemorate the centennial of peace between these two States, is one such

---

signed on 14 May 1954 in The Hague, and on other instruments of international law concerning such protection (1996).

105 Almost all architectural structures made of stone are built with the aim that they last for a long period of time. However, other cultural objects, made of other materials have also survived for centuries or even millennia.

106 See, eg, *Prosecutor v Mladen Naletilić, aka 'Tuta'and Vinko Martinović, aka 'Štela',* Sentencing Judgement Statement, Trial Chamber I, 31 March 2003, Case No. IT-98-34-T, para 16, <http://www.un.org/icty/naletilic/trialc/judgement/nal-state030331e.htm> (Judge Clark, describing the Old Bridge of Mostar as '[t]he *painfully beautiful* old arched footbridge which stood over the Neretva River for four centuries') (emphasis added) [*Naletilić* Sentencing Judgement Statement].

107 See Fechner, above n 1, 381.

108 See Merryman and Elsen, above n 59, xvi.

109 See Merryman, *Elgin Marbles*, above n 52, 110-111 (noting that cultural property is valuable and is a form of wealth, and that it plays a significant role in the tourist industry). Similarly, see Caruthers, above n 1, 161; Forbes, above n 1, 241-42.

110 See Merryman and Elsen, above n 59, xvi.

111 Ibid.

112 See Moustakas, above n 7, 1217.

113 See Bator, above n 98, 306.

example. This is the longest undefended border in the world, and one of the few landmarks in the world listed on the National Historic Registries of two different States.[114]

Today, intercultural dialogue ranks more highly on the international agenda than ever before. The mandate of the United Nations Educational, Scientific and Cultural Organization (UNESCO) places this organisation at the very heart of the promotion of cultural diversity and cultural dialogue. This organisation fosters the belief that in the context of globalisation and the current international political climate, culture, including cultural property, is becoming a vital instrument for maintaining peace, world unity and conciliation,[115] and is 'perhaps even a key to a shared planetary future'.[116]

Concern for culture, including cultural property, does not stop with UNESCO. Other organisations have also been using culture and cultural property to spread peace. For instance, the World Culture Open, an international non-profit organisation which held its inaugural conference at the United Nations in 2004, is designed to create breakthroughs in peace and reconciliation between individuals and societies through celebration of the world's diverse artistic and cultural traditions.[117] In his message, the UN Secretary-General recognised that the goals and ideals of the World Culture Open matched those of the United Nations. He specifically referred to cultural heritage (of which, as noted, cultural property is a constitutive part) emphasising the importance of its role in achieving these goals: 'The sharing and mutual appreciation of *cultural heritage*, customs and traditions [at the World Culture Open festival] bridge[s] the dangerous gap of intolerance, ignorance and miscommunication between cultures'.[118]

Therefore, the utility and expressive value of cultural property are immense. Because of them people care about cultural property deeply. While each of the reasons why people care about cultural property could justify its protection at some level, there are several major explanations as to what has motivated international legal protection of cultural property in armed conflict.

---

114 For information on the Peace Arch, visit http://www.peacearchpark.org/peacearch.htm.

115 Ibid para 3.

116 UNESCO, 'The Word of the Assistant Director-General for Culture: Reconsidering Culture', http://portal.unesco.org/culture/en/ev.php [5].

117 For information on the World Culture Open, visit http://www.worldcultureopen2004.org.

118 UN Press Release, 'Secretary-General's Message to the World Culture Open [delivered by Mr Maurice Strong, Special Adviser and Personal Envoy of the Secretary-General]', 10 September 2004, http://www.un.org/apps/sg/sgstats.asp?nid=1071 [2] (emphasis added).

B *The Rationales for the International Protection of Cultural Property*

1 Universal Value and Concern

International law concerning cultural property is premised on the idea that cultural property is valuable to all humankind. This heritage of humankind doctrine came onto the stage with the arrival of liberalism and its focus on the individual. The law asserts unambiguously that cultural property is part of the joint heritage of all inhabitants of the planet and that the concern about cultural objects stretches beyond national borders and ethnicity.[119] To reiterate, the *1954 Convention* spells out that 'damage to cultural property belonging to any people whatsoever means damage to the cultural heritage of all [hu]mankind, since each people makes its contribution to the culture of the world'.[120]

This shared heritage testifies to the universal nature of the human spirit in all its creations. Cultural objects are human creations and are made to be of use for fellow human beings. Through cultural property, all humanity is interrelated to so great an extent that when one social entity's cultural property is destroyed the whole international community is disinherited and mourns the loss. The concern about cultural property spills across national borders because human beings have a natural propensity to love and appreciate the creative work of their fellow human beings.[121] As one poet observed, 'No man is an island.... Do not ask for whom the bell tolls. It tolls for thee'.[122] By analogy, just as no single people in the world is 'an island' but is a constitutive part of the international community, no cultural property, to whomever it may most immediately 'belong', is an isolated 'island' either, because it forms part of the whole called the cultural heritage of all humankind. When part of this heritage is destroyed, all humanity is disinherited.

The international community raises its voice in reaction to the various situations that endanger the survival of cultural property, including situations of armed conflict. The events relating to cultural property in the former Yugoslavia during the armed conflicts in the 1990s have been strongly condemned worldwide. They have been considered by the international community a 'cultural

119 UNESCO, 'Cultural Heritage Sites', http://portal.unesco.org/culture/ev.php.

120 *1954 Convention*, Preamble para 2.

121 As far back as the fifth decade BC, Cicero said: 'We have a natural propensity to love our fellow man, and this after all is the foundation of all law'.

122 With these words, John Donne, the British poet of the sixteenth century, emphasised the essential relatedness of all humankind – when one human being dies the whole of humanity is diminished.

catastrophe'[123] and to constitute war crimes,[124] and perpetrators are being brought to justice.[125]

2 National Value and Concern

Another explanation as to why cultural property warrants international protection derives from a group or nation's attachment to cultural objects. Here, cultural property is seen as representative of the cultural specificity of a people or a nation. The emergence of cultural property laws reflected the importance of cultural property to the nation-state. These laws came with the development of national self-determination and the nationalist movement of eighteenth century Europe, which soon spread to other parts of the world.[126]

The modern idea of self-determination emerged at the time of the French and American revolutions, which coincided with the arrival of liberalism and the heritage of humankind doctrine. Unlike liberalism which, as noted, focused on the individual, the concept of self-determination and the accompanying doctrine of cultural national patrimony put 'people' and group identity on centre stage. A group calling for self-determination would also call for the preservation of its cultural property because such property, *inter alia*, gave the group a sense of distinctiveness. By providing it with evidence of historical presence – a

123 See Committee on Culture and Education of Parliamentary Assembly of Council of Europe (COE), *First Information Report*, doc 6756, 2 February 1993, 2 ('A cultural catastrophe in the heart of Europe. The wars in Croatia and Bosnia-Herzegovina are a tragedy for the peoples of these countries for all the communities of the war zone…and also for our…heritage, which will emerge from the war singularly amputated') [*First COE Report*].

124 See *Statute of the International Criminal Tribunal for the Prosecution of Persons Responsible for Serious Violations of International Humanitarian Law Committed in the Territory of the Former Yugoslavia since 1991*, adopted by the UN Security Council Res 827, 25 May 1993, UN SCOR, 48th sess, 3217th mtg at 29 UN Doc S/827/1993, as amended by Res 1166, 13 May 1998 and by Res 1329, 30 November 2000, arts 3(d) and 5(h). The Statute is contained in UN Doc S/25704, Annex (1993), and attached to the 'Report of the Secretary-General Pursuant to Paragraph 2 of Security Council Resolution 808' [*ICTY Statute*].

125 A number of ICTY indictments include charges relating to cultural property, some of which already resulted in convictions. See, eg, Dubrovnik Initial Indictment, *Prosecutor v Pavle Strugar, Miodrag Jokić, Milan Zec and Vladimir Kovačević*, Indictment, 22 February 2001 (unsealed 2 October 2001), Case No. IT-01-42-I; *Jokić* Sentencing Judgement; *Strugar* Trial Judgement, *Prosecutor v Pavle Strugar*, Judgement, Trial Chamber II, 31 January 2005, Case No. IT-01-42-T [*Strugar* Trial Judgement].

126 See Nieć, above n 71, 1089.

'historical identity card',[127] as some put it – cultural property helped a group or nation to 'determine' its existence.[128]

Some commentators argue that on acquiring statehood, States entered into international agreements in order to protect their own cultural treasures, and with that their national identity, from the destructive effects of armed conflict and not because of the notion of the shared heritage of humankind.[129] Today, however, international law protecting cultural property in armed conflict merges the two doctrines (heritage of humankind and cultural patrimony). The *1954 Convention* makes it clear that each people of the world contributes to humanity's common cultural heritage and that consequently, 'damage to cultural property belonging to any people whatsoever means damage to the cultural heritage of all [hu]mankind'.[130] At the same time, by prescribing that cultural property will cover 'movable or immovable property of great importance to the cultural heritage of every people',[131] the *Convention* acknowledges the importance of, or rather attachment to, cultural property at the national level. It is at this level that property will be deemed cultural property and as such be considered part of humankind's shared heritage.

3 Future Generations

Today, all peoples in every corner of the world have the right to, and a share in, cultural property.[132] This right is explicitly recognised by a number of international instruments, including the *UN Charter*,[133] the *Universal Declaration of Human Rights*,[134] the *International Covenant on Economic, Social and Cultural Rights*,[135] the *International Covenant on Civil and Political Rights*[136] and the

127 Stanislav Nahlik, *Pillage of Works of Art* (1958) [*Pillage*] 155.

128 See Frid, above n 11, 7.

129 Ibid.

130 *1954 Convention*, Preamble para 2.

131 Ibid art 1(a).

132 See, eg, Prott, 'Understanding', above n 44, 163 *et seq*; Gregory Mose, 'The Destruction of Churches and Mosques in Bosnia-Herzegovina: A Rights-Based Approach to the Protection of Religious Cultural Property' (1996) 3 *Buffalo Journal of International Law* 180, 200-202.

133 *UN Charter*, art 55(b), (c).

134 *Universal Declaration of Human Rights*, adopted and proclaimed by General Assembly Resolution 217 A (III) of 10 December 1948, UN Doc A/71 (1948) arts 17 and 27.

135 *International Covenant on Economic, Social and Cultural Rights*, adopted and opened for signature, ratification and accession by General Assembly Resolution 2200 A (XXI) of 16 December 1966 (entered into force 3 January 1967), arts 1 and 3.

136 *International Covenant on Civil and Political Rights*, adopted and opened for signature, ratification and accession by General Assembly Resolution 2200 A

Universal Declaration on Cultural Diversity (*UDCD*).[137] The *UDCD* reiterates the language of human rights instruments by expressly stating that 'cultural rights are an integral part of human rights, which are universal, indivisible and interdependent'.[138] It declares that the flourishing of creative diversity requires the full implementation of cultural rights as defined in the relevant international instruments governing the protection of human rights. To this end 'all persons should be able to participate in the cultural life of their choice and conduct their own cultural practices'.[139]

The right to enjoy cultural property corresponds with the responsibility to respect cultural property and to transmit it to future generations.[140] The *1970 Convention* points to 'the moral obligations [of every State] to respect its own cultural heritage and that of all nations'[141] and to 'protect the cultural property existing within its territory'[142] against the dangers that threaten its survival. The *1954 Convention* obligates States to 'take all possible steps to protect cultural property'.[143] The *World Heritage Convention* explains this responsibility to respect and protect cultural property by asserting that each State Party has 'the duty of ensuring the...transmission [of the cultural heritage] to future generations'.[144] The *UDCD* stresses that cultural heritage serves as the wellspring of creativity.[145] Its Article 7 stipulates that:

> Creation draws on the roots of cultural tradition, but flourishes in contact with other cultures. For this reason, *heritage in all its forms must be* preserved, enhanced and *handed on to future generations* as a record of human experience and aspirations, so as to foster creativity in all its diversity and to inspire genuine dialogue among cultures.[146]

(XXI) of 16 December 1966 (entered into force 23 March 1976) arts 1(1) and 27.

137 *Universal Declaration on Cultural Diversity*, adopted at 31st UNESCO General Conference of 2 November 2001, arts 4 and 5 [*UDCD*], UNESCO Press No 2001-120-5, http://www.unesco.org/bpi/eng/unescopress/2001/01-120e.shtml.

138 Ibid art 5.

139 Ibid.

140 See, eg, UNESCO Culture Sector, 'Message from the Director-General of UNESCO, Koïchiro Matsuura', http://portal.unesco.org/culture/ev.php. See also Fechner, above n 1, 382; Müller, above n 1, 405.

141 *1970 Convention*, Preamble para 5.

142 Ibid para 4.

143 *1954 Convention*, Preamble para 6.

144 *World Heritage Convention*, art 4.

145 *UDCD*, art 7.

146 Ibid (emphasis added).

But why should we care about the unascertained interests of those who are yet to be born? Professor Jeff McMahan argues that present generations have moral obligations to future generations.[147] In his view, present generations are obligated not to harm future generations in certain ways and also to share the Earth's resources with them in a way that is just.[148] If this reasoning is applied to cultural property, it would follow that if present generations deprive future generations of cultural property, they would harm them and treat them unjustly. Specifically, being a part of the cultural heritage of every people, cultural property involves the notion of inheritance, of handing on. Given that every human being on Earth is entitled to participate in and enjoy their cultural heritage, depriving those who are supposed to 'inherit' such heritage of this entitlement would harm them. At the same time, since cultural property constitutes a non-replenishable and limited resource, present generations must 'use' it responsibly.

The obligation to transmit cultural property to future generations is the essence of the justification for legal protection of cultural property. States enter into international agreements devised to protect cultural property in order to preserve their cultural treasures. As Roger Mastalir correctly observes, '[p]reservation is the first principle of protection of cultural property because if cultural property is destroyed the source nations or peoples, as well as the world heritage at large, are divested of valuable objects'.[149] Numerous centuries-old cultural objects listed in national registries worldwide and now already centuries-old national laws protecting cultural property,[150] as well as countless many-generations-old cultural objects that have been preserved irrespective of whether they have been listed in national or international cultural registers, are evidence of peoples' belief that certain objects must be treated with special care so that they can be preserved for posterity.

But what would provide an adequate account of the foundation of the obligation to transmit cultural property to future generations? Some scholars speak of the notion of intergenerational justice.[151] In their view, just as people today have inherited cultural property from their predecessors, their children and their children's children are entitled to the same inheritance from them. Present generations, who currently are privileged to 'use' cultural property should not disadvantage future, currently unrepresented generations, but owe them the

---

147 See Jeff McMahan, 'Future Generations' in *The Oxford Companion to Philosophy* (1995) 302.

148 Ibid.

149 Mastalir, above n 10, 1045.

150 See Nieć, above n 71, 1093-96.

151 See Moustakas, above n 7, 1205. See also, E. Partridge (ed), *Responsibilities to Future Generations* (1981); Annette Baier, 'For the Sake of Future Generations' in J. Regan (ed), *Earthbound: New Introductory Essays in Environmental Ethics* (1984) 214; Edith Brown-Weiss, *In Fairness to Future Generations: International Law, Common Patrimony, and Intergenerational Equity* (1989).

same opportunity to use cultural property for all those benefits inherent in it.[152] John Moustakas argues that if cultural objects are not passed on to future generations, those generations might lose that important sense of being part of something larger than themselves.[153] At the same time, by failing to pass on cultural property to future generations, present generations interrupt the 'continuity' of preceding generations which is symbolised in the existence and transfer of cultural objects that have been inherited from them.

By emphasising the interests of future generations, one theorist argues that the failure to transfer cultural property to future generations might seriously cripple those generations culturally: 'Suppose we destroyed all of our literary, artistic, and musical heritage; suppose we left to future generations only pot-boiler romance, fluorescent velvet paintings, and disco songs. We would then surely ensure a race of *uncultured* near-illiterates'.[154] This view might be problematic to the extent that present generations cannot know whether their definition of 'cultured' will coincide with that of the future generations. As McMahan correctly observes, '[t]here are, of course, problems with predicting how our acts will affect future people, what their needs and interests will be'.[155] Consequently, future generations' taste might differ from that of present generations. Future generations might prefer 'pot-boiler romance, fluorescent velvet paintings, and disco songs'. In fact, these might well be their cultural property too. Notwithstanding this, they should have an *opportunity* to evaluate other forms of expression and to experience an informed 'freedom of choice'.[156]

Other scholars take a duty-based approach to cultural property protection.[157] Here, although future generations benefit from cultural property protection, protecting cultural property is based not merely on showing concern or respect to future generations but is due to a duty to cultural property. Under this view, a duty to cultural property is based on the special value of such property.[158] Cultural property is considered valuable because it represents an expression or intimate part of human experience.[159] Because cultural property is so valuable, a duty to protect it is not limited only to present generations. This duty is infinite, thus also extending to future generations.

152 See, eg, Corzo, above n 79, 15.

153 Ibid.

154 Mark Sagoff, 'We Have Met the Enemy and He is Us or Conflict and Contradiction in Environmental Law' (1982) 12 *Environmental Law* 283, 300 (emphasis added).

155 McMahan, above n 147.

156 UNESCO, *Declaration on Responsibility of Present Generations towards Future Generations* (1997) art 2, http://www.unesco.org/culture.

157 See Harding, above n 13, 324. See also, Moustakas, above n 7, 1217.

158 Harding ibid.

159 Ibid 317.

Since present generations are protecting cultural property for the benefit of future generations, in so doing present generations are not only making it clear for whom they are acting, they are also emphasising their expectations *vis-à-vis* 'the appropriate normative attitude'[160] relating to preservation of cultural property. As Sarah Harding reasons:

> We would be mortified if the next generation failed to respect those things we have strived so hard to protect, just as we are when our own generation disregards this obligation. We do not protect cultural heritage to give future generations the option of neglect and mistreatment, we protect it because we think it should, to the extent possible, be around for all generations.[161]

In Harding's view a duty to protect cultural property can exist independently of a right.[162] She explains that just as individual human beings do have obligations to themselves in the absence of a right, a duty of future generations to protect cultural property, too, can be founded on a duty in the absence of a right.[163]

Imposing obligations to future generations might involve difficulties. By imposing an infinite duty to cultural property, generations might be seen as being put into an unequal position. Present generations expect future generations to take over the same duty of protecting cultural property because cultural property will promote their flourishing just as it improves human wellbeing and enhances human flourishing of present generations. On the other hand, while benefiting from cultural property themselves, future generations cannot benefit present generations. By the same token, whereas present generations may harm future generations, for instance, by failing to fulfil their duty to protect cultural property, future generations cannot harm present generations (at least not directly). Even if future generations neglect a duty to respect cultural property, present generations cannot hold them accountable if they are gone by the time future generations take over cultural property. Besides, future generations might well be happy with their own quality of life even in the absence of cultural property which their predecessors considered so valuable.

But again, certain things are so much greater than themselves that they demand intergenerational respect irrespective of the 'cultural taste' of a given generation. The existence of countless centuries- or even millennia-old cultural objects confirms that their preservation derives from an ongoing sense of respect and duty, stretching from one generation to another. In a continuing process of handing over, each generation benefits not only during its existence but also posthumously because when future generations take on their duty of

---

160 Ibid 325.

161 Ibid.

162 Ibid.

163 Ibid.

protecting cultural property, they preserve the memory and the legacy of their predecessors thereby ensuring cultural perpetuation. In this sense there is reciprocity between generations with respect to cultural property. Since respect for cultural property is beneficial for both present and future generations, the failure to do so produces a mutually detrimental result. Consequently, in handling cultural property the present and the future 'can' both benefit from each other and harm each other.

Because preservation of cultural property always benefits future generations, intergenerational fairness should be a concern in dealing with cultural property. No one can afford frivolous dealing with cultural property. To ensure the preservation of cultural property, its protection and transfer to future generations is not only elevated to an ethical level but is also a normative imperative extended to all peoples and applicable to all objects of cultural property at all times, including times of armed conflict – the most testing of all times where the survival of cultural property is concerned.

IV Armed Conflict as a Threat to the Survival of Cultural Property

A Cultural Property as the Target of Warfare

Although precious to all humanity, cultural property is continuously exposed to various threats. While some of the threats, such as earthquakes and floods, are nature-based and largely untameable forces, others, such as neglect, urban development and armed conflict are human-made. Ironically, although made by humans, cultural property is, in fact, most seriously endangered by humans. Of all human-made disasters and threats to cultural property, armed conflict appears to be the least controllable and it inflicts the most serious damage on such property. Immovable cultural property is particularly fragile in armed conflict. Although an armed conflict also takes a terrible toll on movable cultural property, such property at least can be removed from the theatre of war and taken to safer areas. Immovable cultural property, on the other hand, for obvious reasons, stays where it is.

Ever since there has been armed conflict and there have existed cultural objects, there has been destruction of such objects. It may be argued that armed conflict is an inherently destructive phenomenon and that the destruction of cultural property is an inevitable consequence of combat. Indeed, some destruction of cultural property does occur accidentally. However, sometimes cultural objects are targeted for destruction deliberately. In some instances the justification for the destruction is sought by advancing the argument of military necessity. This argument has been raised as a standard defence by accused war criminals in the post-WWI and -WWII trials,[164] as well as by the defendants

164 See Merryman, 'Two Ways', above n 9, 839.

at the ICTY.[165] Nonetheless, throughout history, when destroyed wilfully, cultural property has most often been destroyed without any military justification.

For centuries, the destruction of the enemy's monuments, temples, religious sites, libraries and other cultural objects has been considered part and parcel of military victory. Victors could destroy cultural property of conquered nations with no repercussions and had the right to seize whatever cultural objects they could carry as the 'spoils of war'. The history of looting of cultural objects as 'trophies of war' can be traced back to the ancient Roman Empire in 400 BC.[166] It is believed that the Romans originated 'the idea of the triumph as the rape of the works of art in which a nation gloried, and their display in the triumphal procession upon the conqueror's return to Rome'.[167] The loot was displayed to demonstrate the prowess of their victories. But the Romans were also known for their savagery in destroying immovable cultural property. The destruction of Carthage – Rome's old rival and enemy – in 146 BC is a case in point. Cato, a Roman statesman, constantly cautioned that 'Carthage must be destroyed' (*Delenda est Carthago*). It was Scipio Africanus the younger, the Roman general famed for his exploits during the Third Punic War,[168] to whom the destruction of this city was attributed. As François Bugnion writes, '[n]ot a monument, not a temple, not a tomb was spared'.[169] After adding Carthage to the Roman Empire as the new Roman province of Africa, Scipio returned to Rome for a triumph and to be hailed as the second Africanus. This ancient practice of destroying cultural treasures and of gaining promotion afterwards, among other things, has, unfortunately, been extended to present times. This was the common practice during the 1990s Balkan conflicts. For instance, Captain Vladimir Kovačević, who most immediately commanded the 6 December 1991 attack on the Old Town of Dubrovnik, was promoted some eight days after the attack.[170]

When it comes to the fate of cultural property on the battlefield, Carthage-like distressing scenes have been found in war-ravaged areas across the globe

---

165 See, eg, proceedings in the *Milošević* case, *Prosecutor v Slobodan Milošević*, Case No. IT-02-54 [*Milošević* or *Milošević* case] and in the *Strugar* case, *Prosecutor v Pavle Strugar*, Case No. IT-01-42 [*Strugar* or *Strugar* case]. Transcripts [T] at, http://www.un.org/icty/cases/indictments-e.htm.

166 See, eg, Leonard DuBoff, *Art in a Nutshell* (2nd ed 1993) 30; Myerowitz, above n 1, 1962; Wilhelm Treue, *Art Plunder: The Fate of Works of Art in War and Unrest* (1961).

167 Treue, ibid 13.

168 The Third Punic War lasted from 149 to 146 BC.

169 François Bugnion, 'The Origins and Development of the Legal Protection of Cultural Property in the Event of Armed Conflict', http://www.icrc.org/Web/eng/siteeng.nsf/html/65SHTJ.

170 See *Strugar* Trial Judgement, para 174.

throughout the history of humankind.[171] From the fall of ancient Rome, the Crusades, the Thirty Years' War and French Revolution to the World Wars and the recent events in Cambodia, Afghanistan, Kuwait, Iraq and the former Yugoslavia, there are numerous examples of purposeful devastation inflicted on cultural property in armed conflict,[172] which, as Humphreys appropriately puts it, 'provokes dark reflections on the malicious vandalism of our species'.[173] Although deliberate destruction of cultural property has been expressly prohibited by international law since the end of nineteenth century, the law has not been able to curb the destructive appetite of the human species.[174]

One cannot even begin to imagine the quantity of cultural property that has been lost forever throughout history due to armed conflicts. Research shows that destruction of cultural property in the former Yugoslavia during the 1990s conflicts alone amounted to 'cultural catastrophe', the worst seen in post-WWII Europe.[175] The horrendous scale, pattern and intensity of destruction there show

---

171 See Boylan, *Review*, above n 5, para 2.4 (noting that '[t]he destruction, defacing or conversion to a deliberately inappropriate use of monuments of special cultural value to the identity and spiritual values of a conquered people – such as religious buildings and national historic sites – has been widely used throughout history as a sign of conquest and subjugation'); Humphreys, above n 90, para 7 (observing that one can find 'countless examples' of purposeful destruction of cultural property 'at all periods and among all cultures').

172 In addition to the destruction of Carthage by the Romans in the second century BC, some of the precedents for malicious destruction of immovable cultural property include the destruction of Ayutthaya in Thailand by the Burmese in 1767, the Library of Louvain, Belgium in 1915, and old Warsaw in 1944. For a historical overview of the deliberate destruction of cultural property in armed conflict, see, generally, Leonard DuBoff and Sally Holt Caplan, *The Deskbook of Art Law* (2nd ed 1996). See also Boylan, *Review*, above n 5, paras 2.2-2.6; Toman, above n 104; Myerowitz, above n 1, 1961-63; Humphreys, above n 90, paras 4-14; Bevan, above n 53.

173 Humphreys, ibid para 4. In times of extreme stress such as in armed conflict, it is the most primitive level of human brain activity that is often acted upon, rather than the most rational part of the brain which would comply with the rules and follow the implicit mandate of social responsibility. See, eg, ICOMOS Sweden/Central Board of National Antiquities/Swedish National Commission for UNESCO, *Information as an Instrument for Protection against War Damages to the Cultural Heritage. Report from a Seminar, June 1994* Stockholm, Svenska Unescoradets skriftserie, 4/1994 (1994) Stockholm: ICOMOS Sweden [*Information as an Instrument*]; Rebecca Knuth, *Burning Books and Leveling Libraries* (2006).

174 For a detailed evolution of the international rules on the protection of cultural property in armed conflict see, eg, Roger O'Keefe, *The Protection of Cultural Property in Armed Conflict* (2006). See also Toman, above n 104; Kevin Chamberlain, *War and Cultural Heritage: An Analysis of the Hague Convention for the Protection of Cultural Property in the Event of Armed Conflict* (2004).

175 *First COE Report*, above n 123.

that the destruction was largely carried out deliberately.[176] Experts assessed the cultural damage and loss in the first few months of the conflict in Croatia as being greater than in the four years of WWII in the region.[177] Sadly, this was just the beginning. What followed there and elsewhere in the former Yugoslavia during the 1990s, particularly in Bosnia and Herzegovina, amounted to a cultural onslaught.[178] Since cultural property is part of the shared cultural heritage of humanity and as such belongs to everyone, including both the 'holder' and the 'attacker' of cultural property, it would follow that no one could possibly benefit from its destruction. Why is this property, despite the imperative of its preservation, being deliberately targeted from one armed conflict to another?

B Why is Cultural Property Targeted in Armed Conflict?

While the approach to the fate of cultural treasures on the battlefield has historically shifted from the 'lawfulness' of deliberate targeting to explicit prohibition at the international level at the end of the nineteenth century, the underlying motives, such as the marking of military victory, demoralisation of the enemy, enforcement of ethnic cleansing, satisfaction of territorial ambitions, imposition of control, re-writing of history, eradication of the achievements of the enemy and revenge, have remained more or less the same. But why exactly is cultural property targeted? It is precisely because it is precious that this property is destroyed.[179] In the final analysis, cultural objects are targeted in armed conflicts for the very same reasons that people care about such objects and are trying to preserve them. When deliberately targeting cultural objects, the perpetrators' ultimate aim is to annihilate the enemy and to degrade the people on the 'other' side – to crush them psychologically. John Yarwood contends that

---

176 Ibid. See also Herscher and Riedlmayer, *Kosovo Report*, above n 10; András Riedlmayer, 'Destruction of Cultural Heritage in Bosnia-Herzegovina, 1992-1996: A Post-war Survey of Selected Municipalities' 2002, [*BH Report*]; Boylan, *Review*, above n 5, 117-118.

177 *First COE Report*, above n 123; Boylan, *Review*, ibid.

178 See *First COE Report*, above n 123 and subsequent COE Reports (*Second Information Report*, doc 6869, 17 July 1993; *Third Information Report*, doc 6904, 20 September 1993; *Fourth Information Report*, doc 6999, 19 January 1994; *Fifth Information Report*, doc 7070, 12 April 1994; *Seventh Information Report*, doc 7308, 15 May 1995; and *Eighth Information Report*, doc 7341, 28 June 1995); Riedlmayer, *BH Report*, above n 176.

179 See, eg, Yarwood, above n 33, 197 (arguing that in the Balkans, cultural property is destroyed in armed conflict for the same reasons for which such property is considered special).

'cultural warfare'[180] is associated with nationalism and that '[a]n enemy will seek to weaken the will to fight or even to exist, by undermining identity'.[181]

Although other types of material property are destroyed in armed conflict, cultural objects are attacked specifically because the perpetrators know that the end result of such targeting will impact deeply upon the people concerned. Dr Colin Kaiser, who as the UNESCO representative often travelled to the former Yugoslavia during the 1990s, summarises the impact of the destruction of religious and cultural property on the affected people as follows:

> The destruction of a mosque or a church is different from the destruction of a Bosnian's house. What happens to you, everybody knows that you're mortal. Your life is a series of accidents. But the mosque or the church, it represents an order to the world. When you destroy that, you are sort of tampering or threatening their existence. It's often been said to me in my travels during the war, and not only about churches and mosques, but about other major cultural buildings, that, 'We get used to being killed. We know that human life is no more tangible or permanent than the life of a butterfly. But when we see these other buildings being destroyed, we see the rest of the world starting to crumble around us, and we become lost'.[182]

Attackers know that by striking at cultural property they are striking at the social fabric of the community to which they think the cultural object is most immediately linked.[183] War tactics aimed at denigrating and destroying the social fabric of a community are nothing new. They are age-old tactics which happen to be among the most effective tools of warfare. The deliberate destruction of cultural property on a massive scale in the former Yugoslavia demonstrates that these tactics are also part of modern warfare.[184]

---

180 Yarwood identifies five categories of deliberate destruction of cultural property, the fourth of which is called 'cultural warfare' which occurs 'in situations where this assists neither military nor ethnic cleansing operations [and which] may be done at considerable cost to the attacker and may be either an uncontrolled sporadic psychopathic efflorescence, or, more probably, a deliberately planned psychological operation'. Ibid 192.

181 Ibid 194.

182 'War and Cultural Property' in National Arts Journalism Program, *Who Owns Culture?* (statement of Dr Colin Kaiser, quoted by Peter McCloskey, Office of the Prosecutor, ICTY), 68 (Copy on file with author).

183 See, eg, Bevan, above n 53 (arguing that the cultural war rages behind architectural annihilation, and that in this subliminal assault lies the complex aim of exterminating a people).

184 See, Patrick Boylan, 'Protecting the World's Cultural Heritage in Times of Armed Conflict' paper tabled at the symposium in the absence of the author, Towards a Museology of Reconciliation, 1998, http://kafka.uvic.ca/`maltwood.tmr/boylan.html (noting that the deliberate targeting of cultural property has become an

Ironically, however, when wilfully damaging the enemy's cultural objects, perpetrators not only harm the opposing side but also ultimately harm themselves. At the same time, they harm the rest of the international community as an unlawful attack on cultural property 'represents a violation of values especially protected by the international community'.[185]

V The Necessity for Justice for Cultural Property-Related Wartime Atrocities

A The Benefits of International Justice

Under international law, unlawful attacks on cultural property in armed conflict may constitute war crimes. These international crimes can be prosecuted and tried at either a national or international tribunal.[186] Despite grave losses of cultural property in armed conflict, States have been reluctant to prosecute crimes involving cultural property. In fact, States have been perennially reluctant to prosecute war crimes generally, especially if these crimes involved their own nationals.[187] This, however, does not preclude the exercise of jurisdiction by international tribunals. Nevertheless, except for the Nürnberg trial and Tokyo trial, there has been a failure to prosecute through international jurisdiction prior to the establishment of the ICTY in 1993, not only in relation to cultural property but generally *vis-à-vis* all crimes.[188]

The establishment of the ICTY has been the turning point in this regard. Since this court became operational, the international community has been taking unprecedented steps to limit the impunity all too often associated with various wartime atrocities such as mass killings, torture, rape as a weapon of war, and extensive destruction of cultural property. There has been a proliferation of international criminal justice mechanisms[189] and the application of uni-

increasingly common feature of both international and non-international armed conflicts, and pointing to the role of nationalism as one of the root causes) ['Protecting the World's Cultural Heritage'].

185 *Jokić* Sentencing Judgement, para 46.

186 See Cherif Bassiouni, 'Reflections on Criminal Jurisdiction in International Protection of Cultural Property' (1983) 10 *Syracuse Journal of International Law and Commerce* 281, 285-86 ['Reflections'].

187 See, eg, Antonio Cassese, 'On the Current Trends towards Criminal Prosecution and Punishment of Breaches of International Humanitarian Law' (1998) 9 *European Journal of International Law* 1, 2-4 ['Current Trends']; Timothy McCormack, 'Their Atrocities and Our Misdemeanours: The Reticence of States to Try Their "Own Nationals" for International Crimes' in Mark Lattimer and Philippe Sands (eds), *Justice for Crimes against Humanity* (2003) 107 ['Their Atrocities'].

188 Cassese, ibid 4.

189 See, eg, Diane Amann, 'Assessing International Criminal Adjudication of Human

versal jurisdiction to hold perpetrators of the most serious crimes to account.[190] The establishment of the ICTY was followed by the creation of the International Criminal Tribunal for Rwanda (ICTR) in 1994.[191] These two tribunals are *ad hoc* in nature. Their creation by the UN Security Council reflected, *inter alia*, the stark failures of national court systems. Various suspects have been tried irrespective of their official status, including the first trial of a sitting head of state, Slobodan Milošević, by the ICTY, and the trial of the former Prime Minister of Rwanda, Jean Kambanda, by the ICTR. With the recent arrest of four major suspects, including two Bosnian Serb leaders, Ratko Mladić and Radovan Karadžić, accused, along with others, for the Srebrenica genocide, the ICTY has been successful in arresting all of its 161 indictees. As of 17 January 2012, the ICTR's record is slightly less impressive as nine of its 90 indictees are still at large. These Tribunals do not have police or any other form of enforcement mechanism of their own, which impacts on their arrest records. The search for those at large continues, nevertheless.[192]

Notwithstanding this and some other shortcomings, such as the remoteness from victims, slow pace of trials and high cost, the two tribunals have compiled an admirable record in bringing to justice and providing a fair trial for a number of indictees. In the process, they have developed, as the former ICTY Judge Patricia Wald put it in reference to the ICTY, 'a phenomenal body of jurisprudence that brings life to the abstract precepts of international law'[193] and have made a significant contribution to the development of international crimi-

---

Rights Atrocities' in *Third World Legal Studies–2000-2003: Into the 21st Century: Reconstruction and Reparations in International Law* (2003), 170; Fausto Pocar, 'The Proliferation of International Criminal Courts and Tribunals' (2004) 2(2) *Journal of International Criminal Justice* 304-308. For information on international courts and tribunals see also the Project on International Courts and Tribunals (PICT) at, http://www.pict-pcti.org.

190 See, eg, Steven Ratner and Jason Abrams, *Accountability for Human Rights Atrocities in International Law* (2001); O'Connell, above n 14, nn 109-112 and accompanying text; Madeleine Davis, *The Pinochet Case: Origins, Progress, and Implications* (2003); Mark Lattimer and Philippe Sands (eds), *Justice for Crimes against Humanity* (2003); Stacie Jonas, 'The Ripple Effect of the Pinochet Case' (2004) 11(3) *Human Rights Brief* 36-38. It should be noted that generous application of universal jurisdiction continues to meet serious objections. Also, according to research, universal jurisdiction has not been contemplated for an unlawful attack on cultural property.

191 See *Resolution on establishment of an International Tribunal for Rwanda and adoption of the Statute of the Tribunal*, Security Council Resolution 955 (1994) of 8 November 1994, UN Doc. S/RES/955 (1994) [ICTR].

192 See ICTY's and ICTR's websites, http://www.un.org/icty and http://www.un.org/ictr.

193 Patricia Wald, 'UN Should Stay the Course in The Hague' *The Korea Herald* 10 November 2007, http://listserve.buffalo.edu/archives/justwatch-l.html [5].

nal law. Their experience revived the idea of creating a permanent international criminal tribunal where justice can be rendered for the gravest crimes when national courts are unable or unwilling to do so.

In 1998, negotiations to establish the ICC, a permanent international criminal court, were completed by the adoption of the *Statute* of this Court, which four years later, after sixty states ratified this treaty, came into force. Ever since the adoption of its *Statute*, the ICC has engendered great expectations. Meanwhile, the Court has become operational and is closely looking into seven situations (involving 14 cases), including Ituri province of the Democratic Republic of Congo, Uganda, the Sudanese district of Darfur and Libya. As of 17 January 2012, the ICC has several suspects in its custody, including former Congolese warlord Thomas Lubanga and Germain Katanga, the alleged leader of the Patriotic Resistance Force in Ituri.[194]

The beginning of this millennium marked another development in international criminal justice mechanisms, the so-called 'hybrid' national-international tribunals. Such tribunals, where international judges sit together with local judges, were established in East Timor (the so-called Special Panels for Serious Crimes), Kosovo (the Regulation 64 Panels), Sierra Leone (the Special Court for Sierra Leone), BH (the War Crimes Chamber within the Criminal Division of the State Court of Bosnia and Herzegovina) and in Cambodia (the Khmer Rouge Extraordinary Chambers).[195] All these tribunals have faced problems at some stage, including serious budgetary constraints.[196] Despite some failings, they, together with the *ad hoc* tribunals and the ICC, represent a tremendous effort made by the international community towards ending impunity for the most serious international crimes.

As Justice Robert H. Jackson, who was the chief US prosecutor at the Nürnberg trial, explained, and indeed urged, in his opening statement,

> [t]he wrongs which we seek to condemn and punish have been so calculated, so malignant, and so devastating, that civilization cannot tolerate their being ignored, because it cannot survive their being repeated.[197]

---

194 For information about the ICC, including situations and cases, see, http://www.icc-cpi.int/home.html.

195 See, eg, Steven Roper and Lilian Barria, *Designing Criminal Tribunals: Sovereignty and International Concerns in the Protection of Human Rights* (2006).

196 See, eg, Richard Dicker and Elise Keppler, 'Beyond The Hague: The Challenges of International Justice', Human Rights Watch, World Report 2004, at http://hrw.org/wr2k4/ and at http://www.globalpolicy.org/intljustice/general/2004/0205beyond.htm.

197 Opening Statement of Justice Jackson (21 November 1945) in *Trial of Major War Criminals before the International Military Tribunal* (1948) vol 2, 98-99.

Sadly, many of the 'wrongs' Justice Jackson referred to have been repeated in numerous armed conflicts that have occurred since WWII. Why now and not sooner this sudden influx of enforcement of international law through international criminal law adjudication? The end of the Cold War and the ever increasing use of television and other technological tools to screen and thereby make public disturbing images of wartime atrocities worldwide greatly contributed to more being seen and greater insistence than before that something be done.[198] Now, for the first time since the immediate post-WWII period, international criminal tribunals are adjudicating crimes that, even if they occur within a state's borders, offend the entire international community.

The strides made in the area of international justice have been felt at the national level as well. Using domestic universal jurisdiction laws in domestic courts, several States, including Belgium, Denmark and Germany, have tried individuals found on their territory accused of crimes committed in other countries.[199] In October 1998, British authorities arrested former Chilean President Augusto Pinochet on an extradition request from a Spanish judge who brought charges of genocide, torture and other crimes during his rule in the 1970s and 80s. The Pinochet case prompted other litigation for the past wrongs in Chile, as well as in Argentina, Chad, Uruguay and elsewhere,[200] which further demonstrates how efforts to bring justice at the international level influenced developments at the national level, for instance, access to national courts where the crimes occurred, in cases which were previously barred from litigation.

The proliferation of international justice mechanisms tells us about the importance of international criminal adjudication in redressing wartime atrocities. Various claims as to the objectives and functions of this method have been made, including retribution, redress, deterrence and the promotion of peace.

Retribution is considered the first and foremost goal of international criminal adjudication. According to the jurisprudence of international criminal tribunals, 'the individual must be punished because he broke the law' and retribution is an important function of punishment.[201] By holding accountable those who violate international law, international tribunals restore confidence in the rule of law.[202] In the opinion of Antonio Cassese, the first President of the ICTY, trials at international criminal tribunals demonstrate the will of the international community to break with the past by punishing those who have

198 For discussion about the role of international criminal adjudication of violations of international law see generally, Amann, above n 189.

199 See, eg, Ratner and Abrams, above n 190, 160-186; O'Connell, above n 14.

200 See, eg, Jonas, above n 190.

201 *Prosecutor v Furundžija*, Judgement, Trial Chamber II, 10 December 1998, Case No. IT-95-17/1-T, para 288 [*Furundžija* Trial Judgement]. See also *Jokić* Sentencing Judgement, paras 31 and 35 (pointing to the retributive and rehabilitative purpose of punishment, respectively).

202 See Cassese, 'Current Trends', above n 187, 5.

deviated from acceptable standards of human behaviour. However, Cassese stresses that the purpose of punishment 'is not so much retribution as stigmatisation of the deviant behaviour'.[203] Notwithstanding this, Cassese notes that in exercising its retributive function, 'an international criminal tribunal may serve to fill the vacuum left by national legislation on amnesty' and 'may thus do justice where national jurisdictions are unable to do so and where victims would otherwise have no remedy'.[204]

Also, in calling the offenders to account, an international criminal tribunal determines their individual criminal responsibility. By individualising guilt, it detracts from the notion of collective guilt under which an entire people is to blame for the crimes committed by certain individuals fighting in its name. The individualisation of guilt is seen to have the potential to contribute to the process of national reconciliation and to promote peace.[205]

Rendering justice to the victims of war crimes is considered the next major objective of international criminal tribunals. The protection of the weak and vulnerable in times of armed conflict is among the major goals of international humanitarian law.[206] As the *Erdemović* Trial Chamber observed, international criminal trials 'contribute to appeasement and give the chance to the people who were sorely afflicted to mourn'.[207]

International criminal tribunals also have the role of deterring future crimes. The ICTY, for instance, stresses that through punishment it aims to discourage the commission of similar crimes. This is a twofold aim: to turn the specific perpetrator away from future wrongdoing (special deterrence) and to discourage others from committing the same kind of crime (general deterrence).[208]

Furthermore, an international criminal tribunal is considered an independent tribunal, composed of impartial judges of various nations not parties to the conflict, who are well versed in international law. The 'impartial justice' applied by an international criminal tribunal can, as Cassese notes, 'serve to

---

203 Ibid.

204 Ibid.

205 Ibid. See also *Prosecutor v Jean Paul Akayesu*, Judgement, Trial Chamber, 2 September 1998, Case No. ICTR-96-4-T, para 2 [*Akayesu* Trial Judgement].

206 See, eg, *Prosecutor v Dražen Erdemović*, Judgement, Appeals Chamber, 7 October 1997, para 75 (Joint Separate Opinion of Judge McDonald and Judge Vohran), [*Erdemović* Appeal Judgement]. http://www.un.org/erdemovic/appeal/judgement/erd-asojmcd971007e.htm.

207 *Prosecutor v Erdemović*, Sentencing Judgement, Trial Chamber I, 29 November 1996, Case No. IT-96-22-T, para 65 [*Erdemović* Sentencing Judgement], http://www.un.org/erdemovic/trial/judgement/erd-tsj961129e.htm.

208 See *Jokić* Sentencing Judgement, para 33.

blunt the hatred of the victims and their desire for revenge'[209] and contribute to re-establishing peaceful relations on the ground.

Moreover, it has been claimed that international criminal proceedings build a historical record. This is an impartial and objective record of events which, unlike a fact-finding commission or truth commission, passes the rigorous test of judicial scrutiny.[210] The historical record contributes to establishing the truth, which in turn adds to the process of reconciliation and peace. Only when the former foes confront the past can they go forward into the shared future. The failure to do so and to bring to justice the perpetrators of the past wrongdoings breeds more crimes. Where there is silence at the national level, international wrongs must be addressed by an international criminal tribunal. In fact, since the entire international community is offended by international crimes, the message that impunity is not an option resonates much more loudly worldwide if it comes from an international criminal tribunal which acts as a representative of the international community.

International criminal adjudication is an imperfect mechanism and cannot alone fulfil its promises, particularly that of promoting peace.[211] This is above all the case where war crimes have been committed on a massive scale, and in the search for truth and reconciliation additional methods must be considered. International criminal justice is widely seen as random and selective, which greatly affects the goal of retribution and deterrence. Moreover, international tribunals are structured to limit the victim's role. The pacification role of international tribunals is also debatable. This is evidenced by the prolongation of conflicts in the former Yugoslavia well after the establishment of the ICTY. Similar scepticism is attached to the goal of historic record making; namely, what emerges out of international criminal proceedings is likely to be an incomplete record as the trials are focused on particular accused individuals and only on those events that are included in the indictment. However, as long as serious international crimes are being committed and states are unwilling or unable to bring the perpetrators to justice, there is the necessity for international criminal justice for such crimes. There is the need to deal with the past in order to have a future. The failure to do so may risk producing a generation-long hatred and desire for revenge.

---

209 Cassese, 'Current Trends', above n 187, 5.

210 Ibid.

211 See, eg, Amann, above n 189, 173-181; Dicker and Keppler, above n 196.

B Cultural Property at the International Criminal Tribunals

1 Historical Antecedents

(a) The Leipzig Trials

Although wartime cultural destruction has a long history it was not until devastation occurred on a global scale during the World Wars that the international community reacted collectively to cultural wrongs. However, the first steps made in this regard have been cautious. During WWI, norms of international law relating to cultural property were grossly violated across the battlefields resulting in widespread and extensive damage and destruction of cultural property, including the infamous bombing of the Rheims Cathedral, the burning of the Louvain University Library and the destruction of cultural property in Arras.[212] After the war, in January 1919, the Commission on Responsibility for War and Guarantees was established to collect evidence concerning attacks against cultural property.[213] The subsequently adopted *Treaty of Peace with Germany*, also known as the *Treaty of Versailles*, envisaged that Germans accused of war crimes would be tried by military tribunals of the victorious Allies.[214] This was categorically rejected by the Germans who even threatened the resumption of the war if the Allies pressed the matter. Eventually it was agreed that Germans accused of war crimes would be tried by their own national court, namely the high court, the Reichsgericht in Leipzig.[215] The obligation to apply international law introduced the 'international' component into the Leipzig trials.

Notwithstanding this, the Leipzig trials proved to be ineffectual. The number of persons accused of war crimes that were tried in Leipzig and the sentences imposed upon them prove the point. Specifically, when the agreement was reached to conduct trials in Leipzig, the Allies drastically reduced the initial list of 896 war crimes suspects to 45 alleged war criminals, but the Germans agreed to try only 12 of them. In the end, only six persons were tried and convicted. The sentences were also grossly inadequate. To add to the farce, those who were eventually imprisoned immediately 'escaped'.[216] No one was tried for offences involving cultural property. Still, peace treaties concluded after WWI included clauses providing for the restitution of cultural property and for reparations and the Joint Arbitral Tribunal was established to adjudicate the amount

212 See, eg, Boylan, *Review*, above n 5, 27, para 2.16; Bassiouni, 'Reflections', above n 186, 291.

213 See Toman, above n 104, 14.

214 *Treaty of Peace with Germany*, 28 June 1919, 2 Bevans 43, art 228, 11 Marthens Nouveau Recueil (ser. 3) (1919) 323 [*Treaty of Versailles*].

215 See Merryman, 'Two Ways', above n 9, 836, fn 18.

216 Ibid. For an account and evaluation of the Leipzig trials, see C. Mullins, *The Leipzig Trials* (1921).

of reparations, which indicate that cultural property was not completely overlooked.

(b) The IMT

The first truly international enforcement of international law protecting cultural property in armed conflict took place in the immediate aftermath of WWII with the establishment of an international military tribunal at Nürnberg. The Nürnberg International Military Tribunal for the Trial of the Major War Criminals of the European Axis (IMT) was established by the *London Agreement of 8 August 1945* (*London Agreement*).[217] The establishment of the IMT was a response to the massive atrocities committed by the German forces during WWII. Among those atrocities were the destruction and plunder of cultural property carried out wilfully, systematically and on an unprecedented scale. Although the IMT dealt with cultural property, such property was not included in the *Charter* annexed to the London Agreement (*IMT Charter*). Under Article 6 of the *Charter*, the IMT had jurisdiction over crimes against peace, war crimes and crimes against humanity. Cultural property was covered by war crimes under the rubric of 'plunder of public or private property'.[218]

Although cultural property suffered grave damage during WWII, it was not given as prominent a place at the IMT as is often thought to be the case. In addition to the absence of any direct reference to cultural property in the *IMT Charter*, cultural property did not have a prominent place in the IMT Indictment either. The Indictment included four counts: Count One – The Common Plan or Conspiracy; Count Two – Crimes against Peace; Count Three – War Crimes; and Count Four – Crimes against Humanity. Each count consisted of the Statement of the Offence and the Particulars. Cultural property was mainly included in the Particulars. It was most extensively dealt with in Count Three of the Indictment. Curiously, 'plunder' of movable cultural property and 'destruction' of immovable cultural property were covered under the same crime of '*plunder* of public and private property'.[219] Cultural property was

---

217 See *Agreement by the Government of the United States of America, the Provisional Government of the French Republic, the Government of the United Kingdom of Great Britain and Northern Ireland and the Government of the Union of Soviet Socialist Republics for the Prosecution and Punishment of the Major War Criminals of the European Axis*, 8 August 1945 [*London Agreement*], http://www.yale.edu/lawweb/avalon/imt/proc/imtchart.htm. Article 2 of the Agreement provides that the constitution, jurisdiction and functions of the IMT shall be set in the *Charter* annexed to the Agreement, which *Charter* shall form an integral part of the Agreement [*IMT Charter*]. The IMT was established by Article 1 of the *IMT Charter*.

218 *IMT Charter*, art 6(b).

219 Trial of the Major War Criminals before the International Military Tribunal, Indictment, Nürnberg, 20 November 1945, Official Documents, vol I, 27 [*IMT*

addressed in an unsystematic manner in the Indictment and was squeezed in between other types of property, such as raw materials or agricultural stock including cows, pigs, poultry and agricultural machines of all kinds.[220] Where movable cultural property is concerned, the Indictment focused mainly on the economic aspect of art plunder. The approach taken to immovable cultural property slightly differed as the Indictment occasionally emphasised the importance of cultural property as a special type of property.

Nevertheless, the IMT focused on the 'seizure' of movable cultural property and centred its discussion on the defendant Alfred Rosenberg, the organiser of the 'Einsatzstab Rosenberg', and infamous for carrying out the massive art seizure. The IMT held that this defendant was responsible for structuring a system of organised plunder of both public and private cultural and other property throughout the invaded countries of Europe.[221] The IMT noted that the defendant's own records showed the extent of the plunder. The IMT found Rosenberg guilty on all four counts of the Indictment[222] and sentenced him to death by hanging.[223]

As Matthew Lippman correctly observes, the inclusion of Rosenberg in the IMT trial was aimed at highlighting the Reich's theft of cultural property.[224] Even if the plunder of cultural property was just one of the charges, it still ranked high in the discussion and in the determination of the sentence in this defendant's case. In Lippman's words, the imposed sentence was an 'unprecedented criminal punishment for art theft by the International Military

---

Indictment] Count Three: War Crimes, (E) Plunder of Public and Private Property, http://www.yale.edu/lawweb/avalon/imt/proc/count3.htm.

220 See *IMT Indictment*, Count Three, Plunder of Public and Private Property, Particulars, Eastern Countries, para 21, http://www.yale.edu/lawweb/avalon/imt/proc/count3.htm. The International Military Tribunal for the Far East, established by a Special Proclamation by the Supreme Commander for the Allied Powers at Tokyo, 19 January 1946, TIAS No. 1589, 4 Bevans 20 [IMTFE], to prosecute Japanese war crimes, took an even less impressive approach to cultural property. See Sanja Zgonjanin, 'Destruction of Libraries and Archives as a War Crime' (2005) 40 *Libraries and Culture* 128, 131-134 (discussing the case of the Shanghai Library).

221 See Trial of the Major War Criminals before the International Military Tribunal, Judgement, Nürnberg, 1 October 1946, Official Documents, vol I, 171 [*IMT Judgement*], The Accused Individuals, 6.Rosenberg – War Crimes and Crimes against Humanity, para 1, http://www.derechos.org/nizkor/nuremberg/cap9.html.

222 Ibid para 5.

223 *IMT Judgement*, The Sentences, para 7, http://www.derechos.org/nizkor/nuremberg/judgment/cap17.html.

224 See Matthew Lippman, 'Art and Ideology in the Third Reich: The Protection of Cultural Property and the Humanitarian Law of War' (1998) 17 *Dickinson Journal of International Law* 1, 48-49.

Tribunal'.[225] As far as the international criminal tribunals are concerned this kind of punishment for crimes against cultural property has never been repeated since. It is regrettable, however, that the IMT in its Judgement did not discuss or explicitly impose punishment for the plunder of cultural property in relation to other defendants, for instance, Herman Göring[226] and Wilhelm Keitel,[227] who were also involved in the seizure of artworks and other objects of cultural property.

It is also disappointing that the IMT Judgement did not discuss the destruction of immovable cultural property. Despite massive destruction of cultural monuments and other immovable cultural property, the Judgement made only a few brief references to the destruction of museums and to the burning and demolishing of synagogues,[228] for instance.

Notwithstanding these and other shortcomings, the inclusion of cultural property in the IMT Indictment and in the IMT Judgement was a significant recognition of the importance of cultural property. Since the IMT was the first international tribunal ever convened, some shortcomings were understandable. Given the enormity of other crimes committed by the Nazis, as well as the limited time and resources allocated to the Tribunal to deal with those crimes, the mere fact that the offences against cultural property were dealt with by this Tribunal is of enormous significance. This makes the conviction of the defendant Rosenberg relating to crimes involving cultural property even more significant.

However, the temporary character of this international criminal tribunal has seriously reduced its deterrent effect. In the absence of a permanent international enforcement mechanism, cultural property has continued to be the victim of warfare and to be deliberately destroyed, damaged and misappropriated with impunity. It was not until the destruction of cultural property reached catastrophic proportions in the territory of the former Yugoslavia half a century after Nürnberg that the international law protecting cultural property in armed conflict was enforced again at the international level.

2 The ICTY

While chapter six of this book deals more closely with the ICTY and its approach to cultural property, it is important to note here that like its predeces-

225 Ibid 49.

226 Various documents evidencing Göring's involvement in the plunder of cultural property can be accessed at http://www.ess.uwe.ac.uk/genocide/appropriation.htm.

227 For documents evidencing Keitel's involvement in cultural property-related atrocities visit http://www.ess.uwe.ac.uk/genocide/Rosenberg17.htm.

228 See *IMT Judgement*, War Crimes and Crimes against Humanity, (E) Persecution of the Jews, para 8, http://www.derechos.org/nizkor/nuremberg/judgment/cap7.html.

sor, the IMT, the ICTY is also an *ad hoc* criminal tribunal. The ICTY, however, was established by the UN Security Council in response to atrocities with a specific geographical and temporal scope, namely, those committed in the territory of the former Yugoslavia during the 1990s armed conflicts. Unlike the *IMT Charter*, which makes no reference to cultural property, the *Statute of the ICTY*, although it does not use the term 'cultural property', does refer to some types of objects that constitute cultural property. Whereas the IMT centred on movable cultural property, the ICTY's focus has been immovable cultural property. A number of individuals have been prosecuted and tried, *inter alia*, for unlawful attacks on cultural property. Some of the accused have already been convicted for cultural property-related war crimes and are serving their sentences. The so-called 'Dubrovnik' cases relating to the 1991 attack on the Old Town of Dubrovnik by the YA forces, have most prominently dealt with cultural property.

However, as with the IMT, cultural property at the ICTY is not as prominent as it ought to be. Due to various factors, including the magnitude of other crimes and the ICTY's limited resources, cultural property-related offences have to some extent been treated as second class at this Tribunal. Nevertheless, since the ICTY's convictions for the blatant attacks on cultural property in the 'Dubrovnik' cases, there has been no major deliberate wartime damage and destruction of cultural property. Also, the prosecutions and trials of the unlawful attacks on cultural property at the ICTY have influenced the criminalisation of such attacks by the ICC.

3 The ICC

The ICC is the first permanent international criminal tribunal. It was established by the *Rome Statute* which was adopted on 17 July 1998 by the United Nations Diplomatic Conference of Plenipotentiaries (*ICC Statute*). The Court has jurisdiction over persons for the most serious crimes of international concern. Acts against cultural property are among those crimes. Being an 'international' permanent criminal court, the ICC, through its *Statute*, emphasises the universal impact of crimes under its jurisdiction. '[S]uch grave crimes threaten the peace, security and well-being of the world',[229] and 'deeply shock the conscience of humanity'.[230] The *Statute* confirms that all peoples of the world are united by common bonds and that 'their cultures [are] pieced together in a shared heritage'.[231] Cultural property is part of humankind's shared heritage. The inclusion in the *ICC Statute* of crimes against cultural property among 'the

229 *ICC Statute*, Preamble para 3.

230 Ibid para 2.

231 Ibid para 1.

most serious crimes of concern to the international community as a whole'[232] demonstrates the determination of the international community to 'put an end to impunity for the perpetrators of these crimes',[233] and, at the same time, shows the significance of preserving cultural property.

Under the *ICC Statute*, States are obligated to take effective measures at the national level, as well as to enhance international cooperation in order to bring to justice those responsible for international crimes.[234] The *Statute* spells out that it is the primary '*duty* of every *State* to exercise its criminal jurisdiction over those responsible for international crimes'.[235] In situations where a State is unwilling or unable to prosecute,[236] on the basis of the principle of complementarity,[237] 'an independent permanent International Criminal Court',[238] established 'for the sake of present and future generations',[239] steps in.

The ICC has jurisdiction over crimes against cultural property under the rubrics of war crimes[240] and crimes against humanity (persecution).[241] When war crimes are involved, cultural property is placed among 'other serious violations of the laws and customs...of international law'. Like the *ICTY Statute*, the *ICC Statute* accords protection only to certain objects of cultural property. In regard to prosecution of unlawful acts against cultural property as a crime of persecution, the *ICC Statute*, like the *ICTY Statute*, takes an anthropocentric approach to cultural property, which somewhat conflicts with the universal nature of cultural property. All cultural property is ultimately considered part of humanity's shared cultural heritage, but to be prosecuted as a crime against humanity, under the *ICC Statute*, cultural property needs to be linked to an 'identifiable group or collectivity'. It appears that cultural property not claimed by any group or collectivity might remain unprotected no matter how significant it may be from the point of view of art, history or on some other grounds. Even if a cultural object is otherwise considered to 'belong' to more than one group or collectivity, for the purpose of prosecution it must be taken that it 'belongs' to a specific group or collectivity which has been persecuted. This somewhat undermines the universal value of cultural property.[242] Besides

232 Ibid para 4.

233 Ibid para 5.

234 Ibid paras 4 and 6.

235 Ibid para 6 (emphasis added).

236 Ibid art 17(1)(b).

237 Ibid Preamble para 10.

238 Ibid para 9.

239 Ibid.

240 Ibid arts 8(2)(b)(ix) and 8(2)(e)(iv).

241 Ibid art 7(1)(h).

242 This is merely an observational comment and it does not imply that objects should be ranked higher than human beings.

this limitation, the Court also has jurisdiction *ratione temporis* only with respect to crimes committed after the entry into force of its *Statute*.[243] Consequently, all damage to cultural property occurring prior to that date, that is, before 1 July 2002, will be left unpunished unless it is redressed by other mechanisms.

Time will tell how high crimes against cultural property will rank at the ICC. It does not seem likely that the ICC will consider isolated or low-profile cases of destruction of cultural property. It is more probable that the Court will consider cases that involve attacks on cultural objects which are 'a part of a plan or policy or as part of *large-scale* commission of such crimes'[244] rather than cases involving single acts of destruction of cultural objects. Still, unlike the *ICTY Statute*, the *ICC Statute* does not require that the attacks directed against cultural property 'result' in actual damage. The *ICC Statute* covers acts which involve 'intentionally *directing* attacks against [protected cultural objects] provided they are not military objectives'.[245]

Another reason not to become overly enthusiastic about the prosecution of crimes involving cultural property relates to the principle of complementarity. Under this principle, prosecution of crimes over which the ICC has jurisdiction lies primarily with nation states. Yet, prosecution of crimes involving cultural property has not been a priority at the national level. A general reluctance of States to prosecute and to impose adequate penalties has been the major characteristic of the approach to cultural property-related crimes taken at the national level.[246] Nevertheless, since the *ICC Statute* criminalises unlawful attacks on cultural property, the possibility always exists for the prosecution to be carried out at the international level in the event that a State fails to act. This possibility is particularly important, and more likely to be realised, where extensive damage to cultural property occurs. Additionally, the knowledge that unlawful attacks on cultural property are criminalised may save at least some cultural property as the criminalisation will cause at least some potential attackers to think twice before they act. Thus, the inclusion of cultural property-related crimes in the *ICC Statute* is of great importance in both responding to and preventing unlawful attacks against cultural property. Also, as a permanent mechanism, the ICC is, as Professor Diane Amann puts it, 'an essential step toward the *consistency* necessary so that international criminal adjudication properly may serve as one, though not the only, means to societal reconstruction'.[247]

Although this book is concerned only with the enforcement of IHL relating to cultural property through international criminal adjudication mecha-

243 Ibid art 11.

244 Ibid art 8(1) (emphasis added).

245 Ibid arts 8(2)(b)(ix) and 8(2)(e)(iv). Unlike the *ICC Statute*, the *ICTY Statute* fails to refer to a 'military objective'.

246 See, generally, James Nafziger, 'International Penal Aspects of Protecting Cultural Property' (1985) 19 *International Lawyer* 835 ['Penal Aspects'].

247 Amann, above n 189, 181 (emphasis added).

nisms, the role of national courts in enforcing rules on respect of cultural property should not be overlooked.[248] In addition to the potential for domestic courts to try violations of these rules as 'international crimes', in many States, the national legislature has written them into the domestic criminal code, under the heading of 'war crimes' or otherwise.[249] Bosnia and Herzegovina is one of those States. The *Criminal Code of the former Yugoslavia*[250] and the *Criminal Code of BH*,[251] along with the *Criminal Code of the Federation of BH*,[252] have criminalised violations of rules protecting cultural property. The fact that States have generally been reluctant to prosecute war crimes, including those concerning

---

248 See, eg, Ruth Wedgwood, 'National Courts and the Prosecution of War Crimes' in Gabrielle Kirk McDonald and Olivia Swaak-Goldman (eds), *Substantive and Procedural Aspects of International Criminal Law: The Experience of International and National Courts* (1999) 393-413, 393 ('The complementarity roles of national and international courts in processing war crimes is a durable feature of the international legal system. Even with the creation of new international tribunals in this decade, national tribunals remain essential in deterring and remedying violations of the laws of war').

249 See, eg, *UNESCO Reports on the Implementation of the 1954 Convention*, UNESCO Documents: CA/RBC/1/3 and Add. 1-6, SHC/MD/1 dated 19 May 1967; SHC/MD/6 dated 30 April 1970; CC/MD/41 of July 1979; CLT/MD/3 of December 1984; CC/MD/11 of December 1989; CLT-95/WS/13 of December 1995; CLT-2005/WS/6, 2005, available at, http://unesdoc.unesco.org/images/. See also, UNESCO, *National Implementation of the Penal Provisions of Chapter 4 of the Second Protocol of 26 March 1999 to the Hague Convention of 1954 for the Protection of Cultural Property in the Event of Armed Conflict*, Report prepared by Dr Roger O'Keefe, University of Cambridge, UNESCO Doc. CLT/CIH/MCO/2002/PI/H/1, Paris, 29 March 2002; Nafziger, 'Penal Aspects', above n 246.

250 Under Article 151 of the *Criminal Code of the Socialist Federal Republic of Yugoslavia* (SFRY):

> Whoever in time of war or armed conflict destroys cultural or historical monuments, buildings or establishments devoted to science, art, education or humanitarian purposes in violation of the rules of international law, shall be punished by imprisonment for not less than one year.

See *Criminal Code of SFRY*, art 151(1), adopted by the SFRY Assembly at the session of the Federal Council held on 28 September 1976, declared by a decree of the President of the Republic on 28 September 1976, published in the Official Gazette SFRY No. 44 of 8 October 1976, to which a correction was made in Official Gazette SFRY No. 36 of 15 July 1977 which took effect on 1 July 1977.

251 See *Criminal Code of Bosnia and Herzegovina*, arts 179(d) and 183, Official Gazette of Bosnia and Herzegovina No. 3/03, 32/03, 37/03, 54/04, 61/04, 30/05, entered into force 1 March 2003, consolidated version of December 2006 available at, http://www.legislationonline.org/upload/legislations/d2/.

252 See *Criminal Code of the Federation of Bosnia and Herzegovina*, arts 321 and 322, Official Gazette of the Federation of Bosnia and Herzegovina No. 36/03, entered into force 1 August 2003, available at, http://www.legislationonline.org/upload/legislations/b4/b2/5863a4917995d1a282d020fb.

cultural property, particularly if these crimes have involved their own nationals, does not mean that the matter should be allowed to rest there. In addition to the ICTY, Bosnia and Herzegovina itself should play an important role in prosecuting perpetrators of war crimes committed during the siege of Mostar, including the destruction of the Old Bridge.[253]

VI Summary and Observations

Since cultural property is considered so significant, and touches on so many peoples' concerns, there is a high degree of universal interest in its preservation. International rules have been defined to combat various threats to the survival of precious cultural treasures. The rules that emerged first dealt with the protection of cultural property in armed conflict. Although in devising laws protecting cultural property nationalist ideas and State self-interest have played a role (and, perhaps, still do to some extent), it has been the notion of the shared heritage of humankind that has compelled States to realise that objects of cultural property should be respected irrespective of their origin. States began to recognise that cultural property is of value to human society as a whole and also that an enemy's cultural property should be spared from the ravages of war as far as possible so that it can be preserved for future generations. The tragic cultural devastation that occurred during WWI and even more extensively during WWII increased international concern for cultural property. By institutionalising this concern through UNESCO, and the categorical declaration made in the *1954 Convention* that cultural property belonging to any people constitutes the cultural heritage of all humankind, the international community demonstrated a solemn commitment to do its best with respect to its duty to cultural property.

The international criminal adjudication of cultural property-related crimes has been one of the ways in which the international community has honoured its commitment *vis-à-vis* its duty to cultural property. However, international criminal adjudication is neither the only nor the perfect mechanism. The international criminal tribunals have highlighted many problems of international criminal justice, both of a general and cultural property-specific nature. International criminal justice has, *inter alia*, been random and selective, and cultural property has not been as prominent as it is often thought that it should be. Nevertheless, the enforcement of international law through criminal adjudication is an ever-evolving area. The past and present international tribunals have produced an impressive body of jurisprudence, a part of which concerns cultural property. The recently established permanent international criminal tribunal, the ICC, has the potential to enrich this body much further and to ensure the much needed consistency in the realm of international criminal adjudication.

International criminal adjudication is an indispensable method for redressing wartime atrocities, particularly where there is a failure in this regard at the

253 For efforts made in this direction, see chapter six of this book.

national level. Despite its imperfections, this method, together with the prosecution and punishment of offenders within national jurisdictions, remains, as the former ICTY President observes, 'the most effective means of enforcing international humanitarian law'.[254] In fact, 'the rule of international humanitarian law depends on its enforcement through the prosecution and punishment of its offenders'.[255] Where cultural property is concerned, history has shown time and again that failure to bring to justice those responsible for violations of the rules designed to protect this property encourages further such violations.

254 Cassese, 'Current Trends', above n 187, 10.

255 Ibid.

Chapter 3

The Old Bridge: Knowing the Facts

I An Overview

Cultural destruction in the former Yugoslavia during the 1990s is sad testimony to the fate of cultural treasures in times of armed conflict and to the consequences of the loss incurred. Immovable cultural property embodied in objects of both cultural specificity and cultural unity was deliberately targeted, *inter alia*, to cause people to flee and never return, to destroy evidence of coexistence and to rewrite history. Cultural property was destroyed to such an extent that the terms 'cultural genocide' and 'cultural cleansing' were coined.[1] Cities in particular were deliberately targeted because they contained visible physical evidence of the shared past and present. Burnt buildings of exceptional artistic value, burnt archives and libraries containing rare collections of books and manuscripts, and centuries-old places of worship after being dynamited and historic bridges blown up are just a few examples of what cities such as Vukovar, Dubrovnik, Sarajevo and Mostar endured. The urban devastation was so profound that it was labelled 'urbicide'.[2] The damage done to cultural property in the former Yugoslavia during the 1990s was considered the worst in post-WWII Europe; 'a major cultural catastrophe'[3] is how the COE described it. This catastrophe turned yesterday's neighbours, friends and relatives into 'us' and 'them', dividing cities in the process and erasing memories.

While cultural heritage in all parts of the former Yugoslavia suffered significant losses, the cultural heritage of Bosnia and Herzegovina paid a particularly high price.[4] All parties to the conflict bear their share of guilt in destroying or forever scarring numerous churches, mosques, libraries, archives,

1 Colin Kaiser, 'Crimes against Culture' *UNESCO Courier* Sept 2000, 41, http://web1.infotrac.galegroup.com/itw/infomark/109/511/ ['Crimes against Culture'].

2 The term 'urbicide' was coined by Belgrade architect, Bogdan Bogdanović.

3 Committee on Culture and Education of Parliamentary Assembly of Council of Europe (COE), *First Information Report*, doc 6756, 2 February 1993, 3 [*First COE Report*].

4 J. Tunbridge and G. Ashworth, *Dissonant Heritage: The Management of the Past as a Resource in Conflict* (1996).

monuments and other culturally significant structures. Nevertheless, the case that has attracted the greatest publicity[5] is the destruction of the Old Bridge of Mostar by the Croat forces. Built in 1566 by the Ottoman architect Hayreddin and admired by everyone for its technical perfection and aesthetic beauty, the Old Bridge had become a heritage treasure of Mostar, the city named after a bridge,[6] and of all Bosnia and Herzegovina.[7]

In addition to its artistic and scientific value, this masterpiece of architecture embodied the history of all people (Muslims, Croats, Serbs, Jews and others) who lived on the two banks of the Neretva River, which it gracefully linked for 427 years. The Bridge was a public monument, free of ethnicity. It symbolised the peaceful co-existence of different ethnic and religious communities. It was the city's landmark, which distinguished the city itself and its citizens from others, giving them a special identity. The Mostarians shared both the city and the Bridge and were deeply attached to and proud of both of them.

On 9 November 1993, Mostar, Bosnia and Herzegovina and the rest of the world were shocked by the news of the destruction of the world's largest single stone arch. Croatian army tanks deliberately targeted this steep, slippery footbridge.[8] As the Bridge crumbled into the icy waters of the Neretva, the HVO sent the message that, in the absence of the elegant connection between the banks of the River and the symmetry of the towers on each of its ends, the union and harmony of different cultures in Mostar was no longer preserved. Ultimately, this was a symbolic confirmation of the intention of Croatia, which controlled the HVO, to redraw the borders of Bosnia and Herzegovina. The destruction of the Bridge occurred during armed conflict between Croats and Muslims in Bosnia and Herzegovina, referred to as 'a war within the war'.[9] With Croatia's support, the conflict was aimed at establishing HVO control over certain territories in Bosnia and Herzegovina, which would eventually secede and become

5 Amir Pašić, *The Old Bridge (Stari Most) in Mostar* (1995) [*The Old Bridge*].

6 The name 'Mostar' means 'a bridge keeper'. But as Belgrade architect Bogdan Bogdanović observes, 'the name of the city of Mostar is much layered information'. It puts together two pictures and two categories – a bridge and a city – and connects them into an indivisible semantic pair, which is, by further language magic, packed into a united name with multiple meanings. See Bogdan Bogdanović, 'Može li grad bez svog mosta, može li most bez svog grada' ('Can the City be without Its Bridge; Can the Bridge be without Its City?'), *Most*, No. 139, June 2001, http://wl.500.telia.com/~u5000875/50/010.htm [*Most*].

7 Pašić, *The Old Bridge*, above n 5, 3.

8 Rabia Ali and Lawrence Lifschultz, 'An Interview with Ivo Banac: The Last Days of Bosnia?' *Boston Review*, February 1994, http://bostonreview.mit.edu/BostonReview/BT19.1/banac.html [Banac Interview].

9 Gordan Malić, 'Herzeg-Lager' *Bosnia Report*, Issue 15, April-June 1996, http://www.bosnia.org.uk/bosrep/aprjun96/herzeg.cfm [4] (quoting Roy Gutman).

a part of the 'larger' Croatia.[10] Ironically, at the beginning of the armed conflict in Bosnia and Herzegovina, Croats and Muslims fought as allies against the predominantly Serb YA.[11] However, driven by Croatia's expansionist desires and the Croat-Serbian plan to partition Bosnia and Herzegovina,[12] they soon turned against each other. Fighting between Croats and Muslims in Mostar was some of the fiercest during the Balkans conflicts. Mostar appeared to be a test case for the future of Bosnia and Herzegovina; that is, the outcome of this conflict was to be very much an indication of whether Bosnia and Herzegovina would survive as an independent sovereign, internationally recognised state or be partitioned. The damage done to the predominantly Muslim eastern part of the city and suffering inflicted upon its inhabitants were incomparable with that which other cities endured.

The Old Bridge was targeted because it was an object of cultural unity, symbolising the shared past. Its destruction caused immeasurable pain and loss not only to citizens of Mostar but also to other people by disinheriting them all of this particular part of the cultural heritage of all humankind. In addition to the cultural dimension, the destruction of the Bridge widened the distance between the two banks of the Neretva making them unbridgeable for the long term.[13] Once a multicultural city, in which people of different ethnic backgrounds lived, worked and worshipped side by side,[14] Mostar became partitioned along ethnic lines, right across the front line, into Muslim east and Croat west, turning people into 'us' and 'them' and 'ethnicizing'[15] everything that used to be the 'shared' past and the 'shared' pride. Despite many efforts by the international community to reunify the city, Mostar is still divided into Muslim east

---

10 Ibid. See also testimony of Belinda Giles, a television producer, Prosecution witness in the *Prlić* case (*The Prosecutor v Jadranko Prlić, Bruno Stojić, Slobodan Praljak, Milivoj Petković, Valentin Ćorić and Berislav Pušić*, Case No. IT-04-74-T [*Prlić* or *Prlić* case]), 15 May 2006, T 2034 *et seq* (The testimony was based on Giles' film 'A Greater Croatia', made shortly after the destruction of the Old Bridge. The film was played in the courtroom and was admitted into evidence), http://www.un.org/icty/transe74/060515ED.htm [Giles testimony or 'A Greater Croatia'].

11 Malić, ibid.

12 See Interview with Stjepan Mesić, the last chairman of the former Yugoslavia Presidency and the current President of Croatia, 'Division of Bosnia was Tudman's Only Option', *Tjednik* (Zagreb, Croatia), 16 May 1997, translated on 21 February 2001, http://www.cdsp.neu.edu/info/students/marko/tjednik/tjednik2.html [Mesić Interview]

13 See, Banac Interview, above n 8.

14 See, András Riedlmayer, 'Killing Memory: The Targeting of Bosnia's Cultural Heritage', Testimony presented at a Hearing of the Commission on Security and Cooperation in Europe, US Congress, 4 April 1995, Community of Bosnia Foundation, http://www.haverford.edu/relg/sells/killing.html ['Killing Memory'].

15 Kaiser, 'Crimes against Culture', above n 1.

(the left bank of the Neretva and a narrow belt of the right bank, by this river) and Croat west Mostar (the right bank of the Neretva). Although the division line was physically removed several years ago, the division line in people's hearts and minds is unlikely to fade any time soon.[16]

Soon after the destruction of the Old Bridge, while the fighting was still ongoing, local architects and heritage experts began to plan its reconstruction to keep the memory alive and to show that the history and people's spirit were not capable of being destroyed.[17] They then set the date for the grand opening of a new bridge.[18] Mostarians looked forward to that event, hoping that the resurrection of their city's emblem would bring them closer to each other.[19] Thus, once a symbol of co-existence, and later, through its destruction, a symbol of conflict and partition, the Bridge was/is again a metaphor, this time symbolising the hope for peace and reconciliation. The Bridge was indeed rebuilt. The rebuilding of the Old Bridge was an international project.[20] The grand re-inauguration ceremony, attended by a number of Heads of State and other highest level State officials, was held on 23 July 2004.

During the rebuilding process there was much talk about the money required and already spent, and much talk about the power of the reconstruction to accelerate the process of reconciliation.[21] However, there was no talk about the legal implications of the loss of the Old Bridge, no talk about the responsibility for its destruction. Since this book is concerned with such matters, the purpose of this chapter is to provide some factual background for the legal analysis in the following chapters. This chapter first outlines the socio-political circumstances surrounding the building of the Old Bridge. Then, it considers the event of the destruction of the Bridge and examines the major motivations behind this destruction. Thereafter, the chapter looks at the impact of the loss of the Old Bridge on people.

---

16 Banac Interview, above n 8.

17 See Carnegie Endowment for International Peace, 'A Symposium on Destruction and Rebuilding of Architectural Treasures in Bosnia and Herzegovina', Monday, 2 May 1994, especially the presentation by Amir Pašić, http://www.kakarigi.net/many/carnegie.htm [Carnegie Symposium].

18 Ibid.

19 See Michael Ignatieff, 'When a Bridge Is Not a Bridge' *The New York Times* Sunday, 27 October 2002, http://www.nytimes.com/2002/10/27/magazine/27MOSTAR.html.

20 Detailed information on the rebuilding of the Old Bridge can be accessed at http://portal.unesco.org/culture/en/ev.php.

21 See Ignatieff, above n 19.

II Construction of the Old Bridge

> From everything that man erects and builds in his urge for living nothing is in my eyes better and more valuable than bridges. They are more important than houses, more sacred than shrines. Belonging to everyone and being equal to everyone, useful, always built with a sense, on the spot where most human needs are crossing, they are more durable than other buildings and they do not serve anything secret or bad.
>
> *Ivo Andrić, The Bridges*[22]

A Mostar: Geography, Demography and History of the Place

The Old Bridge was the landmark of the city of Mostar. Mostar is the largest city of Herzegovina, the southern part of Bosnia and Herzegovina. The city is situated in the fertile Neretva River Valley, about 120 km southwest of Sarajevo, the capital of Bosnia and Herzegovina, and about 60 km north of Neum, the Bosnian and Herzegovinian town on the Adriatic coast. Mostar is situated in close proximity to the southeast border of Croatia.

Before the conflict, Mostar had 120,000 inhabitants, just over thirty per cent of whom were of Muslim ethnicity, approximately the same percentage Croat, around seventeen per cent Serb and the rest other ethnicities.[23] The city had the highest percentage of ethnically mixed marriages in the former Yugoslavia.[24] Before the 1990s armed conflicts, Mostar was renowned for its cosmopolitanism, harmony and urban spirit. It was the city of artists and writers who were constantly inspired by the emerald waters of the volatile Neretva that flows through the middle of the city, decorated by bridges densely sited over it. All of the bridges of Mostar were beautiful and loved by the citizens of Mostar, but the Old Bridge was of exceptional beauty. It had a very special meaning in every Mostarian's heart. It gave them all a sense of belonging and linked them to the shared past.

The Mostar valley has been inhabited since very ancient times. Evidence points to the old settlements in the immediate vicinity of Mostar in the prehistoric era and Roman times.[25] However, the first historical reference to present-day Mostar goes to 1440, and the first mention of the name 'Mostar' dates to

---

22 Quoted in Ljubomir Pajic, 'End of the Century' 27 December 2000, http://news.beograd.com/english/articles_and _opinion/pajic/.

23 See *Prosecutor v Jadranko Prlić, Bruno Stojić, Slobodan Praljak, Milivoj Petković, Valentin Ćorić and Berislav Pušić*, Amended Indictment, 16 November 2005, Case No. IT-04-74-PT, para 88 [*Prlić* Indictment].

24 Colin Woodard, 'Stillborn', *Bulletin of the Atomic Scientists* 1 July 2000, vol 56, 7/1/00Bull. Atom. Scientists 1719 2000 WL 10491163, http://web2.westlaw.com.

25 Pašić, *The Old Bridge*, above n 5, 7.

the year 1474.[26] The small settlement was named after a wooden bridge over the Neretva, a predecessor of the Old Bridge.[27] This wooden bridge and the fortresses close to it were not only of strategic importance but also of economic significance. Since the main road connecting Bosnia and Herzegovina to the Adriatic coast used the crossing over the Neretva, the bridge brought about a rapid expansion of the city and the development of crafts and trade. The city also became the centre of culture and education.

Bosnia and Herzegovina was ruled by the Ottoman Empire from the fifteenth century until the nineteenth century. Within this period, Mostar had the greatest growth and prosperity under the reign of Sultan Suleyman II the Magnificent.[28] Cultural development, especially in art and architecture,[29] is evidenced not only by the Old Bridge but also by numerous other structures of extraordinary beauty such as mosques, schools, baths and other public architectural structures. The city continued to grow and prosper with the annexation of Bosnia and Herzegovina to the Austro-Hungarian monarchy and later as a city of the former Yugoslavia. Each period left traces embodied in monuments, buildings of a religious and secular character, and other objects of immovable cultural property. All such objects, irrespective of origin, were maintained as symbols of the shared past so well that, prior to the 1990s armed conflicts, Mostar was not only a modern, industrialised European city, but also rich in cultural property.

The Old City (Stari Grad) of Mostar, with the Old Bridge as a focal point, was under the special care of the citizens of Mostar because it was the place from which their city arose. From 1955 until 1991, under the guidance of the Mostar Institute for Preservation of Cultural Heritage, they made a tremendous effort, including the making of plans and legislation, to restore the Old Bridge and the rest of the Old City.[30] In 1986, the city was given one of the world's most prestigious architectural awards, the Aga Khan Award, for exceptional historic restoration.[31] The award was a confirmation of the importance of buildings, spaces, settlements and cities in the process of human development. 'From a lifeless relic of an historic past, [the Mostarians] turned [the Old City

26 Ibid.

27 See, eg, K. Grujic, 'The Most Beautiful Bridges in Bosnia and Herzegovina' *Gajret* 1934, 54; Evlija Čelebi, *Putopis* [*Book of Travel*] (1996 ed) 469.

28 Sultan Suleyman II the Magnificent reigned from 1520 to 1566.

29 Pašić, *The Old Bridge*, above n 5. Architecture was considered art – the most developed area of Ottoman art.

30 Ibid 32-36. This included repairs, conservation and regular maintenance works. Regular wear and tear, some changes made to the Old Bridge during the Austro-Hungarian occupation, and damage caused by the Nazis during WWII, necessitated the restoration works (1955-1991). Ibid 30-31.

31 Nicholas Adams, 'Architecture as the Target' (1993) 52 *Journal of the Society of Architectural Historians* 389.

of Mostar, including the Old Bridge] into a city thriving in its culture, exploding in economic opportunity'.[32] The restoration works carried out in Mostar illustrated how powerful cultural continuity was in contributing to human well-being. In 1991, a commission was appointed and given the task of providing permanent maintenance for the Old Bridge.[33] According to UNESCO, the Old Bridge 'was in a perfect state of conservation before the outbreak of military hostilities in the region'.[34] The Bridge was designated a monument of invaluable significance for the city of Mostar and later was added to a list of national monuments of Bosnia and Herzegovina.[35] Together with the rest of the Old City of Mostar, the Old Bridge was also recommended for inscription on the World Heritage List,[36] which was realised after the conflict, on 15 July 2005.

B Building the Old Bridge

1 Architecture and Engineering

A bridge, as the link across water or a mountain pass, not only connects two areas, but also symbolises the victory of the human spirit over capricious nature.[37] As Professor Amir Pašić, an expert in Ottoman architecture, observes, conquering the Neretva was a challenging task for the sixteenth century builders.[38] Both the design of the Bridge and the material used in constructing it needed to be strong if the Bridge was going to tame the incredibly fast and cold waters of the river. At the time of building the Old Bridge, wood and stone were the materials used for the construction of bridges. Stone bridges were more complicated and more expensive to build, and thus less numerous. The semicircular or occasionally pointed arches of these bridges normally spanned a distance of ten to fifteen metres. While bridges over wide rivers consisted of several arches, those spanning a narrow, deep riverbed usually had a single arch. Prior to construction of the Old Bridge, there was only one stone bridge in Mostar. It was a

32 Mawlana Hazar Imam's statement at the World Congress of Architects in Chicago, 18 June 1993, http://w3.tycnct.com/kozlich/congress.htm.

33 See Pasic, *The Old Bridge*, above n 5, 36.

34 UNESCO's activities, 'Mostar and Its Historical Monuments', http://www.unesco.org/culture/heritage/tangible/mostar/html_eng/monument.shtml.

35 UNESCO, 'Rebuilding of Stari Most (Old Bridge) and the Rehabilitation of the Old Town of Mostar', http://www.unesco.org/opi2/starimost.htm.

36 See Committee on Culture and Education of Parliamentary Assembly of Council of Europe (COE), *Second Information Report*, doc 6869, 17 July 1993 [*Second COE Report*] and Committee on Culture and Education of Parliamentary Assembly of Council of Europe (COE), *Fourth Information Report*, doc 6999, 19 January 1994 [*Fourth COE Report*].

37 Pašić, *The Old Bridge*, above n 5, 11.

38 Ibid.

small bridge, built in 1558 over the tiny, narrow, tranquil Radobolja river, some one hundred and fifty metres from the Neretva and the Old Bridge.[39]

Since the old wooden bridge suspended on thick iron chains over the Neretva was worn out, and the town was growing rapidly, Mostar needed a new and more solid bridge. At the request of the inhabitants of Mostar, Sultan Suleyman the Magnificent ordered its construction. The Bridge was the work of Mimar Hayreddin, a disciple of Mimar Sinan, the greatest Ottoman architect. The length of time spent on building the Old Bridge is disputed. While some argue that the Bridge was built over the period 1557 to 1566,[40] others point to the construction taking two years.[41] In any case, it was a patient and delicate process, the outcome of which was a gentle, but very solid, beautiful single stone arch. At the time, that was 'a very "brave" arch'[42] with a span of 28.70 metres. The supporting vault was only 77 cm deep, 3.97 m wide, and its height was 20.34 m above the river level measured during summer.[43]

The stone used for building the Bridge was the local limestone which is of exceptional physical and chemical qualities. It was used for the entire Bridge including the balustrade. Its sides were cut so smoothly that there was no need for any adhesive material to hold them together. The structure was fragile, so the master builder took care not to overload it with a single unnecessary stone. The deck stairs, also made of limestone to resist the wear from people and animals crossing the Bridge, aided walking on both the incline and decline of the steep deck and steadied the feet, preventing them from slipping.[44] Pieces of stone in the Bridge's construction were joined to each other by iron clamps and then filled with lead.[45] The result was 'an incredibly elegant and delicate vaulted structure'.[46]

Two symmetric, half-cylindrical massive towers, one at each end of the Bridge, were built later.[47] They were keepers of the Bridge's stability. By being supported this way, the Old Bridge looked like an old man leaning on the mas-

---

39 Ibid 12.

40 Suha Özkan, 'The Destruction of Stari Most' (1994) 14 *Development Network* 5. Other research shows that the Bridge was built in two years and cost 300,000 silver coins. See A. Polimac, 'Some New Data about the Old Bridge' (1977) *Most* 1977, 14-15; M. Vasić, 'About the Building of the Old Bridge of Mostar' *Balcanica* 1977, VII.

41 Polimac, ibid; Vasić, ibid.

42 Pašić, *The Old Bridge*, above n 5, 12.

43 Ibid 14.

44 Ibid 12.

45 Ibid 15.

46 Ibid 21.

47 According to Pašić, one tower was built in 1676 and the other in 1736-37. Ibid.

sive armrests of his luxurious armchair.[48] In this way, the Bridge also represented a replica of the city of Mostar – the Bridge, squeezed between the giant towers, resembled the urban landscape of the city of Mostar, developed around the Bridge on both of its sides and squeezed between mountains and hills.[49] Urban settlement around the Bridge developed to an extent before, but for the most part during, the sixteenth and seventeenth centuries. All buildings were built from a bright limestone, roofed with stone slabs the same colour as the walls. Over time, due to Mostar's long and generous autumn rains and merciless summer heat, the colour of the roofs would fade and become brighter. The imposing arch of the Bridge together with the surrounding buildings – combining limestone on limestone – looked like stalagmites,[50] and made a harmonic entity of the untamed scenery of the Neretva and the rocky landscape that 'resembled a huge rock with crystals grown on top'.[51] Although Mostar continued to grow and to catch up to modernity in all of its components, it was 'an incredible [B]ridge', with an early urban ensemble collected around it, that introduced the city, gave it 'personality' and took up the noblest role of being the city's interpreter forever.[52]

2 Aesthetics

Described as a wondrous 'rainbow arch soaring up to the skies and extending from one cliff to the other…an archer's bow with which an arrow has just been shot, forever leaving the bow in its stretched position…thrown from rock to rock as high as the sky… with water flowing across it[53] and underneath it…the splendid stone work [which] had never before been displayed by anyone',[54] it was predicted that the Old Bridge would be 'a great work of art that [would] amaze all the masters of the world'.[55] Indeed, people coming to Mostar from different corners of the world were impressed by this construction and admired its beauty. For instance, in 1658, the Frenchman A. Poullet considered the structure of 'a bridge across the Neretva River…without any doubt, more courageous and more impressive than the Rialto in Venice, although the latter bridge is spoken

48 Bogdanović, *Most,* above n 6.

49 Ibid.

50 Pašić, *The Old Bridge*, above n 5, 28.

51 Ibid.

52 Bogdanović, *Most*, above n 6.

53 Pašić, *The Old Bridge*, above n 5 (referring to water pipes).

54 Čelebi, above n 27, 464. Pašić observes that 'the master builder raised an arch using geometry which until then was unknown in bridge construction'. Pašić, *The Old Bridge*, above n 5, 21.

55 Grujić, above n 27, 55.

of as a real miracle'.[56] An Austrian traveller, Robert Michel, saw the Old Bridge as a 'gigantic seagull' turned to stone in flight, at the moment when the tips of its wings touched the rocky banks of the Neretva, and deemed it 'the most beautiful bridge in the world'.[57]

The Old Bridge, which to some 'looked like a white pearl necklace around the neck of the river',[58] represented an accomplishment which was feared to be impossible. Every crossing of this Bridge was something of a miracle: while the pliable green mass of the Neretva moved quickly under one's feet, a person would feel that what held him or her so strongly and reliably in the blue endlessness of the Mediterranean sky, where he or she would be exposed to the direct touch of eternity, was not stone, but a pure thought into which the stone was transformed[59] – the thought about unity, continuity and great courage.

From the time of its completion, the Old Bridge has been the jumping-off point in a fabled diving competition held every summer.[60] Those brave jumps have always been something of a ritual.[61] They were each a test of courage and passage into manhood. For this 'annual rite of passage', local boys would begin training at age seven,[62] 'fly[ing] like birds through the air, each doing some kind of acrobatic – some div[ing] with their heads down, others with their legs crossed, while yet others div[ing] in groups of two or three and immediately com[ing] safely out of the water and climb[ing] the rocky bank…. It [wa]s indeed highly daring for children to dive into such a river'.[63]

Perfection in construction, logic and the elegance of 'a splendid stone structure'[64] made the Old Bridge a monument of exceptional value from both an artistic and scientific point of view.[65] Over time it grew into a great symbol of tolerance of diversity – a bridge which bridged cultures – a symbol of Mostar and Bosnia and Herzegovina as a whole which marked an important episode in the cultural history of a nation.

---

56 *National Museum Herald* XX, 49.

57 Robert Michel, *Mostar, Prague* (1909) 31-36.

58 Nedim Gürsel, 'The Soul of a Bridge', http://www.atlasturkey.com/990503/97november/bosnia/mostar.html.

59 Ivan Lovrenović, 'Svijet bez mosta – Mostar, devet godina poslije' ['The World without the Bridge – Mostar, Nine Years Later'] *Dani*, archives, No. 256, http://www.bhdani.com/arhiva/256/t25614.shtml.

60 'Bosnian Leaps of Faith' *Sports Illustrated* 18 September 1995 v83 n12 p18 (1) ['Leaps of Faith'].

61 Bogdanović, *Most*, above n 6.

62 'Leaps of Faith', above n 60.

63 Ibid; Pašić, *The Old Bridge*, above n 5.

64 'Leaps of Faith', above n 60.

65 UNESCO's activities, 'Mostar and Its Historic Monuments', above n 34.

III Destruction of the Old Bridge

A The First Siege

According to legend, upon completion of the construction works, the architect Hayreddin went into hiding because he feared that the fragile construction of the Old Bridge would not manage to hold the stones but would collapse into the Neretva. However, 'a thin, soaring structure of exceptional beauty... [which] seemed impossibly delicate, too thin to take the weight of a...man'[66] was incredibly solid. It endured centuries of earthquakes, harsh weather conditions and the wear of many thousands of locals' and tourists' feet. It also survived centuries of wars fought in that region, including both World Wars. The Old Bridge even supported the passage of tanks during WWII, when the Nazis filled the steps leading up and down its platform with sand in order to create a ramp, 'or perhaps to protect the delicate stone steps of the [B]ridge', as Suha Özkan, Secretary-General of the Aga Khan Award for Architecture put it.[67] The retreating Nazis could have blown up the Bridge as they put explosive charges on both of its ends, at a distance of one-fourth of the span,[68] but the Bridge was spared as they, perhaps, decided not to deprive the world of this extraordinary creative achievement, 'one of the building miracles of 16th century Europe'.[69] Sadly, it was the people who had called the Old Bridge 'their' monument that sentenced it to death.

From 1992 to 1994, Mostar was the site of not one, but two armed conflicts fought in the territory of Bosnia and Herzegovina. In 1992, from April to June, during the first siege or 'first war' in Mostar, Croat and Muslim forces fought as allies against the Serb-led YA and other Serbian forces. Neighbouring Croatia provided weapons and supplies.[70] In June 1992, the Serbs retreated from Mostar, leaving behind horrifying damage done to objects of cultural property.

According to the *First COE Information Report*, which covers in great detail war damage to cultural heritage in the lower Neretva River Valley and the environs of Mostar, '[a] cultural catastrophe' took place 'in the heart of Europe'.[71] This catastrophe was characterised as 'a major cultural catastrophe for all the communities of the war zone – whether Croat, Bosnian or Serb – and also for...European heritage, which [was deemed to] emerge from the war singularly amputated'.[72] In Mostar, everything was targeted, irrespective of archi-

66 Ignatieff, above n 19.

67 Özkan, above n 40.

68 Pašić, *The Old Bridge*, above n 5, 31.

69 Ibid 39.

70 Woodard, above n 24.

71 *First COE Report*, above n 3, 2.

72 Ibid.

tectural or artistic style and the period from which it dated: churches, mosques, monasteries, galleries, libraries, museums, archives, historic buildings from the Ottoman, Austrian and other periods and styles, war memorials, bridges.[73] While cases of reprisals[74] against the cultural heritage of the Serbs were not an isolated instance,[75] the vast majority of the damage was done to the cultural heritage of the Muslims and to a lesser extent to that of the Croats.[76] Ethnic cleansing of Muslims on the left bank of the Neretva in Mostar, and on the left bank and part of the right of the Neretva south of Mostar, which were controlled by Serbian forces from April to June 1992, went hand in hand with cultural cleansing.[77] Cultural cleansing then brought about economic cleansing as industry and tourism in Mostar and its surroundings were destroyed.[78]

According to the report based upon a fact-finding mission carried out for the Parliamentary Assembly of the COE by a consultant expert, Dr Colin Kaiser, in Croatia and Bosnia and Herzegovina from 29 November to 20 December 1992, the damage done to cultural property in Mostar during offensive or defensive military action was especially high because the YA used a considerable quantity of heavy artillery, mortars and rockets,[79] 'virtually every kind of projectile in the Yugoslav Army panoply'.[80] Targeting cultural property was psychological warfare against a civilian population. However, for similar psychological reasons, much damage occurred outside the bounds of offensive or defensive military action, when a building, historic complex or a village was burnt or dynamited.[81]

The bombardment of Mostar began in the second week of April 1992, reaching a crescendo from 6 May to 13 May, when the Serbian forces occupied the entire left bank.[82] Amplified by 'psychological' shooting from snipers, the bombardment caused a mass exodus, and the population of Mostar fell from 120,000 to 30,000.[83] Interestingly, the Serbian forces never made a major

---

73 Ibid.

74 The term 'reprisals' is used here in its household sense rather than as a term of art. For a damage survey in relation to war damage in Mostar, see, eg, John Yarwood, 'Cultural Warfare' (2003) 8 (2) *Art Antiquity and Law* 191, 191 fn 1 (noting, *inter alia*, that '[s]omeone had their revenge by dynamiting the exquisite Orthodox cathedral…so comprehensively that not a wall remained').

75 Ibid.

76 Ibid.

77 Ibid.

78 Ibid 3.

79 Ibid 13.

80 Ibid 14.

81 Ibid.

82 Ibid para 127.

83 Ibid para 128.

attempt to cross the Neretva, remaining content to occupy the 'Serbian', east side of the city.[84] Reportedly, after blowing up bridges over the Neretva, other than the Old Bridge, they unexpectedly withdrew from the left bank in June 1992. The devastation of cultural property they caused pales in comparison with that caused half a year earlier in the Old Town of Dubrovnik, Croatia.[85]

The historic Ottoman district – the Old City of Mostar and its surroundings – suffered the heaviest damage. The Old Bridge was not exempt. Its parapet was hit in two different places. Still, experts did not consider this damage to be too alarming.[86] Nevertheless, it was feared that the innumerable detonations in the Old City and surroundings had weakened the structure of the Bridge.[87] Although some protective measures had previously been implemented including placement of car tyres aimed at cushioning the Bridge[88] and a wooden screen on scaffolding above the Bridge, to trigger detonation of projectiles before they reached the surface of the Bridge and to protect both pedestrian traffic and the Bridge surface from fragments, a vertical wooden and rubber screen on the south side to trigger detonation at a point away from the Bridge's structurally weaker centre was not in place at the time of the fact-finding mission's visit to the city.[89] In its recommendations, Kaiser asked the local Ministry of Culture and the Public Office of Building and Reconstruction to add these elements of protection[90] and to further improve protective measures.[91] Because of the importance of cultural property in Mostar to the entire international community, Kaiser also recommended drawing up and submitting to UNESCO '[a] proposal for inscription of the historic centre of Mostar (together with the Old Bridge) and the adjoining mixed historic zone on the List of World Heritage in Danger'.[92]

B The Second Siege

After the Serbian forces withdrew from the left bank of the Neretva, relations between Mostar Croats and Muslims soured. Although the 'second war' in Mostar, as the locals preferred to call it, or the 'war within the war'[93] as Roy

---

84 Ibid.

85 Ibid para 129.

86 Ibid para 138.

87 Ibid.

88 Kaiser, 'Crimes against Culture', above n 1, 4.

89 *First COE Report*, above n 3, para 138.

90 Ibid.

91 Ibid p 41

92 Ibid p 42

93 Malić, above n 9 (quoting Roy Gutman who wrote about the Croat-Muslim conflict in the 1990s).

Gutman put it, began with the 9 May 1993 siege of Mostar,[94] fighting between the Croatian HVO and the predominantly Muslim ABH began earlier.[95] With it began the expulsion of Muslims from the right bank of the Neretva, which was controlled by the HVO, and the second phase of ethnic and cultural cleansing.[96] Reportedly, 20,000 to 25,000 Muslims were expelled from the right bank of the Neretva to the left, predominantly populated by the Muslims.[97] Cultural property, especially sacral cultural property, was targeted on the right bank of the Neretva along with the expulsion of the Muslim population to inflict psychological damage upon them – to make them wish not to return. However, there was fear that the ethnic cleansing carried out in Central Bosnia by the ABH would provoke a massive retaliation in Mostar that would spare no cultural property of Ottoman origin, not only on the right bank of the Neretva but throughout the city.[98] Indeed, the situation soon became 'particularly explosive'[99] and 'catastrophic…on the left-bank zone around the [B]ridge'.[100] The heaviest guns available to the HVO ruthlessly shelled objects of cultural property.[101] Artillery calibres included those used by tanks and howitzers.[102] The shelling created one of the worst cultural disasters of the entire conflict in Bosnia and Herzegovina.[103] Again, this pointed to the need to urgently place the historic core of Mostar together with the Old Bridge on UNESCO's World Heritage in Danger List because they were located close to the front line between the HVO and ABH forces.[104] However, before inscription on the List could happen, the Bridge and much of the historic centre of Mostar were destroyed.

Although in this phase of cultural cleansing in Mostar the targets were both the symbols of unity and the symbols of cultural specificity,[105] it was the

94 According to people who resided in Mostar at the time, the attack was vicious: 'On that day 5,000 grenades fell on small space [of East Mostar]. We thought that no one would survive'. See Svetlana Broz, *Good People in an Evil Time: Participants and Witnesses* (1999) 244.

95 *Second COE Report*, above n 36, paras 41-49.

96 Ibid para 49.

97 Paul Hockenos, 'In Sheltered Mostar, Tentative Rebuilding' *National Catholic Reporter* 16 December 1994, 9, http://web1.infotrac.galegroup.com/itw/infomark/.

98 Committee on Culture and Education of Parliamentary Assembly of Council of Europe (COE), *Third Information Report*, doc 6904, 20 September 1993, para 15 [*Third COE Report*].

99 Ibid (Dr Kaiser's contribution to the Report).

100 *Fourth COE Report*, above n 36, para 74.

101 Ibid para 80.

102 Ibid para 74.

103 Ibid para 80.

104 *Third COE Report*, above n 98 (Dr Kaiser).

105 *Fourth COE Report*, above n 36, para 118.

Old Bridge representing the former that created the most tragic loss of the city's cultural heritage. Some contend that the HVO brought in architects to determine which stones should be targeted to assure the collapse of the delicate arch.[106] Tanks 'at point-blank range' shelled the Bridge.[107] According to the *Fourth COE Information Report*, the shelling by tanks 'probably of Croatian origin'[108] lasted two days. On 8 November 1993, numerous shells were shot at the Bridge.[109] The following day, a few tank shells, which landed at the base of the eastern side of the arch on the south side of the Bridge, brought it down.[110] Ramiz Pandur, an artist from Mostar, who happened to be in his gallery located near the Old Bridge at the time, and was one of the rare eyewitnesses, recalls this horrifying act:

> I heard every grenade when they fired it. I would peep out through the window of the cellar each time when the splinters would disperse and watched the wounded bridge. I am one of a few, if not the only witness who watched the first day of the destruction of the bridge from that proximity.
>
> The following day three grenades were enough to tumble down the whole bridge into the Neretva.[111]

As András Riedlmayer, one of the world's leading experts on Ottoman cultural heritage in the Balkans, observes, the date of the destruction of the Bridge – 9 November 1993 – coincided with 'the 55th anniversary of Kristallnacht, the night when Jewish synagogues and institutions were smashed and burned throughout Hitler's Great German Reich'.[112]

At 10.16 on Tuesday morning, one of the great cultural treasures of the world, one of the greatest cultural treasures of Bosnia and Herzegovina, and the greatest cultural treasure of the city of Mostar was reduced to limestone blocks

106 Jerrilynn Dodds, 'Bridge over the Neretva' (1998) 51 *Archaeology* 3.

107 Ibid.

108 *Fourth COE Report*, above n 36, para 69.

109 Ibid.

110 Ibid.

111 Broz, above n 94, 247.

112 Riedlmayer, 'Killing Memory', above n 14. See also Robert Bevan, *The Destruction of Memory: Architecture at War* (2006), 9-10 (pointing to the numerals which 'mark a day for destruction': 'Numerologists could have a field day with this *matériel*: Kristallnacht began just before midnight on 9 November, the 9/11 of 1938. On the same date in 1989, the first sections of the Berlin Wall began to tumble. Four years later on 9/11, Stari Most, Mostar's historic bridge, was finally brought down into the Neretva River by Croat gunners. Then…came 9/11 in New York – a different day, of course, given the date sequencing used in North America – but the numerals do seem to mark a day for destruction').

and fragments.[113] The scene was recorded on camera and televised throughout the world. The footage showed a puff of smoke and the elegant, soaring arched backbone of the Bridge collapsing into the Neretva, 'like a dead beast'.[114] It was 'a tragic splash, as if the Neretva was shedding tears for the millions of people who had now lost a cherished piece of memory'.[115] It took years of artistic and scientific work to produce and preserve the extraordinary Bridge of invaluable cultural significance, it took centuries of love and admiration to make this mass of stones more special than many others have ever been, and only minutes of complete mindlessness to destroy it and erase memories.

IV Motives Behind the Destruction

A The Ancient Hatreds Argument

People are often told that the destruction of immovable cultural property in Bosnia and Herzegovina during the 1990s conflicts occurred because of 'ancient hatreds', comprising ethnic and religious animosity.[116] On this view, the Old Bridge was targeted as an object of cultural specificity. In other words, since the Old Bridge was built by the Ottoman Empire, with which the Mostar Muslims are linked through shared religious beliefs, the Croats considered it a Muslim monument. Presumably, while ruled by the Ottoman Empire, the Catholic Croats were subjected to centuries of intolerance and, thus, waited for 'a historic opportunity'[117] to remove the Bridge because it was a reminder of an unpleasant past.

However, the view that the destruction occurred due to the 'ancient hatreds' must be rejected. As Riedlmayer notes, 'both buildings and documents, speak eloquently of centuries of pluralism and tolerance in Bosnia [and Herzegovina]'.[118] As far back as the medieval Kingdom of Bosnia, three Christian churches existed side by side: Roman Catholic, Eastern Orthodox and a local Bosnian Church.[119] Islam arrived with the occupation of Bosnia and Herzegovina by the Ottoman Empire. During Ottoman rule, religious and cultural plurality and tolerance in Bosnia and Herzegovina were not sup-

---

113 *Final Report of the United Nations Commission of Experts Established Pursuant to Security Council Resolution 780 (1992), Annex XI: Destruction of Cultural Property Report*, S/1994/674/Add.2 (Vol V) 28 December 1994 [*Final Report*].

114 Ignatieff, above n 9, 2.

115 Özkan, above n 40.

116 See, Riedlmayer, 'Killing Memory', above n 14.

117 Özkan, above n 40.

118 Riedlmayer, 'Killing Memory', above n 14.

119 Ibid.

pressed.[120] Throughout this period, and afterwards, under Austro-Hungarian rule and within the former Yugoslavia, until the dissolution of the latter in the 1990s, irrespective of ethnicity and religious belief, people lived, worked and worshipped side by side. Architecture is particularly powerful evidence of the degree of tolerance in this region: people built their houses, churches, mosques and synagogues close to each other.[121]

The city of Mostar exemplified the multicultural character of Bosnia and Herzegovina. Its old Ottoman architecture was interwoven with other architectural styles. Mostar had a highly developed urban culture. The coexistence of religious traditions led to a sense of further integration developed through a common attachment to places and shared spaces and to a sense of shared ownership of cultural property. The Mostarians shared the city and the Bridge and were all deeply attached to and proud of them both.[122] Thus, the proposition that 'ancient' hatreds comprising religious intolerance led to the destruction of the Mostar Bridge should be refuted.

Animosities are of more recent origin.[123] It was the resurgence of nationalism and the subsequent armed conflicts that destroyed a common civic identity.[124] As Kaiser observes, the Old Bridge became 'ethnicized' in war.[125] Before the war, no one in Mostar would have said that the Old Bridge was a 'Muslim' monument. The shelling first by the Serbs and later by Croats and its final destruction by Croat tanks turned it into one.[126] In a sad testimony to the changes taking place with respect to the approach to cultural property, as the conflict progressed, an increasing number of Muslim soldiers were looking at the Old Bridge not as a symbol of bridging the cultures but as a purely Islamic symbol. In the words of one of them, Kemal Kemo, a local commander: 'This [B]ridge shows the beauty of our Muslim culture. Croats don't have anything here that can compare'.[127] In turn, HVO soldiers were looking at the Bridge as the 'Muslim' relic which along with the 'cleans[ing of] Mostar of the Muslims… [ought to] also be destroyed'.[128] Pero Džidić, a Croat fighting with what was, as

---

120 Ibid.

121 Ibid.

122 Pašić, *The Old Bridge*, above n 5.

123 See Michael Sells, *The Bridge Betrayed: Religion and Genocide in Bosnia* (1996).

124 See, eg, Yarwood, above n 74, 194; Banac Interview, above n 8; Kaiser, 'Crimes against Culture', above n 1.

125 Kaiser, ibid.

126 Ibid 3.

127 John Pomfret, 'A Bridge Becomes a Wedge as Span Crumbles, Unity Dreams Die' *The Seattle Times*, Monday, 30 August 1993, A3 1993 WL 6014999, http://web2westlaw.com.

128 Robert Block, 'Croatian Death Squad Talks Tough around the Pool Table' *The Independent* (London), 6 September 1993, http://listserv.acsu.buffalo.edu.

mentioned, the predominantly Muslim ABH, summed it up sadly: 'Before the war, it belonged to all of us. Now one side wants to claim it as its own and the other wants to destroy it. Nobody is winning here'.[129]

B The Rural v Urban Argument

Another explanation for the destruction of the Old Bridge that has been put forward is based on so-called 'urbophobia'.[130] Under this view, the battle of Mostar is seen as 'the battle between city lovers and city haters',[131] and the destruction of cultural property is seen as the destruction of the physical symbols of the urban environment that stood for coexistence. For the city haters, coming from rural, often ethnically 'pure' areas, the common civic identity characteristic of urban areas was considered the worst enemy as their idea was 'to be alone among our own people',[132] surrounded with relics that symbolise 'our own' past. As a former high-ranking judge of Bosnia and Herzegovina's Supreme Court explained, the idea of coexistence 'is a thing from the city…the people from rural areas do not believe in it. So they want to destroy it. The bridge is a metaphor – to them it must be finished'.[133] In other words, the urban, as synonymous with pluralism, cosmopolitanism, cultural inclusiveness clashed with narrow particularism and xenophobia of nationalistic exclusiveness.[134] Since Mostar, as a city, embodied dignity, sophistication and unity,[135] it was an obstacle to the fulfilment of the aim of uniformity, and, thus, ought to be disassembled altogether. By removing evidence of the shared past, the rural nationalists wanted the city people to whom this past was precious to be eliminated as well. When interviewed by Robert Block of the London newspaper *The Independent* in Mostar at the end of the summer of 1993, an HVO soldier named Branimir stated: 'It is not enough to clean Mostar of the Muslims – the relics must also be removed'.[136]

Indeed, in an insane effort to turn Mostar into something the extreme opposite of what it had been for centuries, a cleansing of the city of its citizens took place, followed by a huge population shift.[137] Namely, while city people who were forcefully expelled from their apartments and houses were now homeless,

---

129 Pomfret, above n 127.

130 See Darko Radović, 'War in Yugoslavia and the Right to the City', http://www.arbld.unimelb.edu.au/envjust/papers/.

131 Pašić, *The Old Bridge*, above n 5, 37.

132 Kaiser, 'Crimes against Culture', above n 1, 2.

133 Pomfret, above n 127.

134 Radović, above n 130.

135 Pašić, *The Old Bridge*, above n 5.

136 Block, above n 128.

137 On the use of destruction of cultural property to implement ethnic cleansing, see generally Bevan, above n 112.

into their homes now moved rural people, mainly from neighbouring villages (often occupying more than one apartment or house previously belonging to the expelled Mostarians). While in some instances the newly arrived people were refugees, themselves expelled from their homes, it is common knowledge that in the majority of cases the new 'citizens' of Mostar were peasants mainly from the nearby villages who never lost their homes in the places they came from.

The cleansing of Mostar of its citizens was accompanied by the destruction of cultural property which symbolised the shared past – the symbols of the urban environment that stood for coexistence. These symbols were targeted from the very beginning of the conflict.[138] The first target was the War Memorial because the attackers deemed it to be holding 'somebody else's memory'.[139] For the same reason historic buildings, museums, galleries, archives and libraries soon also became the target. The Old Bridge was the last major urban target. Since the Bridge represented 'an urbogenetic sparkle that caused Mostar',[140] as long as it was connecting its east and west side, there was hope that the city would survive.[141] Its destruction eliminated the 'other' at all levels[142] and, therefore, symbolically sentenced the city to death.[143] The famous Yugoslav architect, Bogdan Bogdanović, who labelled an attack on cities as 'urbicide', voiced his response to the destruction of cities in the following words:

> I do not understand this military doctrine that seems to be centered on burning cities. The civilized world will one day grow tired of us killing each other, but will never forget the annihilation of these cities.[144]

C *The Territorial Grab Argument*

While hatred flared up during the conflict and nationalistic exclusiveness in opposition to urban multiculturalism played a significant role in the destruction of the Old Bridge, the underlying motive behind the destruction was actually the ultimate aim of the entire Croat-Muslim armed conflict – the division of Bosnia and Herzegovina with Croatia taking up part of the territory of Bosnia

138 Radović, above n 130.

139 Bogdan Bogdanović, *Grad i smrt* (*City and Death*) (1994) [*City and Death*].

140 Radović, above n 130.

141 See, eg, Bogdanović, *Most*, above n 6; Bogdanović, *City and Death*, above n 139; Pomfret, above n 127.

142 Kaiser, 'Crimes against Culture', above n 1, 2. Although Kaiser refers to rural areas, this is applicable to Mostar as well. During and after the conflict there was a significant population shift in Mostar, resulting in a dramatic increase in the percentage of rural population living in Mostar.

143 Radović, above n 130.

144 Nedim Gürsel, 'Bosnia after the Destruction: Urbicide and an Architect', http://www.atlasturkey.com.

and Herzegovina, including Mostar as the main prize.[145] It is believed that this aim was backed up by the Croat-Serb deal to partition Bosnia and Herzegovina and by the subsequent cooperation between the two parties to make it happen.[146] Nationalism, 'urbophobia' and ethnic and cultural cleansing were only instruments used to achieve this aim. As Pašić observes, since the Old Bridge 'contained the meaning and the spirit of all Bosnia and Herzegovina: the essence of the bridge was meeting and joining together; the country, like the bridge, could be divided only by destroying it'.[147]

It appears that even before the former Yugoslavia began to break up officially,[148] Croatia took part in planning the division of Bosnia and Herzegovina. Allegedly, at the famous Karađorđevo meeting held in March 1991, Franjo Tuđman and Slobodan Milošević, the Croatian and Serbian leaders respectively, forged such a plan.[149] According to Croatia's subsequent President, Stjepan Mesić, after the Karađorđevo meeting, Tuđman 'was definitely pleased with the results…absolutely satisfied, even ecstatic'.[150] The meeting was followed by Croatia's declaration of independence in June 1991 and its recognition by the European Community in January 1992. Furthermore, shortly after the Karađorđevo meeting, in Bosnia and Herzegovina both the Republika Srpska and the Croatian Community Herceg-Bosna (the latter to be renamed the Croatian Republic Herceg-Bosna,[151] both of which are hereinafter referred to as (HB)) were formed. This fact 'clearly indicates what the topic of those discussions was and that Milošević and Tuđman agreed about the same concept'.[152]

The HB was set up as a new community or entity for Croats in Bosnia and Herzegovina in November 1991 by the principal Bosnian-Herzegovinian Croat political party, the Croatian Democratic Union of Bosnia and Herzegovina (HDZ-BH), an offshoot of its Croatian parent, the HDZ, a nationalist party.[153]

145 Malić, above n 9, para 4 (referring to Roy Gutman).

146 For evidence on the subject of the carve-up of Bosnia and Herzegovina (BH) see, eg, testimony of the following Prosecution witnesses in *Prlić*: Dr Ćiril Ribičić, 11 December 2007; Raymond Lane, 17 October 2007; Stjepan Kljuić, 26-28 June 2006; Josip Manolić, 3-6 July 2006; and Herbert Okun, 2-5 April 2007. Transcripts at, <http://www.un.org/icty/cases-e/index-e.htm>. See also Oliver Bullough, 'Transcripts suggest Croatia Conspired to Break up Bosnia' Institute for War and Peace Reporting, IWPR's Tribunal Update No. 524, 2 November 2007.

147 Pašić, *The Old Bridge*, above n 5, 39.

148 The break up of the former Yugoslavia began in June 1991 when Slovenia declared independence.

149 Mesić Interview, above n 12.

150 Ibid 5.

151 On 28 August 1993 the HVO proclaimed the Croatian Republic Herceg-Bosna (HB) with Mostar as its capital.

152 Mesić Interview, above n 12.

153 See *Prosecutor v Dario Kordić and Mario Čerkez,* Judgement, Trial Chamber III, 26

The goal of the HDZ-BH 'was to secure the right of the Croatian people to self-determination, including the right to secession'.[154] The HB was described as 'a separate and distinct cultural, economic and territorial whole'.[155] Mostar was to be the capital of this entity.[156]

Bosnia and Herzegovina, disagreeing with its partition, declared independence in March 1992, and was recognised one month later by the European Community as an independent, sovereign state.[157] The same month, the HDZ-BH created the HVO, the supreme executive and defence authority of HB. Local municipal HVO units were subsequently established from June 1992 as the executive and military power in the municipalities.[158] According to President Mesić, 'the HVO quickly replaced legally elected leadership in the municipalities that were under their control even though the HDZ had already held power in them'.[159]

In 1993, the meeting between Radovan Karadžić and Mate Boban, the leaders of Serb and Croat entities in Bosnia and Herzegovina, respectively, was held in Graz.[160] The outcome of the meeting is best summed up by Boban's statement 'that in practice there were no unresolved problems between Croats and Serbs in Bosnia and Herzegovina',[161] meaning that 'a separate agreement was reached on the account of Bosniaks-Muslims'.[162] Mostar was part of this agreement. The siege of the city began on 9 May 1993, only a few days after the meeting in Graz. Prior to the siege all the patriotic media and politicians from HB spread propaganda about 'Croatian Mostar'.[163]

A number of factors, including the absence of the Muslim side at both the Karađorđevo and Graz meetings, the formation of HB, the attack on Mostar, the suspicious withdrawal of Croatian forces from certain regions in northern Bosnia and Herzegovina to surrender them to Serb forces although 'there was no military justification to order the withdrawal',[164] the suspicious withdrawal of Serbian forces from areas, such as Mostar, where they were militarily stronger

February 2001, Case No. IT-95-14/2-T, para 5(b) [*Kordić* Trial Judgement or *Kordić* case or *Kordić*].

154 Ibid.

155 Ibid para 5(c).

156 See 'A Greater Croatia', above n 10 (interview with Jadranko Prlić, the then HB Prime Minister, who explained why Mostar was to be HB's capital).

157 See *Prlić* Indictment, para 19.

158 Ibid paras 25-26.

159 Mesić Interview, above n 12, 5.

160 Ibid.

161 Ibid.

162 Ibid 6.

163 Ibid 6.

164 Ibid 3.

at the time,[165] cooperation between Serbian and Croatian forces in Bosnia and Herzegovina at the expense of Muslims,[166] and war crimes committed on a massive scale against the Muslim population of Bosnia and Herzegovina by both Serbian forces and Croatian forces, demonstrate that there was the plan to divide Bosnia and Herzegovina.

As far as Croatia's territorial claim in Bosnia and Herzegovina was concerned, in President Tuđman's view Croatia needed to reflect its natural borders, which meant incorporating 'the whole of western Herzegovina and Mostar, as well as Bosnian districts where Croats had a clear majority'.[167] To implement the plan of annexation of Bosnian and Herzegovinian territories, the HDZ planned and then implemented, particularly through the HVO, a campaign of persecution and ethnic cleansing. The Croat-Muslim conflict began in January 1993 in Central Bosnia, to be followed by the series of attacks which included the Neretva Valley region. The Vance-Owen Peace Plan provided the pretext for removing the Bosnian and Herzegovinian Muslims.[168] The battle of Mostar was described as one of the bloodiest in the Balkan conflicts.[169] Gutman ascribed it to causes which he heard from the HVO commander Slobodan Praljak – *Lebensraum* (living space) - the very German word used by the Nazis to justify their expansion into Eastern Europe.[170]

Therefore, Mostar, falling within Croatia's 'natural' borders, was attacked in an attempt to redraw those borders, within which there would be space for Croatian people only. Mostar was an important part of the territory within such borders. The HVO headquarters were located in Mostar, and the city was proclaimed the capital of HB on 28 August 1993. Since the percentage of the Mostar population of Serb ethnicity was drastically reduced in 1992, it was the ethnic Muslim population which posed an obstacle to the 'Croatianisation' of Mostar. Hence the ethnic cleansing. Hoping to accelerate the process of ethnic purification, the HVO accompanied it with cultural cleansing. The city's landmark was subsequently targeted and demolished to symbolically confirm this objective.[171] In the same way as everyone else in the former Yugoslavia, the attackers, too, knew about the unifying grandeur of the Old Bridge. Its presence was so noticeable that no one could miss it in either the physical or cultural sense. By intentionally targeting the Old Bridge as a span between the cultures,

165 See, generally, *Kordić* Trial Judgement; *Prosecutor v Mladen Naletilić aka 'Tuta' and Vinko Martinović aka 'Štela'*, Judgement, Trial Chamber, 31 March 2003, Case No. IT-98-34-T [*Naletilić* Trial Judgement or *Naletilić* case or *Naletilić*]; *Prlić* Indictment.

166 Ibid.

167 *Kordić* Trial Judgement, para 135.

168 Ibid para 10.

169 Malić, above n 9, para 4.

170 Ibid.

171 See, eg, Bevan, above n 112, 10-11.

the HVO was at the same time emphasising the historical origins of the Bridge, thereby turning the Bridge from an object of cultural unity into an object of cultural specificity. The HVO shelling attached to the Bridge a specific ethnicity and religion, and thereby sent the message that the people and objects of this origin were undesirable within Croatian borders.

When asked how he felt about the conflict, the then chief commander of the HVO stated that he achieved his war goals and felt 'a victor in every sense of that word'.[172] At that time, since '[v]irtually every war finds generals exulting over a bridge brought down',[173] given the importance of the Old Bridge, its destruction must have been a significant part and parcel of military victory. Celebrating the elimination of the last physical and most symbolic span of Mostar, the HVO cheered and fired their guns in the air:[174] 'thousands of bursts of fire…hugging…screech…happiness, euphoria…not one hundredth part of that clinking was in Mostar even on 9 May 1945 when it was announced that Berlin fell, Germany capitulated and WWII was over'.[175]

At the same time, 'the true Mostarians'[176] cried on both sides of the city.[177] Reportedly, after months of hiding from the constant HVO shooting, people on the left bank of the Neretva, without fearing any longer whether they would be shot, left their cellars and other shelters and headed towards the beloved Bridge: 'People were walking slowly, the way people do when passing-by a coffin of a deceased human being. Some were crying, some were passing by [the fallen Bridge] silently.… It was heartbreaking to watch them'.[178] Then a 'day of mourning' was proclaimed in the municipality of Mostar.[179]

---

172 *Tjednik* interview with General Slobodan Praljak: 'People are Guilty, not Blaškić or Kordić', *Tjednik*, Zagreb, Croatia, 9 May 1997, 9 [Praljak Interview], http://free.freespeech.org/ex-Yupress/tjednik/tjednik1.html> (Copy on file with author).

173 James Yuenger, 'Crossing into History: War Brings Down a Bridge that Spanned Centuries and Linked Memories' *Chicago Tribune* Thursday, 25 November 1993, http://web2westlaw.com/.

174 Dodds, above n 106, 1.

175 Džemal Humo, 'Prličev pucanj u Hajrudina' ['Prlić's Shot at Hayreddin'], *Most*, No. 110-111, February 1999, 4, http://ww1.500.telia.com/~u50008760/2122/2122_056.htm (Copy on file with author).

176 Ibid 4-5.

177 Ibid.

178 Broz, above n 94, 247.

179 See Republic of Bosnia and Herzegovina, Wartime Presidency of the Mostar Municipality, *Decision about Proclaiming 10 November 1993 a Day of Mourning in the Mostar Municipality*, 9 November 1993, published in *Most*, No. 108-109 November-December 1998, http://www.most.ba/01920/006.htm (Copy on file with author); Alija Kebo, 'A Two-Year Mourning Day', a letter of the editor, *Most*, No. 91, November/December 1995, http://w1.500.telia.com/~u50008760/91_2/most2_6.htm (Copy on file with author).

V Effects of the Destruction

> Why lament the destruction of a bridge?
>
> A bridge is, after all, not an organic being but a thing of height and distance and stress resistance, the product of someone at a table scratching out physical calculations, figuring the angles.
>
> Yet a well-conceived bridge is majesty wrought by civil engineering and can consume the eye, not only for its graceful arch across water or a mountain pass but also because of something deeper.
>
> A bridge is a connection, firmly rooted.... To gauge [its] power...consider its reverse....[180]

A Citizens of Mostar

Love for the Old Bridge was passed from one generation of Mostarians to another. To each citizen of Mostar this bridge was much more than a beautiful, well-constructed structure. To some it was even of greater value than their own parents or ancestors.[181] The Mostarians perceived the Old Bridge to be like a human being. They called it 'Stari' ('the old man').[182] They lived with 'Stari'; 'Stari' was a part of them.[183] The Bridge was a place where friendships were strengthened,[184] where some enjoyed their first kiss,[185] the divers' jumping-off point,[186] an open stage, a permanent patient model to artists, an inexhaustible inspiration to poets and much more – a place where East met West. Mostarians did not make friendships or fall in love along ethnic lines. Being a Jew, Serb, Muslim, Croat, Hungarian or simply a Yugoslav was not the basis on which people were considered to be more or less good. It was the character qualities that mattered.[187] Despite the hardship which the conflict imposed on them, people were hoping that the conflict would spare the Old Bridge, and with it centuries-old human links within their equally loved city. For this reason some

---

180 Yuenger, above n 173, 1.

181 *Final Report*, above n 113, 7.

182 See Predrag Matvejević, 'Old Bridges, Old Values', Institute for War and Peace Reporting, War Report Issue, 23 December 1993, http://www.iwpr.net/index.pl?archive/war/war_23_199312_01.txt [2].

183 Broz, above n 94, 247.

184 Matvejević, above n 182.

185 Yuenger, above n 173, 2.

186 Pomfret, above n 127.

187 Matvejević, above n 182.

Croats joined the ABH and took up arms against their own Croat people. Not long before the destruction of the Bridge and the city, and he himself was killed by the HVO, one of them stated:

> I am fighting for the [B]ridge. It's my world – the Old Bridge and Mostar. If the [B]ridge falls, Mostar falls with it. It's our heart.[188]

B Other Citizens of the Former Yugoslavia

The destruction of the Old Bridge caused profound shock and deep pain. By destroying the Bridge, the HVO destroyed a part of every Mostarian[189] and attacked 'the heart of shared history and culture'[190] of the whole of Bosnia and Herzegovina. But the destruction of the landmark Mostar span was not only felt deeply in Mostar and elsewhere in Bosnia and Herzegovina. In one of the ironies that the bloody Balkans armed conflicts gave rise to in abundance, Croats, Muslims and Serbs – three major warring parties – were united in their grief over the loss of a cultural treasure that symbolised what were once thought to be unbreakable bonds between Christian and Muslim, West and East in the entire former Yugoslavia. All spoke with a single voice in denouncing the tank artillery shelling of the Bridge. Even TV stations, which had never mentioned other atrocities committed against cultural property during the conflicts in the former Yugoslavia, carried extensive coverage, including aerial footage of the void left behind by the Bridge's collapse.[191] 'I felt sick when I saw the pictures. No one has the right to destroy our history',[192] lamented a Belgrade student. 'It is a tragic loss for everyone, not just the Muslims but for the Croats who live there as well', said one Zagreb citizen.[193]

C The International Community

The sense of loss was not limited to the Balkans. The entire international community was affected. Throughout the world, the media, particularly the western press, extensively covered the tragic loss of the Old Bridge. International organ-

188 Pomfret, above n 127, 1.

189 Broz, above n 94, 247.

190 'This is an attack on the heart of our history and culture', said Muhamed Filipovic, a Muslim politician and historian in Sarajevo. 'It was a beautiful piece of art, so harmonious'. 'Up to 9 Dead in Shelling at Sarajevo School' *Los Angeles Times* Wednesday, 10 November 1993, http://web2.westlaw.com/.

191 Carol Williams, 'Destruction of Landmark Mostar Span Felt Deeply – Warring Foes United in Grief' *The Seattle Times* Sunday, 14 November 1993, http://web2.westlaw.com.

192 Ibid.

193 Ibid.

isations dealing with cultural property joined them. '[T]he perpetrators of this disgraceful act are trying to eradicate the history of a country and its people',[194] declared Federico Mayor, the then Director-General of UNESCO, the organisation that had worked to add the Old Bridge to the World Heritage in Danger List. 'They are thereby also destroying the bridges of mutual understanding built by people of different origins and religious beliefs who had learnt to live in harmony',[195] said the UNESCO Director-General. 'It is an attack against the values cherished by the international community and dear to the lovers of freedom. The destruction of the Stari Most Bridge has robbed all the communities of Bosnia and Herzegovina of a symbol of hope, ruptured their links with a time of peace and struck at the very roots of their cultural heritage'.[196]

The emotional international outcry relating to the destruction of the Old Bridge, as in the case of the similar outcry after the shelling by the YA of the walled Croatian city of Dubrovnik in 1991, tells of the importance of cultural property to human well-being irrespective of the origins of that property.[197] As discussed previously, the whole world feels a sense of loss when it is deprived of one of its cultural treasures and is united in condemnation of acts that cause its cultural disinheritance. Given the horror of the concentration camps, mass rape and thousands of deaths that occurred in the territory of the former Yugoslavia, to some, these outcries might be signs of indifference to human suffering.[198] But monuments are exceptional objects. They are built on the idea of a future – not only for us, but also for our children and our children's children. This explains why people other than Mostarians cried and felt more pain looking at the images of the void left behind by the Old Bridge's collapse than, for instance, the image of a massacred woman, published approximately at the same

---

194 *Fourth COE Report*, above n 36.

195 Ibid.

196 Ibid.

197 The importance of the survival of immovable cultural property for the rehabilitation of psychologically devastated communities has been the subject of a number of publications. See, eg, John Yarwood, *Rebuilding Mostar: Urban Reconstruction in a War Zone* (1999) [*Rebuilding Mostar*]; Yarwood, 'Cultural Warfare', above n 74; Robert Layton, Julian Thomas and Peter Stone (eds), *Destruction and Conservation of Cultural Property* (2001); Ismail Serageldin, Ephin Shluger and Joan Martin-Brown (eds), *Historic Cities and Sacred Sites: Cultural Roots for Urban Futures* (2001); Bevan, above n 112; Brian Graham and Peter Howard (eds), *The Ashgate Research Companion to Heritage and Identity* (2008);Esther Charlesworth, *Architects without Frontiers: War, Reconstruction and Design Responsibility* (2006).

198 According to one European diplomat, '[t]he Mostar bombing has sparked another round of debate over whether the world is more interested in preserving stones or people'. Carol Williams, 'Bosnia's Hopes Fall with Historic Bridge in Mostar' *Los Angeles Times* Friday, 12 November 1993, http://web2.westlaw.com/.

time.[199] This is, perhaps, because people saw their own mortality in the collapse of the Bridge, not in the death of the woman. As Croatian author Slavenka Drakulić observes:

> We expect people to die. We count on our own lives to end. The destruction of a monument to civilization is something else. The bridge, in all its beauty and grace, was built to outlive us; it was an attempt to grasp eternity. Because it was the product of both individual creativity and collective experience, it transcended our individual destiny. A dead woman is one of us-but the bridge is all of us, forever.[200]

VI Summary and Observations

The destruction of cultural property in the Balkans during the 1990s is sad testimony to the fate of cultural treasures in times of armed conflict. In an insane race for territory in Bosnia and Herzegovina, cultural cleansing was employed to implement ethnic cleansing. In an attempt to redraw borders and to erase memories, everything that was a reminder of the shared past and that was not deemed 'ours' but considered to be 'theirs' was destroyed mercilessly.

On 9 November 1993, the 'painfully beautiful'[201] Old Bridge was blasted and crumbled into the Neretva over which it had stood for 427 years. The delicate stone arch that adorned the city of Mostar was destroyed by the Croat forces to the loss of all peoples in Mostar and elsewhere. If, by knocking down the Bridge, the HVO hoped to strike right at the hearts of the citizens of Mostar, then this aim was fully accomplished. The pain was profound and the void that this act created was unbearable.

Since cultural property forms part of the cultural heritage of all humankind and ultimately belongs to everyone, by destroying the Old Bridge, the HVO also created a tragedy for its own people, and disinherited them of a cultural treasure of outstanding value. In the process, the HVO even deepened the Croats' tragedy in that the whole Croat nation was labelled a guilty party with respect to the Old Bridge. This is a heavy burden, which cannot be eased until the individuals responsible for the destruction of the Bridge are identified and brought to justice. To determine whether the destruction of the Old Bridge was

---

199 See Slavenka Drakulić, 'Falling Down: a Mostar Bridge' (1993) 209 *The New Republic* 14(2).

200 Ibid.

201 *Prosecutor v Mladen Naletilić, aka 'Tuta' and Vinko Martinović, aka 'Štela'*, Sentencing Judgement Statement, Trial Chamber I, 31 March 2003, Case No. IT-98-34-T, para 16, <http://www.un.org/icty/naletilic/trialc/judgement/nal-state030331e.htm> (Judge Clark, describing the Old Bridge of Mostar as '[t]he *painfully beautiful* old arched footbridge which stood over the Neretva River for four centuries') (emphasis added) [*Naletilić* Sentencing Judgement Statement].

an unlawful act entailing individual criminal responsibility, it is important to examine how international law regulates the protection of cultural property in armed conflict.

Chapter 4

International Law Protecting Cultural Property in Armed Conflict

I An Overview

Armed conflict is perhaps as old as humankind itself. Jiří Toman notes that '[i]n the course of 5,000 years of history, some 14,000 wars have afflicted humanity',[1] causing countless deaths and immeasurable human suffering and destruction. For centuries, the right to resort to war (*jus ad bellum*) had been deemed inseparable from the concept of sovereignty. The accompanying destruction of property had been seen as an inevitable part of warfare. From the nineteenth century onwards, much effort has been made at the international level to make warfare more humane. This effort has resulted in numerous multilateral treaties that impose certain limits on the means and methods of conducting armed conflict. The first half of the twentieth century witnessed a radical change in the area of international law governing the recourse to armed conflict. After WWI, in what is considered the most grandiose peacekeeping effort, the *Treaty Providing for the Renunciation of War as an Instrument of National Policy of 27 August 1928*,[2] also called the *Pact of Paris*, or the *Kellogg-Briand Pact*,[3] prohibited any recourse to armed conflict. Initially, this treaty was intended to be a bilateral non-aggression pact, but it eventually became a multilateral agreement, attracting nearly all the nations of the world, agreeing to renounce war as an instrument of national policy and to settle all international disputes by peaceful means.

The events of WWII proved that the Pact was ineffective. But the international community was unstoppable in its resolve 'to save succeeding generations

---

1 Jiří Toman, *The Protection of Cultural Property in the Event of Armed Conflict: Commentary on the Convention for the Protection of Cultural Property in the Event of Armed Conflict and its Protocol, signed on 14 May 1954 in The Hague, and on other instruments of international law concerning such protection* (1996).

2 See *Treaty Providing for the Renunciation of War as an Instrument of National Policy*, 27 August 1928, art 1, 46 Stat. (1929) 2343, 2346, TS No. 796, 94 LNTS 57, 63.

3 Aristide Briand was the French foreign minister and was the first to suggest a bilateral non-aggression pact in the spring of 1927. Frank B. Kellogg, the US secretary of state, proposed that the pact be converted into a general multilateral treaty, which the French accepted.

from the scourge of war, which…has brought untold sorrow to [hu]mankind'.[4] In its more recent attempt to outlaw armed conflict, the international community in 1945 adopted the *UN Charter* prohibiting the use of force as well as the threat of force. In its pertinent parts, Article 2 of the *Charter* spells out that '[a]ll Members [of the UN] shall refrain in their international relations from the threat or use of force',[5] and that they 'shall settle their international disputes by peaceful means in such a manner that international peace and security, and justice, are not endangered'.[6] The only exception allowing States unilaterally or collectively to resort to military force is self-defence, but even then '[m]easures taken by [UN] Members in the exercise of this right of self-defence shall be immediately reported to the Security Council'[7] – the principal UN organ responsible for the maintenance of international peace and security. Today, war is deemed illegal and the very term 'war' has been abandoned in international instruments.

The prohibition on the use of force and the threat of force has not ruled out the necessity of regulating the means and methods of conducting warfare (*jus in bello*). The numerous occurrences of armed conflict in the post-WWII period is evidence that warfare is not a thing of the past. These conflicts have occurred both between and within States. But what is an armed conflict and exactly when is it said that an armed conflict exists? The generally applicable answer to this question is found in existing treaty law, specifically, the *Geneva Conventions of 12 August 1949* (*1949 Geneva Conventions*)[8] and the *1977 Protocols* additional to these *Conventions* (*Additional Protocol I* and *Additional Protocol II*).[9]

---

4 *Charter of the United Nations*, 26 June 1945, 59 Stat 1031, TS 993, 3 Bevans 1153, Preamble para 1 (entered into force 24 October 1945) [*UN Charter*].

5 Ibid art 2(4).

6 Ibid art 2(3).

7 Ibid art 51.

8 See *Geneva Convention for the Amelioration of the Condition of the Wounded and Sick in Armed Forces in the Field*, 12 August 1949, 75 UNTS 31, arts 2 and 3 (entered into force 21 October 1950) [*1949 Geneva Convention I*]; *Geneva Convention for the Amelioration of the Condition of Wounded, Sick and Shipwrecked Members of Armed Forces at Sea*, 12 August 1949, 75 UNTS 84, arts 2 and 3 (entered into force 21 October 1950) [*1949 Geneva Convention II*], *Geneva Convention relative to the Treatment of Prisoners of War*, 12 August 1949, 75 UNTS 135, arts 2 and 3 (entered into force 21 October 1950) [*1949 Geneva Convention III*] and *Geneva Convention relative to the Protection of Civilian Persons in Time of War*, 12 August 1949, 75 UNTS 287, arts 2 and 3 (entered into force 21 October 1950) [*1949 Geneva Convention IV*]. As at 4 February 2012, there were 194 States parties to each Convention. The 1949 Geneva Conventions are available at http://www.icrc.org/ihl.nsf.

9 See *Protocol Additional to the Geneva Conventions of 12 August 1949, and Relating to the Protection of Victims of International Armed Conflicts*, 8 June 1977, 1125 UNTS 3, art 1 (entered into force 7 December 1978) [*Additional Protocol I*]; *Protocol Additional to the Geneva Conventions of 12 August 1949, and Relating to the Protection of Victims*

Several situations enlisted in the relevant provisions of these instruments have been summarised succinctly in the jurisprudence of the ICTY. According to the ICTY Appeals Chamber in *Tadić*, an armed conflict exists:

> whenever there is a resort to armed force between States or protracted armed violence between governmental authorities and organized armed groups or between such groups within a State.[10]

The distinction must be made between international and non-international armed conflicts. In accordance with Article 2 common to the *1949 Geneva Conventions* and Article 1 of *Additional Protocol I*, armed conflicts that arise between two or more States are characterised as *international* armed conflicts.[11] Conflicts that take place within a State, 'between its armed forces and dissident armed forces or other organized armed groups which, under responsible command, exercise such control over a part of its territory as to enable them to carry out sustained and concerted military operations'[12] are characterised as *non-international* armed conflicts. Under international law, 'situations of internal disturbances and tensions, such as riots, isolated and sporadic acts of violence and other acts of a similar nature'[13] are not considered armed conflicts.

The body of law that governs armed conflict is usually referred to as *international humanitarian law* (IHL). According to the *ICRC Commentary on the Additional Protocols* (*ICRC Commentary*), the expression *international humanitarian law applicable in armed conflict* means

> international rules, established by treaties or custom, which are specifically intended to solve humanitarian problems directly arising from international or non-international armed conflicts and which, for humanitarian reasons, limit the right of Parties to a conflict to use the methods and means of warfare of their choice or protect persons and property that are, or may

of Non-International Armed Conflicts, 8 June 1977, 1125 UNTS 609 art 1(1) (entered into force 7 December 1978) [*Additional Protocol II*]. As at 4 February 2012, there were 171 States parties to *Additional Protocol I* and 166 States parties to *Additional Protocol II*. The *Protocols* are available at http://www.icrc.org/ihl.nsf.

10 *Prosecutor v Duško Tadić aka 'Dule'*, Decision on the Defence Motion for Interlocutory Appeal on Jurisdiction, Appeals Chamber, 2 October 1995, Case No. IT-94-1-AR72 para 70 [*Tadić* Jurisdiction Decision].

11 See *1949 Geneva Conventions*, common art 2 and *Additional Protocol I*, art 1. This includes situations in which 'peoples are fighting against colonial domination and alien occupation and against racist regimes in the exercise of their right of self-determination'. *Additional Protocol I*, art 1(4).

12 *Additional Protocol II*, art 1(1).

13 Ibid art 1(2).

> be, affected by conflict. The expression…is often abbreviated to *international humanitarian law* or *humanitarian law*.[14]

IHL is generally taken to consist of two sets of laws: the so-called Hague law and the so-called Geneva law.[15] Both laws mitigate the negative effects of armed conflict, notably, death and destruction. The former, which finds its principal elaboration in, as Professor Ivan Shearer puts it, 'the now rather dated'[16] *Hague Conventions of 1899 and of 1907*,[17] prohibits or restricts the use of certain means and methods of warfare. The latter, which draws principally on the four *Geneva Conventions of 1949*,[18] imposes a set of rules aimed at the protection of certain classes of persons and objects. In fact, it was with the adoption of the *1949 Geneva Conventions* that the term *international humanitarian law* came into use. At first, the term was used solely in reference to Geneva law, as part of what was traditionally called the law of war or the law of armed conflict.[19] As Professor Kalshoven explains,

> [m]ilitary circles were not enthusiastic at the time about the suggestion that 'their' battlefield law would be referred to as humanitarian as well. They felt that this shift in name masked the true, intrinsically harsh nature of battlefield law and, indeed, risked heralding the introduction of unduly soft, protective, elements into it. Conversely, members of the Red Cross and Red Crescent community were afraid of seeing the notion of protective humanitarian law contaminated with crude battlefield law.[20]

---

14 Yves Sandoz *et al* (eds), *Commentary on the Additional Protocols I and II of 9 June 1977* (1987), xxvii [*ICRC Commentary*].

15 See, eg, William Fenrick, 'Humanitarian Law and Criminal Trials' (1997) 7 *Transnational Law and Contemporary Problems* 23, 27. See also Hirad Abtahi, 'The Protection of Cultural Property in Times of Armed Conflict: The Practice of the International Criminal Tribunal for the Former Yugoslavia' (2001) 14 *Harvard Human Rights Journal* 1, 5; Ivan Shearer, 'Rules of Conduct during Humanitarian Interventions', http://www.unc.edu/depts/diplomat/archives_roll/2001_07-09/hum_intervention/hum [10].

16 Shearer, ibid.

17 The Hague Conventions of 1899 and of 1907 were produced at the First and the Second Peace Conference. The First Peace Conference was convened in The Hague from 18 May to 29 July 1899. It produced three conventions. The Second Hague Peace Conference was held from 15 June to 18 October 1907. It adopted thirteen conventions. Conventions produced at both Hague Peace Conferences are available at http://www.icrc.org/ihl.nsf.

18 See above, n 8.

19 See Frits Kalshoven, 'The Protection of Cultural Property in the Event of Armed Conflict within the Framework of International Humanitarian Law', (2005) 57 *Museum* 61, para 2 ['The Protection of Cultural Property'].

20 Ibid.

However, with the adoption of the two *Additional Protocols* in 1977,[21] which contain a mixture of Hague and Geneva rules, the two sets of laws were brought together in one stream. Today, the terms *international humanitarian law* and *the law of armed conflict* are usually used interchangeably.[22]

Notwithstanding the terminology, the very cautious approach of States to restrictions on their means and methods of waging warfare resulted in less developed rules on the subject than those rules protecting victims of armed conflict.[23] Also, whereas IHL applies to both international and non-international armed conflict, so far as non-international armed conflicts are concerned, only a small fraction of the total number of rules are applicable, namely, only one of the 429 articles of the four *1949 Geneva Conventions* – Common Article 3 – and *Additional Protocol II*, containing 28 articles (in contrast to *Additional Protocol I* which comprises 102 articles). Where cultural property is concerned, the distinction should be made between common Article 3 and *Protocol II*. While the latter does contain provisions relevant to cultural property, the former does not explicitly regulate the protection of any property at all and thus has nothing to say about cultural property. In its document 'The Conduct of Hostilities' of August 2007, the International Committee of the Red Cross (ICRC) reaffirmed that 'Article 3 common to the *1949 Geneva Conventions* only governs the treatment of persons and objects which have fallen into the power of the enemy and does not pertain to the conduct of hostilities'.[24]

In William Fenrick's view, an explanation for the emphasis placed on international armed conflict lies with the notion of State sovereignty.[25] Non-international armed conflicts have long been considered internal matters of a State. From the beginning of the 1990s, with the disappearance of the constraints of the Cold War and with increasing occurrences of non-international armed conflicts, the situation began to change. The response of the international community to the situation in the former Yugoslavia in the 1990s exemplifies that the resolution of these conflicts can no longer be considered exclusively a State responsibility. When expelling the Iraqi forces from Kuwait at the beginning of the 1990s, the international community sent a clear message that States

21 See above, n 9.

22 See Shearer, above n 15. But see Kalshoven, 'The Protection of Cultural Property', above n 19 (noting that the terms 'international humanitarian law' and 'the law of armed conflict' have not necessarily acquired an identical meaning for everyone).

23 See Fenrick, above n 15.

24 ICRC, 'The Conduct of Hostilities', a document written in August 2007 for the 30th Sanremo Round Table on Current Issues of International Humanitarian Law, 'The Conduct of Hostilities: Revisiting the Law of Armed Conflict 100 years after the 1907 Hague Conventions and 30 years after the 1977 Additional Protocols' 6 to 8 September 2007, Sanremo, Italy, http://www.reliefweb.int/rw/rwt.nsf/db900SID/OCHA.

25 See Fenrick, above n 15, 25.

could no longer use the shield of national sovereignty when invading other countries either. Although an armed conflict, irrespective of its character, is increasingly being seen as a concern of the entire international community, its classification as international or non-international still matters because it determines which rules of IHL apply. Even if these rules are not equally developed, the fact remains that in either type of conflict the belligerents must observe certain standards of conduct. As the ICTY Appeals Chamber notes, this obligation to respect the rules of IHL in both types of armed conflict

> begins with the initiation of such armed conflicts and extends beyond the cessation of hostilities until a general conclusion of peace is reached; or, in the case of internal conflicts, a peaceful settlement is achieved. Until that moment, international humanitarian law continues to apply in the whole territory of the warring States or, in the case of internal conflicts, the whole territory under the control of a party, whether or not actual combat takes place there.[26]

While it is understandable that violations of the rules of conduct prescribed by IHL stand out, such rules, as Professor Stanislav Nahlik correctly observes, have in fact often been observed, 'if for no other reason than fear of retaliation'.[27] Another compelling reason to abstain from violating any of the rules governing the conduct of armed conflict is fear of prosecution. As the IMT, ICTY, ICTR and ICC, as well as numerous other hybrid tribunals across the world demonstrate, those responsible for such violations may be brought to justice – not merely before a municipal court, but also before an international criminal court. Needless to say, this would be impossible without addressing the reality of occurrences of armed conflicts by devising rules regulating the conduct of warfare even if these conflicts are legally prohibited.

Whereas the rules of conduct can be divided into several categories, there are two major categories with respect to objects of protection: the rules protecting certain groups of persons and the rules protecting property. Given that an armed conflict is a deadly affair, which takes a great toll on human life, one might argue that rules regulating the protection of persons are far more important than those according protection to property and that the belligerents should concentrate on protecting human life as superior in value to material objects. An examination of the instruments of IHL indeed reveals that a majority contain an incomparably greater number of provisions concerning persons than those relating to property.

---

26 *Tadić* Jurisdiction Decision, para 70. See also *1949 Geneva Convention (I)*, art 5; *1949 Geneva Convention (III)*, art 5; *1949 Geneva Convention (IV)*, art 6; *Additional Protocol I*, art 3; *Additional Protocol II*, art 2.

27 Stanislav Nahlik, 'International Law and the Protection of Cultural Property in Armed Conflict' (1976) 27 *Hastings Law Journal* 1069, 1069 ['International Law'].

Nonetheless, this does not mean that the protection of property is of only modest significance. People are not only concerned with their survival in armed conflict. Their dignity, memory, heart and soul also matter. Where property which has merely a material or financial value is replaceable, sometimes, as Nahlik observes, 'ironically, to the benefit of the apparent loser, who may receive more up-to-date equipment or machinery than that destroyed',[28] certain objects, which are today called cultural property, are, because of their uniqueness, irreplaceable. Since the value of cultural objects is far greater than their worth in material or financial terms and since these objects are so closely linked to human life, no effort should be spared to preserve them during hostilities.

It could also be argued that while human beings have a limited life span, cultural objects of outstanding value could and should last indefinitely if they are adequately protected.[29] Still, the importance of protecting human life should not be weighed against the importance of protecting cultural property and *vice versa* as any comparison of the kind would be quite inappropriate. Human life is invaluable and irreplaceable, and as such imperatively requires protection. However, since cultural property plays an important role in human life, it is also crucial that such property receive adequate protection. Because the two are fundamentally linked, when cultural property is protected, human life also flourishes.[30]

The following sections of this chapter consider international law pertaining to the protection of cultural property in armed conflict. The chapter first briefly surveys the development of rules relevant to wartime protection of cultural property. The chapter focuses only on major internationally binding instruments applicable to wartime protection of cultural property. In order to determine exactly which law, and how much of it, is relevant to the Old Bridge, the chapter then examines the nature of the Bosnian and Herzegovinian Croat-Muslim conflict in Mostar at the time of the destruction of the Old Bridge. This examination highlights the direct intervention and overall control tests. Thereafter, the chapter outlines the law applicable to the destruction of the Old Bridge, specifying the applicability of both customary and treaty IHL.

28 Ibid 1070.

29 Ibid.

30 See, eg, Jean-Marie Henckaerts, 'New Rules for the Protection of Cultural Property in Armed Conflict' (1999) No. 835 *International Review of the Red Cross* 593 ['New Rules'].

II International Rules on Wartime Protection of Cultural Property

A The State of International Law before Adoption of the 1954 Convention

Long before the emergence of the rules of IHL, some, albeit isolated, efforts were made to spare certain objects from the harsh laws of war. But it was not until the First Peace Conference held at The Hague in 1899 and the Second Peace Conference held at The Hague in 1907 that cultural property was accorded international legal protection in armed conflict by a multilateral treaty – an internationally legally binding instrument.

Conventions adopted at these conferences played a significant role in the development of the international protection of cultural property in armed conflict. *Convention (II) with Respect to the Laws and Customs of War on Land* (*1899 Convention (II)*), with its annexed *Regulations Concerning the Laws and Customs of War on Land* (*1899 Regulations*),[31] adopted at the First Peace Conference, was the first international, legally binding instrument that provided some protection to cultural property in armed conflict.

The Second Peace Conference adopted a series of treaties relating to the laws and customs of war. *Convention (IV) Respecting the Laws and Customs of War on Land* (*1907 Convention (IV)*), with annexed *Regulations Respecting the Laws and Customs of War on Land* (*1907 Regulations*)[32] is the most relevant to cultural property, though *Convention (IX) Concerning Bombardment by Naval Forces in Time of War (1907 Convention (IX))*[33] also contains an important prohibition on the bombardment by naval forces of historic monuments, buildings used for artistic purposes and other protected architectural structures and places.

---

31 *Convention (II) with Respect to the Laws and Customs of War on Land*, The Hague, 29 July 1899, 32 Stat. 1803, TS 403 (entered into force 4 September 1900) [*1899 Convention (II)*]; *Regulations Concerning the Laws and Customs of War on Land*, annexed to *Convention (II) with Respect to the Laws and Customs of War on Land*, The Hague, 29 July 1899 (entered into force 4 September 1900) [*1899 Regulations*], available at http://www.icrc.org/ihl.nsf.

32 *Convention (IV) Respecting the Laws and Customs of War on Land*, The Hague, 18 October 1907, 36 Stat 2277 (entered into force 26 January 1910) [*1907 Convention (IV)*]; *Regulations Respecting the Laws and Customs of War on Land* annexed to *Convention (IV) Respecting the Laws and Customs of War on Land*, The Hague, 18 October 1907 (entered into force 26 January 1910) [*1907 Regulations*], reproduced in Adam Roberts and Richard Guelff (eds), *Documents on the Laws of War* (3rd ed, 2000) 69, also available at http://www.icrc.org/ihl.nsf.

33 *Convention (IX) Concerning Bombardment by Naval Forces in Time of War*, The Hague, 18 October 1907, 36 Stat 2351 (entered into force 26 January 1910) [*1907 Convention (IX)*], reproduced in Roberts and Guelff, ibid 112, also available at http://www.icrc.org/ihl.nsf.

These two *Conventions* slightly expanded the protection accorded to cultural property by *1899 Convention (II)*. Articles 27 and 56 of the *1907 Regulations* are of particular interest here. Article 27, which regulates the means of injuring the enemy through sieges and bombardments, added 'historic monuments' to the list of buildings and places already protected by Article 27 of the *1899 Regulations*.[34] Article 27 of the *1907 Regulations* provides that:

> In sieges and bombardments all necessary steps must be taken to spare, as far as possible, buildings dedicated to religion, art, science, or charitable purposes, *historic monuments*, hospitals, and places where the sick and wounded are collected, provided they are not being used at the time for military purposes.
>
> It is the duty of the besieged to indicate the presence of such buildings or places by distinctive and visible signs, which shall be notified to the enemy beforehand.[35]

Article 56 of the *1907 Regulations* refers to the protection of cultural property in occupied territories. There was only a minor difference between the provisions of Article 56 of the *1899 Regulations*,[36] which deals with the same matter, and Article 56 of the *1907 Regulations*. Whereas the former stipulated that the seizure of, destruction or intentional damage to cultural property should be made the subject of 'proceedings', the latter made this provision more precise by spelling out that these were to be 'legal' proceedings.[37] Otherwise, the provisions of Article 56 were worded in a similar way to those contained in the *1899 Regulations*. Article 56 of the *1907 Regulations* states:

---

34 See *1907 Regulations*, art 27(1).

35 Ibid art 27(1) and (2) (emphasis added). Article 27 of the 1899 Regulations is similarly worded:

> In sieges and bombardments all necessary steps should be taken to spare as far as possible edifices devoted to religion, art, science, and charity, hospitals, and places where the sick and wounded are collected, provided they are not used at the same time for military purposes.
>
> The besieged should indicate these buildings or places by some particular and visible signs, which should previously be notified to the assailants.

1899 Regulations, art 27.

36 See *1899 Regulations*, art 56 ('(1) The property of the communes, that of religious, charitable, and educational institutions, and those of arts and science, even when State property, shall be treated as private property. (2) All seizure of, and destruction, or intentional damage done to such institutions, to historical monuments, works of art or science, is prohibited, and should be made the subject of *proceedings*') (emphasis added).

37 See *1907 Regulations*, art 56(2).

> The property of municipalities, that of institutions dedicated to religion, charity, and education, the arts and sciences, even when State property, shall be treated as private property.
>
> All seizure of, destruction or wilful damage done to institutions of this character, historic monuments, works of art and science, is forbidden, and should be made the subject of *legal proceedings*.[38]

Although both referred to a 'distinctive and visible sign', neither the *1899 Regulations* nor the *1907 Regulations* specified the sign that was to be used for marking protected property. This was remedied by Article 5 of *1907 Convention (IX)* which provided the description of such a sign.[39]

The provisions of the Hague Conventions of 1899 and 1907 are still in force today and are generally considered part of customary international law. It should be noted that it was intended that *1907 Convention (IV)* replace *1899 Convention (II)* as between States Parties to both treaties. However, of forty-six States which had become parties to the *1899 Convention*, eighteen did not become party to the *1907 Convention*, and, thus, continued to be bound by the *1899 Convention*.[40] Application of these *Conventions* was further complicated by the so-called 'general participation clause', contained in Article 2 of *1907 Convention (IV)*, pursuant to which the provisions contained in *1907 Convention (IV)* and in the annexed *Regulations*, as referred to in Article 1 of the *1907 Convention*, 'do not apply except between Contracting Powers, and then only if all the belligerents are parties to the Convention'.[41] However, to the extent that provisions of the *Hague Conventions* have gained customary law status, those provisions are binding on all States and not only on the parties to these treaties. In 1946, the IMT expressly recognised *1907 Convention (IV)* as declaratory of customary international law:

> The rules of land warfare expressed in the convention undoubtedly represented an advance over existing international law at the time of their adoption. But the convention expressly stated that it was an attempt 'to revise the general laws and customs of war', which it thus recognized to be then existing, but *by 1939 these rules laid down in the convention were recognized by all civilized nations, and were regarded as being declaratory of the laws and customs of war* which are referred to in Article 6(b) of the Charter.[42]

---

38 Ibid art 56(1) and (2) (emphasis added). Other provisions of the *1899* and *1907 Regulations* that are relevant to the protection of cultural property, notably, Articles 23, 25, 27, 28, 46 and 47, are also worded in a similar way.

39 See *1907 Convention (IX)*, art 5(2).

40 See Roberts and Guelff, above n 32, 68.

41 *1907 Convention (IV)*, art 2.

42 *Judgement of the International Military Tribunal* (1946), The Law relating to War Crimes and Crimes against Humanity (emphasis added), at http://www.derechos.

The *Report of the United Nations Secretary-General to the Security Council in May 1993* concerning the establishment of the ICTY (*Report of the Secretary-General*) affirmed that *1907 Convention (IV)* and the annexed *Regulations* formed part of international customary law.[43]

During WWI and WWII, the *1899* and *1907 Conventions* were the only applicable international law that contained provisions on the subject of cultural property protection in armed conflict. The extent of the destruction proved that those provisions were ineffective. The drafting of the *1954 Convention*, which many called the 'Red Cross Charter for cultural property',[44] was aimed at providing more comprehensive protection to cultural property in times of armed conflict. Its adoption represented a further – and thus far the most significant – development in the protection of cultural property in armed conflict.

B The 1954 Convention

The *1954 Convention* was adopted by the Intergovernmental Conference on the Protection of Cultural Property in the Event of Armed Conflict, convened by UNESCO and held at The Hague, Netherlands, from 21 April to 14 May 1954.[45] The Conference also produced the *Protocol for the Protection of Cultural Property in the Event of Armed Conflict*, three Resolutions and the Final Act of the Conference. The *1954 Convention* was the first international multilateral treaty to deal exclusively with cultural property. It was also the first treaty to

---

org/nizkor/nuremberg/judgment/cap7.html and http://www.yale.edu/lawweb/avalon/imt/proc/judwarcr.htm.

43 See *Report of the Secretary-General Pursuant to Paragraph 2 of Security Council Resolution 808 (1993)*, paras 41-42, UN Doc S/of 3 May 1993, 32 ILM 1159 [*Report of the Secretary-General*].

44 Toman, above n 1, 21.

45 *Convention for the Protection of Cultural Property in the Event of Armed Conflict*, 14 May 1954, 249 UNTS 240 (entered into force 7 August 1956) [*1954 Convention*]. The *Regulations for the Execution of the Convention for the Protection of Cultural Property in the Event of Armed Conflict* [*1954 Regulations*] annexed to the *Convention* are considered an integral part thereof. See also *Protocol for the Protection of Cultural Property in the Event of Armed Conflict*, 14 May 1954, 249 UNTS 358-64 (entered into force 7 August 1956) [*1954 Protocol*] and *Protocol for the Protection of Cultural Property in the Event of Armed Conflict*, 26 March 1999, 38 ILM 769-82 (entered into force 9 March 2004) [*1999 Protocol*]. For the verbatim record of the 1954 Hague Conference, see Intergovernmental Conference on the Protection of Cultural Property in the Event of Armed Conflict, *Records of the Conference Convened by the United Nations Educational, Scientific and Cultural Organization, Held at The Hague from 21 April to 14 May 1954*, published by the Government of the Netherlands, The Hague, Staatsdrukkerijen Uitgevrijbedrijf (1961) [*1954 Records*]. For a detailed discussion of the drafting history of the *1954 Convention* and analysis of the *1954 Records*, see Toman, above n 1.

introduce the term 'cultural property' into international law. The forty articles of the *1954 Convention* and twenty-one articles of the annexed *Regulations* for its execution aimed to provide more adequate and comprehensive protection to cultural property in the event of armed conflict than the few basic provisions scattered in the *1899* and *1907 Conventions*. Those scattered provisions were the only binding international law on the subject prior to the adoption of the *1954 Convention*, and proved ineffective during both World Wars. Unlike its predecessors (the *1899* and *1907 Conventions*), the *1954 Convention* includes provisions which protect cultural objects not only during hostilities but also in peacetime.

The *1954 Convention* covers both movable and immovable cultural property. In accordance with its first Article, the following categories of objects are protected under the rubric 'cultural property':

> (a) movable or immovable property of great importance to the cultural heritage of every people, such as monuments of architecture, art or history, whether religious or secular; archaeological sites; groups of buildings which, as a whole, are of historical or artistic interest; works of art; manuscripts, books and other objects of artistic, historical or archaeological interest; as well as scientific collections and important collections of books or archives or of reproductions of the property defined above;
> (b) buildings whose main and effective purpose is to preserve or exhibit the movable cultural property defined in subparagraph (a) such as museums, large libraries and depositories of archives, and refuges intended to shelter, in the event of armed conflict, the movable cultural property defined in subparagraph (a);
> (c) centres containing a large amount of cultural property as defined in subparagraphs (a) and (b), to be known as 'centres containing monuments'.[46]

The *Convention's 1954 Protocol* deals only with movable cultural property, prohibiting its export from occupied territory. The *Regulations* set out the procedures relating to monitoring the application of the *Convention*, special protection, transport of movable cultural property and the distinctive emblem. The *1954 Convention*, its annexed *Regulations* and the *1954 Protocol*, along with the *1999 Protocol*, undoubtedly constitute the most important instruments for the protection of cultural property. They form, as Toman puts it, 'a true code for cultural property'.[47] The *Convention* is founded on the idea that the preservation of cultural property is not only of importance to the State in which such property is located but to the entire international community and that it is, thus, 'important that this [property] should receive international protection'[48] in times of armed

46 *1954 Convention*, art 1.

47 Toman, above n 1, 24.

48 *1954 Convention*, Preamble para 3.

conflict. To be effective, such protection needs to be organised in time of peace by taking both national and international measures.[49] In the event of armed conflict, both parties to the conflict are obligated to respect cultural property.[50] In other words, pursuant to Article 4 of the *Convention*, they are precluded from using cultural property and its immediate surroundings for military purposes and from attacking cultural property except in cases of military necessity:

> The High Contracting Parties undertake to respect cultural property situated within their own territory as well as within the territory of other High Contracting Parties by refraining from any use of the property and its immediate surroundings or of the appliances in use for its protection for purposes which are likely to expose it to destruction or damage in the event of armed conflict; and by refraining from any act of hostility directed against such property.

49 Ibid para 5. See also arts 2, 3, 6, 7, 8, 24, 25 and 28 of the *1954 Convention*. Note that the 'effectiveness' referred to here relates to the necessity of national and international peacetime measures for the international wartime protection of cultural property, as mentioned in the Preamble to the *1954 Convention* ('such protection cannot be *effective* unless both national and international measures have been taken to organize it in time of peace', *1954 Convention*, Preamble para 5 (emphasis added)) and it does not imply the 'ineffectiveness' of the *1954 Convention* generally. The 'ineffectiveness' of the *1954 Convention* is a separate problem. However, it is not argued in this book that a problem of 'ineffectiveness' of international treaties is unique to the protection of cultural property and that a perfectly drafted and widely accepted legal instrument would prevent all damage to and destruction of cultural property. The 'ineffectiveness' of treaties is characteristic of international law in general, and not only that for protection of cultural property. Irrespective of how 'perfect' it may be, law alone will never be sufficient to prevent all damage to and destruction of cultural property. See, generally, ICOMOS Sweden/Central Board of National Antiquities/Swedish National Commission for UNESCO, *Information as an Instrument for Protection against War Damages to the Cultural Heritage. Report from a Seminar, June 1994* Stockholm, Svenska Unescoradets skriftserie, 4/1994 (1994) Stockholm: ICOMOS Sweden [*Information as an Instrument*]; *Resolution on Information as an Instrument for Protection against War Damages to the Cultural Heritage* (Sweden, 10 June 1994), adopted at an expert meeting convened by the Swedish Central Board of National Antiquities, the Swedish National Commission for UNESCO and ICOMOS Sweden [*Resolution on Information as an Instrument*]. See also Lyndel Prott, 'The International Movement of Cultural Objects' (2005) 12 *International Journal of Cultural Property* 225, 245 ['International Movement']; Rino Büchel and Peter Hostettler, 'Protection of Cultural Property: Reflections from a Civilian and a Military Point of View' in Edwin Micewski and Gerhard Sladek (eds), *Protection of Cultural Property in the Event of Armed Conflict – A Challenge in Peace Support Operations* (2002) 9-14, 14.

50 *1954 Convention*, arts 2, 4, 5, 8, 9 and 11.

> The obligation mentioned in paragraph 1 of the present Article may be waived only in cases where military necessity imperatively requires such a waiver.[51]

Like the *1899* and *1907 Conventions*, the *1954 Convention* does not define the notion of military necessity, which is considered one of the shortcomings of this instrument.

Notwithstanding this, and in contrast to the *1899* and *1907 Conventions*, which accord equal protection to an entire, albeit very narrow, list of forms of cultural property, the *1954 Convention* provides for a system of so-called 'general protection'[52] for all property that meets the definition of cultural property in its Article 1, and the system of so-called 'special protection'[53] for a limited number of particular forms of immovable cultural property. The *Convention* applies to both international and non-international armed conflict.[54] In the event of the latter, the *Convention* does not apply in its entirety.[55] For breaches of its provisions, the *Convention* envisages individual criminal responsibility.[56] Consistent with Article 28 of the *1954 Convention*, the High Contracting Parties are required to make provision in their domestic criminal legislation for prosecution and punishment of the perpetrators of breaches of the *Convention*.[57] This provision applies to breaches in both international and non-international armed conflict.

The *Convention's* major weaknesses, including the absence of specific breaches that give rise to criminal responsibility and the ambiguity of the provisions relating to the concept of military necessity, were addressed in the *1999 Protocol*, the adoption of which represented the most important development since the *1954 Convention* with respect to instruments dealing directly with the

---

51 *1954 Convention*, art 4(1), (2). Article 4 of the *1954 Convention* also prohibits theft, pillage or misappropriation of cultural property, any acts of vandalism directed against such property, requisitioning movable cultural property and reprisals against cultural property. Ibid paras (3) and (4).

52 Ibid Chapter 1.

53 Ibid Chapter 2. The *1999 Protocol* introduced the third system of protection, so-called 'enhanced protection'. As discussed in chapter five of this book, the system of special protection for all practical purposes has remained a dead letter.

54 Ibid Chapter 6.

55 Ibid art 19.

56 Ibid art 28.

57 The former Yugoslavia had done this. See Article 151 of the *Criminal Code of the SFRY* (envisaging imprisonment of not less than one year for destruction of cultural property and imprisonment of not less than five years for destruction of especially protected cultural objects). See also *Prosecutor v Miodrag Jokić*, Case No. IT-01-42/1-S, Sentencing Judgement, Trial Chamber I, 18 March 2004, Case No. IT-01-42/1-S, paras 104-111 (discussing the general practice regarding prison sentences in the courts of the former Yugoslavia) [*Jokić* Sentencing Judgement].

protection of cultural property in armed conflict. The *1999 Protocol* specified the breaches of the *Convention* which give rise to criminal responsibility and linked the definition of military necessity in Article 4 of the *1954 Convention* with the concept of 'military objective' as introduced in *Additional Protocol I* in 1977, which, in effect, is the main achievement of the *1999 Protocol*. This *Protocol* reflects developments in international law and supplements the *1954 Convention* with regard to relations between the Parties, in particular those concerning respect for cultural property and the conduct of hostilities, through measures to reinforce their implementation. Yet the *1954 Convention* remains the main and most significant IHL instrument according protection to cultural property in armed conflict. As at 4 February 2012, there were 123 States Parties to this *Convention*.[58] Some of its provisions, including those regulating respect for cultural property, are considered part of customary international law.[59]

C *The State of International Law after the Adoption of the 1954 Convention*

In addition to activities supported by UNESCO, significant development of rules governing the protection of cultural property has also reflected the reaffirmation and development of IHL under the patronage of the ICRC. Of particular relevance to the protection of cultural property in armed conflict are the relevant provisions of the *Protocols Additional to the 1949 Geneva Conventions*. The *Protocols* were adopted on 8 June 1977 at the Diplomatic Conference on the Reaffirmation and Development of International Humanitarian Law Applicable in Armed Conflicts held in Geneva from 1974 to 1977. *Protocol I* relates to the protection of victims of international armed conflicts and *Protocol II*, which is less detailed than *Protocol I*, relates to the protection of victims of non-international armed conflicts. These *Protocols* contain several articles relevant to the protection of cultural property in armed conflict, two of which – namely, Article 53 of *Protocol I* and Article 16 of *Protocol II* – are in their entirety devoted to the 'protection of cultural objects and places of worship'.[60] Article 53 of *Protocol I* states:

---

58 An updated list of States parties to the *1954 Convention* and its *protocols*, as well as other relevant IHL instruments is available at, http://www.icrc.org/ihl.nsf and http://portal.unesco.org/la/convention_p.asp?language=E&KO.

59 See, eg, *Tadić* Jurisdiction Decision, para 127; Patrick Boylan, *Review of the Convention for the Protection of Cultural Property in the Event of Armed Conflict* (1993), para A.3 [*Review*]; David Meyer, 'The 1954 Hague Cultural Property Convention and its Emergence into Customary International Law' (1993) 11 *Boston University International Law Journal* 349; Jean-Marie Henckaerts and Louise Doswald-Beck (eds), *Customary International Humanitarian Law* (2005) vol I *Rules*, 129; vol II *Practice*, Chapter 12: Cultural Property, 723 *et seq* [*Customary IHL*].

60 See *Additional Protocol I*, art 53 and *Additional Protocol II*, art 16.

> Without prejudice to the provisions of the Hague Convention for the Protection of Cultural Property in the Event of Armed Conflict of 14 May 1954, and of other relevant international instruments, it is prohibited:
> (a) to commit any act of hostility directed against the historic monuments, works of art or places of worship which constitute the cultural or spiritual heritage of peoples;
> (b) to use such objects in support of the military effort;
> (c) to make such objects the objects of reprisals.[61]

The references to 'other relevant international instruments' and the prohibition of reprisals are not included in Article 16 of *Additional Protocol II*, but the remainder of the text of Article 53 of *Protocol I* is identical to Article 16 of *Protocol II*.

Nevertheless, the *1954 Convention* constitutes an instrument of paramount importance for the international protection of cultural property in armed conflict and its application is in no way prejudiced by those two articles of the *Additional Protocols*. Those Articles contain an explicit clause on the subject.[62] In fact, the ICRC's original draft did not contain any provisions directly relating to cultural property because the protection of such property had already been provided for by the *1954 Convention*, specially designed for this purpose.[63] Cultural property-related provisions were included into the *Additional Protocols* partly due to concern for the cultural heritage of humanity[64] and partly because it was felt that there was the need to strongly reaffirm the principles behind the *1954 Convention* and draw fresh attention to it considering that the *Convention* had not attracted worldwide acceptance by the time of adoption of the two *Additional Protocols*.[65]

According to the *ICRC Commentary*, Articles 53 and 16 were intentionally kept short, 'limited to the essential points, prohibiting the making of cultural objects into military objectives, as well as prohibiting their destruction'.[66] It was

---

61 *Additional Protocol I*, art 53.

62 Ibid ('[w]ithout prejudice to the provisions of the Hague Convention for the Protection of Cultural Property in the Event of Armed Conflict of 14 May 1954'). See also Resolution 20, 'Protection of Cultural Property', 4th sess., 55th plen. mtg., paras 1 and 2, reproduced in ICRC, *Protocols Additional to the Geneva Conventions of 12 August 1949* (revised edition 1996) 114; also available at, http://www.icrc.org/ihl.nsf.

63 See *ICRC Commentary*, above n 14, 640, para 2039.

64 Ibid para 2040.

65 Ibid. It was hoped that the cultural property provisions in the two *Additional Protocols* would obligate the large number of States which in 1977 were Parties to the *1949 Geneva Conventions* and which were thought to be likely to ratify the *Additional Protocols*. See also Meyer, above n 59, 363-64.

66 *ICRC Commentary*, ibid.

agreed that there was no need to revise the existing rules on the subject, but only to confirm the protection and respect for such objects,[67] and thus to state at the beginning of these Articles that they did not modify the *1954 Convention* and other relevant existing instruments, the latter being mentioned only in Article 53 and not in Article 16. In the event of a contradiction between these Articles and a rule of the *1954 Convention*, the latter is applicable if the parties concerned are bound by the *Convention*. If one of the parties is not bound by the *Convention*, Article 53 or Article 16 applies.[68] It is important to know which instrument applies in a particular situation especially with respect to the exception of military necessity. Whereas the *1954 Convention* allows for the waiver of military necessity from the prohibition on direct acts of hostility against cultural property and from the prohibition on using cultural property for military purposes, Articles 53 and 16 of *Protocol I* and *Protocol II* respectively do not allow for any such waiver.

Notwithstanding this, Articles 53 and 16 represent statements of general principles which reflect the provisions of *1907 Convention (IV)* concerning cultural property and the entire *1954 Convention*. These Articles are deemed 'the portions of cultural protection law that have most clearly reached customary international law status'.[69] The provisions of the *1954 Convention* relating to general protection of cultural property, although not those which provide specific protection, are considered to provide the most evidence in support of the customary international law status of Articles 53 and 16.[70] David Meyer notes that numerous States involved in devising the *Additional Protocols* 'in effect restated the principles of general cultural property protection of the *1954 Convention* without the specific provisions on how to actually protect property'.[71]

As already mentioned, in addition to the *1954 Convention*, Article 53 of *Protocol I* refers to 'other relevant international instruments'.[72] Here, reference is implicitly being made to the relevant provisions of the *1899* and *1907 Conventions* and the *Washington Pact* of 15 April 1935, also known as the *Roerich Pact*,[73] and also to the *1970 Convention* and the *World Heritage Convention*. Of primary importance now are the provisions of *1907 Convention (IV)* concerning cultural

67 Ibid 641, para 2046.

68 Ibid.

69 Meyer, above n 59, 362. See also Christopher Greenwood, 'Customary Law Status of the 1977 Geneva Protocols' in Astrid Delissen and Gerard Tanja (eds), *Essays in Honour of Frits Kalshoven* (1991) 93, 110.

70 Meyer, ibid.

71 Ibid 363.

72 *Additional Protocol I*, art 53.

73 *Treaty on the Protection of Artistic and Scientific Institutions and Historic Monuments*, Washington, 15 April 1935, League of Nations, TS CLVII 1936, 290 (entered into force 26 August 1935), [*Roerich Pact*], available at http://fletcher.tuffs.edu/multi/www/roerich.html.

property because of their customary law status. These provisions remain applicable to property not covered by the *1954 Convention*, namely, property which is not 'of great importance for the cultural heritage of peoples'[74] (i.e., property not designated by the competent national authority as worthy of preservation), and thereby bind even the High Contracting Parties to this *Convention*.

With respect to *Additional Protocol I*, property protected by *1907 Convention (IV)*, which does not fall within the scope of Article 53 of *Protocol I*, that is, cultural objects and places of worship which constitute the cultural or spiritual heritage of peoples, is protected by virtue of its civilian character. Article 52 of *Additional Protocol I* ('General protection of civilian objects') provides protection for civilian objects by prohibiting attacks on non-military objectives. The definition of 'military objective'[75] provided in this Article significantly remedies one of the major weaknesses of the *1954 Convention*, specifically, the ambiguity surrounding the concept of military necessity.[76] Article 52 also prohibits making civilian objects 'the object of attack or of reprisals'.[77] The provisions of Article 52 of *Additional Protocol I* have attained the status of customary international law.[78]

Additional Protocol II does not contain provisions corresponding to these. Notwithstanding this, the general rule prohibiting attacks on civilian objects is also considered applicable to non-international armed conflicts.[79] Some other important provisions relevant to cultural property protection, however, which are included in *Protocol I*, are also absent from *Protocol II*. For instance, only *Protocol I* contains provisions on grave breaches. In accordance with Article 85 of *Protocol I*, attacks directed against cultural property may qualify as a grave breach and may thus be regarded as a war crime.[80]

All in all, international legal protection of cultural property in armed conflict has come a long way since the First Peace Conference. A few brief provisions of *1899 Convention (II)* providing for very modest protection of cultural property evolved into a proliferation of legally binding norms protecting cultural property from effects of warfare in a relatively short – a century-long – span of time. These norms are contained in *1899 Convention (II)*, *1907 Conventions (IV)*

74 *1954 Convention*, art 1(a).

75 Ibid art 52(2).

76 See *ICRC Commentary*, above n 14, 648, fn 30.

77 *Additional Protocol I*, art 52(1).

78 See, eg, *Prosecutor v Pavle Strugar*, Judgement, Trial Chamber II, 31 January 2005, Case No. IT-01-42-T, para 223 [*Strugar* Trial Judgement]; *Tadić* Jurisdiction Decision, para 127.

79 See, eg, *Strugar* Trial Judgement, para 224; *Tadić* Jurisdiction Decision, paras 100, 111 and 127. See also UN General Assembly Resolution 2675 'Basic principles for the protection of civilian populations in armed conflicts', adopted during the 25th Session of the General Assembly, on 9 December 1970, http://www.un.org/documents/resga.htm; *Customary IHL*, above n 59, 26-36.

80 *Additional Protocol I*, art 85(4)(d).

and *(IX)*, the *1954 Convention* and its two *Protocols*, and in the two *1977 Protocols Additional to the 1949 Geneva Conventions*. All these instruments are now in force and their provisions are considered an important part of IHL. Although not all of these instruments have achieved universal acceptance, their most important provisions have nevertheless acquired customary law status. Despite some weaknesses, those provisions provide for comprehensive protection of cultural property in armed conflict. When combined, they make it almost impossible for belligerents to justify an attack on cultural objects. To determine exactly which of these provisions apply to the case of the Old Bridge, this chapter now turns to an examination of the nature of the conflict in Mostar at the time of the destruction of the Bridge.

III The Nature of the Conflict in Mostar

The Bosnian and Herzegovinian Croat-Muslim conflict began in April 1993.[81] The HVO attack on the city of Mostar occurred on 9 May 1993. The attack was followed by fierce fighting between military formations of the HVO and of the ABH. The fighting was particularly hard and bitter around the Bulevar, a street in Mostar which separated the two forces. There, they fought for each metre and each building, being constantly on guard against attacks and shooting from the other side as the opposing forces took up positions within shouting distance of each other.[82] As noted, Muslims from the HVO-controlled West Mostar were forced from their homes in large numbers. They were driven into the Muslim-dominated East Mostar, which was under siege until the beginning of 1994. East Mostar was under constant bombardment as the HVO was trying to gain control of the whole of Mostar and aimed at eventually cleansing the city of all Muslims. The humanitarian situation on the Eastern side of Mostar was horrific.[83] The Old Bridge of Mostar was destroyed, as the Prosecution in the *Prlić* case alleges, '[a]s part of and in the course of the East Mostar siege'.[84]

81 The Appeals Chamber in *Kordić* upheld the finding of the Trial Chamber in that case that the Bosnian and Herzegovinian Croat-Muslim conflict existed even before April 1993, namely that 'in the time following October 1992 there was serious fighting for an extended period of time'. *Prosecutor v Dario Kordić and Mario Čerkez*, Judgement, Appeals Chamber, 17 December 2004, Case No. IT-95-14/2-A, para 341 [*Kordić* Appeal Judgement].

82 See *Prosecutor v Mladen Naletilić aka 'Tuta' and Vinko Martinović aka 'Štela'*, Judgement, Trial Chamber, 31 March 2003, Case No. IT-98-34-T, para 49 [*Naletilić* Trial Judgement or *Naletilić* case or *Naletilić*].

83 Ibid paras 50-51. See also *Prosecutor v Jadranko Prlić, Bruno Stojić, Slobodan Praljak, Milivoj Petković, Valentin Ćorić and Berislav Pušić*, Amended Indictment, 16 November 2005, Case No. IT-04-74-AU, paras 110-117 (Initial Indictment, 4 March 2004 (kept confidential until its unsealing on 2 April 2004)) [*Prlić* Indictment].

84 *Prlić* Indictment, para 116.

The Bosnian and Herzegovinian Croat-Muslim conflict lasted until the end of February 1994. The *Washington Agreement*, concluded between 28 February and 1 March 1994, established the Croat-Muslim federation and ended the large-scale open fighting between the two sides.[85]

The very destruction of the Old Bridge of Mostar was preceded by shelling of the Bridge by the Croat forces for two consecutive days, from 8 November to 9 November 1993.[86] Allegedly, there was no fighting between the HVO and ABH forces at the time.[87] However, this absence of actual combat does not affect the existence of an armed conflict and the application of the norms of IHL. IHL applies from the beginning to the end of the conflict.[88] It is not necessary that actual combat takes place in a particular part of the territory affected by the conflict.[89] The combat need not take place in a particular area all the time. It is sufficient that the context of an armed conflict can be established. To reiterate the finding of the Appeals Chamber in *Tadić*, an armed conflict exists:

> whenever there is a resort to armed force between States or protracted armed violence between governmental authorities and organized armed groups or between such groups within a State. International humanitarian law applies from the initiation of such armed conflicts and extends beyond the cessation of hostilities until a general conclusion of peace is reached; or, in the case of internal conflicts, a peaceful settlement is achieved. Until that moment, international humanitarian law continues to apply in the whole territory of the warring States or, in the case of internal conflicts, the whole territory under the control of a party, *whether or not actual combat takes place there.*[90]

In accordance with the Appeals Chamber's reasoning, the destruction of the Old Bridge took place in the context of an armed conflict. The Croat-Muslim conflict, including the fighting between the HVO forces and ABH forces in

85 *Naletilić* Trial Judgement, para 179. See also *Prlić* Indictment, para 42; *Prosecutor v Dario Kordić and Mario Čerkez*, Judgement, Trial Chamber III, 26 February 2001, Case No. IT-95-14/2-T, para 759 [*Kordić* Trial Judgement or *Kordić* case or *Kordić*].

86 See *Final Report of the United Nations Commission of Experts Established Pursuant to Security Council Resolution 780 (1992), Annex XI: Destruction of Cultural Property Report*, S/1994/674/Add.2 (Vol V) 28 December 1994, III. Mostar bridge, A. The facts [*Final Report*]. See also Committee on Culture and Education of Parliamentary Assembly of Council of Europe (COE), *Fourth Information Report*, doc 6999, 19 January 1994 [*Fourth COE Report*].

87 Ibid. See also testimony of Miro Salčin, the Prosecution witness in *Prlić*, 15 and 19 February 2007 [Salčin testimony] and of Mustafa Hadrović, the Prosecution witness in *Prlić*, 21-22 February 2007 [Hadrović testimony].

88 See *Tadić* Jurisdiction Decision, para 70.

89 Ibid.

90 Ibid (emphasis added).

Mostar, did not end until the *1994 Washington Agreement*. In regard to the Mostar area, there was fighting between the warring parties both prior to and after the destruction of the Bridge although not at the time of that particular incident. Additionally, the Bridge was destroyed by the HVO forces which took part in the hostilities as a party to the conflict.

The existence of the Croat-Muslim conflict in the Mostar area around the time of the destruction of the Bridge is well documented and is an adjudicated fact.[91] In fact, the existence of the conflict has not been disputed.[92] What has been disputed, however, is the nature of the conflict.[93] Since the legal regime pursuant to the protection of cultural property in non-international armed conflict is more limited than that of an international conflict it is important to examine the exact nature of the conflict in order to identify the relevant IHL provisions applicable to the destruction of the Old Bridge.

Thus, the obvious next question is: when is an armed conflict internal, when international; specifically, does third-party intervention into an initially internal armed conflict, on this or the other side, change the situation? Existing treaty law does not resolve the issue and state practice is uncertain. The ICJ *Nicaragua* Judgement of 27 June 1986[94] is not relevant either as it deals with state responsibility, which is not the point at issue here. Thus, the general conclusion appears to be that the point is undecided.

As noted, the Croat-Muslim conflict was taking place in Mostar at the time of the destruction of the Old Bridge. Did it amount to an international

---

91 See, eg, *Naletilić* Trial Judgement, para 179; *Prosecutor v Tihomir Blaškić*, Judgement, Trial Chamber I, 3 March 2000, Case No. IT-95-14-T, paras 7, 94 [*Blaškić* Trial Judgement].

92 See *Naletilić* Trial Judgement, para 178.

93 Ibid and discussion in paras 185-202. See also *Prosecutor v Mladen Naletilić aka 'Tuta' and Vinko Martinović aka 'Štela'*, Judgement, Appeals Chamber, 3 May 2006, Case No. IT-98-34-A, 107 [*Naletilić* Appeal Judgement]; *Kordić* Trial Judgement, paras 47-48; *Kordić* Appeal Judgement, paras 295-374; *Blaškić* Trial Judgement, paras 79-80, 160. In the *Blaškić* Appeal, the Appellant does not challenge the Trial Chamber's finding that the conflict was international. The Appellant challenges the Trial Chamber's finding that Croatia and Bosnia and Herzegovina were not co-belligerents. See *Prosecutor v Tihomir Blaškić*, Judgement, Appeals Chamber, 29 July 2004, Case No. IT-95-14-A, paras 183-189 [*Blaškić* Appeal Judgement]. It has been contended that the presence of the CA in Bosnia and Herzegovina enabled an agreement on friendship and cooperation between Bosnia and Herzegovina and Croatia that was signed by the then Presidents of these two States, Alija Izetbegović and Franjo Tuđman in Zagreb on 21 July 1992. See Sense News Agency, ICTY, 'Praljak's "Bearable Misfortune"', The Hague, 9 January 2006, http://www.sense-agency.com/en/stream.php?sta=3&pid=9016&kat=3.

94 *Military and Paramilitary Activities in and against Nicaragua (Nicaragua v United States of America)*, Merits, Judgement of 27 June 1986, ICJ Reports [1986] 14, available at, http://www.icj-cij.org/docket/files/70/6503.pdf.

armed conflict? Given that both parties to the conflict – the HVO and the ABH – came from the same State, Bosnia and Herzegovina, and protracted armed violence between them took place within that State, it might appear that the conflict was non-international in character.[95] Since the fighting took place within the boundaries of one State, and the level and nature of fighting exceeded that of common Article 3, an initial examination of the position under *Additional Protocol II* and Article 19 of the *1954 Convention* is required.

Under Article 1(1) of *Additional Protocol II*, an armed conflict is deemed 'non-international' if it takes place 'in the territory of a High Contracting Party between its armed forces and dissident armed forces or other organized armed groups which, under responsible command, exercise such control over a part of its territory as to enable them to carry out sustained and concerted military operations and to implement [the] *Protocol*'.[96] The conflict in Mostar was between the ABH – armed forces of the Republic of Bosnia and Herzegovina, which was, at the time, already an independent, sovereign State, recognised by the UN[97] – and the HVO forces, which were organised armed forces and were under responsible command (with an established chain of command, with a 'Commander of the Main Staff' as the military head of the HVO armed forces).[98] The HVO forces exercised full control over West Mostar, which enabled them to 'carry out sustained and concerted military operations' in East Mostar and to keep that side of the city under siege. Therefore, it appears that the requirements in Article 1(1) of *Additional Protocol II* are met. If the conflict was 'non-international', parties to the conflict were still under obligation to respect cultural property. Article 19 of the *1954 Convention*, provides that '[i]n the event of an armed conflict not of an international character occurring within the territory of one of the High Contracting Parties, each party to the

95 In *Blaškić*, the Defence referred to the agreement signed in May 1992 under the auspices of the ICRC between the three main national parties in Bosnia and Herzegovina, namely, the Croatian Democratic Community (HDZ), the Serbian Democratic Party (SDS) and the Party of Democratic Action (SDA), according to which these three parties were committed to honouring the provisions relevant to internal armed conflicts covered in Article 3 common to the *1949 Geneva Conventions* and to observing certain rules applicable to international armed conflict. By making this reference, the Defence considered that the agreement demonstrated the conviction of the ICRC that the conflict was non-international in character. However, the Trial Chamber held that the parties to the conflict may not agree between themselves to change the nature of the conflict. In this Chamber's view, it is the Chamber itself which is responsible for evaluating the facts before it and determining the true nature of the conflict. See *Blaškić* Trial Judgement, paras 80–82.

96 *Additional Protocol II*, art 1(1).

97 For details on the admission to the UN membership, see below n 131.

98 See, eg, *Prlić* Indictment.

conflict shall be bound to apply, as a minimum, the provisions of the [*1954*] *Convention* which relate to *respect for cultural property*'.[99]

A non-international armed conflict may, nonetheless, be rendered international if 'another State intervenes in that conflict through its troops or...some of the participants in the internal armed conflict act on behalf of that other State'.[100] To establish that the conflict is international in character it is sufficient to prove that one of the two tests – the test of direct intervention or the overall control test – is satisfied.[101] In the Mostar Bridge case, ample evidence supports the claim that the conflict was international because of Croatia's involvement in the conflict both through the active participation of its army in Bosnia and Herzegovina, fighting together with the HVO against the ABH, and because Croatia exercised overall control over the HVO.[102]

A The Direct Intervention Test

The direct intervention test fairly straightforwardly converts an internal armed conflict into an international one, namely through the direct participation of foreign troops on the territory of a state. According to the jurisprudence of the ICTY, Croatia was directly involved in the armed conflict between the HVO and the ABH through both the actual presence of its troops in the area of the conflict, and through the appointment of Croatian officers in the command of the HVO.[103] A range of arguments aimed at denying Croatia's involvement have been raised. They include the contention that Croatia intervened in the conflict in Bosnia and Herzegovina in 1992 and not in 1993 and that such intervention was aimed at fighting against Serb forces rather than the ABH; that despite the participation of Croatia's Army (CA) units in some operations in Bosnia, the CA was never present in any significant numbers in Herzegovina; and that the soldiers and officers present on the territory of Bosnia and Herzegovina

---

99 *1954 Convention*, art 19 (emphasis added). See also *1954 Convention*, art 4 and *Additional Protocol II*, art 16.

100 *Prosecutor v Duško Tadić aka 'Dule'*, Judgement, Appeals Chamber, 15 July 1999, Case No. IT-94-1-A, para 84 [*Tadić* Appeal Judgement].

101 See *Naletilić* Trial Judgement, para 197.

102 See *Naletilić* Appeal Judgement, para 122 and fn 267; *Naletilić* Trial Judgement, paras 191-202; *Kordić* Trial Judgement, paras 38-45, 65-102, 108-146; *Kordić* Appeal Judgement, paras 295-321, 342-374; *Blaškić* Trial Judgement, paras 75-123; *Blaškić* Appeal Judgement, paras 185, 187-188.

103 See, eg, *Naletilić* Trial Judgement, paras 189-196; *Blaškić* Trial Judgement, paras 115-117; *Kordić* Trial Judgement, paras 80-110 (discussing extensively evidence on Croatia's direct intervention in the Bosnian and Herzegovinian Croat-Muslim conflict). But see *Kordić* Appeal Judgement, paras 355-360 (the Appeals Chamber found that no reasonable trier of fact could have found that Croatia directly intervened in the armed conflict in Central Bosnia).

were actually citizens of Bosnia and Herzegovina who had previously joined the CA and voluntarily returned to the HVO after the armed conflict ended in Croatia.[104] However, there is an overwhelming amount of evidence to the contrary. For instance, according to the evidence presented in the *Naletilić* case – the geographical scope of which comprises the conflict in the Mostar area, and the time frame of which includes the time surrounding the destruction of the Old Bridge – personnel from the European Community Monitoring Mission (ECMM) and United Nations Protection Force (UNPROFOR) 'witnessed the presence and direct intervention of [CA] troops in Bosnia and Herzegovina in general, and in the area of Mostar in particular, throughout 1993'.[105] Evidence of the involvement of Croatia in the Bosnian and Herzegovinian Croat-Muslim conflict was also set out in numerous UN documents, including the UN Secretary-General's information to the Security Council in early 1994 that

> the Croatian Army [CA] has directly supported the HVO in terms of manpower, equipment and weapons for some time.... It is assessed that in total, there is the equivalent of three Croatian Brigades of regular Army personnel in Bosnia and Herzegovina, approximately 3,000 to 5,000.[106]

According to the testimony of many eyewitnesses, CA troops belonging to different units were seen in several locations in and around Mostar.[107] But even if CA troops were not directly involved in the conflict in Mostar, that would still not affect the applicability of the *Geneva Conventions*. As the *Naletilić* Trial Chamber held,

> [t]here is no requirement to prove that [CA] troops were present in every single area where crimes were allegedly committed. On the contrary, the conflict between the ABiH and the HVO must be looked upon as a whole and, if it is found to be international in character through the participation of [CA] troops, then Article 2 of the Statute will apply to the entire territory of the conflict.[108]

This does not mean, however, that a decision that an internal conflict in a particular area was internationalised leads necessarily to the conclusion that another internal conflict in another area was also internationalised.[109] As the Appeals

104 See *Naletilić* Trial Judgement, para 190.

105 Ibid 192. See also *Blaškić* Trial Judgement, para 94 (noting that 'the evidence demonstrated that...the [CA] soldiers were primarily in the Mostar' region).

106 *Naletilić* Trial Judgement, ibid exhibit PPIAC-82.

107 Ibid para 193 and nn 531-536.

108 Ibid para 194.

109 See, eg, *Kordić* Appeal Judgement, para 320; *Kordić* Trial Judgement, para 70.

Chamber held in *Tadić*, 'the conflicts in the former Yugoslavia have both internal and international aspects'.[110] Thus, '[t]he determination as to whether the conflict is international or internal has to be made *on a case-by-case basis*'.[111]

With respect to Croatia's appointment of Croatian officers in the command of the HVO, contrary to the above-mentioned argument that the CA soldiers present in Bosnia and Herzegovina were predominantly Bosnian and Herzegovinian volunteers in the conflict in Croatia who had returned to defend their homeland,[112] the Trial Chamber in *Naletilić* refused to accept 'this version of the facts'.[113] In the Chamber's view, based on evidence it heard and received, it was Croatia that sent the vast majority of its officers. However, Croatia tried to conceal the presence of its troops, for instance, by replacing their uniforms and insignia with those of the HVO. Moreover, CA troops in Bosnia and Herzegovina received their monthly salary from Croatia and maintained their other rights as members of the CA.[114] General Slobodan Praljak, who was the Chief of the HVO Main Staff from around mid-July 1993 until November 1993, admitted that he did not resign from the CA when he departed because the CA tolerated departures and the 'struggle against evil' in Bosnia and Herzegovina.[115] After all, in early 1994, while insisting on the 'voluntary' nature of the CA presence in Bosnia and Herzegovina, limited only to the border areas, the Government of the Republic of Croatia itself admitted the presence of regular CA units in another, sovereign state.[116] Hence, the direct intervention test, which requires the direct participation of foreign troops on the territory of a state, seems to be satisfied.

B The Overall Control Test

The overall control test is defined by the Appeals Chamber in *Tadić* as follows:

> control by a State over subordinate armed forces or militias or paramilitary units may be of an overall character (and must comprise more than the mere provision of financial assistance or military equipment or training). This requirement, however, does not go so far as to include the issuing of specific orders by the State, or its direction of each individual operation. Under

110 *Tadić* Jurisdiction Decision, para 77.

111 *Kordić* Trial Judgement, para 70 (emphasis added). This finding is confirmed by the Appeals Chamber. See *Kordić* Appeal Judgement, para 320.

112 See Testimony of defence witness Slobodan Praljak in *Naletilić*, T 9322-9823, 2 April 2002. [Praljak testimony].

113 *Naletilić* Trial Judgement, para 195. See also *Blaškić* Trial Judgement, para 115.

114 *Naletilić* Trial Judgement, ibid.

115 Ibid fn 537.

116 Ibid para 195.

> international law, it is by no means necessary that the controlling authorities should plan all the operations of the units dependent on them, choose their targets, or give specific instructions concerning the conduct of military operations and any alleged violations of international humanitarian law. *The control required by international law may be deemed to exist when a State (or, in the context of an armed conflict, the Party to the conflict) has a role in organising, coordinating or planning the military actions of the military group, in addition to financing, training and equipping or providing operational support to that group.*[117]

Applying the Appeals Chamber's definition to the Croat–Muslim conflict, two requirements must be met in order for the overall control test to be satisfied, namely that Croatia provided financial and training assistance, military equipment and operational support, and that it participated in the organisation, coordination or planning of military operations. As with the direct intervention test, the application of the overall control test in Croatia's case has been dealt with in several cases before the ICTY.[118] The evidence presented in those cases showed that Croatia financed and provided military equipment and logistical support to the HVO, provided training to the HVO in the military academy of the CA, paid salaries to members of the HVO and participated in managing the HVO personnel.[119] Croatia also took part in the organisation, planning or coordination of military operations conducted in the context of the conflict between the HVO and the ABH.[120] As the Trial Chamber in *Naletilić* held, the ultimate common goal of Croatia and the HB was 'the incorporation of Croatian provinces of Bosnia and Herzegovina into a single Croatian State'.[121] In the words of President Tuđman, it was 'Herceg-Bosna [HB]…where the future borders of the Croatian state are being resolved'. That is why 'it was very important that they defended the positions and the territory the HVO was holding there'.[122] In an attempt to implement this common goal, and ensure control over the HVO, the Croatian leadership issued orders for HVO or CA troop movements and military strategies and appointed CA officers at the most senior positions in the HVO command structure.[123] Consequently, the requirements for the overall control test appear to be met.

---

117 *Tadić* Appeal Judgement, para 137 (emphasis added).

118 See, generally, the *Naletilić* case; the *Kordić* case; the *Blaškić* case, http://www.un.org/icty/cases-e/index-e.htm.

119 See *Naletilić* Trial Judgement, para 199.

120 Ibid para 200.

121 Ibid.

122 Statement by President Tuđman made during a meeting held on 22 October 1993. Quoted in *Naletilić* Trial Judgement, para 200.

123 See, eg, *Naletilić* Trial Judgement, para 201; *Blaškić* Trial Judgement, para 115.

Therefore, armed conflict between Bosnian and Herzegovinian Croats and Bosnian and Herzegovinian Muslims, or rather between military formations of the HVO and the ABH, existed in Mostar on 9 November 1993 – the date of destruction of the Old Bridge. To the extent that Croatia directly intervened in that conflict through its troops and that this State exercised overall control over the HVO in the context of the conflict (which, according to the evidence, appears to be the case), the Croat-Muslim conflict could be deemed to have been internationalised. The nature of the conflict determines the scope of application of the relevant instruments of IHL. As noted, a much larger body of IHL norms apply to international than to non-international armed conflict. Some of those norms by virtue of their customary nature are binding on all States. Others are binding only on those States for which a particular treaty is in force. The following section outlines the law according protection to cultural property in armed conflict that is applicable to the destruction of the Old Bridge.

IV The Law Applicable to the Destruction of the Old Bridge

The international character of the Croat-Muslim conflict in Mostar determines the relevance of several IHL instruments that prohibit destruction of cultural property in international armed conflict. The applicable law includes: *1907 Convention (IV)*; *1949 Geneva Convention (IV)*; the *1954 Convention* and *Additional Protocol I*.

A Customary IHL

1907 Convention (IV) and *1949 Geneva Convention (IV)* form part of customary IHL and as such apply to all States irrespective of whether a State in question is a party to them or not. They are specifically listed in the *Report of the Secretary-General* regarding the establishment of the ICTY as constitutive of international customary law. In its pertinent part the *Report* specifies:

> The part of conventional international humanitarian law which has beyond doubt become part of international law is the law applicable in armed conflict as embodied in: the Geneva Conventions of 12 August 1949 for the Protection of War Victims; the Hague Convention (IV) Respecting the Laws and Customs of War on Land and the Regulations annexed thereto of 18 October 1907; the Convention on the Prevention and Punishment of the Crime of Genocide of 9 December 1948; and the Charter of the International Military Tribunal of 8 August 1945.[124]

With respect to *1907 Convention (IV)*, several provisions are relevant to the protection of cultural property. Although this *Convention* provides protection to a

124 *Report of the Secretary-General*, above n 43, para 35 (footnotes omitted).

limited number of categories of cultural property, such protection is nevertheless of the utmost importance in cases where particular objects belonging to the listed categories are not protected by other instruments. 'Historic monuments' are included in the list of categories of objects protected by this *Convention*. Since the Old Bridge can be so categorised, the *Convention* undoubtedly applies in an analysis of the legal nature of its destruction.

In regard to the *1949 Geneva Conventions*, *Convention (IV)*, or to be precise, its Article 53 – which prohibits any destruction of property by the occupying power except where such destruction is rendered absolutely necessary by military operations – is applicable to the extent that it is considered that Mostar was under occupation by the HVO at the time of the destruction of the Bridge.[125] According to the *Prlić* Indictment,

> a state of armed conflict, international armed conflict and *partial occupation* existed in Bosnia and Herzegovina, which involved, in whole or part, the State of the Republic of Croatia and its government, armed forces and representatives in an armed conflict against the State of the Republic of Bosnia and Herzegovina and/or against the ABiH and/or Bosnian Muslims on the territory of the State of the Republic of Bosnia and Herzegovina.[126]

But, as held by the Trial Chamber in *Naletilić*, the law of occupation is only applicable to 'those areas *actually controlled* by the occupying power'.[127] Where the occupying power no longer exercises actual authority over the occupied area, the law of occupation cannot apply. Consequently, as the state of occupation is dependent on the actual authority over the given area, the exercise of such authority must be determined 'on a case by case basis'.[128] This Trial Chamber distinguished the actual authority test, which is applicable to the determination of the existence of an occupation, from the overall control test, which is applicable to the existence of international armed conflict. Because in its view the former requires a further degree of control than the latter, the Chamber 'respectfully disagree[d] with the finding in the *Blaškić* Trial Judgement argued by the Prosecution'.[129] In determining whether the authority of the HVO was actually established in Mostar at the time relevant to the destruction of the Old Bridge, various factors should be weighed, including the presence of sufficient HVO forces in Mostar and the HVO's capacity to send troops within a reasonable time to make its authority felt, the abolition of the local government by the HVO and establishment of its own administration over Mostar, and the encir-

---

125 See *Prlić* Indictment, para 232.

126 Ibid (emphasis added).

127 *Naletilić* Trial Judgement, para 218 (emphasis added).

128 Ibid.

129 Ibid para 214.

clement and siege of East Mostar and its constant bombardment by the HVO in an attempt to ethnically cleanse Mostar of the Bosnian and Herzegovinian Muslims.[130]

B Treaty IHL

The *1954 Convention* and *Protocol I Additional to the 1949 Geneva Conventions* form part of the applicable law because these treaties were binding on both Bosnia and Herzegovina and Croatia as contracting States at the time of the destruction of the Old Bridge, irrespective of whether their specific provisions are part of customary international law. The *1954 Convention* was ratified by the former Yugoslavia on 29 December 1955. It continued to apply to Bosnia and Herzegovina and Croatia as from their dates of independence, following their deposit of notification of succession. Bosnia and Herzegovina deposited notification of succession on 12 July 1993. Croatia deposited its notification of succession a year earlier, on 6 July 1992. In accordance with the law of treaties, a State which makes a declaration of succession is considered to have been a party to the relevant treaty as from its date of independence. Both Bosnia and Herzegovina and Croatia were recognised by the UN and admitted to its membership on 22 May 1992, a factor that has important implications for the question of the 'international' or 'non-international' character of the conflict.[131]

Additional Protocol I was ratified by the former Yugoslavia on 11 June 1979. Bosnia and Herzegovina deposited its declaration of succession on 31 December 1992. It declared that it became party to the *Geneva Conventions*[132] and the *Additional Protocols* as of the date of its independence, 6 March 1992. Croatia deposited its declaration of succession on 11 May 1992. It declared that it was a party to the conventions to which the former Yugoslavia was a party as of 8 October 1991. Consequently, as of 1 January 1993, the two States were bound by the provisions of *Additional Protocol I*, whatever its status within customary

---

130 For guidelines on determining whether the authority of the occupying power has been actually established, see *Naletilić* Trial Judgement, para 217.

131 Bosnia and Herzegovina was admitted as a Member of the UN by General Assembly Resolution A/RES/46/237 of 22 May 1992. Croatia was admitted as a member of the UN by General Assembly Resolution A/RES/46/238 of 22 May 1992.

132 The Appeals Chamber in *Čelebići* held that, as of the date of its independence from the former Yugoslavia, Bosnia and Herzegovina was automatically bound by the provisions of the *1949 Geneva Conventions* under customary law 'irrespective of any findings as to formal succession' because '[i]t may now be considered in international law that there is automatic State succession to multilateral humanitarian treaties in the broad sense, *i.e., treaties of universal character which express fundamental human rights*'. *Prosecutor v Zejnil Delalić, Zdravko Mučić, aka 'Pavo', Hazim Delić, Esad Landžo, aka 'Zenga'*, Judgement, Appeals Chamber, 20 February 2001, Case No. IT-96-21-A, para 111 [*Čelebići* Appeal Judgement] (emphasis in original).

international law. Also, in the abovementioned agreement signed on 22 May 1992 under the auspices of the ICRC, Bosnia and Herzegovina and Croatia expressly agreed that they would be bound during the conflict by the provisions of *Additional Protocol I*.

V Summary and Observations

As with other areas of international law, development in rules providing protection to cultural property in times of armed conflict has generally been a result of reaction to certain events that have already occurred. However, this situation is not necessarily a negative one. The international community has been continuously aiming to improve protection of its cultural treasures from the horrors of warfare. Those efforts have produced a considerable number of norms of international law relevant to the protection of cultural property in armed conflicts. Today, those norms are considered an important part of IHL. They form part of both customary international law, applicable to all States, and treaty law, applicable only to the contracting parties. The norms of IHL in relation to cultural property provide protection to a wide range of categories of objects by, *inter alia*, prohibiting their destruction except in cases of military necessity. The scope of application of legal instruments containing provisions relevant to the wartime protection of cultural property depends on the nature of an armed conflict. A substantially smaller number of norms on cultural property protection apply in the case of non-international as against international armed conflict.

However, an internal armed conflict can be internationalised provided that either the direct intervention test or the overall control test is satisfied. Both of these tests seem to be met with respect to the Bosnian and Herzegovinian Croat-Muslim conflict in and around Mostar because of Croatia's involvement in this conflict at the time of the destruction of the Old Bridge. To be exact, the conflict is internationalised through the presence of CA troops in this city fighting together with the HVO against the ABH. Croatia also exercised an overall control over the HVO.

The international character of the conflict in Mostar is conclusive of the applicability of IHL instruments containing numerous provisions relevant to the protection of cultural property in international armed conflict. Both customary IHL and treaty IHL apply. The specific provisions of the applicable IHL instruments which are relevant to the protection of cultural property provide the basis for an analysis of the legal nature of the destruction of the Old Bridge.

Chapter 5

The Legal Nature of the Destruction of the Old Bridge

I An Overview

As discussed in the preceding chapters, there was an attack on the Old Bridge of Mostar. It appears that the attack was carried out by the HVO and that the HVO targeted the Old Bridge and destroyed it wilfully. Wilful destruction of cultural property is prohibited under IHL. Such destruction may be justifiable only in cases of imperative military necessity, when cultural property becomes a military objective. This chapter deals with the legal nature of the destruction of the Old Bridge, and it aims to apply the specific provisions of the relevant IHL to the destruction of the Old Bridge, with an emphasis on the question of targeting cultural property in armed conflict.

The first part of this chapter examines whether the destruction of the Old Bridge was lawful, focusing on two major questions. It first looks at the question of whether the Old Bridge was a protected object and examines whether the Bridge was a legitimate military target. In addressing the first question, three areas of protection of cultural property in armed conflict are considered: (a) the subject matter of protection under the relevant IHL instruments; (b) the measures of safeguard, i.e., physical protective measures against structural collapse; and (c) distinctive marking. The chapter argues that the Bridge was a protected object within the scope of IHL. With respect to the first of these areas relating to protection of cultural property in armed conflict, the Bridge represented an object to which IHL accords dual protection in armed conflict, namely the indirect protection attached to all civilian objects and the direct protection provided specifically for cultural property. As regards the second of these areas, some measures had been taken to protect the Old Bridge physically from damage emanating from the shelling. However, although they play an important role in the preservation of cultural property, under the existing law, safeguarding measures are not central in determining the lawfulness of the deliberate destruction of cultural property. A similar sentiment could be expressed in relation to the third area of protection. Despite its general value in making cultural property recognisable, and thereby in minimising the danger of damage to or destruction of such property, distinctive marking is not a deciding factor in the legal characterisation of an attack on cultural property, at least with respect to cultural property under the so-called general protection, as was the case with the Old Bridge.

The second major question (as to whether the Old Bridge was a legitimate military target) concerns the prohibition of the use of cultural property for military purposes, the prohibition of direct attacks against cultural property, the exception of military necessity, the rule of distinction (in pursuance of which, attacks must be limited to military objectives during a military operation) and precautionary measures. It has been alleged that the ABH used the Old Bridge for military purposes thereby turning it into a military target. IHL prohibits the use of cultural property for military purposes in the absence of military necessity. This is so because the use of cultural property for military purposes makes such property a potential military target and thereby exposes it to the danger of damage or destruction. However, under the existing law, not every use of cultural property for military purposes automatically turns such property into a legitimate military target. The attack on cultural property must also be justified by military necessity. Attacks on cultural objects are permissible if such objects become military objectives. But even then additional, precautionary measures must be taken. The Old Bridge did not have military value and it did not constitute a military objective at the time of its destruction. The HVO's attack on the Bridge was not justified by military necessity and it was generally carried out in disregard of the rules of IHL.

The application of IHL to the Old Bridge case exposes certain weaknesses in IHL instruments concerned with protection of cultural property in armed conflict and raises a number of issues, which are the subject of the discussion in the second part of this chapter. The discussion will focus on underlining the major problems in general terms. The discussion first focuses on the issue of the definition of a military objective. This definition is an important factor in determining what can and what cannot be targeted in armed conflict. The indeterminacy on the subject may pose a difficulty for military commanders in making decisions regarding the list of military targets. The discussion then highlights the problem of arbitrariness with respect to the obligation to issue advance warning. Thereafter, attention is drawn to the difficulties related to the rule of distinction when it comes to the urban battlefield. Fighting in such a battlefield takes place in densely populated residential areas, which may also be spatially very restricted, as in the case of East Mostar where everything is only a few minutes or few hundred metres away. This, at the same time, raises an associated problem of guarding cultural property in such areas where it may be difficult to distinguish combatants from persons empowered to guard cultural objects. In turn, the issue of guarding – specifically, the question, by whom should cultural property be guarded in times of armed conflict? – raises yet another issue, the problem of State sovereignty in matters of cultural property. The issue of sovereignty is followed by a brief discussion of the problem of indeterminacy in the battlefield.

II Applying the Law

A Was the Old Bridge a Protected Object?

1 Dual Immunity

IHL provides two types of protection for cultural property. First, cultural property is protected indirectly under the rubric of civilian objects. Second, cultural property is protected directly as such. As far as the Old Bridge is concerned, it has been claimed that it was an ordinary object, 'just an old bridge'[1] as General Slobodan Praljak – who is allegedly responsible for the destruction of the Old Bridge – has put it. This claim implied that there should be no legal repercussions for the destruction of the Bridge. But was the Old Bridge really just like any other bridge in the eyes of IHL and, even if it was, would it still be protected in any event?

(a) The Old Bridge as a Civilian Object - Indirect Protection

The indirect protection of cultural property stems from the general protection accorded to civilian objects. Cultural property is considered to be essentially civilian property.[2] Under IHL, civilian objects must be respected and protected

---

1 Agence France Presse (AFP), 'Croat General Shows No Regret for Shelling of Mostar Bridge', Mostar, Bosnia and Herzegovina, 23 July 2004, http://listserv.buffalo.edu/archives/justwatch-l.html. For similar statements, see, eg, Radio-Most, Interview with Safer Halilović, in Sarajevo, and Slobodan Praljak, in Zagreb, on who is responsible for the Croat-Muslim armed conflict in Bosnia and Herzegovina, 28 February 1999, 13:45 [Radio-Most], http://www.danas.org/programi/most/1999/02/19990228074536.asp#form (Transcript on file with author); Ivica Đikić, 'ABC of Croatian Crimes in Bosnia-Herzegovina', *Bosnia Report* No. 21/22, January-May 2001, http://www.bosnia.org.uk/bosrep/report_format.cfm?articleD=717&reportid=150; *Slobodna Bosna* (Sarajevo), 'Praljak u Hagu: General mrtvih mostova' ['Praljak in The Hague: The General of Dead Bridges'] uploaded 27 May 2002, Bosnian Institute, *Bosnia Report*, http://www.bosnia.org.uk/news_body.cfm?newsid=1617; Mostarlija, *Luciferov pohod na Mostar* [*Devil's Campaign on Mostar*] (1998).

2 For instance, Article 53 of *Additional Protocol I*, which deals with cultural property, is included in Chapter III – Civilian Objects. See *Protocol Additional to the Geneva Conventions of 12 August 1949, and Relating to the Protection of Victims of International Armed Conflicts*, 8 June 1977, 1125 UNTS 3, art 1 (entered into force 7 December 1978) [*Additional Protocol I*]. See also *Geneva Convention for the Amelioration of the Condition of the Wounded and Sick in Armed Forces in the Field*, 12 August 1949, 75 UNTS 31, arts 2 and 3 (entered into force 21 October 1950) [*1949 Geneva Convention I*]; *Geneva Convention for the Amelioration of the Condition of Wounded, Sick and Shipwrecked Members of Armed Forces at Sea*, 12 August 1949, 75 UNTS 84, arts 2 and 3 (entered into force 21 October 1950) [*1949 Geneva Convention II*], *Geneva*

in armed conflict and must be prohibited from being targeted during a military operation. It is the basic rule of IHL that a distinction must always be made between the civilian population and combatants and between civilian objects and military objectives and that military operations must be directed only against military objectives. The rule of distinction forms part of customary international law.[3] In its Advisory Opinion on the *Legality of Nuclear Weapons*, the International Court of Justice (ICJ) stressed that the principle of distinction and the principle of protection of the civilian population are 'the cardinal principles contained in the texts constituting the fabric of humanitarian law', and held that '[t]hese fundamental rules are to be observed by all States whether or not they have ratified the conventions that contain them, because they constitute intransgressible principles of international customary law'.[4] The principle of distinction is contained in *Additional Protocol I*. Article 48 of the *Protocol* explicitly enunciates this principle as a basic rule.[5] Article 48 states:

> In order to ensure respect for and protection of the civilian population and civilian objects, the Parties to the conflict shall at all times distinguish between the civilian population and combatants and between civilian objects and military objectives and accordingly shall direct their operations only against military objectives.[6]

The definitions of a civilian and the civilian population are contained in Article 50 of *Additional Protocol I*[7] which Article refers to Article 4 of *Geneva Convention III*. These two Articles stipulate that a civilian is any person who does not belong to one of the following categories of persons: members of the armed forces of a party to the conflict as well as members or volunteer corps forming part of such armed forces; members of other militias and members of other volunteer corps, including those of organised resistance movements,

---

Convention relative to the Treatment of Prisoners of War, 12 August 1949, 75 UNTS 135, arts 2 and 3 (entered into force 21 October 1950) [*1949 Geneva Convention III*] and *Geneva Convention relative to the Protection of Civilian Persons in Time of War*, 12 August 1949, 75 UNTS 287, arts 2 and 3 (entered into force 21 October 1950) [*1949 Geneva Convention IV*]; *Protocol Additional to the Geneva Conventions of 12 August 1949, and Relating to the Protection of Victims of Non-International Armed Conflicts*, 8 June 1977, 1125 UNTS 609 art 1(1) (entered into force 7 December 1978) [*Additional Protocol II*].

3 See Yves Sandoz *et al* (eds), *Commentary on the Additional Protocols I and II of 9 June 1977* (1987), 598, paras 1863-1867 [*ICRC Commentary*].

4 *Legality of the Threat or Use by a State of Nuclear Weapons in Armed Conflict*, Advisory Opinion of 8 July 1996 [1996] ICJ Reports 66, para 78 [*Nuclear Weapons* Case].

5 See *ICRC Commentary*, 598, paras 1868-1871.

6 *Additional Protocol I*, art 48.

7 Ibid art 50(1), (2). This is a 'negative' definition (i.e., defined by what they are not).

belonging to a party to the conflict and operating in or outside their own territory, even if this territory is occupied, provided that such militias or volunteer corps, including such organised resistance movements, are being commanded by a person responsible for his subordinates, have a fixed distinctive sign recognisable at a distance, carry arms openly and conduct their operations in accordance with the laws and customs of war; members of regular armed forces who profess allegiance to a government or an authority not recognised by the detaining power; and inhabitants of a non-occupied territory, who on the approach of the enemy spontaneously take up arms to resist the invading forces, without having had time to form themselves into regular armed units, provided they carry arms openly and respect the laws and customs of war.[8] The civilian population consists of all persons who are considered civilians.[9] Combatants, on the other hand, are, in accordance with Article 43 of the *Protocol*, members of the armed forces except medical personnel and chaplains.[10] In regard to military objectives, these include the armed forces and their installations and transport. In order to ensure the highest respect for and protection of the civilian population in armed conflict, in line with Article 50 of the *Protocol*, in case of doubt as to whether a person is a civilian, that person is to be considered a civilian.[11] Also, the presence within the civilian population of non-civilians does not change the civilian character of the population.[12]

As far as civilian objects are concerned, consistent with Article 52 of the *Protocol*, these include all objects which are not military objectives.[13] Pursuant to the same Article, military objectives relating to objects are limited to

> those objects which by their nature, location, purpose or use make an effective contribution to military action and whose total or partial destruction, capture or neutralisation, in the circumstances ruling at the time, offers a definite military advantage.[14]

This Article further stipulates that, in case of doubt as to whether an object which is normally dedicated to civilian purposes is being used to make an effective contribution to military action, it must be presumed 'not to be so used'.[15] Such situations require strict compliance with the precautions spelt out in

---

8 *1949 Geneva Convention III*, art 4A(1), (2), (3) and (6) and *Additional Protocol I*, art 43.

9 *Additional Protocol I* art 50(2).

10 Ibid art 43(2).

11 Ibid art 50(1).

12 Ibid art 50(3).

13 Ibid art 52(1).

14 Ibid art 52(2).

15 Ibid art 52(3).

Article 57 of *Additional Protocol I*. In attacks, precautions must be taken at the highest level of command. That is, 'those who plan or decide upon an attack' are the ones who, *inter alia*, must ascertain whether the object is indeed making an effective and not merely a potential contribution to military action.[16] Sometimes the situation might not be clear-cut, which may create difficulties in the battlefield for making adequate judgement. This, however, does not diminish the overall importance of the rule in the protection of the civilian population according to which belligerents cannot arbitrarily and unilaterally declare any civilian object to be a military objective.

With respect to cultural property, such property, as noted, is considered to be essentially civilian property. The *ICRC Commentary* notes that cultural property enjoys dual immunity, namely, that attached to civilian objects and that accorded to cultural property as such.[17] ICTY jurisprudence also points to the double protection of cultural property.[18] The Appeals Chamber in *Kordić* observed that 'international instruments provide two types of protection for cultural, historical and religious monuments'.[19] First, '[t]here is the general protection [which] applies to civilian objects'[20] and, then, there is 'special protection' given to 'certain objects'.[21] This Chamber explains that

> the general protection…is provided for, *inter alia*, under Article 52 of Additional Protocol I and applies to civilian objects. The protection provided is that the building or monument cannot be destroyed unless it has turned into a military object by offering the attacking side 'a definite military advantage' at the time of the attack.[22]

As far as the Old Bridge is concerned, it was considered a civilian, public monument. As such it warranted the protection that it could not be targeted during military operations. Civilian objects can nevertheless become military objects, and thus legitimate military targets, if used for military purposes. Some com-

16 Ibid art 57(2)(a).

17 See *ICRC Commentary*, above n 3, 647, para 2067.

18 See, eg, *Prosecutor v Dario Kordić and Mario Čerkez,* Judgement, Trial Chamber III, 26 February 2001, Case No. IT-95-14/2-T, para 361 [*Kordić* Trial Judgement or *Kordić* case or *Kordić*]; *Prosecutor v Dario Kordić and Mario Čerkez*, Judgement, Appeals Chamber, 17 December 2004, Case No. IT-95-14/2-A, para 89 [*Kordić* Appeal Judgement]; *Prosecutor v Miodrag Jokić*, Case No. IT-01-42/1-S, Sentencing Judgement, Trial Chamber I, 18 March 2004, Case No. IT-01-42/1-S, para 50 [*Jokić* Sentencing Judgement]; *Prosecutor v Pavle Strugar*, Judgement, Trial Chamber II, 31 January 2005, Case No. IT-01-42-T, paras 277 *et seq.* [*Strugar* Trial Judgement].

19 *Kordić* Appeal Judgement, ibid.

20 Ibid.

21 Ibid para 90.

22 Ibid para 89.

mentators stress that certain objects are typically regarded in customary law as legitimate military targets. Gaby Rado explains that '[t]he logic is that they can usually be put to military use and are essential for the functioning of any modern military in time of conflict'.[23] As far as bridges are concerned, they are considered legitimate infrastructure targets. These targets include 'lines and means of communication, command and control – railway lines, roads, *bridges*, tunnels, and canals – that are of fundamental military importance'.[24] With respect to bridges, some military commanders argue that '[i]t's enough for one soldier to cross a bridge and the bridge becomes a military target'.[25]

However, an object cannot be deemed to be a legitimate military target just because it 'can *usually* be put to military use'. An object must actually be used for military purposes. But even then it does not automatically become a military objective.

Unless all the requirements spelt out in Article 52(2) of *Additional Protocol I*, which defines military objective, are met cumulatively – i.e., an object concerned makes not merely any but an 'effective' contribution to military action, 'and' total or partial destruction, capture or neutralisation thereof offers not merely any but 'definite' military advantage, 'and' definite military advantage is not determined in relation to merely any past use of an object for military purposes but in the circumstances ruling 'at the time' – an object concerned remains to be deemed civilian. When there is doubt about whether an object is being used to make an effective contribution to military action in accordance with Article 52(3) of *Protocol I* it must be presumed that it is not. Consistent with observations made by the Appeals Chamber in *Kordić*, the imperative 'in case of doubt' is limited to 'the expected conduct of a member of the military'.[26] If, however, all the conditions in Article 52(2) are met, an attack cannot proceed if damage to civilians and civilian objects would be excessive when compared to the concrete and direct military advantage anticipated.[27] A range of other precautionary measures must be taken, including the choice of means and methods of attack, and effective advance warning. When there is a choice between several military objectives in obtaining a similar military advantage, the attacking force must choose the one which would be expected to cause the least damage to civilian lives and civilian objects.[28]

---

23 Gaby Rado, 'Legitimate Military Targets' in *Crimes of War Project*, http://www.crimesofwar.org/thebook/legit-military-target.html [3].

24 Ibid [6] (emphasis added).

25 Statement of the accused General Praljak made during cross-examination of the Prosecution witness Enes Vukotić in *The Prosecutor v Jadranko Prlić, Bruno Stojić, Slobodan Praljak, Milivoj Petković, Valentin Ćorić and Berislav Pušić*, Case No. IT-04-74-T, 7 February 2007, T 13698 [*Prlić* or *Prlić* case].

26 *Kordić* Appeal Judgement, para 53.

27 *Additional Protocol I*, art 57(2)(iii).

28 Ibid art 57.

Allegedly, the Old Bridge was used by the ABH in support of the military effort during the conflict. It has been claimed that the ABH used the Bridge for the movement of military personnel as well as for transport of ammunition and food.[29] Consistent with statements made by the Muslim side, the ABH did use the Bridge at some point,[30] but briefly and mainly for carrying wounded soldiers and wounded civilians from one bank of the Neretva to the other – that is, from the narrow strip of Muslim held territory in West Mostar where the front line was, to the hospital in Muslim-controlled East Mostar – and for getting home.[31]

However, crossing the Old Bridge was extremely dangerous due to the frequency of the shelling by the HVO. According to Jeremy Bowen, who made a documentary about East Mostar from August to early October 1993, 'shelling was a pretty constant fact of life. Shelling could happen at any time...and the shells could land anywhere'.[32] Sniper fire posed an additional difficulty. The prospect of being shot dead by a sniper was ever present for people in East Mostar. Throughout the conflict, everyone there lived under a constant fear of being hit by a sniper.[33] In regard to the area of the Old Bridge, the HVO positions, including the sniper spots, were on the nearby hills, Hum and Stotina, which overlooked the area.[34] The HVO also had heavy weapons, heavy mortars and tanks there.[35] According to Bowen, the HVO used 'the big anti-aircraft weapon that was set up on Hum'[36] to target East Mostar, 'and this was a weapon that terrified everybody on the east side because it was a large-calibre weapon

29 See testimony of Miro Salčin, the Prosecution witness in *Prlić*, 15 February 2007, T 14252 [Salčin testimony].

30 Ibid.

31 See the *Naletilić* case, proceedings of 15 November 2001, T 5774, 5776 (BBC documentary about East Mostar, made by Jeremy Bowen from August to October 1993) [Bowen Documentary or Bowen testimony in *Naletilić*]. *Prosecutor v Mladen Naletilić aka 'Tuta' and Vinko Martinović aka 'Štela'*, Judgement, Trial Chamber, 31 March 2003, Case No. IT-98-34-T [*Naletilić* Trial Judgement or *Naletilić* case or *Naletilić*] and *Prosecutor v Mladen Naletilić aka 'Tuta' and Vinko Martinović aka 'Štela'*, Judgement, Appeals Chamber, 3 May 2006, Case No. IT-98-34-A [*Naletilić* Appeal Judgement].

32 Bowen testimony in *Naletilić*, ibid, T 5809-5810.

33 See, eg, Bowen testimony in *Naletilić*; ibid; testimony of Jeremy Bowen in *Prlić*, 23-24 January 2007, T 12711 *et seq*. [Bowen testimony or Bowen Documentary in *Prlić*]; testimony of Omer Dilberović in *Prlić*, 31 January 2007 [Dilberović testimony]; testimony of Grant Finlayson in *Prlić*, 7 May 2007 [Finlayson testimony]; testimony of Ratko Pejanović in *Prlić*, 4 May 2006 [Pejanović testimony].

34 See, eg, Bowen testimony in *Prlić*, ibid; Salčin testimony, above n 29; testimony of Enes Delalić in *Prlić*, 17 May 2007 [Delalić testimony].

35 See, eg, Salčin testimony, ibid; testimony of Witness QQ in *Naletilić*, 21-22 November 2001 [Witness QQ testimony].

36 Bowen testimony in *Prlić*, 23 January 2007, T 12757.

which could cause quite a bit of damage'.[37] There was not much difference in night-time with respect to the risks associated with crossing the Bridge as the HVO had weapons and other equipment designed for night-time use.[38] When all of this is added to the fact that the Old Bridge was a narrow (3.97 m wide) footbridge and a structure 20.34 m tall, on which everyone was exposed and in the sights of HVO weapons, it seems unlikely that the Bridge could have been of much use to the ABH. In fact, various reports, statements of eyewitnesses and other sources stress that the Old Bridge was devoid of any military significance at the time of its destruction.[39] At some point this was even admitted by the Croat side itself. Shortly after the destruction of the Old Bridge, in an interview with Belinda Giles for her film 'A Greater Croatia', Jadranko Prlić, Prime Minister of the then HB and the second most powerful official in the HB/HVO political and governmental structures,[40] could not see why it was necessary to destroy the Old Bridge. Although he did not name the responsible party, Prlić emphasised that there were 'no[t] any political and *military* reason[s] to destroy this bridge'.[41]

As there was no fighting between the ABH and the HVO in the immediate vicinity of the Old Bridge at the time, it seems that the HVO targeted and destroyed the Bridge deliberately without any military necessity. It appears that the HVO was aiming, *inter alia*, at stopping any crossing of the Bridge by the Muslim side by whomever that might have been done, and to demoralise the opponent. Therefore, in all probability the Old Bridge was a civilian object at the time of its destruction, and as such was protected by IHL. In other words, even if it was 'just an old bridge' as claimed by General Praljak, the Old Bridge still enjoyed protection and could not be considered a legitimate military target. This chapter now turns to an examination of the protection of the Old Bridge under the rubric of cultural property.

(b) *The Old Bridge as an Object of Cultural Property - Direct Protection*

Certain objects are protected by IHL directly under the rubric of cultural property. In the words of the Trial Chamber in *Jokić*, '[t]his immunity is clearly *addi-*

37 Ibid T 12757-12758.

38 Ibid T 12757.

39 See *Final Report of the United Nations Commission of Experts Established Pursuant to Security Council Resolution 780 (1992), Annex XI: Destruction of Cultural Property Report*, S/1994/674/Add.2 (Vol V) 28 December 1994 [*Final Report*].

40 See *Prlić* Indictment, paras 2-3.

41 Statement of Jadranko Prlić made in November 1993 during an interview with Belinda Giles for her film 'A Greater Croatia' (emphasis added). This film was produced for British television and was aired in December 1993 on Channel 9 in Great Britain. The Prlić interview videotape was played in the Court, in the *Prlić* trial during the proceedings of 15 May 2006, T 2073.

tional to the protection attached to civilian objects'.[42] IHL accords this additional immunity to a wide range of objects. The broadest spectrum of objects that enjoy immunity in armed conflict is provided for under the *1954 Convention*. The *Convention* distinguishes between the so-called 'general protection' of cultural property and the so-called 'special protection' of cultural property. The former is granted to all property which meets the definition of 'cultural property' given in the first article of the *Convention*. The latter applies only to a limited number of select categories of cultural property.

In accordance with Article 1 of the *1954 Convention*, general protection is accorded to both movable and immovable property that is 'of great importance to the cultural heritage of every people'.[43] The *Convention* sets up several categories of property that are to be considered 'cultural property'. The listed property is protected by virtue of its intrinsic value. Article 1 of the *1954 Convention* begins with the statement that protection is granted 'irrespective of origin or ownership'[44] of the property concerned. Moreover, the character of property is irrelevant in obtaining protection. The *Convention* enunciates explicitly that protection is to be accorded to property 'whether religious or secular'.[45] Pursuant to Article 1, property is to be considered 'cultural property' if it falls into one of the following three groups of objects: (a) immovable and movable objects which are themselves of intrinsic artistic, historic, scientific or other cultural value; (b) objects which themselves do not have cultural value but serve to house – to preserve or exhibit – movable objects that have such value, that is, movable cultural property; and (c) centres containing a substantial number of objects falling into the two preceding groups, such centres being further referred to as 'centres containing monuments'.[46] Article 1 of the *1954 Convention* states:

> Definition of cultural property
>
> For the purposes of the present Convention, the term 'cultural property' shall cover, irrespective of origin or ownership:

---

42 *Jokić* Sentencing Judgement, para 50 (emphasis in the original).

43 *Convention for the Protection of Cultural Property in the Event of Armed Conflict*, 14 May 1954, 249 UNTS 240 (entered into force 7 August 1956), art 1(a) [*1954 Convention*]. The *Regulations for the Execution of the Convention for the Protection of Cultural Property in the Event of Armed Conflict* [*1954 Regulations*] annexed to the *Convention* are considered an integral part thereof. See also *Protocol for the Protection of Cultural Property in the Event of Armed Conflict*, 14 May 1954, 249 UNTS 358-64 (entered into force 7 August 1956) [*1954 Protocol*] and *Protocol for the Protection of Cultural Property in the Event of Armed Conflict*, 26 March 1999, 38 ILM 769-82 (entered into force 9 March 2004) [*1999 Protocol*].

44 *1954 Convention*, ibid introductory statement in art 1.

45 Ibid art 1(a).

46 Ibid art 1(c).

(a) movable or immovable property of great importance to the cultural heritage of every people, such as monuments of architecture, art or history, whether religious or secular; archaeological sites; groups of buildings which, as a whole, are of historical or artistic interest; works of art; manuscripts, books and other objects of artistic, historical or archaeological interest; as well as scientific collections and important collections of books or archives or of reproductions of the property defined above;
(b) buildings whose main and effective purpose is to preserve or exhibit the movable cultural property defined in sub-paragraph (a) such as museums, large libraries and depositories of archives, and refuges intended to shelter, in the event of armed conflict, the movable cultural property defined in subparagraph (a);
(c) centres containing a large amount of cultural property as defined in sub-paragraphs (a) and (b), to be known as 'centres containing monuments'.[47]

The definition of cultural property in Article 1 of the *1954 Convention* is one of the most comprehensive in international law.[48] Article 1 provides the High Contracting Parties with an illustrative but non-exhaustive list of objects and sites that qualify as cultural property within the meaning of the *Convention*.[49] It also sets up the criteria on the basis of which international legal protection is to be provided to particular categories of objects. Some objects are protected because of their nature and others because of their purposes. With respect to the former, the leading example of cultural property given in subparagraph (a) illustrates that not all kinds of monuments will be afforded protection under the *1954 Convention*.[50] To qualify for the protection, a monument needs to be of architectural, artistic or historic significance.[51] Not all of these requirements need to be met cumulatively. One of them will suffice in order that a monument becomes eligible for protection in times of armed conflict. It is irrelevant whether a monument is of religious or secular character or what its origin or ownership is. It is its importance from the point of view of architecture, art or history that mat-

---

47 Ibid art 1.

48 See, eg, Karen Detling, 'Eternal Silence: The Destruction of Cultural Property in Yugoslavia' (1993) 17 *Maryland Journal of International Law and Trade* 41, 46; Jiří Toman, *The Protection of Cultural Property in the Event of Armed Conflict: Commentary on the Convention for the Protection of Cultural Property in the Event of Armed Conflict and its Protocol, signed on 14 May 1954 in The Hague, and on other instruments of international law concerning such protection* (1996), 54.

49 See Gregory Mose, 'The Destruction of Churches and Mosques in Bosnia-Herzegovina: A Rights-Based Approach to the Protection of Religious Cultural Property' (1996) 3 *Buffalo Journal of International Law* 180, 183.

50 See Roger O'Keefe, 'The Meaning of "Cultural Property" under the 1954 Hague Convention' (1999) XLVI *Netherlands International Law Review* 26, 47.

51 See *1954 Convention*, art 1(a).

ters.[52] In regard to the latter, examples of buildings listed in subparagraph (b) illustrate that the protection can be accorded because of an object's 'main and effective purpose'[53] rather than its nature. As long as a building 'preserve[s] or exhibit[s]'[54] objects defined as movable cultural property of artistic, historical, archaeological or scientific interest, it is entitled to protection under the *1954 Convention*. Conversely, once the movable cultural property that was housed, for instance, in a museum or a large library, is removed, the protection is lost, unless a building itself is of importance from the point of view of architecture, art or history.[55] Centres containing monuments – the third group of cultural property in Article 1 – are protected as a whole. For instance, important historic cities fall into this group. The Old Town of Dubrovnik, Croatia, is one such example. Everything within the walls of this medieval town, including the residential buildings, is considered a 'centre' within the meaning of Article 1(c) of the *1954 Convention*.[56] Vatican City (Citta del Vaticano) is another example. This city in its entirety is protected by the *1954 Convention*.

Identification of objects deserving international legal protection is in the contracting States' domain.[57] Property that is to be considered cultural property within the meaning of Article 1 of the *1954 Convention*, i.e., property 'of great importance to the cultural heritage of every people' is 'classified' or 'scheduled' in accordance with national cultural heritage laws by the competent national authorities. All designated cultural property ultimately forms part of the cultural heritage of all humankind. Since the list given in Article 1 of the *1954 Convention* of objects and sites that qualify as cultural property is only an illustrative list, in designating their cultural property, the High Contracting Parties seem to be free to either follow the list or introduce new categories of objects they deem worthy of preservation. As the *Convention* does not impose limits on the numbers of cultural objects and sites entitled to international protection, the High Contracting Parties also appear to be at liberty to identify as many objects as they consider are deserving of being saved from destruction by an armed conflict. This freedom to expand the list of cultural property in Article 1 and to determine the volume of cultural property eligible for protection makes the scope of application of the *1954 Convention* dependent on the discretion of the High Contracting Parties.[58] Such discretion might be considered to be restric-

52 See, eg, Toman, above n 48, 50-51; O'Keefe, above n 50, 47 fn 93. See also UNESCO Docs 5C/PRG/6, Annex I, para XV and 7C/PRG/7, Annex I, 7.

53 *1954 Convention*, art 1(b).

54 Ibid.

55 See Toman, above n 48, 53-54.

56 See, eg, *Jokić* Sentencing Judgement, para 51; *Strugar* Trial Judgement, paras 279 and 285.

57 See O'Keefe, above n 50, 50.

58 Ibid 47-50.

tive of the scope of Article 1, that is, to be limiting the international protection in armed conflict only to cultural property which is already designated by the competent national authorities. Accordingly, property that was not designated would be left without the *Convention's* protection in armed conflict even if it was of a high cultural value.[59]

On the other hand, States' discretion may cause the scope of application of the Convention to become too broad as protection is accorded to all the national cultural heritage of each High Contracting Party as defined by that State.[60] In other words, every object of cultural property that a High Contracting Party holds in its territory which it has protected by its national cultural heritage laws is considered to be 'of great importance' to the cultural heritage of the State concerned and as such automatically qualifies for the protection envisaged by the *Convention*.[61] Roger O'Keefe observes that '[a]n overwhelming majority of the High Contracting Parties appear to apply the Convention to all movable and immovable property comprising their respective national cultural heritages (or to a substantial and representative range thereof)'[62] and that they 'effectively deem international importance to attach to property of national significance'.[63] Since the average national register of cultural property comprises 'tens and perhaps hundreds of thousands'[64] of objects of cultural property, it would mean that the *Convention* applies to a massive volume of cultural property in each High Contracting Party.[65]

Theoretically, the enormity of the scope of application of Article 1 is not inconsistent with the object and purpose of the *Convention*. According to its

---

59 However, a competent tribunal may well decide that property not designated by the State in question is covered by the definition in Article 1 of the *1954 Convention*.

60 O'Keefe, above n 50, 30. See also Toman, above n 48, 49-50; Maja Seršić, 'Protection of Cultural Property in Time of Armed Conflict' (1996) 27 *Netherlands Yearbook of International Law* 3, 9; Address by HE Nagendra Singh, Judge at the International Court of Justice, at the celebration of the thirtieth anniversary of the Hague Convention, in UNESCO, *Information on the Implementation of the Convention for the Protection of Cultural Property in the Event of Armed Conflict, The Hague, 1984 Reports*, UNESCO Doc. CLT/MD/3, Paris, December 1984, 15 [Address by HE Nagendra Singh].

61 See O'Keefe, ibid 36.

62 Ibid 48.

63 Ibid 49.

64 Ibid 29.

65 In his dissenting opinion in the *Legality of Nuclear Weapons* case, Judge Weeramantry takes the Federal Republic of Germany as an example. In 1986 this State had around one million listed monuments. The city of Cologne alone had around 9,000 listed buildings. Judge Weeramantry observes that '[a] nuclear attack on a city such as Cologne would thus deprive Germany, in particular, and the world community in general, of a *considerable segment* of their cultural inheritance'. *Nuclear Weapons* Case, 226, 467 (emphasis added).

Preamble,[66] the object and purpose of the *Convention* is the international protection of 'the cultural heritage of all [hu]mankind'.[67] Paragraph 2 of the Preamble stipulates that 'damage to cultural property belonging to any people whatsoever means damage to the cultural heritage of *all [hu]mankind*, since *each people* makes its contribution to the culture of the world'.[68] In a sense, the term 'all humankind' represents a whole and the term 'each people' represents a part. As O'Keefe argues, this suggests that the term 'every people' in the phrase 'of great importance to the cultural heritage of every people' contained in Article 1(a) of the *Convention* should be read as 'every people *individually*'.[69] Accordingly, the cultural heritage of all humankind within the meaning of the *Convention* is the sum of movable and immovable cultural property of all High Contracting Parties as identified under their national laws.[70] Since the *Convention* explicitly acknowledges that 'each people makes its contribution to the culture of the world',[71] and does not impose any restrictions whatsoever as to the number of objects and sites that are to be protected, 'each people' is entitled to make 'its contribution' as colossal as they deem appropriate. If the enormity of the scope of application of Article 1 of the *Convention* is perceived as problematic on these grounds, that is, if it is so extensive that it is impossible to engage in the necessary military activity, the exception of 'military necessity' comes into play.

In contrast to the general protection of cultural property, which provides protection for all movable and immovable cultural property that is of 'great importance' to the cultural heritage of every people, and which, as noted, can be broad in scope, the special protection within the meaning of the *1954 Convention*[72] applies only to a limited number of cases of immovable cultural

66 The Preamble to a treaty is considered an integral part of a treaty and hence primary means of its interpretation. See *Vienna Convention on the Law of Treaties*, art 31(2). *Vienna Convention on the Law of Treaties*, 23 May 1969, 1155 UNTS 331.

67 *1954 Convention*, Preamble para 2.

68 Ibid (emphasis added).

69 O'Keefe, above n 50, 38.

70 Ibid. See also Address by HE Nagendra Singh, above n 60, 15; John Merryman, 'The Public Interest in Cultural Property' (1989) 77 *California Law Review* 339, 343 ['Public Interest'].

71 *1954 Convention,* Preamble para 2.

72 The so-called 'special protection' under the *1954 Convention* is often confused with protection of cultural property generally as opposed to protection accorded to civilian objects. Protection provided for cultural objects under Article 53 of *Additional Protocol I* is often referred to as 'special protection' in order to distinguish it from protection accorded to civilian objects under the same *Protocol*. Yet 'special protection' under *Protocol I* is completely different from the special protection under the *1954 Convention*, both in terms of the subject of protection as well as the requirements accompanying those two types of protection. Moreover, the special protection under the 1954 Convention is often confused with the protection accorded to cultural and natural heritage under the *World Heritage Convention*. It is often

property, namely, 'a limited number of refuges intended to shelter movable cultural property in the event of armed conflict, of centres containing monuments and other immovable cultural property of *very great importance*'.[73] To be granted special protection, cultural property must also satisfy other very rigorous conditions spelt out in Article 8 of the *Convention*.[74] If those requirements are satisfied, cultural property is granted special protection by its entry in the International Register of Cultural Property under Special Protection.[75] Entry in the Register is the *conditio sine qua non* for acquiring special protection.

However, in reality, due to the stringent requirements in Article 8 and resulting practical difficulties with the application of this Article, there is a very modest number of entries in the mentioned International Register. Only one centre containing monuments[76] and eight refuges intended to shelter movable cultural property have been listed in the Register.[77] However, even this already modest number of entries was cut back following requests for the cancellation

---

assumed that World Heritage sites are automatically entitled to the special protection within the meaning of the *1954 Convention*. Yet, in times of armed conflict property inscribed on the World Heritage List can enjoy the special protection under the *1954 Convention* only if it is also listed as cultural property under special protection in the International Register of Cultural Property under Special Protection. Otherwise, such sites enjoy the 'general protection' under the *1954 Convention* as with any other property deemed to be 'of great importance to the cultural heritage' of the people concerned. It should be noted that the conditions in which a site can be nominated for special protection under the *1954 Convention* are so narrow that the majority of sites on the World Heritage List would not qualify for listing in the Special Register. Nevertheless, they do have some protection under Articles 6(1) and (3) and 11(4) of the *World Heritage Convention*. This *Convention* has a different set of States Parties and its provisions may be helpful if the *1954 Convention* does not apply.

73 *1954 Convention*, art 8(1) (emphasis added).

74 But see *Kordić* Trial Judgement, para 362 ('there is little difference between the conditions for the according of general protection and those for the provision of special protection [as] protection of whatever type will be lost if cultural property... is used for military purpose').

75 See *1954 Convention*, art 8(6).

76 The Vatican City State was first to be listed. It entered the Register as a whole on 11 March 1960. See UNESCO, *Information on the Implementation of the Convention for the Protection of Cultural Property in the Event of Armed Conflict*, The Hague 1954, 1995 Reports, CLT-95/WS/13, Paris, December 1995 [*1995 Periodic Reports*]. For other periodic reports see *UNESCO Reports on the Implementation of the 1954 Convention*, UNESCO Documents: CA/RBC/1/3 and Add. 1-6, SHC/MD/1 dated 19 May 1967; SHC/MD/6 dated 30 April 1970; CC/MD/41 of July 1979; CLT/MD/3 of December 1984; CC/MD/11 of December 1989; CLT-2005/WS/6, 2005, available at, http://unesdoc.unesco.org/images/. See also UNESCO Doc CLT-97/WS/12, August 1997.

77 The eight refuges for cultural property include six refuges in the Netherlands, one refuge in Austria and one refuge in the Federal Republic of Germany. See *1995 Periodic Reports*, ibid 6.

of inscription of three refuges for cultural property on the Register in 1994 and one refuge in 2000.[78]

At the time of its destruction, the Old Bridge was not inscribed on the International Register of Cultural property under Special Protection. In fact, neither the former Yugoslavia nor any of its successor States has ever had any immovable cultural property inscribed on this register. Thus, the provisions of the *1954 Convention* relating to special protection are not applicable to the Old Bridge case. This type of protection is mentioned here only in passing, only to make the distinction between the special protection within the meaning of the *1954 Convention* and the protection accorded to cultural property under Article 53 of *Additional Protocol I*. Protection accorded to objects under Article 53 is often referred to as 'special protection'. For instance, the *ICRC Commentary* refers to '[t]he special protection conferred by Article 53'.[79] The ICTY jurisprudence, relying on the *Commentary* as authority, also makes reference to special protection when discussing protection under Article 53 of *Additional Protocol I*.[80] However, the special protection of cultural property under the *1954 Convention* and the 'special protection' under Article 53 of *Additional Protocol I*, are very different concepts. Whereas the former is a type of protection accorded to cultural property 'of very great importance' that requires a higher degree of protection than cultural property under general protection (i.e., property 'of great importance' to the cultural heritage of the people concerned), the latter is the term that is used to distinguish the protection accorded to all civilian objects from the protection given to objects listed in Article 53 of the *Protocol*. As far as objects that constitute the cultural heritage of peoples are concerned, there is no difference between general protection accorded by Article 1 of the *1954 Convention* and that under Article 53 of *Additional Protocol I*. Under both instruments the High Contracting Parties are free to designate those objects they deem to be worthy of preservation and to list, in accordance with national heritage laws, as many objects in quantity terms as they wish. Under both instruments, listed objects automatically become entitled to the international legal protection in armed conflict.

The definition of protected objects in Article 53 of *Additional Protocol I* is built on the *1954 Convention*. In its pertinent part, Article 53 states:

---

78 In January 1994, the Netherlands requested the cancellation of the inscription on the Register of three of its refuges for cultural property. This was followed by Austria's request to cancel the inscription on the Register of one of its refuges. See UNESCO, CLT/CIH/MCO/2008/PI/46, 2000, available at http://unesdoc.unesco.org/images/0015/001585/158587eb.pdf . See also *1995 Periodic Reports*, ibid.

79 *ICRC Commentary*, above n 3, 646, para 2063.

80 See *Kordić* Appeal Judgement, para 90.

> Without prejudice to the provisions of the Hague Convention for the Protection of Cultural Property in the Event of Armed Conflict of 14 May 1954, and of other relevant international instruments, it is prohibited:
> (*a*) to commit any acts of hostility directed against the historic monuments, works of art or places of worship which constitute the cultural or spiritual heritage of peoples.[81]

The wording of Article 53 makes it apparent that protection accorded to objects enumerated in paragraph (a) does not modify the *1954 Convention*. According to the *ICRC Commentary*, the inclusion of Article 53 in *Additional Protocol I* was not intended to amount to a revision of the existing rules on the subject but that protection and respect for cultural objects was to be confirmed.[82] Because of the 'without prejudice' clause, in case of contradiction, the *1954 Convention* has primacy over Article 53 of *Additional Protocol I*.[83]

Article 53 of *Additional Protocol I* provides protection for three categories of objects: historic monuments, works of art, and places of worship. Protection is granted on condition that these objects constitute the cultural or spiritual heritage of people. This Article uses terminology different from that used in Article 1 of the *1954 Convention*. Whereas Article 53 refers to objects which 'constitute the cultural or spiritual heritage', Article 1 of the *1954 Convention* makes reference to property which is 'of great importance to the cultural heritage'. However, according to the *ICRC Commentary*, despite the difference in terminology, 'the basic idea is the same'.[84]

Historic monuments and works of art fall into the category of 'cultural objects', while 'spiritual objects' comprise places of worship. Still, there are instances when one object falls into both categories or an object passes from one category into another. When in doubt with respect to categorisation, according to the *ICRC Commentary*, the views of the people concerned as to how they see an object as part of their heritage should be taken into account.[85] The *Commentary* emphasises that 'all objects of sufficient artistic or religious importance to constitute the heritage of peoples are protected [under Article 53] including those which have been renovated or restored'.[86] Article 53 does not further define the protected categories of objects. As far as cultural objects are concerned, the *Commentary* notes that historic monuments and works of art

81 *Additional Protocol I*, art 53(a).
82 *ICRC Commentary*, above n 3, para 2046.
83 Ibid.
84 Ibid para 2064.
85 Ibid para 2065.
86 Ibid para 2066.

must be considered as generic terms, but that in case of doubt reference should be made to the detailed definition given in Article 1 of the *1954 Convention*.[87]

In contrast to the *1954 Convention* and *Additional Protocol I*, the *1907 Regulations* refer only to components of cultural property.[88] Two articles of the *1907 Regulations* encompass components of cultural property: Article 27 (appli-

87 Ibid para 2068.

88 See, eg, Hirad Abtahi, 'The Protection of Cultural Property in Times of Armed Conflict: The Practice of the International Criminal Tribunal for the Former Yugoslavia' (2001) 14 *Harvard Human Rights Journal* 1, 6-7 (noting that most instruments relating to armed conflict, including the *1907 Regulations*, *the Roerich Pact*, the *ICTY Statute* and the *ICC Statute*, refer to the components of cultural property, not to cultural property explicitly, and implying that this should not be problematic because these instruments apply to almost identical components of cultural property and illustrate the century-long approach adopted by the majority of international instruments). See *Convention (II) with Respect to the Laws and Customs of War on Land*, The Hague, 29 July 1899, 32 Stat. 1803, TS 403 (entered into force 4 September 1900) [*1899 Convention (II)*]; *Regulations Concerning the Laws and Customs of War on Land*, annexed to *Convention (II) with Respect to the Laws and Customs of War on Land*, The Hague, 29 July 1899 (entered into force 4 September 1900) [*1899 Regulations*], available at http://www.icrc.org/ihl.nsf; *Convention (IV) Respecting the Laws and Customs of War on Land*, The Hague, 18 October 1907, 36 Stat 2277 (entered into force 26 January 1910) [*1907 Convention (IV)*]; *Regulations Respecting the Laws and Customs of War on Land* annexed to *Convention (IV) Respecting the Laws and Customs of War on Land*, The Hague, 18 October 1907 (entered into force 26 January 1910) [*1907 Regulations*], reproduced in Adam Roberts and Richard Guelff (eds), *Documents on the Laws of War* (3rd ed, 2000) 69, also available at http://www.icrc.org/ihl.nsf; *Convention (IX) Concerning Bombardment by Naval Forces in Time of War*, The Hague, 18 October 1907, 36 Stat 2351 (entered into force 26 January 1910) [*1907 Convention (IX)*], reproduced in Roberts and Guelff, ibid 112, also available at http://www.icrc.org/ihl.nsf. See also *Treaty on the Protection of Artistic and Scientific Institutions and Historic Monuments*, Washington, 15 April 1935, League of Nations, TS CLVII 1936, 290 (entered into force 26 August 1935), [*Roerich Pact*], available at http://fletcher.tuffs.edu/multi/www/roerich.html; *Statute of the International Criminal Tribunal for the Prosecution of Persons Responsible for Serious Violations of International Humanitarian Law Committed in the Territory of the Former Yugoslavia since 1991*, adopted by the UN Security Council Res 827, 25 May 1993, UN SCOR, 48th sess, 3217th mtg at 29 UN Doc S/827/1993, as amended by Res 1166, 13 May 1998 and by Res 1329, 30 November 2000, contained in UN Doc S/25704, Annex (1993), and attached to the 'Report of the Secretary-General Pursuant to Paragraph 2 of Security Council Resolution 808' [*ICTY Statute*]; and *Rome Statute of the International Criminal Court*, UN Diplomatic Conference of Plenipotentiaries on the Establishment of an International Criminal Court, UN Doc A/CONF 183/9 (17 July 1998) 2187 UNTS 3 (entered into force 1 July 2002), [*ICC Statute*], http://www.igc.org/icc/Rome/html.

cable to sieges and bombardments), and Article 56 (relating to military authority over the territory of the hostile state). In its pertinent part, Article 27 provides:

> In sieges and bombardments all necessary steps must be taken to spare, as far as possible, buildings dedicated to religion, art, science, or charitable purposes, historic monuments, hospitals, and places where the sick and wounded are collected, provided they are not being used at the time for military purposes.[89]

Article 27 provides protection only for a few categories of objects that are today considered cultural property. Moreover, this Article does not apply to the components of cultural property exclusively. Those are mixed together with other property such as buildings dedicated to charitable purposes, hospitals and places where the sick and wounded are collected, which are essentially not cultural property objects. This mixing together of cultural property with non-cultural property demonstrates that the *Regulations* do not sufficiently recognise the uniqueness of cultural property. However, considering that this instrument was devised a century ago, even the mere inclusion at that time of the components in the list of other property, let alone the reference to cultural property together with hospitals and places where the sick and wounded are collected (which connotes the imperativeness of the protection of the highest value of all, human life, and implies that the preservation of cultural property is just as important), emphasises the recognition of the significance of cultural property.[90] Article 56 of the *1907 Regulations* accords protection to 'institutions dedicated to religion, charity and education, the arts and sciences, historic monuments, and works of art and science'.[91] This Article proclaims that,

> [t]he property of municipalities, that of institutions dedicated to religion, charity and education, the arts and sciences, even when State property, shall be treated as private property.
>
> All seizure of, destruction or wilful damage done to institutions of this character, historic monuments, works of art and science, is forbidden, and should be made the subject of legal proceedings.[92]

Both Articles include historic monuments among the protected objects. But they do not define this category of cultural property just as they do not define any other object to which they grant protection. Historic monuments are also referred to in Article 53 of *Additional Protocol I* under the rubric of cultural

89 *1907 Regulations*, art 27(1).

90 See Abtahi, above n 88, 6.

91 *1907 Regulations*, art 56.

92 Ibid.

objects. Apart from requiring a historic monument to constitute 'the cultural heritage of people', this Article does not provide any further definition of historic monuments either. However, because of the 'without prejudice' clause, reference should be made to the definition in Article 1 of the *1954 Convention*. As discussed, 'monuments' are the leading example in subparagraph (a) of Article 1 of the *1954 Convention*. Article 1 does not refer to historic monuments in general terms but it specifies them as 'monuments of architecture and art'. To be considered cultural property within the meaning of Article 1, a monument must be deemed to be 'of great importance to the cultural heritage' of the people from the point of view of history, architecture or art. The requirement of 'great importance' is met in legal terms through the designation of a monument in accordance with national cultural heritage laws, which is carried out by the competent national authorities. It is completely irrelevant whether a monument is religious or secular, or who designed or built it, or who owns it. It is its historico-architectural-artistic value that counts. Once the monument is listed in accordance with national cultural heritage laws, it is considered 'cultural property' within the meaning of Article 1 of the *1954 Convention* and it automatically becomes eligible for protection under the *Convention*, provided the State concerned is a party to the *Convention*. Such monuments also automatically form part of the cultural heritage of all humankind.

However, the *1954 Convention* does not prescribe criteria or standards on the basis of which a monument is to be categorised as historic, architectural or artistic, or a combination of those kinds. UNESCO offers some guidance in this regard, defining monuments as 'construction[s] of a certain age and design, whatever their purpose, as well as monuments, in the more limited sense, erected to commemorate some event or person'.[93] It is also useful to consider the definition of monuments provided for in the *Venice Charter*. The *Charter* specifies that the concept of a historic monument embraces not only the single architectural work but also the urban or rural setting in which the evidence of a particular civilization, significant development or historic event is found, and stresses that this applies not only to great works of art but also to more modest works of the past which have acquired cultural significance with the passing of time.[94] The *World Heritage Convention* provides assistance as to the kinds of objects which are to be considered 'monuments'. It specifies the following items under this category of cultural property: 'architectural works, works of monumental sculpture and painting, elements or structures of an archaeological nature, inscriptions,

---

93 UNESCO Docs 5C/PRG/6, Annex I, para XV and 7C/PRG/7, Annex I, 7.

94 *International Charter for the Conservation and Restoration of Monuments and Sites*, adopted at the 2nd International Congress of Architects and Technicians of Historic Monuments, which met in Venice from 25 to 31 May 1964 [*Venice Charter*], art 1, http://www.icomos.org/docs/venice_charter.html.

cave dwellings and combinations of features,[95] which are of outstanding universal value from the point of view of history, art or science'.[96]

Because Bosnia and Herzegovina was bound by the *1954 Convention* and by *Additional Protocol I*, as well as by *1907 Convention (IV)*, at the time of the destruction of the Old Bridge, these instruments were the main applicable law. Since the *1954 Convention* provides for the most detailed definition of cultural property (which reflects *1907 Convention (IV)*, and which, together with the *1907 Convention*, is reflected in Article 53 of *Additional Protocol I*), this chapter discusses the question of whether the Old Bridge was considered a protected object under the rubric of 'cultural property' with reference to the requirements given in Article 1 of the *1954 Convention*. The chapter first assesses which category of property the Bridge came within and then considers whether it was deemed to be property 'of great importance' to the cultural heritage of the citizens of Mostar and of the whole of Bosnia and Herzegovina.

First of all, the Bridge was a fixed architectural structure, a permanent crossing from the East to the West bank of the Neretva. Thus, it belonged to the category of immovable property. As discussed, the Bridge was considered to be a public monument of exceptional artistic and scientific value. It also illustrated a significant stage in the history and development of the city of Mostar and of the wider region. Because of its age – that is, its 427-year lifespan – the Old Bridge easily fell into the category of 'historic monuments'. The sixteenth and seventeenth century documents retrieved in the archives in Turkey for the purposes of the reconstruction of the Old Bridge, describe it as the Bridge of

95 The *Dayton Accords* seem to encompass elements of both the definition of cultural property given in Article 1 of the *1954 Convention* and the definition of monuments in Article 1 of the *World Heritage Convention* into their own definition of national monuments. See *General Framework for Peace in Bosnia and Herzegovina*, initialled in Dayton, 21 November 1995, signed in Paris, 14 December 1995, Annex 8 on Commission to Preserve National Monuments, art VI ('The following shall be eligible for designation as National Monuments: movable or immovable property of great importance to a group of people with common cultural, historic, religious or ethnic heritage, such as monuments of architecture, art or history; archaeological sites; groups of buildings; as well as cemeteries') [*Dayton Accords, Annex 8*].

96 *World Heritage Convention*, art 1. To be included on the World Heritage List, sites must satisfy the selection criteria. These criteria are explained in the Operational Guidelines for the Implementation of the World Heritage Convention. See *Convention concerning the Protection of the World Cultural and Natural Heritage*, 16 November 1972, 1037 UNTS 151 (entered into force 17 December 1975), [*World Heritage Convention*]; see also *Convention for the Safeguarding of the Intangible Cultural Heritage*, 17 October 2003, http://www.unesco.org/culture/laws/2003/html. The Operational Guidelines and other information on the World Heritage are available at http://whc.unesco.org.

Sultan Suleyman, the Ottoman ruler at the time.[97] There was also an inscription cut into the Bridge which paid homage to the Sultan 'who ruled when the bridge was being finished', and which gave the year 1566 as the year of construction of the Bridge.[98]

The Bridge was designed by Ottoman architect Mimar Hayreddin, who was a student of another Ottoman architect, the famous Kodja Mimar Sinan. Its association with these prominent architects of the time is additional evidence of the historic significance of the Old Bridge. The Old Bridge was one of the oldest and best known architectural structures in the Balkans and even beyond. Moreover, throughout the period of its lifespan, the Bridge existed and was continuously used on the original site in an unaltered original state. According to UNESCO, the Old Bridge 'was in a perfect state of conservation before the outbreak of military hostilities in the region'.[99] The Bridge was representative of the highest Ottoman achievements in engineering and architecture in the Balkans at the time. Because of its architectural design and its nature as a masterpiece of construction, the Bridge was a monument of exceptional scientific and aesthetic value. Since it was such a well preserved monument, it had a great educative potential; for instance, by contributing to the understanding of early architectural design and early building techniques. In general, the Bridge represented historical evidence of the Ottoman presence in the region which influenced the way of life for centuries. In particular, the Bridge was evidence of an important four-centuries-long phase in the development of the city of Mostar.

But was the Old Bridge considered to be 'of great importance' to the cultural heritage of the people concerned within the meaning of Article 1 of the *1954 Convention*? The Old Bridge was the landmark of Mostar. It stood as a symbol of unity and harmony of Mostar's multicultural milieu. The Bridge was so deeply ingrained in Mostar's every pore that over the years the city and its Old Bridge became an inseparable whole. To the citizens of Mostar, the city was unimaginable without its Old Bridge.[100] This bridge was considered the heart of Mostar's (and the whole of Bosnia and Herzegovina's) history and culture.[101] In

97 See Mirjana Belanov, 'The Mostar Bridge Conservation Issues' December 1995, 3.2.1, http://www.gen-eng.florence.it/starimost/10_contr/belanov/belanov01.htm.

98 Ibid 3.2.2.

99 See UNESCO's activities, 'Mostar and Its Historical Monuments', http://www.unesco.org/culture/heritage/tangible/mostar/html_eng/monuments.html.

100 See Belanov, above n 97, 3.2.

101 See, eg, Amir Pašić, *The Old Bridge (Stari Most) in Mostar* (1995) [*The Old Bridge*]; Associated Press, 'Ethnic Strife Destroys Mostar's Symbol of Diversity', *San Francisco Chronicle*, Wednesday, 10 November 1993, A 10, 1993 WL 6434487 ('This is an attack on the heart of our history and culture', said Muhammed Filipović, a Muslim politician and historian in Sarajevo. 'It was a beautiful piece of art, so harmonious').

the words of the Director-General of UNESCO, '[t]he bridge was exceptional both artistically and structurally, and was considered the most outstanding monument in Bosnia and Herzegovina. It also came to represent the relations of mutual understanding between the various communities of the region'.[102] The Bridge was well known not only to those with an interest in culture and science but also to other people in the region, irrespective of their ethnicity, and was one of the most famous monuments in the entire former Yugoslavia.

The Old City of Mostar, with the Old Bridge as its focal point, was under the special care of the citizens of Mostar. From 1955 until 1991, under the guidance of the Mostar Institute for the Preservation of Cultural Heritage, tremendous effort was made to restore the Old Bridge and the rest of the Old City.[103] That effort resulted in the world's most prestigious architectural award, the Aga Khan Award, for exceptional historic restoration.[104] The award was a confirmation of the importance of buildings, spaces, settlements and cities in the process of human development. The Earth's cultural non-renewable resources such as monuments of art, architecture and history shape the values of a society. The Old Bridge, together with the adjacent area of the Old City of Mostar, was an example of how the built environment can be the embodiment and bearer of those values. In addition to being a beautiful object symbolising a significant part of Mostar's past, the Old Bridge and the area around it was put to many uses. For instance, it became an open stage for various cultural activities, a meeting place for thousands of Mostar's youth coming from both banks of the Neretva, and a tourist attraction. In short, '[f]rom a lifeless relic of an historic past [the Mostarians] turned [the Old City of Mostar] into a city thriving in its culture, exploding in economic opportunity'.[105] The restoration work carried out in the Old City of Mostar illustrated how powerful cultural continuity was in contributing to human well-being.

In 1991, a commission was appointed and given the task of providing permanent maintenance for the Old Bridge.[106] In accordance with the *Law of the Socialist Republic of Bosnia and Herzegovina on the Protection and Utilisation of Cultural-Historic and Natural Heritage*, the Bridge was designated a monument of invaluable significance for the city of Mostar and was later added to a list of national monuments of Bosnia and Herzegovina.[107] Together with 136 other

---

102 UNESCO, 'Director-General Appeal for Reconstruction of Mostar's Bridge', Paris, 10 March 1994, www.unesco.org.

103 See Pašić, *The Old Bridge*, above n 101.

104 See Nicholas Adams, 'Architecture as the Target' (1993) 52 *Journal of the Society of Architectural Historians* 389.

105 Mawlana Hazar Imam's statement at the World Congress of Architects in Chicago, 18 June 1993, http://w3.tyenet.com/kozlich/congress.htm.

106 See Pašić, above n 101, 36.

107 See *Law on Protection and Use of Cultural-Historic and Natural Heritage*, Official Gazette of SR BH, Nos 20/85 and 12/87. See also UNESCO, DRG Operational Unit,

monuments that represented the cultural heritage of Bosnia and Herzegovina, the Old Bridge was also added to the list of national monuments of the former Yugoslavia.[108] As Kaiser explains:

> in ex-Yugoslavia there was a fairly precise classification for cultural heritage. At the top level there was the so called zero monument. The zero monument was a monument of world class importance and in Bosnia-Herzegovina there was only one. It was the Old Bridge at Mostar; however, which was never on the UNESCO list, in spite of what has been said. Monument value (1) was a national monument; (2) was a regional monument and (3) was a local monument.[109]

That the Old Bridge was also a monument of exceptional value for the entire international community is demonstrated by the fact that it was one step away from being added to the World Heritage treasures as it had been, together with the Old City of Mostar, recommended for inscription on the World Heritage in Danger List.[110]

Mostar/Stari Most, 'Rebuilding of Stari Most (Old Bridge) and the Rehabilitation of the Old Town of Mostar', http://www.unesco.org/opi2/starimost.htm.

108 See Presentation of Professor Amir Pašić at the Carnegie Symposium, Carnegie Endowment for International Peace, 'A Symposium on Destruction and Rebuilding of Architectural Treasures in Bosnia and Herzegovina', Monday, 2 May 1994, http://www.kakarigi.net/many/carnegie.htm [Carnegie Symposium].

109 Testimony of Dr Colin Kaiser, the Prosecution witness, Public hearing in *The Prosecutor of the Tribunal v Radovan Karadžić and Ratko Mladić*, Tuesday, 2 July 1996, Case No. IT-95-18-R61 and IT-95-5-R61, Tuesday, T 433 [Kaiser testimony in *Karadžić*].

110 See Committee on Culture and Education of Parliamentary Assembly of Council of Europe (COE), *First Information Report*, doc 6756, 2 February 1993, 42 [*First COE Report*] (Dr Colin Kaiser, consultant expert, in his report based upon a fact-finding mission carried out for the Parliamentary Assembly of the COE, in Croatia and in Bosnia and Herzegovina from 29 November to 20 December 1992, with respect to Mostar vis-à-vis damage done to cultural property by the YA forces, recommended the drawing up and submitting to UNESCO of '[a] proposal for inscription of the historic centre of Mostar (together with the Old Bridge) and the adjoining mixed historic zone on the List of World Heritage in Danger'). See also Committee on Culture and Education of Parliamentary Assembly of Council of Europe (COE), *Third Information Report*, doc 6904, 20 September 1993 [*Third COE Report*] (following the heavy shelling of cultural property in Mostar by the HVO at that time, Dr Kaiser again pointed to the need for urgently placing the historic core of Mostar together with the Old Bridge on UNESCO's World Heritage in Danger List as this area was near the front line between the HVO and ABH forces. However, before the inscription on the List could happen, the Bridge and much of the Old City of Mostar were destroyed). It should be noted that, pursuant to Article 11(4) of the *World Heritage Convention*, a site must be on the World

Therefore, the Old Bridge was a historic monument, as well as an architectural monument, which was 'of great importance' to the cultural heritage of Mostar and Bosnia and Herzegovina, and as such it was clearly eligible for protection under the rubric of cultural property within the meaning of the *1954 Convention*. At the same time, the Old Bridge was a historic monument which constituted part of the cultural heritage of peoples within the meaning of Article 53 of *Additional Protocol I*, as well as a historic monument entitled to the protection under *1907 Convention (IV)*.

2 Physical Protection

Turning now to the question of physical protection of the Old Bridge, it has been contended that the Old Bridge was neither marked[111] nor adequately protected against collapse,[112] but does that really matter in determining whether the Bridge was a legitimate military target?

(a) Distinctive Marking

The main purpose of marking cultural property by a distinctive emblem is to facilitate its recognition. Distinctive marking is envisaged in *1907 Convention (IV)*. Article 27(2) of its *Regulations*, which concerns immovable cultural property in sieges and bombardments, expressly states:

> It is the duty of the besieged to indicate the presence of such buildings or places by distinctive and visible signs, which shall be notified to the enemy beforehand.[113]

The wording of this Article suggests that distinctive marking is compulsory. It is 'the duty' of the besieged, that is, the holder of cultural property, to mark the presence of cultural property with 'signs'. The signs must be 'distinctive and visible' and must be notified to the opposing side beforehand. However, *1907 Convention (IV)* does not specify the details of the signs.[114]

Heritage List before it can be placed on the World Heritage in Danger List. This process is painstaking and relatively long (it takes at least 18 months). As there are over 800 sites already on the List, the criteria for listing are detailed and all need to be considered by ICOMOS and by the World Heritage Committee.

111 See General Praljak's statement in an interview with Radio-Most, above n 1.

112 See, eg, *Final Report*, above n 39, Appendix I, Record: cultural property in the former Yugoslavia, Meeting of 15 February 1994, IV.c; *First COE Report*, above n 110, 41.

113 *1907 Regulations*, art 27(2).

114 The question is dealt with in Article 5 of *1907 Convention (IX)*, relevant to the protection of cultural property in bombardment by naval forces. See *1907 Convention (IX)*, art 5(2).

The *1954 Convention* also envisages distinctive marking. This *Convention* does specify the form of the distinctive emblem. In accordance with its Article 16, the distinctive emblem of the *Convention*

> shall take the form of a shield, pointed below, per saltire blue and white (a shield consisting of a royal blue square, one of the angles of which forms the point of the shield, and of a royal-blue triangle above the square, the space on either side being taken up by a white triangle).[115]

The emblem defined in Article 16 of the *1954 Convention* may be used 'alone or repeated three times in a triangular formation (one shield below)',[116] under the conditions specified in Article 17 of this *Convention*.

As far as *Additional Protocol I* is concerned, it does not contain provisions defining the emblem for cultural objects. But because the *Protocol* deals with cultural property only briefly, since there is a specialist treaty governing cultural property matters in detail, and because of the explicit 'without prejudice' clause, the provisions of the *1954 Convention* relating to the distinctive marking are applicable in that case as well.

The *1954 Convention* treats separately the distinctive marking of cultural property under general protection and the distinctive marking of cultural property under special protection. The distinctive marking for cultural property under general protection is not compulsory and, consequently, is not a condition for the obligation to exercise respect for cultural property.[117] Article 6 of the *1954 Convention*, which is relevant to the general protection of cultural property, states that such property '*may* bear a distinctive emblem so as to facilitate its recognition'.[118] According to Toman, although the absence of a distinctive emblem is not a *conditio sine qua non* for the obligation to respect cultural property under general protection, it might, nevertheless, lessen the responsibility of the opposing party in the event of bombardment if the presence of cultural property is not clearly visible.[119]

In contrast, in accordance with Article 10 of the *1954 Convention*, cultural property under special protection must be marked with the distinctive emblem during an armed conflict.[120] As noted, the distinctive emblem may be repeated three times or used alone.[121] The former applies to immovable cultural prop-

---

115 *1954 Convention*, art 16(1).

116 Ibid art 16(2).

117 See Toman, above n 48, 90.

118 *1954 Convention*, art 6 (emphasis added).

119 See Toman, above n 48, 90.

120 *1954 Convention*, art 10.

121 Ibid art 16(2).

erty under special protection,[122] as well as to the transport of cultural property[123] and to improvised refuges, under the conditions provided for in the *1954 Regulations*.[124] The latter applies to cultural property under general protection and also to the persons responsible for the duties of control in accordance with the *Regulations*, to the personnel engaged in the protection of cultural property and to the identity cards.[125] Article 17(4) provides that the distinctive emblem 'may not be placed on any immovable cultural property unless at the same time there is displayed an authorisation duly dated and signed by the competent authority of the High Contracting Party'.[126] As the Convention does not define the form of the authorisation, that would depend on the national regulations of each contracting State. In accordance with Article 20 of the *Regulations*, the placing of the distinctive emblem and its degree of visibility is also left to the discretion of the competent national authorities of each State.[127] However, the emblem must be clearly visible in daylight from the air as well as from the ground.[128]

Some States hold suspicions in relation to distinctive marking because they believe that such marking provides the enemy with a potential 'target list'. For instance, although it shelled Iran's cultural property during the 1980s Iran-Iraq armed conflict, Iraq refused to mark its own cultural property with the distinctive emblem of the *1954 Convention* because of the belief that this emblem would attract aerial bombardment.[129] Sadly, events in the territory of the former Yugoslavia during the 1990s conflicts provide many examples of how marked cultural property was indeed a particularly favoured target. For instance, a huge sign as specified by the *1954 Convention* that was placed on the museum in Vukovar, Croatia, almost immediately prompted shelling by YA forces.[130] The protective flags displaying the distinctive emblem of the *1954 Convention* that flew in the Old Town of Dubrovnik in 1991 also attracted shelling by the YA forces.[131]

122 Ibid art 17(1)(a).

123 Ibid art 17(1)(b) and arts 12 and 13.

124 Ibid art 17(1)(c).

125 Ibid art 17(2).

126 Ibid art 17(4).

127 *1954 Regulations*, art 20(1).

128 Ibid art 20(2).

129 Jeffrey Levin, 'Cultural Heritage under Fire', Newsletter 7.1 1992 (Conservation at the Getty), <http://www.getty.edu/conservation/publications/newsletters/7_1/cultural.html> [5].

130 For a discussion of the shelling of Vukovar museum following the display of the distinctive emblem of the *1954 Convention*, see National Arts Journalism Program, 'Who Owns Culture? War and Cultural Property', 68, <http://www.whoownsculture/058-071WarandCulturalProperty.pdf>.

131 For a discussion of the shelling of cultural property in Croatia which was marked by the distinctive sign in 1991, see Detling, above n 48, 66-68 and nn 155 and 156.

Still, marking should not be regarded as giving rise to a 'target list'. This is not to say that more marking should be encouraged. In the situation where a major motivation for the hostilities was the desire to obliterate the cultural monuments of the opposing side, it would be quite impractical to insist on marking as a way to ensure protection of these monuments as it may well ensure their destruction. Rather, marking should be seen merely as a measure aimed at facilitating identification of cultural property and its protection from attack where appropriate. In that regard, advantage should be taken of new technology to assist in identification. For instance, a hand-held global positioning system (GPS) can provide a very accurate measurement of the location concerned. As Hays Parks explains, '[w]hen target intelligence people are building [their] maps for conducting campaigns, they have to have very accurate data. So GPS readings can help not only to establish the location of targets, but the location of cultural property so it can be protected from attack'.[132] As far as the marking of cultural property is concerned, there has been some criticism that the marking in and of itself is very inadequate because the signs are small and thus not visible from an altitude of 10,000 feet.[133] However, as expressed at the Carnegie Endowment for International Peace Symposium on Destruction and Rebuilding of Architectural Treasures in Bosnia and Herzegovina,

> Question: If you bomb the bridge at Mostar, you shouldn't be able to plead ignorance.
>
> Mr Parks: That's correct. This is probably easier because everyone knows of its cultural significance. Perhaps, as was said, that's why it was bombed.[134]

Indeed, the Old Bridge was clearly identifiable as an object of cultural property. Under ICTY case law, the destruction of cultural property may amount to a violation of the laws or customs of war if it is, *inter alia*, committed intentionally to objects of cultural property which may clearly be identified as such. In the *Blaškić* case the Trial Chamber held that 'the damage or destruction must have been committed intentionally to institutions which may *clearly be identified* as dedicated to religion or education'.[135] Although the *Blaškić* Indictment deals mainly with institutions dedicated to religion, when Article 3(d) of the *ICTY Statute* is considered in its entirety, the same reasoning could be applied to other objects protected by this Article, including historic monuments (as objects of cultural property). As discussed, the Old Bridge was a monument of history. It was 'well known to all of the population in the region, whether

132 Presentation of Hays Parks, Carnegie Symposium, above n 108, 7.

133 Ibid 8.

134 Ibid 9.

135 *Prosecutor v Tihomir Blaškić*, Judgement, Trial Chamber I, 3 March 2000, Case No. IT-95-14-T, para 185 (emphasis added) [*Blaškić* Trial Judgement].

Serbian, Croatian or Muslim'.[136] However, 'identification' should not be equated with 'marking'. Whereas distinctive marking is a means of identification, some cultural property, including the Old Bridge, is easily identifiable even in the absence of the marking. As seen, under the *1954 Convention*, marking is compulsory only for cultural property under special protection. Since the Old Bridge has never been placed under special protection, only the rules regarding general protection, in accordance with which cultural property 'may', but is not required to, bear the distinctive emblem apply. Allegedly, the Old Bridge did bear the emblem defined by the *1954 Convention* during the conflict, but the marking was removed at some stage,[137] perhaps for fear it would make the Old Bridge a target.

Nevertheless, as the distinctive marking of cultural property under general protection is not compulsory, in accordance with the *Commentary on the 1954 Convention*, 'it is not a condition for the respect of cultural property'.[138] As noted, the absence of the distinctive marking as a means of identification of cultural property might lessen the responsibility of the opposing party in the event of bombardment since that party might claim that the damage or destruction was due to lack of knowledge about the presence of an object of cultural property.[139] In the case of the Old Bridge such ignorance could not be pleaded. To reiterate, in the former Yugoslavia the Bridge was classified as the 'zero' monument of world class importance.[140] The Bridge was well known to its destroyers. It was a dominant feature of the Old City of Mostar and of the whole of Mostar. Because of its size, especially because of its height, and because of its shimmery-white colour, the Bridge was very visible from afar. Besides, no aerial bombardment was employed in its destruction. There is ample evidence that the Bridge was targeted and shelled almost at point-blank range from the ground by Croat tanks for two consecutive days on 8 and 9 November 1993, during daylight when its presence could not be missed at all. Therefore, it was not compulsory for the Old Bridge to be marked by the distinctive emblem of the *1954 Convention* in order to be spared from attack. But even if the distinctive marking was required, its absence would still not affect the (visual) recognition of the Bridge as this monument was plain to see at a distance and was obvious to the HVO forces on 8 and 9 November 1993.

---

136 *Final Report*, above n 39.

137 See Radio-Most, above n 1.

138 Toman, above n 48, 90.

139 Ibid.

140 See above, n 109 and accompanying text.

(b) Protective Measures

It has been contended that the Old Bridge was not adequately protected in a physical sense prior to its destruction. But does that affect the obligation to respect cultural property? The *1954 Convention* is the only applicable instrument that includes provisions regarding protective measures. The *Convention* refers to these measures as safeguarding cultural property. In fact, the protection of cultural property, within the meaning of the *1954 Convention*, comprises the safeguarding of and respect for such property.[141] Whereas respect for cultural property is mainly applicable to times of armed conflict, the former is mainly applicable to so-called peacetime. The safeguarding of cultural property is defined in Article 3 of the *1954 Convention* as follows:

> The High Contracting Parties undertake to prepare in time of peace for the safeguarding of cultural property situated within their own territory against the foreseeable effects of an armed conflict, by taking such measures as they consider appropriate.[142]

In accordance with this Article, the safeguarding of cultural property consists of all preparatory measures which are designed to ensure the best possible material conditions for its protection against the foreseeable effects of armed conflict. The *Convention* places the duty of safeguarding cultural property on the contracting States in the territory of which cultural property is situated. Within the meaning of Article 3, States should carry out preparation for safeguarding in time of peace. The *Convention* does not specify preparatory measures. Rather, it leaves the decision to States to take 'such measures as *they* consider appropriate'.[143] This certainly allows each State to organise the safeguarding of cultural property in accordance with its financial, material and technical resources. According to States' periodical reports on the implementation of the *1954 Convention*, some States, such as Germany, the Holy See, the Netherlands, Sweden and Switzerland, have made great effort to fulfil their duty of safeguarding cultural property.[144]

However, some States have not addressed the question of safeguarding in their reports, and some States have failed to send a report to the Director-General altogether despite their obligation to do so 'at least once every four years'.[145] The failure to send a report or the absence of information on the measures of safeguarding in the reports which were sent does not in itself mean that

141 *1954 Convention*, art 2.

142 Ibid art 3.

143 Ibid (emphasis added).

144 See *1995 Periodical Reports*, above n 76.

145 *1954 Convention*, art 26(2).

those States have not taken such measures. Still, the internal freedom provided for in Article 3 of the *Convention* may lead to the taking of inadequate or insufficient preparatory measures or, worse, to the taking of no such measures at all. While the *Convention* obligates each High Contracting Party 'to take all necessary measures to ensure its effective application within a period of six months after [its] entry into force'[146] with respect to the State concerned, in effect, the Convention does not explicitly envisage any consequences for failures relating to safeguarding even if they may result in the loss of cultural property and thereby in the impoverishment of the cultural heritage of all humankind. If interpreted broadly, Article 28 of the *Convention* might constitute the exception to this position. This Article provides for prosecution and punishment of persons responsible for 'a breach of the...Convention'.[147] As the *Convention* does not provide a list of crimes against cultural property, or identify specific provisions the breach of which give rise to individual criminal responsibility, the phrase 'a breach of the *Convention*' could mean a breach of 'any' provision of the *Convention*, thus including a breach of its Article 3. The matter of sanctions is left to the state domain, however, to be regulated 'within the framework of [States'] ordinary criminal jurisdiction'.[148]

There have been no published cases relating to the safeguarding of cultural property. In fact, according to States' reports, sanctions are mainly envisaged for acts arising from the failure to 'respect' cultural property during hostilities, notably destruction of cultural property.[149] There has been a doctrinal attempt to enumerate a list of crimes against cultural property. In 1959, Nahlik published a list of thirty prohibitions and injunctions, the twenty-third of which (placed in Section 6: 'Injunctions Concerning Property Belonging to the Enjoined State Itself') concerned the safeguarding of cultural property.[150]

Despite its imperfection, Article 3 of the *Convention* is an important provision, and it represents a substantial improvement in the protection of cultural property in armed conflict. As noted, the *1899* and *1907 Conventions* did not include any such provision. As for the weakness of the safeguarding aspect of the protection of cultural property in Article 3, this is remedied to some extent by

146 Ibid art 34.

147 Ibid art 28.

148 Ibid.

149 See *1995 Periodic Reports*, above n 76, 17, 19, 37, 42-43. See also Toman, above n 48, 294-95.

150 See Stanislav Nahlik, 'Des crimes contre les biens culturels' (1959) 29 *Annuaire de l'Association des auditeurs et anciens auditeurs de l'Académie de droit international de La Haye* 14, 24-27 ('23. Injunction addressed to all the Contracting Parties to prepare in time of peace for the safeguarding of cultural property situated within their own territory against the foreseeable effects of an armed conflict (Article 3 of the *1954 Convention*)') ['Des crimes']. Professor Nahlik's list is reproduced in Toman, above n 48, 296.

other provisions of the *Convention*. To be precise, the *Convention* provides States with an opportunity to call upon UNESCO for technical assistance in organising the protection of cultural property situated in their territories, or in relation to any other problem arising out of the application of the *Convention*.[151] Importantly, UNESCO is also authorised to make, on its own initiative, proposals on the subject to States concerned.[152] The involvement of UNESCO in the safeguarding of cultural property means that responsibility for safeguarding does not lie solely with the State in the territory of which cultural property is located but also with the international community, adding an element of universality which, in turn, is consistent with the concept of the cultural heritage of all peoples.

Confirmation that safeguarding is primarily, but not exclusively, the responsibility of a State in whose territory cultural property is situated can be additionally found in Article 5 of the *Convention* relating to occupation. Under this Article the occupying power has the responsibility to support, to the extent possible, the competent national authorities of the occupied State in safeguarding and preserving cultural property situated in the occupied territory,[153] and in cases where the competent national authorities are unable to take measures necessary to preserve cultural property in territory which has been occupied and damaged by military operations, to take, again to the extent possible, and in close cooperation with such authorities, those measures most necessary to preserve cultural property.[154]

The establishment of adequate and sufficient safeguarding measures before an armed conflict occurs considerably increases the chances of survival for cultural property during conflict. Since cultural property belonging to any of the world's people is part of humanity's shared heritage, and since its protection is aimed at its transmission to future generations, the safeguarding of that property should be an imperative. However, the *1954 Convention* does not condition the duty to respect cultural property during armed conflict on the fulfilment of the obligation to safeguard that property. Rather, the *Convention* explicitly states that the failure to apply safeguarding measures does not absolve any State from its duty to respect the cultural property of another State:

> No High Contracting Party may evade the obligations incumbent upon it under the present Article, in respect of another High Contracting Party, by reason of the fact that the latter has not applied the measures of safeguard referred to in Article 3.[155]

---

151 See *1954 Convention*, art 23(1).

152 Ibid art 23(2).

153 Ibid art 5(1).

154 Ibid art 5(2).

155 Ibid art 4(5). This equally applies to parties to a non-international armed conflict and members of a resistance movement. Ibid arts 19(1) and art 5(3), respectively.

With respect to the Old Bridge, certain protective measures were undertaken in order to protect the Old Bridge from the effects of warfare. According to the report based upon a fact-finding mission carried out for the Parliamentary Assembly of the COE by Kaiser, a consultant expert, in Croatia and Bosnia and Herzegovina from 29 November to 20 December 1992, the damage done to cultural property in Mostar during offensive or defensive military action was especially high because the YA used a considerable quantity of heavy artillery, mortars and rocket, 'virtually every kind of projectile in the Yugoslav Army panoply'.[156] The devastation such ordnance inflicted on cultural property half a year earlier in the Old Town of Dubrovnik, Croatia, pales in comparison with the devastation of Mostar.[157] Mostar's historic Ottoman district – the Old City of Mostar – and its surroundings suffered the heaviest damage. The Old Bridge was not exempt. Its parapet was hit in two different places. However, experts did not consider this damage to be alarming.[158] Nevertheless, it was feared that the innumerable detonations in the Old City of Mostar and surroundings weakened the structure of the Bridge.[159] Some protective measures had already been implemented, including placement of car tyres aimed at cushioning the Bridge,[160] and of a wooden screen on scaffolding above the Bridge to trigger detonation of projectiles before they reached the Bridge surface and to protect pedestrian traffic and the Bridge surface from shrapnel. However, vertical wooden and rubber screens on the south side, to trigger detonation away from the Bridge's structurally weaker centre, were missing at the time of the fact-finding mission's visit to the city.[161] In its recommendations, Kaiser asked the local Ministry of Culture and the Public Office of Building and Reconstruction to add these elements of protection to the Bridge[162] and to further improve protective measures.[163]

When the conflict between Croats and Muslims began, the situation soon became 'particularly explosive'[164] and 'catastrophic…on the left-bank zone around the [B]ridge'.[165] The heaviest guns available to the HVO mercilessly

156 *First COE Report*, above n 110, 13.

157 Ibid 129.

158 Ibid para 138.

159 Ibid.

160 See Colin Kaiser, 'Crimes against Culture' *UNESCO Courier* Sept 2000, 4, http://web1.infotrac.galegroup.com/itw/infomark/109/511/ ['Crimes against Culture'].

161 See *First COE Report*, above n 110, para 138.

162 Ibid.

163 Ibid 41.

164 *Third COE Report*, above n 110, para 15.

165 Committee on Culture and Education of Parliamentary Assembly of Council of Europe (COE), *Fourth Information Report*, doc 6999, 19 January 1994, para 74 [*Fourth COE Report*].

shelled objects of cultural property.[166] Artillery calibres included those used by tanks and howitzers.[167] Reportedly, the shelling created one of the worst cultural disasters of the entire war in Bosnia and Herzegovina.[168] The Old Bridge remained protected during this part of the conflict in Mostar up until its destruction in November 1993. General Praljak, one of the six accused in the *Prlić et al* case, claims that he 'personally issued the order to use very thick boards and put up a structure around the bridge so that mortar projectiles would not destroy it, and [that] two soldiers of the Croat Defence Council were killed in the process'.[169] According to the General, '[t]his structure protected the bridge *for months*, and there is a sufficient number of photographs'.[170] Several witnesses in the *Naletilić* and *Prlić* cases have testified that they saw 'some scaffolding…a rope and some old tyres hanging on a concrete pillar'[171] in 1993. According to Miro Salčin, who was an eyewitness to the two-day shelling and the destruction of the Old Bridge, the Bridge was protected until its last day. Together with some fifteen to twenty other people, this witness went to the Bridge in the evening of 8 November 1993 and, while standing at the top of the Bridge,[172] saw 'some sort of protection'[173] there. However, according to the *Final Report of the United Nations Commission of Experts*, the Old Bridge was not 'adequately' protected.[174] The Parliamentary Assembly of the COE made similar findings. Consistent with its *Fourth Information Report*, the competent local authorities did not respond to the requests regarding improvement of the measures of safeguard:

> On the basis of a video taken of Mostar Bridge in August [1993], showing damage to the parapets on the north side, and at the request of Mr Tummers, General Rapporteur on the Architectural Heritage, the consultant wrote to Mr Vučina, President of the Cabinet of the Government of Herzegovina, drawing attention to the damage and asking him what steps were being taken to ensure protection of the bridge (18 August). No response was received. Bosnia-Herzegovina Heritage Rescue also published an appeal.[175]

166 Ibid para 80.

167 Ibid para 74.

168 Ibid para 80. See also Bowen testimony in *Naletilić*, above n 31, T 5799.

169 Statement of General Slobodan Praljak, Testimony of defence witness Slobodan Praljak in *Naletilić*, T 9322-9823, 3 April 2002. [Praljak testimony], T 9375. See also hearing of 19 February 2007 in *Prlić*, T 14270.

170 Praljak testimony in *Naletilić*, ibid (emphasis added).

171 Witness QQ testimony, above n 35, 22 November 2001, T 6273. See also testimony of Milivoj Gagro in *Prlić*, 29 May 2006 [Gagro testimony].

172 Salčin testimony, above n 29, 15 February 2007, T 14212.

173 Ibid T 14213.

174 See *Final Report,* above n 39, Appendix IV.c.

175 *Fourth COE Report*, above n 165, Contribution by Dr Kaiser, para 68.

Although the protective measures needed improvement the HVO nevertheless could not (in line with Article 4(5) of the *1954 Convention*) on those grounds evade the obligation to refrain from acts directed at destruction of the Bridge.

Thus, it appears that the Old Bridge was a protected object within the scope of IHL. It enjoyed dual immunity: the protection accorded to civilian objects and that granted to cultural property. Even though it was allegedly not marked with a distinctive sign at the time of its destruction, distinctive marking of the Old Bridge was not compulsory under IHL. Seemingly, the Bridge was not protected adequately against the shelling. Even so, IHL does not absolve any party to the conflict from the duty to respect cultural property if the opposing side has not applied safeguarding measures.

B Was the Old Bridge a Legitimate Military Target?

IHL requires the parties to the conflict to respect cultural property at all times. Only exceptionally, in cases of military necessity, can the duty to respect cultural property be overridden by other considerations such as the protection of troops. In an attempt to justify the destruction of the Old Bridge, the HVO has claimed that it was necessary to target the Bridge because of its strategic position and its use for military purposes by the ABH. But was the Old Bridge really a legitimate military target under IHL on 9 November 1993 and was its destruction truly a military necessity?

Acts against cultural property are prohibited by Article 27 of the *1907 Regulations*,[176] by the *1954 Convention*, notably by its fourth Article, and by Article 53 of *Additional Protocol I*.

Article 27 of the *1907 Regulations* states in its pertinent part:

> In sieges and bombardments all necessary steps must be taken to spare, as far as possible, buildings dedicated to religion, art, science, or charitable purposes, historic monuments, hospitals, and places where the sick and wounded are collected, provided they are not being used at the time for military purposes.[177]

Article 4 of the *1954 Convention*, titled 'Respect for cultural property', demands that the High Contracting Parties:

---

176 Article 56 of the *1907 Regulations* also prohibits acts against cultural property, i.e., seizure of, destruction or wilful damage done to protected objects, but this Article is applicable in occupied territory, i.e., in a situation where the objects listed for protection are under the occupation of the occupying power. Since the attack on the Old Bridge does not appear to be an 'occupied territory' event, Article 56 is irrelevant here.

177 *1907 Regulations*, art 27(1).

1. [...] undertake to respect cultural property situated within their own territory as well as within the territory of other High Contracting Parties by refraining from any use of the property and its immediate surroundings or of the appliances in use for its protection for purposes which are likely to expose it to destruction or damage in the event of armed conflict; and by refraining from any act of hostility directed against such property.
2. The obligations mentioned in paragraph 1 of the present Article may be waived only in cases where military necessity imperatively requires such a waiver.

...

4. They shall refrain from any act directed by way of reprisals against cultural property.[178]

Article 53 of *Additional Protocol I*, called 'Protection of cultural objects and of places of worship', specifies that,

> [w]ithout prejudice to the provisions of the Hague Convention for the Protection of Cultural Property in the Event of Armed Conflict of 14 May 1954, and of other relevant international instruments, it is prohibited:
> (a) to commit any acts of hostility directed against the historic monuments, works of art or places of worship which constitute the cultural or spiritual heritage of peoples;
> (b) to use such objects in support of the military effort;
> (c) to make such objects the object of reprisals.[179]

The *1907 Regulations* protect cultural property if it is not used at the time for military purposes.[180] Further, the *Regulations* allow for the destruction of cultural property during hostilities if that is 'imperatively demanded by the necessities of war'.[181] The *Regulations* neither define the concept of military necessity nor specify the nature of the distinction which is intended by the word 'imperatively'.

The *1954 Convention* emphasises the duty to respect cultural property. This duty comprises the obligation to refrain 'from any use of the property and its immediate surroundings or of the appliances in use for its protection for purposes which are likely to expose it to destruction or damage in the event of

178 *1954 Convention*, art 4(1), (2), (4).

179 *Additional Protocol I*, art 53.

180 Article 27 of the *1907 Regulations* reads in the relevant part: 'provided they are not being used at the time for military purposes'.

181 *1907 Regulations*, art 23(g).

armed conflict'[182] and the obligation to refrain 'from any act of hostility directed against such property'.[183] The Convention stresses that these obligations may be waived only when 'military necessity imperatively requires such a waiver'.[184] This applies to all cultural property, which is under the so-called general protection. Special provisions, which, *inter alia*, envisage the concept of 'unavoidable' military necessity,[185] apply to cultural property under the special protection. Since the Old Bridge was not under special protection, the concept of 'unavoidable' military necessity will not be considered here. Instead, only the provisions pertinent to the respect for cultural property under the general protection will be discussed.

Additional Protocol I prohibits the use of cultural objects 'in support of the military effort'.[186] However, as the Trial Chamber in *Strugar* observed, the *Protocol* makes 'no explicit provision for the consequence of such a use, *i.e.*, whether it affords a justification for acts of hostility against such property'.[187] Moreover, the *Protocol* proscribes acts of hostility directed against cultural objects, but makes no explicit reference to military necessity. However, since the relevant provisions of the *Protocol* are to be applied 'without prejudice' to the provisions of the *1954 Convention*, the *Protocol*, as the *Strugar* Trial Chamber noted, 'may not have affected the operation of the waiver provision of the Convention of 1954 in cases where military necessity imperatively requires waiver'.[188] Since the *1954 Convention*, as the specialist treaty takes primacy in the Old Bridge case, this chapter now turns to a discussion of the provisions of Article 4 of this *Convention*.

1 Respect for Cultural Property

Article 4 of the *1954 Convention*, titled 'Respect for Cultural Property', is the most important article of all the general provisions of the *Convention*. Under this Article States must respect cultural property situated within their own territory as well as property situated within the territory of other States. Article 4 thus provides for the maximum protection of cultural property possible by imposing the responsibility to protect such property during hostilities on both parties to the conflict, namely the holder of cultural property and the attacker of cultural property. Respect for cultural property within the meaning of Article 4 comprises the obligation to refrain from the use of cultural property and its

---

182 *1954 Convention*, art 4(1).

183 Ibid.

184 Ibid art 4(2).

185 Ibid art 11.

186 *Additional Protocol I*, art 53(b).

187 *Strugar* Trial Judgement, para 309.

188 Ibid (italics omitted in original).

immediate surroundings or of the appliances for military purposes, and the obligation to refrain from directing any hostile act against cultural property. These obligations can be waived only on the grounds of imperative military necessity. Respect for cultural property also includes a prohibition on, and, if necessary, a requirement to prevent or stop any form of theft, pillage or misappropriation and any acts of vandalism,[189] as well as a prohibition on acts of reprisal directed against cultural property.[190] The *Convention* does not allow for the exception of military necessity for these acts. This exception applies only to cases involving the use of cultural property for military purposes and hostile acts directed against cultural property. But even then, not any military necessity would justify the attack on cultural objects. To be justifiable, the attack, in accordance with the second paragraph of Article 4, must be 'imperatively' required by military necessity. Accordingly, in the absence of 'imperative' military necessity, a party to the conflict is bound by the obligation to respect cultural property even if such property is being used for military purposes by the opposing party.[191] Before discussing the concept of military necessity within the meaning of Article 4 of the *1954 Convention*, it is necessary to touch upon the two components of the duty to respect cultural property. The first component is the prohibition of the use of cultural property or its surroundings for military purposes and the second component is the prohibition on directing attacks against cultural property.

(a) The Prohibition of the Use of Cultural Property for Military Purposes

With the first prohibition in Article 4 of the *1954 Convention* – the use for military purposes – the distinction should be made between the use of cultural property itself for military purposes and the use of the immediate surroundings of cultural property or of the appliances in use for its protection for purposes which are likely to expose it to destruction or damage in the event of armed conflict. Article 4 of the *1954 Convention* does not specify when cultural property or its surroundings are to be considered to be 'used' for military purposes.

Unlike Article 4 of the *1954 Convention*, Article 53 of *Additional Protocol I* does not mention the use of immediate surroundings of cultural property for military purposes or of the appliances in use for its protection. It limits the prohibition to the 'use [of] such objects in support of the military effort'.[192] The 'military effort' is a very broad concept. It encompasses all military activities connected with the conduct of armed conflict. Support of the military effort can be passive or active. The *ICRC Commentary* notes that in the case of the 'passive'

189 *1954 Convention*, art 4(3).

190 Ibid art 4(4).

191 See, eg, Toman, above n 48, 70.

192 *Additional Protocol I*, art 53(b).

military effort, a party to the conflict benefits from protected objects. So-called 'active' military effort involves the use of such objects, for instance, by including them in a defence position.[193] But, like Article 4 of the *1954 Convention*, Article 53 of *Additional Protocol I* does not itself define the 'use' of cultural property for military purposes or rather the concept of 'support of the military effort'.

Similarly to *Additional Protocol I*, the *1907 Regulations* provide protection to cultural property on the condition that such property is 'not being used at the time for military purposes'.[194] Whereas the *Regulations* refer only to the use of cultural property for military purposes and not to its surroundings or the appliances, they go a step further than the *Protocol*, and Article 4 of the *1954 Convention* for that matter. This is because the *Regulations* specify that it is not the use of cultural property for military purposes at any point in time that is relevant here but only the use 'at the time' concerned. It follows from this that the past use of cultural property for military purposes, or an anticipated future such use, cannot provide justification for an attack.

However, like Article 53 of *Additional Protocol I* and Article 4 of the *1954 Convention*, the *Regulations* are silent on the subject of the definition of 'the use of cultural property for military purposes'. Article 8 of the *1954 Convention* provides some guidance on the subject. Whereas this Article deals with cultural property under special protection, namely centres containing monuments, its provisions regarding the use of cultural property for military purposes can also be applied to other immovable cultural property, including immovable cultural property under general protection. After all, as the Trial Chamber in *Kordić* noted, 'there is little difference between the conditions for the according of general protection and those for the provision of special protection. The fundamental principle is that protection of whatever type will be lost if cultural property ... is used for military purposes, and this principle is consistent with the custom codified in Article 27 of the [1907] Hague Regulations'.[195] Article 8 provides that

> a centre containing monuments shall be deemed to be used for military purposes whenever it is used for the movement of military personnel or material, even in transit. The same shall apply whenever activities directly connected with military operations, the stationing of military personnel, or the production of war material are carried on within the centre.[196]

In accordance with this Article, using a centre containing monuments for the movement of military personnel or material, even in transit, as well as carrying on activities directly connected with military operations, the stationing of

193 See *ICRC Commentary*, above n 3, para 2078.

194 *1907 Regulations*, art 27(1).

195 *Kordić* Trial Judgement, para 362.

196 *1954 Convention*, art 8(3).

military personnel, or the production of war material within the centre are to be considered use for military purposes. In that case, the centre may become a military objective, 'for as long as this violation persists'[197] and, consequently, the opposing party is 'released from the obligation to ensure the immunity of the property concerned'.[198] This temporal limitation is similar to the abovementioned provision of the *1907 Regulations* specifying that protection is provided for cultural property on the condition that it is not being used for military purposes 'at the time' concerned.

Article 4 of the *1954 Convention* is also silent on when the immediate surroundings of cultural property are to be considered to be used for military purposes. As a result, various interpretations of what is to be considered as 'the immediate surroundings' may come into play. Again, an examination of Article 8 dealing with cultural property under special protection could shed some light on this issue. This Article prescribes that cultural property must be

> situated at an adequate distance from any large industrial centre or from any important military objective constituting a vulnerable point, such as, for example, an aerodrome, broadcasting station, establishment engaged upon work of national defence, a port or railway station of relative importance or a main line of communication.[199]

Article 8 further stipulates that cultural property

> situated near an important military objective…may nevertheless be placed under special protection if the High Contracting Party asking for that protection undertakes, in the event of armed conflict, to make no use of the objective and particularly, in the case of a port, railway station or aerodrome, to divert all traffic therefrom. In that event, such diversion shall be prepared in time of peace.[200]

However, neither the *Convention* nor its *Regulations* specifies the meaning of an 'adequate distance'. As Nahlik notes, this can only be assessed on a case by case basis.[201] In reality, however, many great monuments and museums of undisputable world importance[202] are situated within 'large industrial centres' or in their

---

197 Ibid art 11(1).

198 Ibid.

199 Ibid art 8(1)(a).

200 Ibid art 8(5).

201 See, eg, Stanislav Nahlik, 'Protection of Cultural Property' in UNESCO, *International Dimensions of Humanitarian Law* (1988) 208 ['Protection']; Toman, above n 48, 101.

202 See Patrick Boylan, *Review of the Convention for the Protection of Cultural Property in the Event of Armed Conflict* (1993), 76, para 6.4 [*Review*].

vicinity. The proximity of cultural property to military objectives also poses a problem. Because of the practical difficulties involved, States are reluctant to declare that military objectives in the vicinity of cultural property will not be used in the event of armed conflict. The problem of the use of the immediate surroundings of cultural property for military purposes has been addressed in the ICTY jurisprudence. In interpreting Article 3(d) of the *ICTY Statute*, the *Blaškić* Trial Chamber held that

> [t]he damage or destruction must have been committed intentionally to institutions which may clearly be identified as dedicated to religion or education and which were not being used for military purposes at the time of the acts. In addition, the institutions *must not have been in the immediate vicinity of military objectives*.[203]

Because of the specific charges in this case, the *Blaškić* Trial Judgement refers to institutions dedicated to religion or education. However, given that Article 3(d) of the *ICTY Statute* also covers some components of cultural property, it would follow from this that the same reasoning is applicable to such property. The *Naletilić* Trial Judgement rejected the conclusion in *Blaškić* that, in order to be protected, the institutions mentioned therein must not have been located in the immediate vicinity of military objectives.[204] The Trial Chamber in *Naletilić* declared:

> The Chamber respectfully rejects that protected institutions 'must not have been in the vicinity of military objectives'. The Chamber does not concur with the view that the mere fact that an institution is in the 'immediate vicinity of military objective' justifies its destruction.[205]

The *Naletilić* Trial Chamber noted that '[t]his conclusion follows from Article 27 of the [1907] Hague Regulations',[206] thereby highlighting its customary law nature. The Trial Chamber in *Strugar* emphasised 'the established jurisprudence of the Tribunal confirming the "military purposes" exception[[207]] which is consistent with the exceptions recognised by the *Hague Regulations of 1907* and the *Additional Protocols*'.[208] This Chamber noted that 'the protection accorded to cultural property is lost where such property is used for military purposes'.[209] With

203 *Blaškić* Trial Judgement, para 185 (emphasis added).
204 See *Naletilić* Trial Judgement, para 604.
205 Ibid.
206 Ibid fn 1484.
207 *Strugar* Trial Judgement, para 310.
208 Ibid (italics added).
209 Ibid.

respect to the differences between the *Blaškić* and *Naletilić* Trial Judgements regarding the use of the immediate surroundings of cultural property for military purposes, the *Strugar* Trial Chamber instructed that

> the preferable view appears to be that it is the *use* of cultural property and not its *location* that determines whether and when the cultural property would lose its protection.[210]

This Chamber explained that because Article 27 of the *1907 Regulations* explicitly refers to 'in sieges and bombardments', 'it is not because of the location of cultural property, but because of their use when cultural property loses its protection'.[211] To reinforce its view, the *Strugar* Trial Chamber pointed to the *1999 Protocol*, the relevant provisions of which make it clear that the protection of cultural property is waived 'when and for as long as (i) that cultural property has, by its function [and not by its location], been made into a military objective'.[212] Consequently, in the *Strugar* Trial Chamber's view, 'the special protection awarded to cultural property itself may not be lost simply because of military activities or military installations in the immediate vicinity of the cultural property'.[213] Nevertheless, the Chamber warned that in such a case 'the practical result may be that it cannot be established that the acts which caused destruction of or damage to cultural property were "directed against" that cultural property, rather than the military installation or use in its immediate vicinity'.[214]

(b) The Prohibition of an Attack

In accordance with Article 4(1) of the *1954 Convention*, it is prohibited to direct any act of hostility against cultural property. It would follow from this that not only are attacks which result in actual destruction of or damage to cultural property prohibited but 'any' attack directed against cultural property is to be considered a breach of this provision of the *1954 Convention*. As noted, a similar prohibition is contained in Article 53 of *Additional Protocol I*.

Unlike the *1954 Convention*, *Additional Protocol I* provides a definition of attacks. Article 49 of the *Protocol* defines 'attacks' as 'acts of violence against the

---

210 Ibid (emphasis added).

211 Ibid fn 957.

212 Ibid (referring to Article 6 of the *1999 Protocol*). For discussion of the relevance of the 'use' of cultural property for military purposes and not the 'location' of cultural property see, Jean-Marie Henckaerts, 'New Rules for the Protection of Cultural Property in Armed Conflict' (1999) No. 835 *International Review of the Red Cross* 593 ['New Rules'].

213 *Strugar* Trial Judgement, para 310.

214 Ibid.

adversary, whether in offence or in defence'.[215] An act of hostility involves any act arising from the conflict which has or can have a substantial detrimental effect on cultural property. Article 49 further stipulates that the provisions of the *Protocol* relating to attacks 'apply to all attacks in whatever territory conducted, including the national territory belonging to a Party to the conflict but under the control of an adverse party'.[216] Also, those provisions 'apply to any land, air or sea warfare which may affect the civilian population, individual civilians or civilian objects on land'.[217]

The prohibition of attack in both the *1954 Convention* and in *Additional Protocol I* is expressed in stricter terms than that given in Article 27 of the *1907 Regulations*. Whereas the *Convention* obligates the High Contracting Parties to 'refrain from any act of hostility' directed against cultural property and *Additional Protocol I* states that 'it is prohibited to commit' any acts of hostility against cultural property, Article 27 of the *1907 Regulations* simply requires States 'to spare, as far as possible' the protected property. Furthermore, Article 56 of the *Regulations* prohibits all seizure of, destruction or wilful damage 'done' to the protected property. For a violation of this Article to occur it is necessary that the seizure has taken place or that there has been actual destruction or damage to the protected objects.

(c) The Exception of Military Necessity

The protection of cultural property in armed conflict within the meaning of Article 4 of the *1954 Convention* is not absolute. The prohibition on the use of cultural property and its immediate surroundings for military purposes and the prohibition on directing acts of hostility against cultural property may be waived. However, such a waiver may occur only in cases of imperative military necessity. In keeping with the fundamental postulate of IHL, the reservation of military necessity in the *1954 Convention* strikes a balance between humanitarian requirements and military necessity and demands. The reservation of military necessity has a long history; it was included in other international instruments long before the *1954 Convention*. For instance, Article 14 of the *1863 Lieber Code* stresses that '[m]ilitary necessity, as understood in modern civilized nations, consists in the necessity of those measures which are indispensable for securing the ends of war, and which are lawful according to the modern law and usages of war'.[218] Those measures allow, *inter alia*, '*all* destruc-

215 *Additional Protocol I*, art 49(1).

216 Ibid art 49(2).

217 Ibid art 49(3).

218 *Instructions for the Government of Armies of the United States in the Field*, prepared by Francis Lieber, promulgated as General Order No. 100 by President Abraham Lincoln, Washington DC, 24 April 1863, art 14 [*Lieber Code*]. For a definition of military necessity, see also Pietro Vierri, *Dictionary of the International Law of*

tion of property',[219] thus including cultural property. Furthermore, Article 23(g) of the *1907 Regulations* specifically forbids destruction or seizure of the enemy's property 'unless such destruction or seizure [is] *imperatively* demanded by the necessities of war'.[220] This is in line with the assertion that '[t]he right of belligerents to adopt means of injuring the enemy is not unlimited'.[221]

Unlike its predecessors, the *1954 Convention* does not contain a general reservation of military necessity stated in a preambular text. Whereas the Preamble to *1899 Convention (II)* states that the wording of the provisions of this *Convention* 'has been inspired by the desire to *diminish the evils of war so far as military necessities permit*',[222] and the Preamble to *1907 Convention (IV)* makes similar reference to '*military requirements*',[223] the Preamble to the *1954 Convention* does not contain a like phrase. Military necessity is only referred to in Article 4(2) and in the relevant article dealing with special protection of cultural property.[224] In fact, modern international law in general does not embody a general reservation of military necessity. As Toman explains, as far as treaty IHL is concerned, military necessity may only be invoked when the text of a rule of international law is drafted and when the reservation of military necessity is expressly referred to in the text of the rule of international law.[225] The reservation of military necessity cannot be invoked in other cases and treaties must be respected in all circumstances. It should be noted that the above reference to military necessity in a preambular text of *1899 Convention (II)* and *1907 Convention (IV)*, and the absence of such reservation in the Preamble to the *1954 Convention*, does not imply that military necessity is placed 'instead' in Article 4 of the *1954 Convention*. Like the *1954 Convention* (with its Article 4), the *1899 Convention* and the *1907 Convention* contain articles specifically qualified by 'military necessity', including Article 23(g), mentioned in the preceding paragraph. Reference to military necessity in a preambular text does not have the same significance and effect as an express rule.[226]

Notwithstanding this, although the text of the rule concerning military necessity is expressly referred to in Article 4(2) of the *1954 Convention*, the *1954*

Armed Conflict, ICRC (1992) 75 (according to which 'military necessity, in its wider sense, means doing what is necessary to achieve war aims').

219 *Lieber Code*, art 15 (emphasis added).

220 *1907 Regulations*, art 23(g) (emphasis added).

221 Ibid art 22.

222 *1899 Convention (II)*, Preamble para 6 (emphasis added).

223 *1907 Convention (IV)*, Preamble para 5 (emphasis added).

224 See *1954 Convention*, art 11(2).

225 Toman, above n 48, 73.

226 While preambles are constitutive parts of the text of treaties, they do not represent binding law as an express rule but rather, as context, provide useful interpretative guidance.

Convention does not define the concept of 'imperative military necessity'. The lack of clear meaning of the concept of military necessity may create problems in practice and can have fatal consequences for cultural property. As the Allied Supreme Commander in Europe during World War II, General Dwight D Eisenhower observed in his Staff Orders of 29 December 1943 concerning the Mediterranean Theatre, the concept of military necessity can be very elastic.[227] While pointing to the supreme necessity to spare the lives of combatants, General Eisenhower warned that the defence of 'military necessity' should not be read too broadly:

> If we have to choose between destroying a famous building and sacrificing our own men, then our men's lives count infinitely more and the buildings must go. But the choice is not always so clear-cut as that. In many cases the monuments can be spared without any detriment to operational needs. Nothing can stand against the argument of military necessity. That is an accepted principle. But the phrase 'military necessity' is sometimes used where it would be more truthful to speak of military convenience or even of personal convenience. I do not want it to cloak slackness or indifference.[228]

Despite these clear directions to respect and preserve cultural property, the Allied forces failed to spare the Abbey of Monte Cassino, one of the oldest and most significant of European cultural sites.[229] The Allied forces sought to justify the bombing of Monte Cassino and its reduction to rubble by asserting the claim of military necessity. However, they have been widely criticised for this deliberate destruction of cultural property.[230]

The alleged use of cultural property or its surroundings for military purposes by the opposing party has been one of the standard grounds for invoking military necessity by the attacking party during the Balkan conflicts.[231] The shelling of Dubrovnik which occurred on 6 December 1991 is a powerful example of the 'flexibility' of the term 'military necessity'. In this instance, it was claimed that the opposing party used cultural property for military purposes. The alleged use was automatically translated by the attacking party into military necessity to attack irrespective of whether cultural property was actually so

227 Staff Orders issued by the Commander-in-Chief of the Allied Forces, General Eisenhower on 29 December 1943, American Commission for the Protection and Salvage of Artistic and Historic Monuments in War Areas, *Report 48* (1946) [*1946 Report*] 48 (quoted in John Merryman, 'Two Ways of Thinking about Cultural Property' (1986) 80 *American Journal of International Law* 831, 839 ['Two Ways'], and in Boylan, *Review*, above n 202, 55 para 4.9).

228 *1946 Report* ibid.

229 See Merryman, 'Two Ways', above n 227, 839.

230 Ibid. See also Boylan, *Review*, above n 202, 36, para 2.44.

231 See, eg, *1995 Periodic Reports*, above n 76; *Strugar* Trial Judgement, para 182.

used, or whether the alleged use could pose a significant threat to the attacking party. In the *Strugar* case, the Defence claimed that on 6 December 1991 the Croatian forces had their firing positions and heavy weapons within the walls of the Old Town of Dubrovnik and in its immediate vicinity, and that the YA forces were merely responding to fire coming from those positions. However, evidence revealed that there were no such positions or weapons within the Old Town.[232] In the *Strugar* Trial Chamber's view, '[e]ven if…some or all firing positions or heavy weapons referred to in the evidence…was believed to exist in the Old Town or on its walls, the evidence discloses that they were *not* treated as *posing any significant threat* to the [Y]A forces on the day'.[233]

The *Strugar* Trial Chamber followed similar reasoning in relation to the alleged use of the Old Town's vicinity for military purposes. The Chamber found that the evidence indicated that some of the alleged Croatian military positions 'within 500 metres of the Old Town' were not known to the YA on the day or, if known, were not considered worthy of serious attention.[234] The *Strugar* Trial Chamber found that there were no Croatian firing positions or heavy weapons in the Old Town or on its walls on 6 December 1991,[235] and that, consequently, the shelling of the Old Town on the day 'was not a [Y]A response at Croatian firing or other military positions, actual or believed, in the Old Town'.[236]

A sharp contrast with the practices in the Balkans armed conflicts in the 1990s is provided by the approach of the Allied forces to military necessity relating to cultural property during the 1991 'Desert Storm' campaign. Although it was revealed that the Iraqi forces located anti-aircraft defences on the fortification of Ninevah and placed two MiG aircraft inside the walls of Ur, US-led Allied forces refrained from attacking these objects of outstanding cultural significance as commanders recognised that these Iraqi positions did not pose a significant threat to the Allied forces.[237] In the earlier Second Indo-China (Vietnam) War, the High Command also declared the historic zone of Angkor Wat in Cambodia to be absolutely 'off limits' in aerial and land operations, and in a similar way protected the historic Citadel at Hué, in Vietnam.[238]

Under Article 4(2) of the *1954 Convention*, not only can the attacking party invoke military necessity when cultural property is being used for military purposes by the opposing party, but the actual use of cultural property for military purposes may be allowed where imperatively required by military necessity. One of the recent examples of claiming military necessity on these grounds is

232 *Strugar*, ibid paras 202-203.

233 Ibid para 194 (emphasis added).

234 Ibid para 209.

235 Ibid para 193.

236 Ibid para 214.

237 See Boylan, *Review*, above n 202, 105, para 11.9.

238 Ibid 104-105, para 11.8.

the use of the spiral minaret of the nearly twelve centuries-old al-Mutawakkil mosque in Samarra, Iraq, by American armed forces as a sniper post in February 2005. Reportedly, the positioning of US army snipers at the top of the 172 foot high minaret[239] has drastically reduced the number of roadside bombs targeting military vehicles.[240] However, the use of this structure of outstanding historic and architectural importance for military purposes raises concerns for its safety as such a use has drawn the fire of Iraqi insurgents causing damage to the mosque.[241] According to US military spokesman Major Richard Goldenberg, the US presence on the minaret was merely observational and 'the value of safeguarding innocent Iraqis and [Coalition] security force partners, when considered in total, must take precedence'.[242]

The case of the Samarra Minaret exemplifies the complexity involved in subordinating the protection of cultural property to the vagueness of military necessity in Article 4(2) of the *1954 Convention*. The case raises the two interrelated questions of whether the use of the minaret by the US was required by military necessity, and whether the attack which was likely on the minaret by the opponent of the US in order to remove the threat posed by the positioning of snipers on the minaret could be justified by military necessity. As Article 4(2) allows for the waiver of the obligations to refrain from using cultural property and its surroundings for military purposes and from directing any act of hostility against that property 'only in cases where military necessity imperatively requires such a waiver', in this instance, both parties would need to prove the existence of 'imperative' military necessity.

However, the difficulty is that Article 4(2) does not make it clear when military necessity is to be qualified as 'imperative'. This Article does not provide any details as to when and for how long the use of cultural property for military purposes or the attack on that property is to be regarded as constituting imperative military necessity, at what command level the decision to invoke imperative military necessity is to be taken, and whether there are any other additional requirements to be fulfilled by the party concerned. However, even if the use of the minaret turns it into a possible military target, the right to attack is still not unlimited. In accordance with Article 52 of *Additional Protocol I*, attacks must be limited strictly to military objectives.[243] If the minaret becomes a military objec-

---

239 Lucian Harris, 'US Snipers on Samarra's Spiral Minaret', *The Art Newspaper*, London, Friday, 25 February 2005, http://www.theartnewspaper.com/news/article.asp?idart=11727 [1].

240 Ibid [2].

241 Ibid [4], [5], [6].

242 Ibid [10].

243 See *Additional Protocol I*, art 52(2).

tive, the principle of proportionality[244] must be respected and other precautionary measures must be taken.[245]

By stating that the value of safeguarding human lives must take precedence over the protection of cultural property, Major Goldenberg echoed General Eisenhower's words that the 'lives' of members of the Allied forces 'count infinitely more than buildings'. To some military commanders, preventing 'any' kind of danger to which their soldiers might be exposed, and not merely saving soldiers' lives, is worth sacrificing cultural objects no matter how significant they may be. For instance, General Praljak has stated that he would be prepared 'to destroy hundreds of *[O]ld [B]ridges* for the sake of one little finger of his soldier'.[246]

In contrast, there are those who believe that the preservation of cultural property of outstanding importance should be paramount even if it involves sacrificing the most valued human life. Sir Harold Nicolson argued that works of major artistic value should be preserved from destruction even if their preservation entails the sacrifice of human life:

> I should assuredly be prepared to be shot against a wall if I were certain that by such a sacrifice I could preserve the Giotto frescoes; nor should I hesitate for an instant (were such a decision ever open to me) to save St Mark's even if I were aware that by so doing I should bring death to my sons…. My attitude would be governed by a principle which is surely incontrovertible. The irreplaceable is more important than the replaceable, and the loss of even the most valued human life is ultimately less disastrous than the loss of something which in no circumstances can ever be created again.[247]

By contrast, in Merryman's view it is not surprising that military necessity can justify the destruction of cultural property when military necessity sometimes justifies the denial or limitation of the constitutionally guaranteed rights of individuals.[248] Still, in the opinion of some commentators, except in very limited instances where there is no other choice but to sacrifice cultural property in order to save human lives, there are always alternatives which allow cultural property to be avoided.[249]

---

244 Ibid arts 51(5)(b), 57(2)(a)(iii) and 57(2)(b).

245 Ibid arts 57 and 58.

246 Đikić, above n 1 (emphasis added).

247 Sir Harold Nicolson, 'Marginal Comments' *Spectator* 25 February 1944 (quoted in Merryman, 'Two Ways', above n 227, 840), reprinted in full in John Merryman and Albert Elsen, *Law, Ethics and the Visual Arts* 1-2 (4th ed, 2003).

248 Merryman, 'Two Ways', ibid 841, fn 34.

249 See Jean-Marie Henckaerts, 'The Significance of the Second Protocol to the 1954 Hague Convention for the Protection of Cultural Property in the Event of Armed Conflict' (1999) No. 835 *International Review of the Red Cross* 593, para on

There are also critics who question the concept of military necessity altogether.[250] In their view, unique objects of great cultural value should not be legally sacrificed to the ends of armed conflict.[251] Nahlik implies that military necessity is an outdated concept. He points to the origins of inclusion of the clause on military necessity into provisions of international instruments dealing with cultural property, noting that in 1899, when wars were considered lawful, the German delegation insisted on inserting not only a 'necessity of war' clause into Article 23(g) of *1899 Convention (II)* dealing with the destruction or seizure of the enemy's property, but also (as discussed) a general clause concerning 'military necessity' into paragraph 6 of the Preamble to the *Convention*.[252] Both these clauses were accepted, though reluctantly, by the other States in order not to discourage Germany from becoming a party to the *Convention*, and later the clauses passed almost automatically into Article 23(g) of *1907 Convention (IV)* and into paragraph 5 of the Preamble to this *Convention*. However, since then, the *UN Charter* has outlawed war,[253] and the idea that cultural property belongs to all humankind has been accepted. Consequently, in Nahlik's view, the reservation of military necessity in the *1954 Convention* is inappropriate.[254] Merryman, too, finds the concession to military necessity inconsistent with the premises of the *1954 Convention*: '"the cultural heritage of all [hu]mankind" is put at the mercy of the relatively parochial interests of certain belligerents'.[255] But, as Merryman observes, since we live in the world of 'national' States, and these States are parties to an 'international' convention, 'this is perhaps unsurprising and may be unavoidable'.[256]

Nevertheless, to avoid tragic consequences as a result of the 'elasticity' of the concept of military necessity for the cultural heritage of all humankind, the High Contracting Parties have been urged to reconsider the *Convention's* provisions pertinent to military necessity. In his 1993 *Review of the Convention for the Protection of Cultural Property in the Event of Armed Conflict*, Professor Boylan strongly recommended that in any revision of the *1954 Convention* or in any new additional protocol to it, 'High Contracting Parties should *renounce* the provisions of Article 4(2) allowing the waiving of the provisions of the Convention in

imperative military necessity, p 3 of the printed version, http://www.icrc.org/Web/eng/siteengo.nsf/iwpList260/ ['The Significance of the Second Protocol'].

250 See Stanislav Nahlik, 'International Law and the Protection of Cultural Property in Armed Conflict' (1976) 27 *Hastings Law Journal* 1069, 1070 ['International Law'].

251 Ibid.

252 Ibid 1084-1085.

253 The use of force is only legal in self-defence.

254 Nahlik, 'International Law', above n 250, 1069-1070.

255 Merryman, 'Two Ways', above n 227, 841.

256 Ibid.

the case of military necessity'.[257] Unsurprisingly, the concept of military necessity was one of the most hotly debated issues during the review process. High Contracting Parties did not renounce the provisions of Article 4(2) concerning the waiver of imperative military necessity. However, as is discussed in the final chapter of this book, the review of the *1954 Convention* resulted in the *1999 Protocol*, which substantially clarified and strengthened Article 4(2) of this *Convention*.

In contrast to Article 4 of the *1954 Convention*, Article 53 of *Additional Protocol I* (*Protocol Additional to the 1949 Geneva Conventions*) does not envisage the exception of military necessity. However, where the Parties to the *Protocol* are also Parties to the *1954 Convention*, the military necessity exception applies because the Convention takes primacy over the *Protocol*. Notwithstanding this, an attack may never be launched against an objective which is not a military objective in the sense of the *Protocol*. As with a violation of Article 4 of the *1954 Convention*, a violation of Article 53 of *Additional Protocol I* does not automatically give the opposing party the green light to attack cultural objects. In accordance with Article 52 of *Additional Protocol I*, which distinguishes between civilian objects and military objectives, civilian objects must not be made the object of attack. To restate, civilian objects are all objects which are not military objectives. Since cultural objects are essentially civilian objects, they must be exempt from an attack. As the *ICRC Commentary* notes, to the extent that the right to attack these objects of exceptional value exists, such a right would depend on their being a military objective.[258] In so far as objects are concerned, military objectives are defined as

> objects which by their nature, location, purpose or use make an effective contribution to military action and whose total or partial destruction, capture or neutralisation, in the circumstances ruling at the time, offers a definite military advantage.[259]

Under Article 52(2) of *Additional Protocol I*, the mere use of a cultural object or a place of worship does not make it a military objective. To be deemed so, the use of the protected object must make an 'effective' contribution to military action. Also, total or partial destruction, capture or neutralisation of such object must offer a 'definite' military advantage, in the circumstances ruling 'at the time'. These conditions must be fulfilled cumulatively and must apply to the time of a given military action and not to the use of the protected object in support of the military effort (or, to use the language of the *1954 Convention*, for military purposes) at some time in the past or to its anticipated use at a time in the future.

---

257 Boylan, *Review*, above n 202, 57, para 4.15 (emphasis added).

258 *ICRC Commentary*, above n 3, para 2079.

259 Ibid.

Accordingly, 'it is not permitted to destroy a cultural object whose use does not make any contribution to military action, nor a cultural object which has temporarily served as a refuge for combatants, but is no longer used as such'.[260] Since the rule of limiting attacks to military objectives is part of customary international law,[261] the provisions of Article 52, including the definition of military objectives, also apply when the *1954 Convention* takes primacy, as it does in the present case. As observed in the *ICRC Commentary*, this is an important development in the protection of cultural property as Article 52 of *Additional Protocol I* in effect limits the scope of derogations allowed by the vagueness of the provisions relating to the exception of military necessity in Article 4 of the *1954 Convention*.[262]

The requirement to abide by the rule of limiting an attack strictly to military objectives is reinforced by the obligation that constant care must be taken to spare the civilian population, civilians and civilian objects in the conduct of military operations.[263] With respect to attacks, a range of precautionary measures must be taken. These measures are spelt out in Article 57 of *Additional Protocol I*.[264] In addition to precautions in attack, the parties to the conflict must also take precautions against the effects of attacks, as provided for in Article 58 of *Additional Protocol I*. Therefore, IHL provides for a range of safeguards in protecting cultural property. When combined they make it almost impossible for a cultural object to become a legitimate military target. Did the HVO abide by these safeguards on 8 and 9 November 1993 when it targeted and destroyed the Old Bridge?

2 Respect or Disrespect for the Old Bridge?

Allegations have been made that the Old Bridge and its surroundings were used for military purposes. It has been contended that the ABH had its posi-

260 Ibid.

261 See, eg, *Strugar* Trial Chamber Decision on Jurisdiction, paras 17-21; *Strugar* Appeals Chamber Decision on Jurisdiction, para 9; *Strugar* Trial Judgement, para 223; *Prosecutor v Duško Tadić aka 'Dule'*, Decision on the Defence Motion for Interlocutory Appeal on Jurisdiction, Appeals Chamber, 2 October 1995, Case No. IT-94-1-AR72 para 127 [*Tadić* Jurisdiction Decision]; Jean-Marie Henckaerts and Louise Doswald-Beck (eds), *Customary International Humanitarian Law* (2005) vol I *Rules*, vol II *Practice*, Chapter 12: Cultural Property, 723 *et seq* [*Customary IHL*].

262 The ICTY uses the definition of military objective when referring to military necessity. For instance, in *Strugar*, the Trial Chamber 'is of the view that military necessity may be usefully defined…with reference to the widely acknowledged definition of military objectives in Article 52 of Additional Protocol I'. *Strugar* Trial Judgement, para 295.

263 See *Additional Protocol I*, art 57.

264 Ibid art 57(2),(3).

tions near the Bridge, and that the Bridge was used by the ABH for the movement of its military personnel and for transport of ammunition and food. In a radio interview conducted a few years after the destruction of the Old Bridge, General Praljak contended that the Bridge was a military object because it was, *inter alia*, used for crossing the river. According to the General, when cultural objects are being so used then such objects lose their protection. '[I]f there is shooting from a church tower, then that is not a church anymore but a machine-gun post',[265] in the opinion of the General. Also, it seems that to this General it is the original purpose of an object that matters and whether such an object also constitutes cultural property is completely irrelevant. For example, he suggested that since '[t]he walls surrounding the Old Town of Dubrovnik were built for the purpose of defending people',[266] they could also be used for defensive purposes in 1991. With regard to the Old Bridge, the very function of the Bridge – as a means of communication – made it a military objective. In the General's view there is no honourable commander who would not knock down a bridge in order to save lives of their soldiers.[267] In this context, his claim can be noted that he lost two HVO soldiers on the Old Bridge when the scaffolding was to be made to physically protect the Bridge against the shooting.[268]

However, as Sefer Halilović, a former commander of the ABH (and General Praljak's co-interviewee in the same interview), correctly observed, the Old Bridge was a protected object, from which no one was shooting. Although he agrees that the life of a soldier is of the utmost value both in times of armed conflict and in peacetime, in Halilović's view, 'there was no need for destruction of the Old Bridge because this Bridge was not a military objective'.[269]

The loss of soldiers' lives when erecting the scaffolding referred to by General Praljak occurred in 1992 when the HVO and ABH were fighting together against the YA forces. The incident does not have any significance with respect to the allegation that the Old Bridge was a military objective on 8 and 9 November 1993 when the Bridge was targeted and destroyed.

With regard to the contention that the ABH used the Bridge for crossing over to the other bank of the Neretva, there is no information as when that took place. To reiterate, a use of cultural property for military purposes that occurred at some time in the past does not turn cultural property into a military objective. It is 'the circumstances ruling *at the time*'[270] that matter. In the *Prlić* trial, during the cross-examination of the witness Salčin, the accused General Praljak attempted to argue that the ABH had combat positions in the area of

265 Radio-Most, above n 1.

266 Ibid.

267 Ibid.

268 Ibid.

269 Ibid.

270 *Additional Protocol I*, art 52(2) (emphasis added).

the Old Bridge and reiterated his claim that the Bridge was used for military purposes.[271] The witness did not deny that the area surrounding the Old Bridge on the left bank of the Neretva was under ABH control[272] but claimed that ABH combat positions were actually on the right bank.[273]

Contrary to assertions that the Old Bridge was the only remaining bridge over the Neretva at the time, the witness noted that there were two other, make-shift bridges located not far away from the Old Bridge, one on its northern side (the Bunur Bridge) and the other on its southern side (the Kamenica Bridge).[274] The accused contended that the ABH used the Old Bridge and the Kamenica Bridge for military purposes, including the transport of ammunition and food.

> Q. Both bridges were used by the [ABH] soldiers, amongst others, is that correct? The ammunition was being transported across the bridges?
> A. Yes.
> Q. Food as well?
> A. Yes.
> Q. Can we then conclude that, using the military terminology, both bridges were used for the purposes of the war on the part of the [ABH]?
> A. Yes, sir.[275]

The accused further stressed that both the Old Bridge and the Kamenica Bridge were standing intact during the entire conflict despite the proximity of the HVO positions overlooking the area, suggesting that if the HVO wanted to destroy the Old Bridge it could have done so at any time.

> Q. We had a witness here whom I asked the following question: If the HVO controlled Stotina, if that is the case, and it did, it did control Stotina, and if there was a tank up there, how come they did not destroy the Kamenica Bridge and...prevented the supplies coming to the BH army?
> A. I don't know, sir.
> Q. There was another question: Throughout the months how come that the HVO didn't do that with the Old Bridge as well?
> A. I wouldn't know, sir.[276]

---

271 Proceedings in *Prlić*, 15 February 2007, T 14239-14265.

272 Ibid T 14240.

273 Ibid T 14240-14242.

274 Ibid T 14250-14252.

275 Ibid T 14252.

276 Ibid T 14253-14254.

The accused put forward the hypothesis that the HVO did not destroy the Old Bridge but rather that an explosive charge was placed under the Bridge, and it exploded:

> the act of the destruction of the Bridge was not the result of a hit by a tank grenade but an explosive that had been placed on the Bridge and which was detonated from the left bank of the Neretva River.[277]

This hypothesis provoked the following angry response by this witness:

> No, sir. No, General, sir. No, General, sir, no. You needn't tell me about morals. You don't know what bombs and mines and shrapnel mean. No, General, sir. You can take me out of the courtroom dead, but this is a lie. Slavuj 150, 150 howitzers. I have them in my yard. I have the shells in my yard. I didn't bring them into court. They were the shells that destroyed my house too. No, General, sir. I'll stay here for a month, but I say no, no, and no, and you can take me out of here dead. This is nonsense. Are you going to teach me technology? I worked in the aviation industry for 20 years. I'm not going to allow you to do that. You can check out what I've said....270 of my soldiers were killed. This is no doctor. He's got a diploma, but he should be hung from the Bridge. He's no expert. He's no professional. And I have two grenades, two shells that I can show you. I hid them and I have them in safekeeping. I'll bring them in on Monday. Fourteen and a half kilogrammes it was, and it hit...the SpaBat of UNPROFOR received those shells and we listed the places where they were found unexploded.[278]

Whereas General Praljak claims that the ABH did use the Old Bridge in support of military effort but argues that it was not the HVO but rather the Muslims themselves who destroyed the Bridge, the late Croatian President Franjo Tuđman blamed the war-time purpose of the Bridge for its destruction.[279] In President Tuđman's view it was to be deplored that the Bridge as a 'structure for communication' was destroyed 'under war-time conditions'.[280] The phrase 'under war-time conditions' implies an absence of responsibility on the

277 Ibid T 14262.

278 Ibid T 14262-14263.

279 See, eg, Letter from Professor Biserka Nagy, Advisor to President Tuđman to Leni Fischer, Chairperson of the Committee on Culture and Education, Parliamentary Assembly COE, 25 November 1993, *Fourth COE Report*, above n 14 (emphasis added) [Nagy Letter].

280 Statement of President Tuđman, quoted in Letter from Baron Janko Vranyczany-Dobrinović, Ambassador of Croatia in Brussels, to Jonkheer Daniel Cardon de Lichtbuer, Executive President of Europa Nostra, 9 December 1993, *Fourth COE Report*, above n 165 [Baron Vranyczany-Dobrinović Letter].

part of Croatia and the HVO. Nevertheless, with respect to the latter, President Tuđman stated that he 'sent a demand to the people in the leadership of Herceg-Bosna to examine why this occurred and that those who did this should be held accountable'.[281]

There is ample evidence pointing to the HVO's involvement in the destruction of the Old Bridge and which underscores the allegations made by the HVO itself that the Bridge was destroyed because of its strategic importance and because it was used by the opposing party as a means of communication. According to the Prosecution in the *Prlić* case, a report by HVO commander Miljenko Lasić of 9 November 1993 notified the Main Staff of the HVO that 'some fifty tank shells had been fired from the HVO position on Stotina, in the direction of the Old Town and that the Old Bridge had been destroyed that morning'.[282] Reportedly, on the same day, Veso Vegar, a spokesperson for the HVO, admitted that the HVO's 'gunners had targeted the [B]ridge'.[283] Consistent with the HVO spokesperson's statement, the destruction of the Bridge was justified on the grounds of the Bridge's strategic importance:

> Since the [B]ridge is in a place that is strategically important and the Muslim positions are very near, 70 to 100 meters, the [B]ridge has constantly been shelled.[284]

As stated by Vegar, Croats fired ten shells at the span on Monday, 8 November 1993 alone. The following day sixty shells hit the structure.[285]

The hypothesis espoused by General Praljak is further undermined by the fact that the Mostar District Court conducted an investigation into the three members of the HVO – Tomo Topić, Dragan Rezić and Senaid Carčić – who were the crew of the tank that allegedly fired projectiles which destroyed the Old Bridge,[286] and also by the fact that an employee of the Zagreb-based Institute for the Protection of Monuments filed a suit against one of the crew members involved in the incident in which the Old Bridge was 'deliberately fired upon by Croat tanks'.[287]

---

281 Ibid.

282 Sense News Agency, 'Destruction of Old Bridge Seen from Two Angles' 17 May 2007, http://www.sense-agency.com/en/stream.php?sta=3&pid=9676&kat=3 [5].

283 Chuck Sudetić, 'Croatians Destroy Historic Ottoman Bridge in Bosnia', New York Times News Service, 9 November 1993, http://www.members.tripod.com/~UnconqueredBosnia/Mostar3.html [4].

284 Ibid [5].

285 Ibid [5] and [6].

286 See, eg, *Večernji List*, 23 May 2001, http://www.hic.hr/hrvatski/vijesti/arhiv/latest/BiH- POLITIKA_23_5_2001 [1].

287 Ephemera Wired News, 'Bridge Rebuilding', 30 July 1998, http://www.wired.com/news/meanwhile/0,1252,0-1998~7,00.html (Copy on file with author). See

Returning to the claim of use for military purposes, reportedly, the Old Bridge was used by the Muslim side in the conflict, by both the military and the civilian segments: the former 'to take up their positions on the battle lines on the western side of the river' and the latter 'to cross the [B]ridge to the Muslim-controlled east bank, where they could fill plastic containers with drinking water'.[288] Philip Watson, former European Community monitor in Bosnia and Herzegovina, testified in the *Prlić* trial that the accused General Praljak let him know that 'a military solution'[289] had to be achieved in Bosnia and Herzegovina. To realise the solution, among other things, 'the humanitarian aid convoys had to be stopped and power and water supply for the enemy troops had to be cut'.[290]

However, '[t]he enemy troops' could not 'be cut' off without greatly affecting the civilian population in the area under the control of the ABH. Such an area, including the Old City precinct, was, and still is, a densely populated residential area. A number of witnesses have told the ICTY that many ABH soldiers defending the surroundings of the Old Bridge resided there. They actually defended their homes.[291] For instance, Enes Vukotić, the Prosecution witness in *Prlić*, did not dispute the presence of the ABH in Donja Mahala, the neighbourhood in the vicinity of the Old Bridge.[292] He asserted that people who defended this neighbourhood, including himself, were the residents of the area.

Because this area of East Mostar was 'heavily populated with civilians',[293] and the military was mixed with the civilians, this suggests that it was difficult for the HVO to distinguish between civilian and military. This is especially so because of the variety of uniforms worn by ABH members. A number of witnesses testified before the ICTY that the ABH had very limited resources and that its members wore all kinds of clothing, ranging from civilian to mis-

---

also 'The Hague Prepares New Accusations against Herzegovinian Croats', Justwatch-L archives, December 1998, http://listserv.acsu.buffalo.edu/cgi-bin/wa?A2=ind9812&L=justwatch-1&P=R56065 (noting that Josip Silić, an architect from Zagreb who was born in Mostar, sued Mladen Naletilić aka Tuta accusing him of destroying the Old Bridge).

288 Sudetić, above n 283, [8]. See also John Pomfret, 'As Span Crumbles, Unity Dreams Die', *Washington Post*, Monday, 30 August 1993, http://web2.westlaw.com/result/text.wl?RecreatePath-/Search/default.wl&RS=WLW.

289 Sense News Agency, 'Witness: Prlić was "Key Player" in Herceg-Bosna', 21 May 2007, http://www.sense-agency.com/en/stream.php?sta=3&pid=9691&kat=3 [7].

290 Ibid.

291 See Salčin testimony, above n 29; testimony of Mustafa Hadrović, the Prosecution witness in *Prlić*, 21-22 February 2007 [Hadrović testimony]; testimony of Enes Vukotić in *Prlić*, 6 and 7 February 2007 [Vukotić testimony]; testimony of Dževad Hadžizukić in *Prlić*, 1 February 2007 [Hadžizukić testimony]; and testimony of Damir Katica in *Prlić*, 5 February 2007 [Katica testimony].

292 See Vukotić testimony, ibid 6 February 2007, T 13566 *et seq*.

293 Finlayson testimony, above n 33, 7 May 2007, T 18042.

matched clothing.[294] The witness Vukotić testified that he did not have a uniform at all.[295]

Notwithstanding this, according to the witness Vukotić, it was the police that guarded the Kamenica Bridge in Donja Mahala, and there was no military whatsoever anywhere near this bridge.[296] Apparently, 'there were about 30 to 40 men living in the Donja Mahala area that would guard the area around the clock from the HVO, and this bridge was being specifically guarded'.[297] Mustafa Hadrović, another witness in *Prlić*, who was in the reserve police force during the conflict, which was, he claimed, 'a civilian service, a civilian agency',[298] testified that all bridges over the Neretva in Mostar, including the Old Bridge, were guarded by police.[299] After the Serb forces withdrew from Mostar in June 1992 and the Muslim and Croat forces crossed the Neretva,[300] daily duties of the police included guarding the bridges.[301] Since the witness 'knew Donja Mahala well because [he] was born there',[302] he was involved in guarding the bridges there and in the surrounding area.[303] Contrary to the widely held claim that the Serb forces destroyed all bridges in Mostar except the Old Bridge, this witness testified that the bridges were left untouched by the Serbs when they were leaving the area.[304] The witness Hadrović suspects that the Croats, with whom the Muslims at first jointly guarded the bridges, were the guilty party:

> When the Serbs left, crossed over to the other side, there were exchanges of fire but not a single bridge was destroyed by the Serbs. I can prove that. Because at that time I passed across all the bridges, and I can mention some members of the HVO and who are still friends with me today who told me openly, 'Watch out for your bridges'. I don't know how, but I know that all the bridges that were guarded by the [ABH] and the police remained untouched. And then the moving out from Luka began, and all the bridges were destroyed. I personally watched over Lučki Bridge and Hasan Brkić Bridge [both being located not far away from the Old Bridge]. We had our booths there. I never saw, and other people can confirm this, I never observed

294 Vukotić testimony, above n 291, 6 May 2007, T 13279-80, 13655. See also testimony of Patrick van der Weijden in *Prlić*, T 13816 [Weijden testimony].

295 Vukotić testimony ibid T 13661.

296 Ibid 7 February 2007, T 13694.

297 Ibid T 13698.

298 Hadrović testimony, above n 291, 21 February 2007, T 14549.

299 Ibid 14553.

300 Ibid 14552.

301 Ibid 14553.

302 Ibid.

303 Ibid.

304 Ibid 14556.

> anyone from the Serb army approaching those bridges.... The 4th Battalion [of the HVO] came to help us guard the bridges. However, I cannot understand some things to this day. Whenever somebody came to replace us in guarding the bridge, that bridge was destroyed a couple of days later.[305]

This statement implies that the HVO could have easily put the explosive under the Old Bridge while they still had access to this bridge and not the Muslim side to the conflict as argued by the accused Praljak. This statement also implies that by destroying the bridges, and thereby cutting East Mostar from the remainder of the city, the HVO planned the siege of East Mostar well before the conflict began, while the HVO was still perceived to be siding with the Muslims.

With respect to the guarding of the Old Bridge, Hadrović testified that his assignment was to prevent looting of property and to take care to ensure that businesses were not harassed.[306] The witness stated that the guarding of the Old Bridge, which was at some point carried out jointly with the HVO, also involved securing the movement of troops:

> JUDGE MINDUA: ...who was in charge of securing that bridge? What was the size of that force, police or military, because you said on the other side there were members of the HVO. So what was that force securing the bridge?
>
> THE WITNESS: At the outset we [*sic*] were 15 on the old bridge, and we switched, took turns to secure the movement of troops from one bank to the other. Everything went according to plan. There were only members of one ethnic group at that point. Later, in order to establish peace and harmony, from six to seven members of the HVO arrived, and they were with us for a while but not for long. I don't know what the purpose of that was, why they were there, but we watched over that bridge, we members of the army and the police.[307]

According to the witness Hadrović, with the arrival of the HVO to assist in guarding the bridges, 'the bridges began to snap'.[308] The Old Bridge was guarded, *inter alia*, to secure movement of troops from one bank of the Neretva to the other, which means the Bridge was not protected from the effects of armed conflict as cultural property but rather for military reasons. Since the guarding was done together with the HVO, at least at some point, and the guarding involved securing the movement of troops, the HVO itself, even to a limited extent, used the Old Bridge for military purposes. Moreover, the guarding of bridges was

305 Ibid T 14555-14556.

306 Ibid T 14557.

307 Ibid 14559.

308 Ibid.

done not solely by police but also by the army, which differs from the abovementioned testimony of the witness Vukotić.

With respect to the question of who did the guarding – the police or the ABH – in the opinion of General Milivoj Petković, another accused in *Prlić*, there is no difference. General Petković contended that the police were part of the ABH forces, which suggests that the guarded objects constituted potential military objectives.[309]

Regarding the positions of the ABH, General Petković stressed that the ABH had positions throughout East Mostar:

> So we cannot say that apart from the front line, all the rest, all the rest of the area is filled with civilians. The BH army, the brigade of the BH Army took up its positions in the whole of East Mostar, and deployed its men all around, its armed forces.[310]

Bowen, in his documentary and his testimony in both *Naletilić* and in *Prlić*, accounted for the use of the Old Bridge by the ABH as a means of reaching ABH positions on the right bank of the River. But, at the same time, he highlighted the difficulties involved in crossing the Bridge, such as the frequency of the shelling[311] and the ever-present prospect of being shot dead by a sniper,[312] which implies that the crossings could not be overly significant in military terms. A number of other witnesses testified before the ICTY about the problem of sniper fire.[313] To further minimise the significance of the use of the Bridge in support of military effort, Bowen underlined the use of the Bridge by the civil defence for transporting wounded from the right bank to the left bank of the Neretva where the hospital was located, and drew attention to the existence of other bridges in the area. In Bowen's view, the crossing of the Bridge was a risky endeavour.[314]

Even if the Old Bridge and its surroundings were used for military purposes, irrespective of whether the ABH invoked military necessity or not for such use, the HVO's attack on the Bridge could not be justified unless the attack was due to a military necessity on the HVO side, or rather that the Bridge constituted a military objective, and the precautionary measures, including the rule of proportionality, were adhered to by the HVO. Thus, the most immedi-

---

309 Vukotić testimony, above n 291, 7 February 2007, T 13695.

310 Ibid 13696.

311 Bowen testimony in *Naletilić*, above n 31, T 5809-5810.

312 Ibid T 5811.

313 See, eg, Salčin testimony, above n 29; Weijden testimony, above n 294; Katica testimony, above n 291; Hadžizukić testimony, above n 291; and Pejanović testimony, above n 33.

314 Bowen documentary and testimony in *Naletilić*, above n 31, T 5775-5776.

ate question here is whether the use of the Old Bridge and its immediate surroundings was of such significance that it posed a threat to the HVO which required, by military necessity, a response of shelling the Bridge for two consecutive days and completely destroying this exceptional monument. In other words, the question is whether the use of the Bridge and its surroundings by the ABH made an effective contribution to military action and whether on 9 November 1993 the destruction of the Bridge offered a definite military advantage to the HVO.

As noted, there was no fighting in the area of the Old Bridge on 8 and 9 November 1993.[315] In fact, there is no evidence that there had ever been any shooting from the Bridge. Thus, from this perspective, it seems that the Old Bridge could not pose a threat to the HVO. Since the Bridge was used as a means of communication, by both army and civilians, it could be argued that the use of the Bridge by the ABH for transporting water, food, their wounded and dead did have military significance. However, there were other bridges over the Neretva. While the Old Bridge was destroyed, the other bridges were left standing.[316] Given the existence of other bridges over the Neretva at the time, it would not be persuasive to argue that by destroying the Old Bridge, the HVO cut off the only useable avenue of retreat in the event of a Croat offensive against the foothold that the ABH held on the right bank of the Neretva.

Furthermore, the physical characteristics of the Old Bridge rendered it almost impossible to use for military purposes in such a way as to make any effective contribution to military action. The Old Bridge was a narrow bridge, only four metres wide. It was a pedestrian footbridge exclusively. Unless its walkway was significantly modified (which reportedly was only carried out in WWII, to accommodate the passage of Nazi tanks), the Bridge could not be used for the passage of any vehicles. Its entire walkway was covered by white shiny narrow limestone stairs. The walkway formed a steep incline from one bank up to the middle of the Bridge, then declining steeply to the other bank. Accordingly, to cross the Bridge it was necessary to climb up those stairs, and after reaching the midpoint, the highest point on the Bridge, go down the stairs. Due to centuries-long wear and tear, those stairs had become dangerously slippery. Consequently, it was a challenging task to cross the Bridge even in peacetime let alone during the conflict when, due to the danger emanating from the combat activities around the area, a higher degree of caution was required. As one resident of Mostar recalled, '[t]he walkway's stones were rubbed so smooth

315 See Alija Behram, 'Srušen je svijet: Zlocinci srusili Stari most' ['World is Destroyed: Criminals Destroyed the Old Bridge'], *Most*, No. 91, November-December 1995, http://www.most.ba/002/050.htm.

316 Vanessa Vasić-Janeković, Justwatch posting, 12 April 1999, http://listserv.buffalo.edu/archives/justwatch-1.html. On the subject of the destruction of the Old Bridge, see also Justwatch postings of András Riedlmayer, Žarko Modrić, Charles Ingrao, John Pritchard and Ewen Allison, April 1999. Ibid.

by the footsteps that you had to hold on to the rails to avoid slipping even when it was dry'.[317] For some, crossing the Bridge was always quite a terrifying experience. For instance, Ivo Banac, once described as the 'political conscience of modern Croatia',[318] speaking about the destruction of the Old Bridge as 'a watershed',[319] remarks:

> It is curious how certain events, which are by themselves perhaps not as horrifying as concentration camps and strategic rape, become symbolically important. I walked over the Old Bridge at Mostar many times, always with a sense of insecurity and wonder; insecurity, because it was a terrifyingly smooth and slippery edifice; wonder, because of the thrill of temporarily occupying a space that was meant for the birds of the sky. Now, various propagandists of Boban's parastate tell us that this was really a strategic pontoon 'for the new conquests and [*sic*] Islamicization of Croatian lands' (Marko Matić in *Vjesnik*, 8 December 1993). No, for me the destruction of the Old Bridge became the symbol of Tuđman's policy in Bosnia.[320]

Indeed, how could this tall structure, standing twenty metres above the water level in summer be used in support of a military effort so to contribute to military action 'effectively'? Its shiny whiteness made the Bridge visible from afar. Until the very last day of its existence, as John Pomfret saw it, 'despite the bandages and danger of sniper fire, dawn and dusk [would] bathe the bridge in a pink light that ma[d]e it glow'.[321] Furthermore, any traffic across the open Bridge was capable of being easily spotted. More importantly, the height of the Bridge caused it to be exposed to nearby HVO positions on the Hum and Stotina Hills overlooking the area. As discussed, these positions included sniper posts. The HVO was well equipped for both daytime and night-time combat. The weapons included heavy-weapons such as tanks. The frequency of shelling and the ever-present risk of being shot dead by snipers, in both cases emanating from these positions, made any traffic across the Bridge extremely difficult and dangerous.

It might be argued that what is relevant here is not the volume of traffic on the Bridge but rather the extent of the military advantage of destroying the Bridge. Although, for instance, any movement of troops or civilian traffic moving food or other supplies to the military may constitute a military advan-

317 Statement of Borjanka Šantić in Sudetić, above n 283, [11].

318 Rabia Ali and Lawrence Lifschultz, 'An Interview with Ivo Banac: The Last Days of Bosnia?' *Boston Review*, February 1994, http://bostonreview.mit.edu/BostonReview/BT19.1/banac.html [Banac Interview].

319 Ibid 11.

320 Ibid.

321 John Pomfret, 'A Bridge Becomes a Wedge as Span Crumbles, Unity Dreams Die' *The Seattle Times*, Monday, 30 August 1993, A3 1993 WL 6014999, [12], http://web2westlaw.com.

tage, an object becomes a military objective with respect to the military advantage requirement only if a military advantage is 'definite'. IHL does not define this concept. According to the *ICRC Commentary*, 'it is not legitimate to launch an attack which only offers potential or indeterminate advantages. Those ordering or executing the attack must have sufficient information available to take this requirement into account'.[322] Accordingly, if there was, for instance, a major troop movement or a movement of a large burst of civilian traffic the purpose of which was to support the ABH on 8 and 9 November 1993, the HVO might claim definite military advantage.

However, for the reasons discussed above, it is unlikely that the Bridge was capable of being used for any major movement of either military or civilians. In any event, there is no evidence that this was the case at the time of the destruction of the Bridge. Even if such use did happen at some time in the past, that would not be relevant here. In accordance with Article 52(2) of *Additional Protocol I*, destruction of an object whose use makes an effective contribution to military action must offer a definite military advantage to the destroyer of such object 'in the circumstances ruling at the time'. But even if all the requirements prescribed by Article 52(2) are fulfilled, the attack is still not considered lawful if the damage to civilians and civilian objects will be excessive in relation to the concrete and direct military advantage anticipated. Since the walkway of the Bridge was in an exposed position, the movement of foot soldiers over the Bridge, as Riedlmayer observes, 'could be effectively interdicted with small-arms fire',[323] without destroying the Bridge.

Instead, as if they wanted to demonstrate their military strength, the HVO forces opted for the mighty weapons. They shelled the Old Bridge by tanks at point-blank range for two days – on 8 and 9 November 1993 – and knocked it down into the waters of the Neretva on the second day of shelling.[324] Numerous shells were fired in the direction of the Bridge on those two days.[325] According to one eyewitness, on 8 November alone the shelling lasted for hours. The Bridge was targeted four times, at two-hour intervals.[326] Another commentator notes that 'the lengthy onslaught suffered by the historic bridge at Mostar' is probably the best example of how 'the energy and firepower expended upon bridges is often out of all proportion to any military interest the structure might arouse'.[327]

322 *ICRC Commentary*, above n 3, para 2024.

323 András Riedlmayer, Justwatch posting on the subject of 'Blowing up Bridges', 12 April 1999, http://listserv.acsu.buffalo.edu/cgi-bin/wa?A2=ind9904&L-justwatch-1&P-R88581.

324 See *Final Report*, above n 39, para A. The facts.

325 See, eg, Svetlana Broz, *Good People in an Evil Time: Participants and Witnesses* (1999), 247; Salčin testimony, above n 29, T 14208-14214.

326 Salčin testimony, ibid T 14212.

327 Alby Stone, 'The Perilous Bridge' *At the Edge* No. 1 1996, http://www.indigogroup.co.uk/edge/pbridge.htm [10].

This was not the first time during the conflict that the HVO had targeted the Old Bridge, however. Allegedly, 'Croat mortar and tank shells have struck the bridge at least three times since May 9, when the factions, once allies against the Serbs in Bosnia's 17-month-old war, began fighting'.[328] Some noted that the Old Bridge was targeted from various HVO positions.[329] For instance, witness QQ testified in *Naletilić* that while doing forced labour as a prisoner of war at HVO positions on the Brkan Hill, '[o]n two or three occasions, shelling of the Old Bridge, Stari Most, was announced'.[330] This witness told the Court that he overheard an order being given that all guns come to bear on the Bridge.[331] He recalled that the Croat forces had a lot of weapons firing in the direction of the Old Bridge: 'three tanks, three howitzers, a number of rocket launchers, then anti-aircraft guns and machine-guns, the self-propelled recoilless guns, and so on'.[332] These included 'one or two tanks which came from the Croatian army'.[333] According to this witness several HVO officers were present at that location when he saw the tanks firing in the direction of the Old Bridge.[334]

The fact that the Croat forces fired upon the Bridge over a prolonged period of time weakens the argument that the Bridge was destroyed due to military necessity, or because it was considered a military objective. Rather this points to the Croats' determination to bring the Bridge down. The *Final Report of the UN Commission of Experts* asserts that the 'initial objective, it would seem, had been to discourage people from using it…forcing anyone who might be tempted to cross the bridge to refrain from doing so', but that 'the shelling on 8 November 1993 clearly aimed to destroy the bridge'.[335] Some contend that the Croats even brought in architects to determine which stones should be targeted to assure the collapse of the Old Bridge.[336] While studying the film that documented the 8 and 9 November 1993 shelling of the Old Bridge, the firm General Engineering from Florence, Italy, which worked on the final architectural design for the reconstruction of the Old Bridge, made the following observations:

> shelling was coming from south side and hit mostly the south east portion of the bridge over the arch reins…shelling was performed with accuracy almost

328 Pomfret, above n 321, [7]. See also Bowen testimony in *Naletilić*, above n 31, T 5776; Mostarlija, above n 1, 172.

329 See Vukotić testimony, above 291, T 13705.

330 Witness QQ testimony, above n 35, 22 November 2001, T 6268.

331 Ibid T 6273-6274.

332 Ibid T 6275.

333 Ibid.

334 Ibid T 6277.

335 *Final Report*, above n 39, para A. The facts.

336 Jerrilynn Dodds, 'Bridge over the Neretva' (1998) 51 *Archaeology* 3, (abstract), http://www.archaeology.org/9801/abstracts/bosnia.html [3].

> on the same spot in order to cause the collapse using the minimum numbers of shells and the structure was divided in two main parts…the attack has been performed by people that knew the basic functioning of a bridge structure.[337]

These observations suggest that shelling was not random or *ad hoc* but rather that the destruction was premeditated. Two months before the Bridge was knocked down, an interview with members of the HVO by Robert Block revealed the HVO's intention to destroy the Old Bridge. Block warned that 'a few of Tuta's men talked about how it [was] only a matter of time before Mostar's famous Ottoman bridge, the Stari Most, is destroyed'.[338] As noted, when asked why Croat troops were seeking to destroy the Bridge, one soldier explained that it was 'not enough to clean Mostar of the Muslims – the relics [ought] also be removed'.[339]

This explanation suggests that the main reason behind the destruction of the Old Bridge was not its military value but rather its symbolic meaning. Whereas East Mostar was in shock and many people elsewhere were saddened when the Bridge fell, the HVO soldiers 'cheered and fired their guns in the air, celebrating the destruction of a span that had come to symbolize the idea of a multicultural Bosnia'.[340] To the Croat soldiers this particular destruction was a spectacle.[341] To their General Slobodan Praljak, the destruction of the Old Bridge represented the removal of the symbolic reminder of the Ottoman occupation. Allegedly, the General advised that '[n]obody [had] reason to cry over the Old Bridge' because the Bridge 'was and still is the symbol of foreign conquest'.[342] He also reiterated his slogan that he would 'for the sake of his soldiers destroy three Old Bridges'.[343]

There is no evidence to suggest that the HVO soldiers were placed in danger for any reason connected with the Old Bridge on 8 and 9 November 1993, or that any such danger emanated from its immediate vicinity on those two days. Even if that was the case and its use for military purposes turned the Old Bridge into a military objective within the meaning of Article 52(2) of *Additional Protocol I*, the HVO ought still to have respected the rules pertain-

337 General Engineering, The Old Bridge Project, Bridge Description, Part III, 2.3.7. The destruction event, http://www.gen-eng.florence.it/starimost/01_intro/descr/des01c.htm.

338 Robert Block, 'Croatian Death Squad Talks Tough around the Pool Table' *The Independent* (London), 6 September 1993, http://listserv.acsu.buffalo.edu.

339 Ibid.

340 Dodds, above n 336, [3].

341 See Hadrović testimony, above n 291, 22 February 2007, T 14604.

342 Mostarlija, above n 1, 187.

343 Ibid.

ing to the precautions in attack.[344] However, if the Old Bridge did not become a military objective, as argued here, then even if the HVO did take some precautions in attack, for instance, if it gave warning of the attack, that would still not rule out the illegality of the attack because in such a case the Old Bridge would be considered a civilian object and IHL, to restate, explicitly prohibits attacks on civilian objects. Therefore, neither its location nor its use for military purposes justified the attack on the Old Bridge. The Bridge did not constitute a military objective within the meaning of IHL and its prolonged shelling and destruction were unnecessary. Thus the argument that the Old Bridge was a legitimate military target must be rejected.

III Issues

The application of IHL according protection to cultural property in armed conflict to the Old Bridge case raises a number of issues. While some of these highlight difficulties emanating from the modern battlefield, others point to the lack of clarity of the relevant principles of IHL. This section limits itself to a brief consideration of several major problems mainly relating to the rule of distinction. While the law lays out numerous rules that provide protection for cultural property during military operations, applying them in densely populated (as well as spatially challenging) residential areas like East Mostar can be difficult. According to the rule of distinction, the parties to the conflict must at all times distinguish between the civilian population and combatants and between civilian objects and military objectives. The parties are under a duty to direct their operations only against military objectives. During military operations both sides must take constant care to spare civilian lives and property.[345] When targeting a military objective, the attacking side is under an obligation not to cause unnecessary harm to civilians or civilian objects. The side under attack has, *inter alia*, an obligation to avoid locating military objectives within or near densely populated areas. But the first problem here is that it may not be always clear which object constitutes a military objective.

A The Definition of a Military Objective

1 'Effective' Contribution and 'Definite' Advantage

Article 52(2) of *Additional Protocol I* requires that the following two elements be present simultaneously if an object is to be considered a military objective:

---

344 See *Additional Protocol I*, art 57.

345 For a discussion of the principles of proportionality and distinction in the context of targeting decisions, see Dale Stephens and Mike Lewis, 'The Law of Armed Conflict' – A Contemporary Critique' (2005) 6 *Melbourne Journal of International Law* 55.

(1) an object by its nature, location, purpose or use must make an 'effective' contribution to military action and (2) total or partial destruction, capture or neutralisation of that object, in the circumstances ruling at the time, offers a 'definite' military advantage. The wording of the definition of a military objective is, as one commentator describes it, 'seemingly definitive and yet endlessly slippery'.[346] The law does not define the terms 'effective' and 'definite' in this context. Thus, determining what constitutes an 'effective' contribution to military action and whether there is really a 'definite' military advantage can only be assessed on a case-by-case basis. As the *Strugar* Trial Chamber held in this regard, 'each case must be determined on its facts'.[347] This leaves much room for subjectivity on the part of a military commander.

2 Decision-Making Level

Even if it is not difficult to determine 'effective' contribution and 'definite' military advantage, it is still not clear at precisely what level the decisions are to be made that an object becomes a military objective and that it is to be attacked. As discussed, the relevant IHL on the subject, i.e., the *1907 Regulations*, the *1954 Convention* and *Protocol I Additional to the 1949 Geneva Conventions* are silent on the subject of the decision-making level. Such silence leaves especially protected cultural property at the mercy of whoever happens to be the decision-maker on the day.

3 Temporal Issues

The silence of the law stretches further, to the subject of timing. The law does not make it clear which timeframe is to be applied to the existence of a military objective. *Additional Protocol I* requires that total or partial destruction, capture or neutralisation of an object offer a definite military advantage 'in the circumstances ruling *at the time*'. But the law does not specify how long 'at the time' actually is. Is it the very day of an attack that matters, or can the phrase 'at the time' extend to an earlier point, and if the latter, exactly how much earlier could one go?

---

346 Adam Liptak, 'When Letter of the Law Does Not Spell "Clarity"', *The New York Times* Wednesday, 1 May 2002, http://www.nytimes.com/2002/05/01/international/middleeast/01LAW.html [9].

347 *Strugar* Trial Judgement, para 285. Discussing 'the excessive (damage) in relation to the concrete and direct military advantage anticipated', which in his view 'may in many cases be impractical', Kevin Chamberlain has questioned the concept of military advantage: 'How can damage to the cultural heritage be weighted against possible military advantage? It is not comparing like with like': Kevin Chamberlain, 'The Protection of Cultural Property in Armed Conflict' (2003) 8(3) *Art, Antiquity and Law* 209, 233.

According to the ICTY jurisprudence, it is the time of an attack that is relevant. For instance, the Trial Chamber in *Strugar* made it clear that if the Old Town of Dubrovnik and its immediate vicinity were used for military purposes, it would be its use on 6 December 1991, the day of the shelling of the Old Town, and not any supposed possible previous use that would be relevant.[348] It should be noted that the *Strugar* Indictment deals only with one specific attack on the Old Town of Dubrovnik, namely the attack that occurred on 6 December 1991.

4 Issue of Location

The side under attack has obligations *vis-à-vis* the protection of civilian lives and property. Among other requirements, the side under attack must, to the maximum extent feasible, 'avoid locating military objectives within or near densely populated areas'.[349] This obligation is part of the precautions against the effects of attacks envisaged by Article 58 of *Additional Protocol I*. However, as East Mostar exemplifies, it may be difficult to apply this provision in densely populated areas. In East Mostar, as Bowen observes, '[n]othing is more than a few minutes away'.[350] In such a small space, proximity to military objectives is inevitable. The Old Bridge, together with the rest of the Old City of Mostar was not far from the front line, which was in the street called Bulevar, only about 200 metres away. The Prosecution witness Salčin testified in *Prlić* that ABH soldiers were stationed in the 'Ruža' Hotel, which was '[a] maximum of 150 to 200'[351] metres from the Old Bridge, and in close vicinity to the front line.

The issue of location directly impacts upon the definition of a military objective. Consistent with Article 52(2) of *Additional Protocol I*, an object can, *inter alia*, by its 'location' become a military objective. According to the *ICRC Commentary* the location criterion was introduced into *Additional Protocol I* without reasons being given.[352] The *Commentary* includes reference to a bridge among the examples of objects which can by their location become a military objective.[353] But, as Jean-Marie Henckaerts from the ICRC argues, with respect to historic bridges, 'it is really the use of such bridges that can make an effective contribution to military action'.[354] This view was adopted by the trial Chamber in *Naletilić*,[355] which rejected the view of the Trial Chamber in *Blaškić* that cultural property must not be situated in the immediate vicinity of military

348 Ibid para 328, footnotes omitted (emphasis added).

349 *Additional Protocol I*, art 58(b).

350 Bowen testimony in *Naletilić*, above n 31, T 5775.

351 Salčin testimony, above n 29, T 14213.

352 *ICRC Commentary*, above n 3, para 2021.

353 Ibid.

354 Henckaerts, 'New Rules', above n 212, 37.

355 See *Naletilić* Trial Judgement, para 604.

objectives.[356] The *Naletilić* Trial Chamber held that the mere fact that cultural property is situated in the immediate vicinity of a military objective does not justify its destruction.[357] In this Trial Chamber's view it is the use of cultural property for military purposes and not its location that determines whether, as well as when, cultural property would lose its protection.[358] The Trial Chamber in *Strugar* concurs with the view of the *Naletilić* Trial Chamber, stressing that 'the special protection awarded to cultural property itself may not be lost simply because of military activities or military installations in the immediate vicinity of the cultural property'.[359]

B Advance Warning

If the attacking side has given the side under attack advance warning, this raises the question of how long should the time span be between a warning and an attack? 'Advance warning' is not referred to in the definition of a military objective. The duty to give 'effective advance warning' is one of the precautions in attack, envisaged by Article 57(2)(c) of *Additional Protocol I*. As with the clause providing for the 'at the time' requirement referred to in the definition of a military objective, the *Protocol* is silent on the question of how 'advanced' a warning should be.

The duty to give advance warning is not absolute. The phrase in sub-paragraph (c) 'unless circumstances do not permit' allows for derogation. Similar derogation can be found in Article 26 of the *1907 Regulations* which requires the officer in command of an attacking force to warn the authorities before commencing a bombardment, except in cases of assault, when warning, as the *ICRC Commentary* notes, 'may be inconvenient when the element of surprise in the attack is a condition of its success'.[360] But it is precisely because of the element of surprise in the attack that the phrase 'unless circumstances do not permit' is likely to be interpreted as 'never', and thus remain only a dead letter on paper.

C The Rule of Distinction

A further issue arising from the application of IHL to the Old Bridge concerns the difficulty of distinguishing between civilians and combatants which ultimately affects the character of an object concerned. The Old Bridge was used as a means of communication not only by ABH soldiers but also by civilians. In addition to this it was claimed that the Bridge was guarded by the police. At

356 See *Blaškić* Trial Judgement, para 185.

357 See *Naletilić* Trial Judgement, para 604.

358 Ibid para 605.

359 See *Strugar* Trial Judgement, para 310.

360 *ICRC Commentary*, above n 3, para 2223.

the same time, consistent with evidence presented in *Prlić*, there was a variety of uniforms in use in East Mostar, and some soldiers did not have uniforms at all. With respect to the issue of uniforms, the Defence in *Prlić* stressed that it was difficult for the HVO to distinguish between civilians and combatants, suggesting that the presence of ABH soldiers legitimised attacks on East Mostar.

The problem here is that East Mostar, as noted, was a densely populated area at the time. During the conflict, due to forced expulsions of the Muslims from West Mostar by the Croats, the population drastically increased in the besieged East Mostar. In Donja Mahala (a small neighbourhood in the vicinity of the Old Bridge) alone, in three months, from May to August 1993, the population 'swelled' from 2,000 to 5,000 people.[361] Among the civilian population which lived in the area were numerous soldiers who also resided there. Pursuant to Article 50(3) of *Additional Protocol I*, 'the presence within the civilian population of individuals who do not come within the definition of civilians does not deprive the population of its civilian character'.[362] However, if ABH soldiers camouflaged themselves so as to appear to be civilians then they clearly put civilians and civilian objects in danger. According to the *ICRC Commentary*, it would appear that if military objectives located in an urban area are camouflaged – and soldiers are considered legitimate military targets – but the adversary knows that they exist, 'the danger for the population is increased, particularly because of the incidental damage caused by bombing or artillery fire'.[363] Article 51(7) explicitly states that the presence of civilians does not make certain areas immune from military operations:

> The presence or movement of the civilian population or individual civilians shall not be used to render certain points or areas immune from military operations, in particular in attempts to shield military objectives from attacks or to shield, favour or impede military operations. The Parties to the conflict shall not direct the movement of the civilian population or individual civilians in order to attempt to shield military objectives from attacks or to shield military operations.[364]

If the problem of camouflage is removed, this provision may be in contradiction with Articles 50(3) and 48 of the *Protocol* which require that a distinction be made at all times between the civilian population and combatants and between civilian objects and military objectives, and that operations be directed only against military objectives. In any event, the application of Article 51(7) may be difficult where densely populated areas are concerned. In areas such as East

361 See Salčin testimony, above n 29, T 14181, 14307.

362 *Additional Protocol I*, art 50(3).

363 *ICRC Commentary*, above n 3, para 2254.

364 *Additional Protocol I*, art 51(7).

Mostar (which was under siege, where all residents were soldiers to some extent, as one of them put it,[365] where there was a lack of uniforms, shortage of food and where water and electricity were cut off,[366] and where the population had dramatically increased in numbers), fighting was a matter of survival.[367] As Bowen's documentary sums it up, such areas are to those most immediately affected 'law of the jungle'[368] zones into which it is challenging to bring respect for the norms of international law.[369]

D Guarding of Cultural Property

The problem of distinguishing between the civilian sector and the military sector raises the additional issue of guarding cultural property. At the same time, the issue of guarding is intertwined with the issue of the use of cultural property or its immediate surroundings for military purposes. As discussed, it has been claimed that the Old Bridge was guarded by police and ABH forces.[370] The guarding was for the purpose of preventing looting in the area[371] and for securing the movement of troops from one bank of the Neretva to the other.[372] A counterclaim that police formed part of the ABH and that they were armed has been put forward.[373] This implied that the presence of armed police on the Bridge and the purpose of guarding in this particular case made the Bridge a possible military target. It is not clear whether those 'guards' were on guard duty on 8 and 9 November 1993. If the guarding occurred, for example, months before the destruction of the Old Bridge, it would not be relevant to the case at hand. If, however, the Bridge was so guarded on the particular days involving the attack, then the questions of whether the Bridge was guarded as a cultural property object and whether those who did the guarding were empowered to do so warrant attention.

IHL is almost silent on the subject of guarding cultural property. Neither the *1899* nor *1907 Conventions*, nor the two *Additional Protocols*, contain any pro-

365 Bowen testimony in *Naletilić*, above n 31, T 5777.

366 Ibid 5793, 5802. See also Salčin testimony, above n 29, T 14166 *et seq;* Vukotić testimony, above n 291, T 13566 *et seq.*

367 See Bowen documentary and testimony in *Naletilić*, above n 31, T 5777.

368 Bowen documentary, ibid T 5792 (Colonel Esad Humo, Mostar Brigade, stating that in East Mostar the 'law of a jungle' ruled because people were fighting to survive).

369 Ibid T 5790-5791.

370 Hadrović testimony, above n 291, 21 February 2007, T 14553-14560.

371 Ibid T 14557-14558.

372 Ibid 14558-14559. On the question of guarding the bridges over the Neretva, see also Vukotić testimony, above n 291, T 13655 *et seq.*

373 See statement of the accused General Milivoj Petković during cross-examination of witness Enes Vukotić in *Prlić*, 7 February 2007, T 13694-13696.

vision in this regard. The provisions of the *1954 Convention* governing the general protection of cultural property also contain no mention of the guarding of such property. Article 8(4) of the *1954 Convention* is the only provision that does make explicit reference to the guarding of cultural property. However, this Article relates to cultural property under special protection. Article 8(4) states:

> The guarding of cultural property mentioned in paragraph 1 above by *armed custodians specially empowered* to do so, or the presence, in the vicinity of such cultural property, of *police forces* normally responsible for the maintenance of public order shall not be deemed to be use for military purposes.[374]

This provision allows the guarding of cultural property by the custodians who are especially empowered by competent authorities to do so and it also allows the custodians to be armed. The presence of police forces normally responsible for the maintenance of public order in the vicinity of cultural property is permissible as well. Consistent with this Article, the guarding of cultural property by specifically empowered armed custodians and the presence of police forces should not be deemed to be evidence of the use of cultural property for military purposes. The *Convention* does not refer to the use of arms by the personnel involved in the guarding of cultural property, but, as Toman observes, 'it seems quite natural that such personnel cannot be expected to become passive sacrificial victims'.[375] An analogy can be made to the *Commentary on the First Geneva Convention*, according to which it is necessary for medical personnel to be in a position to ensure the maintenance of order and discipline in units under their charge but that such personnel may only resort to arms in self-defence and where obviously necessary.[376] Toman suggests an expansive reading of Article 8(4) in this respect, pointing to the question of good faith of the unit involved in the guarding.[377] The *Convention* does not make any reference to the type of uniform which should be worn by the custodians of cultural property. In his commentary on Article 4 of the *1954 Convention*, which covers respect for cultural property under general protection, Toman notes that it has been recommended, in relation to the area of Angkor Wat in Cambodia, that 'the custodians of cultural property should not wear military or paramilitary uniform and that their clothing should be readily distinguishable from clothes which suggest a military presence'.[378] As Cambodia has never had any cultural property under special protection, this suggests that the provision of Article 8(4) on the guarding

374 *1954 Convention*, art 8(4) (emphasis added).

375 Toman, above n 48, 105.

376 Ibid.

377 Ibid 106.

378 Ibid 80.

of cultural property under special protection could equally be applied to cultural property under general protection.

The guarding of cultural property within the meaning of Article 8(4) of the *1954 Convention* is a measure aimed at protection of certain objects because they are cultural property and not because they are also, for instance, a means of communication. The guarding of the Old Bridge to secure the transport of troops and to prevent looting could not be characterised as guarding for the purpose of protecting the Bridge as an object of cultural property. But even if the Bridge was intended to be guarded as cultural property, the problem of who was to guard it remains, as the presence of ABH forces would require the conclusion as a matter of law that the Old Bridge was being used for military purposes. With regard to police forces, their presence would not be contrary to Article 8(4) of the *1954 Convention*, provided that they belonged to the civilian sector and did not form part of the ABH. Whether they carried arms or not would not affect their status *vis-à-vis* the guarding because personnel involved in the guarding of cultural property are allowed to be armed for self-defence purposes.

Nevertheless, it may be challenging to ensure proper guarding of cultural property in times of armed conflict. In some situations, even if armed custodians from one party to the conflict are specially empowered by the competent authority to perform the guarding, it is still likely that the adversary would translate such guarding into evidence of the use of cultural property for military purposes and, consequently, would seek to justify an attack on cultural property on those grounds. In such situations, only a third, international party could be perceived as a neutral party and provide effective guarding of cultural property, aimed at the prevention of its destruction or damage.

As noted, United Nations forces, specifically the UNPROFOR Spanish Battalion (SpaBat), were present in Mostar throughout the conflict. They were a neutral party of this kind. But these forces did not guard the Old Bridge. The rules of engagement did not encompass such task. Yet, the situation prior to the destruction of the Bridge suggested that the survival of the Bridge was endangered and that something needed to be done to prevent the loss of the Bridge. That is, the Bridge was targeted on several occasions before November 1993. Also, statements given by HVO members in the international media indicated that there was an intention on the HVO side to bring the Bridge down. Moreover, numerous reports by international monitors present in Mostar throughout the conflict and by various international bodies warned that the situation in the area of the Old Bridge was critical. This raises the question of whether the mandate of UNPROFOR could (and should?) have been expanded to include the guarding of cultural property.

Could anyone else have prevented the destruction of the Bridge? Was UNESCO or any other international organisation that deals with cultural property empowered to take steps on the subject? Kaiser, who at the time worked for the Committee on Culture and Education of the Parliamentary Assembly of the COE and for UNESCO, went on missions to Bosnia and Herzegovina, including Mostar, several times during the conflict. His reports to UNESCO and the COE on war damage to cultural property included the situation in the Old City of Mostar.[379] In fact, for UNESCO he has written reports specifically on Mostar.[380] Yet UNESCO was not able to prevent the destruction of the Bridge. A similar situation with respect to UNESCO's powerlessness in this regard occurred in other parts of the former Yugoslavia affected by the 1990s armed conflicts, and elsewhere.[381] As Karen Detling notes in relation to the former Yugoslavia, 'the observers who arrived served only to catalogue the atrocities'.[382]

E State Sovereignty

Under existing international law neither UNESCO nor any other organisation, State or other party is entitled to intervene in the internal matters of a State without its authorisation. Even if preventive in character, intervention in domestic matters without the consent of the State concerned could be seen as an infringement of State sovereignty, which is one of the cornerstones of the *UN Charter*,[383] and an 'identity' card of a State in the world of international relations. While beyond the scope of this book, it is abundantly clear that the conditions under which sovereignty is exercised, and intervention is practised, have dramatically changed since the adoption of the *Charter*.[384] Notwithstanding this, State sovereignty remains an underlying hurdle with respect to several other issues pertaining to the question of the targeting of cultural property in armed

379 See Kaiser testimony in *Karadžić*, above n 109, T 423 *et seq*, http://www.un.org/icty/transe5&18/960702it.htm. See also testimony of Dr Colin Kaiser in *Blaškić*, 16 July 1998, T 10577 *et seq* [Kaiser testimony in *Blaškić*], http://www.un.org/icty/transe14/980716IT.html.

380 Kaiser testimony in *Karadžić*, ibid T 424 (noting that while the reports he has written for the COE are public documents, the reports for UNESCO are 'much more of a confidential institutional sort of document').

381 See Boylan, *Review*, above n 202, 88, para 7.9 (noting various UNESCO efforts to stop the damage to and destruction of cultural property, including Cyprus in the 1970s, Cambodia in 1970 and Lebanon in 1982).

382 Detling, above n 48, 73.

383 The prohibition of intervention in domestic matters of a State is one of the principles of the UN, spelt out in Article 2(7) of its Charter, *Charter of the United Nations*, 26 June 1945, 59 Stat 1031, TS 993, 3 Bevans 1153, Preamble para 1 (entered into force 24 October 1945) [*UN Charter*].

384 See, generally, *The Responsibility to Protect*, Report of the International Commission on Intervention and State Sovereignty, December 2001 [*ICISS Report*], http://www.dfait-maeci.gc.ca/iciss/report2-en.asp. See also Catherine Vernon, 'Common Cultural Property: The Search for Rights of Protective Intervention' (1994) 26 *Case Western Reserve Journal of International Law* 435.

conflict, such as the definition of cultural property and the safeguarding of cultural property. In relation to the former, the issue does not arise directly from the application of IHL to the case at hand. Still, the definition of cultural property may pose difficulties in the battlefield generally. International law lacks a uniform and clear definition of cultural property largely due to the impact of State sovereignty. This can be confusing in times of armed conflict as it may not always be sufficiently clear which objects are 'subject to special protection'.[385] Yet military commanders need to know precisely which objects can, and which cannot, be targeted.

In relation to the issue of safeguarding, a State may neglect cultural property to which it is territorially linked both in time of peace and in armed conflict without any repercussions.[386] Under the *1954 Convention*, protection of cultural property does not mean respect for cultural property only during armed conflict, but also comprises safeguarding of cultural property in times of peace against the foreseeable effects of an armed conflict.[387] Safeguarding of cultural property concerns the taking of measures aimed at its physical protection from artillery fire and other dangers emanating from combat activities.[388] However, States are free to take 'such measures as *they* consider appropriate'.[389] There are no consequences for a State if a chosen measure proves to be inappropriate or insufficient and an object of cultural property is damaged or destroyed as a result. This conclusion also applies in cases where a State considers it 'appropriate' to take no measures at all.

Although the failure to apply the measures of safeguard does not absolve the opposing party to a conflict from the obligation to respect cultural property, the holder of cultural property should bear some responsibility for the failure to adequately protect cultural property. As discussed, some protective measures had been taken to physically protect the Old Bridge against shelling. Allegedly, at some stage prior to the conflict, the HVO itself was involved in erecting the scaffolding over the Bridge.[390] However, the measures taken were

385 *Additional Protocol I*, art 57(2)(b) ('an attack shall be cancelled or suspended if it becomes apparent that the objective is…*subject to special protection*') (emphasis added).

386 See Frank Fechner, 'The Fundamental Aims of Cultural Property Law' (1998) 7 *International Journal of Cultural Property* 376, 380–81 (stressing that '[i]t is dangerous for cultural property when a state does not want to care for its cultural assets or is not able to do so [yet] a group cannot be forced to protect its own cultural heritage').

387 See *1954 Convention*, art 2.

388 Ibid art 3. See also *1999 Protocol*, art 5.

389 *1954 Convention*, ibid (emphasis added).

390 See statement of General Praljak in Radio-Most, above n 1, and in the *Prlić* trial, hearing of 19 February 2007, T 14270.

deemed inadequate[391] and further protection of the Bridge was requested.[392] The Bridge required additional protection to its southern side to protect it from the HVO shelling from that direction. Despite the request, which was made by the COE in mid-August 1993, and despite the fact that a fairly long period of time remained for steps to be taken to ensure protection of the Bridge, nothing was done.[393] When the Bridge was targeted on 8 and 9 November 1993, it was its southern – inadequately protected – side that could not withstand the shelling. One must wonder whether the destruction could have been prevented had adequate safeguard measures been taken.

F Indeterminacy on the Battlefield

Indeterminacy[394] in the battlefield poses an additional problem for the protection of cultural property in armed conflict. It must be taken into account that the legal principles must be applied to harsh conditions on the ground, 'to fast-moving action in the heat and dust of battle'[395] as Adam Liptak so accurately depicts it. As the *ICRC Commentary* observes, the interpretation of any IHL provision which is vague must be a question of common sense and good faith for military commanders, who in every attack must carefully weigh up the humanitarian and military interests at stake.[396] This is, of course, how things should be. But, in reality, military commanders sometimes forget about the required balance. Some military commanders utilise the flexibility in terminology to their own advantage. The enormity of the losses in civilian lives and civilian property in the Balkans during the 1990s suggests that this was the case there.

IV Summary and Observations

Because of its architectural and historical value the Old Bridge was a monument deemed to be of great importance to the cultural heritage of the citizens of Mostar and of the whole of Bosnia and Herzegovina. On 8 and 9 November 1993 the Bridge was deliberately targeted and destroyed by the HVO forces. In an attempt to justify the destruction, various excuses have been put forward, including that the Bridge was 'just an ordinary bridge', that it was inadequately protected against the shelling, that it was not marked with a distinctive

391 See, eg, *Fourth COE Report*, above n 165, para 68; *Final Report*, above n 39, Appendix I Record: Cultural Property in the Former Yugoslavia, Mtg of 15 February 1994, IV. Operational framework, para (c).

392 See *Fourth COE Report*, ibid.

393 Ibid.

394 Liptak, above n 346, [8] (quoting Professor Ruth Wedgwood of Yale Law School who notes that '[i]t's that indeterminacy in the battlefield that makes it so difficult').

395 Ibid [7].

396 *ICRC Commentary*, above n 3, para 2208.

emblem, that the Bridge and its immediate surroundings were used for military purposes and that, in these circumstances, the Bridge was destroyed due to military necessity.

Yet the Old Bridge was not an ordinary object within the meaning of IHL. Because of its exceptional value it was distinguished from other objects and was granted immunity under the rubric of cultural property. Since cultural property is essentially civilian in character, even if the Bridge was just an ordinary bridge, it would still be entitled to the protection accorded to all civilian objects. While it is true that the Bridge was in need of additional protection at the time, the HVO's acts nevertheless could not be justified on that basis as IHL does not absolve an adversary of its obligation to respect cultural property where the holder of cultural property has not applied the measures of safeguard. Since the Old Bridge constituted cultural property under general protection, the distinctive marking was not compulsory. Consequently, its absence could not justify the destruction.

With respect to the claim that the Bridge and its immediate surroundings were used for military purposes, IHL is explicit in its prohibition on such use. This prohibition may be waived only on the grounds of military necessity. However, even if cultural property is used for military purposes on the grounds of military necessity, it does not follow that the adversary can automatically launch an attack on the cultural property concerned. Under IHL, an attack itself must also be justified by military necessity. While the relevant IHL lacks an adequate definition of military necessity, still it is universally accepted that in order to become a legitimate military target, an object must become a military objective. Moreover, an attack must not cause unnecessary harm to civilians or civilian objects. In that regard, the rule of proportionality must be adhered to and other precautionary measures must be taken. IHL imposes the requirement to take the precautions not merely on the attacking party. The side under attack has obligations, too, including the obligation to avoid locating military objectives within or near densely populated areas.

Research shows that ABH positions were located relatively closely to the area of the Old Bridge and that the Bridge was indeed used for military purposes in the period preceding its destruction. However, it has been accepted that it is not the location of cultural property but rather its use that may lead to the loss of immunity. To result in the loss of immunity, the use of cultural property must make 'an effective contribution to military action'. According to the information available, on 8 and 9 November 1993 there was not any fighting in the area of the Old Bridge and neither was there any major movement of troops or supplies across the Bridge. But even if the Bridge and its immediate surroundings were used for military purposes on these two specific days, there is no evidence to suggest that this was treated as posing any significant threat to the HVO forces at the time, or that the HVO forces considered it worthy of serious attention. This suggests that the Old Bridge was devoid of military significance and that, consequently, the targeting and destruction of it, as determined by the World Heritage Committee, were 'in flagrant contradiction with international law'.[397]

Notwithstanding this qualification, the destruction of the Old Bridge draws attention to the lack of clarity in the relevant rules of IHL and points to the difficulty of their application to an urban battlefield. Although destruction of cultural property may be allowed under IHL on the grounds of military necessity, it fails to define the concept. The definition of a military objective can be used to fill in this gap. However, the problem of ambiguity is still not entirely removed as the definition of military objective does not deal with factors which may be crucial to the survival of cultural property, such as determination of the precise military level at which a decision to attack cultural property is to be made, whether there should be warning prior to attack and whether this warning should be compulsory, as well as the question 'for how long' an object of cultural property is to be considered a military objective. As to the factors which the definition of a military objective does deal with, it may not always be easy to determine whether they are simultaneously present, as required by Article 52(2) of *Additional Protocol I*. The same could be said in relation to precautionary measures. The situation is even harder if an attack is assessed *ex post facto*. This may include many fact-driven questions, the resolution of which can only be achieved in a trial.

The lack of clarity in the relevant concepts may cause the problem of indeterminacy in the battlefield. When the battlefield is an urban, densely populated area, application of the relevant rules of IHL is particularly challenging. In spatially restricted areas such as East Mostar, it may not be possible to avoid locating military objectives in the vicinity of cultural property. When such areas are also under siege and the people who are encircled are fighting merely for survival, there may be no choice other than to use cultural property for various purposes, including military purposes. As military personnel may intermingle with civilians, it may be difficult to determine by whom exactly – whether the combatants or civilians – and for what purposes precisely – whether military or civilian – the property is being used at the time concerned. This, in effect, increases the vulnerability of cultural property. The vulnerability of cultural property is further magnified in cases where the side in control of cultural property fails to take adequate measures of safeguard. Although the absence of protective measures does not absolve the adversary from the obligation to refrain from directing hostile acts against cultural property, the failure to apply adequate measures may reduce the prospects of the property's survival.

Despite the challenges emanating from the application of IHL, the law does provide for the protection of cultural property. Its every rule may not be

397 *Declaration of the World Heritage Committee on the Destruction of Cultural Heritage of Bosnia and Herzegovina*, mtg in Cartagena, Colombia, 6-11 December 1993, *World Heritage Newsletter* vol II, No. 6, 11 December 1993, para 2 (Copy on file with author).

as clear as it should be, but since it is aimed at establishing a balance between humanitarian and military interests, the law does impose some important restrictions on arbitrary behaviour in the battlefield. Research points to the conclusion that on 8 and 9 November 1993, the HVO overlooked those restrictions. The failure to abide by the relevant rules of IHL does not seem to have been due to their lack of clarity. Rather, the breaches of applicable norms seem to have been wilful.

Chapter 6

The Question of Justice for the Destruction of the Old Bridge

I An Overview

Wilful breaches of norms of IHL granting protection to cultural property in armed conflict may constitute a war crime giving rise to individual criminal responsibility. Cultural property-related crimes do not usually rank highly on the prosecution priority list, however. This is not surprising given the reluctance to prosecute war crimes generally, at least until recently.[1] It is not rare for calls to be made, usually after the conflict and more often than not by those who might have been implicated in war crimes, to forget the crimes in order to create a precondition for peace and coexistence.[2] The Balkans is not an exception to this. In a perverse switch of roles, those who have waged armed conflict claiming that life together was not possible, and who, in the process, destroyed monuments as evidence of shared life, have suddenly become staunch supporters of coexistence, advocating general amnesty and general amnesia. Declaring himself in favour of a specific general pardon in the name of a new beginning, Croatia's late President Tuđman publicly advised that '[i]t is much more important to create conditions for coexistence of those who waged war against each other until recently than to sentence criminals'.[3] However, without bringing those responsible to justice and punishing them adequately there can be no peace

1 See Antonio Cassese, 'On the Current Trends towards Criminal Prosecution and Punishment of Breaches of International Humanitarian Law' (1998) 9 *European Journal of International Law* 1, 3 ['Current Trends']. See also Cherif Bassiouni, 'Combating Impunity for International Crimes' (2000) 71 *University of Colorado Law Review* 409; Steven Ratner and Jason Abrams, *Accountability for Human Rights Atrocities in International Law* (2001); Timothy McCormack, 'Their Atrocities and Our Misdemeanours: The Reticence of States to Try Their "Own Nationals" for International Crimes' in Mark Lattimer and Philippe Sands (eds), *Justice for Crimes against Humanity* (2003) 107 ['Their Atrocities'].

2 For discussion of the 'peace v justice' struggle see, eg, Frits Kalshoven, 'Introduction' in Frits Kalshoven (ed), *The Centennial of the First International Peace Conference* (2000) 1.

3 'The Whip of the Hague Snapping over Croatia', http://w3.tyenet.com/kozlich/whip.htm [4].

in the long run. Justice cannot be seen to be done properly unless all crimes, including cultural property-related crimes, are treated appropriately.

The destruction of the Old Bridge has been considered a very serious event throughout the Balkans. In the city of Mostar specifically, this has been a major issue.[4] Together with much of the Old City, the Old Bridge has been rebuilt recently. Its rebuilding was an international project,[5] which, *inter alia*, included involvement of experts from Croatia and Bosnia and Herzegovina, in the latter cases comprising both Croat and Muslim representatives, to symbolically demonstrate that the former foes can work and live side by side again. The rebuilt bridge looks exactly as the Old Bridge; but in the final analysis, even though it is an outstanding replica, it is still a new bridge.[6] As the Trial Chamber in *Jokić* observed,

> [r]estoration of buildings of this kind, when possible, can never return the buildings to their state prior to the attack because a certain amount of original, historically authentic, material will have been destroyed, thus affecting the inherent value of the buildings.[7]

In any event, when the original is gone, it is gone forever. Someone is responsible for the loss of the original Old Bridge. Unless the culprits are identified, the whole Croat nation will be deemed a guilty party by many people in the Balkans. Bringing to justice those responsible for the destruction of the Bridge would individualise guilt and help the healing process. At the same time, this would deter the would-be destroyers of irreplaceable cultural resources that are essential for human functioning from such wrongdoings, and it would significantly contribute to ending the impunity for this kind of violation of IHL.

---

4 See, eg, Robert Bevan, *The Destruction of Memory: Architecture at War* (2006); Ismail Serageldin *et al* (eds), *Historic Cities and Sacred Sites: Cultural Roots for Urban Futures* (2001); Martin Coward, 'Community as Heterogeneous Ensemble: Mostar and Multiculturalism', paper prepared for the ISA Annual Convention, Chicago, 21-24 February 2001, Panel SB05: Methodological Options, Political Consequences, Saturday, 24 February, 2001, 10.30, http://www.isanet.org/archive/coward.html.

5 See, eg, John Yarwood, *Rebuilding Mostar: Urban Reconstruction in a War Zone* (1999) [*Rebuilding Mostar*]; Hannah Lawrence, 'The Partnership for Mostar' in Serageldin *et al* (eds), above n 4, 385-390; Esther Charlesworth, *Architects without Frontiers: War, Reconstruction and Design Responsibility* (2006).

6 See, eg, Lawrence, ibid 388, 390; Ascensión Hernández Martinez, 'Conservation and Restoration in Built Heritage: A Western European Perspective' in Brian Graham and Peter Howard (eds), *The Ashgate Research Companion to Heritage and Identity* (2008) 245-266, 249.

7 *Prosecutor v Miodrag Jokić*, Case No. IT-01-42/1-S, Sentencing Judgement, Trial Chamber I, 18 March 2004, Case No. IT-01-42/1-S, para 52 [*Jokić* Sentencing Judgement].

Cases involving violations of IHL should be dealt with at both the national and international level. Since this book focuses on the ICTY response to the destruction of the Old Bridge, this chapter looks at how the law protecting cultural property in armed conflict is enforced at the international level, through criminal prosecution. The chapter first briefly surveys the relevant provisions of the *1907 Regulations*, *1954 Convention* and *Protocol I Additional to the 1949 Geneva Conventions*. It then outlines venues for prosecution relevant to the case at hand. The chapter then examines the approach to cultural property taken by the ICTY. The examination first considers the relevant provisions of the *ICTY Statute* and then applies those provisions to the Old Bridge case. In its final section, the chapter discusses a number of issues pertaining to the question of justice for the destruction of the Old Bridge. Some of the issues arise from the place assigned to cultural property by the *ICTY Statute*, whereas others involve the ICTY's approach taken to cultural property as evidenced in its decisions and indictments. Of special interest here is the *Prlić* Indictment, which, *inter alia*, deals with the destruction of the Old Bridge of Mostar. Some difficulties the ICTY is faced with, which stem from various administrative and technical matters, as well as the political realities, such as the pressure to complete its work by the imposed deadlines, also impact upon the case at hand.

II Applicable Law

Violations of IHL rules according protection to cultural property in armed conflict may entail individual criminal responsibility under both customary international law and treaty international law. This section first considers the relevant provisions of the *1907 Regulations*, which form part of customary international law, and then, in relation to treaty international law, it looks at the applicable provisions of the *1954 Convention* and of *1977 Protocol I Additional to the Geneva Conventions of 12 August 1949*.

A 1907 Regulations

Article 56 of the *1907 Regulations* stipulates that

> [a]ll seizure of, destruction or wilful damage done to institutions [dedicated to religion, charity and education, the arts and sciences],[8] historic monu-

8 *1907 Regulations*, art 56(1). *Regulations Respecting the Laws and Customs of War on Land* annexed to *Convention (IV) Respecting the Laws and Customs of War on Land*, The Hague, 18 October 1907 (entered into force 26 January 1910) [*1907 Regulations*], reproduced in Adam Roberts and Richard Guelff (eds), *Documents on the Laws of War* (3rd ed, 2000) 69, also available at http://www.icrc.org/ihl.nsf. See also *Convention (II) with Respect to the Laws and Customs of War on Land*, The Hague, 29 July 1899, 32 Stat. 1803, TS 403 (entered into force 4 September 1900) [*1899*

ments, works of art and science, is forbidden, and should be made the subject of legal proceedings.[9]

Only acts which result in actual seizure, destruction and wilful damage are to be considered a breach of this Article.

B 1954 Convention

Article 28 of the *1954 Convention* requires the High Contracting Parties to

---

Convention (II)]; *Regulations Concerning the Laws and Customs of War on Land*, annexed to *Convention (II) with Respect to the Laws and Customs of War on Land*, The Hague, 29 July 1899 (entered into force 4 September 1900) [*1899 Regulations*], available at http://www.icrc.org/ihl.nsf; *Convention (IV) Respecting the Laws and Customs of War on Land*, The Hague, 18 October 1907, 36 Stat 2277 (entered into force 26 January 1910) [*1907 Convention (IV)*]; *Convention (IX) Concerning Bombardment by Naval Forces in Time of War*, The Hague, 18 October 1907, 36 Stat 2351 (entered into force 26 January 1910) [*1907 Convention (IX)*], reproduced in Roberts and Guelff, ibid 112, also available at http://www.icrc.org/ihl.nsf. In relation to the Geneva Conventions, see *Geneva Convention for the Amelioration of the Condition of the Wounded and Sick in Armed Forces in the Field*, 12 August 1949, 75 UNTS 31, arts 2 and 3 (entered into force 21 October 1950) [*1949 Geneva Convention I*]; *Geneva Convention for the Amelioration of the Condition of Wounded, Sick and Shipwrecked Members of Armed Forces at Sea*, 12 August 1949, 75 UNTS 84, arts 2 and 3 (entered into force 21 October 1950) [*1949 Geneva Convention II*], *Geneva Convention relative to the Treatment of Prisoners of War*, 12 August 1949, 75 UNTS 135, arts 2 and 3 (entered into force 21 October 1950) [*1949 Geneva Convention III*] and *Geneva Convention relative to the Protection of Civilian Persons in Time of War*, 12 August 1949, 75 UNTS 287, arts 2 and 3 (entered into force 21 October 1950) [*1949 Geneva Convention IV*]; *Protocol Additional to the Geneva Conventions of 12 August 1949, and Relating to the Protection of Victims of International Armed Conflicts*, 8 June 1977, 1125 UNTS 3, art 1 (entered into force 7 December 1978) [*Additional Protocol I*]; *Protocol Additional to the Geneva Conventions of 12 August 1949, and Relating to the Protection of Victims of Non-International Armed Conflicts*, 8 June 1977, 1125 UNTS 609 art 1(1) (entered into force 7 December 1978) [*Additional Protocol II*]. In relation to the 1954 Convention, see *Convention for the Protection of Cultural Property in the Event of Armed Conflict*, 14 May 1954, 249 UNTS 240 (entered into force 7 August 1956), art 1(a) [*1954 Convention*]. The *Regulations for the Execution of the Convention for the Protection of Cultural Property in the Event of Armed Conflict* [*1954 Regulations*] annexed to the *Convention* are considered an integral part thereof. See also *Protocol for the Protection of Cultural Property in the Event of Armed Conflict*, 14 May 1954, 249 UNTS 358-64 (entered into force 7 August 1956) [*1954 Protocol*] and *Protocol for the Protection of Cultural Property in the Event of Armed Conflict*, 26 March 1999, 38 ILM 769-82 (entered into force 9 March 2004) [*1999 Protocol*].

9 *1907 Regulations*, art 56(2).

> undertake to take, within the framework of their ordinary criminal jurisdiction, all necessary steps to prosecute and impose penal or disciplinary sanctions upon those persons, of whatever nationality, who commit or order to be committed a breach of the present Convention.[10]

This Article makes it clear that breaches of the *Convention* incur individual criminal responsibility. It declares that States are vested with the jurisdiction to prosecute and punish offenders. States have jurisdiction over persons 'of *whatever* nationality'[11] who either actually commit a breach of the *Convention* or order such a breach to be committed. But in order to exercise jurisdiction, States must first enact the necessary legislation, incorporating the provisions of the *Convention* into national penal codes.[12] As Toman observes, this legislation must be implemented in peacetime and it should specify penalties for each breach to which it refers.[13]

Article 28 has been the subject of much criticism as it neither provides a list of possible violations of the *Convention* nor spells out the concrete sanctions that should be imposed. This Article merely obliges States to prosecute and impose penal or disciplinary sanctions for 'a breach' of the *Convention*. What is to be considered a breach of the *Convention* is left to be specified in the national criminal codes of the High Contracting Parties. Nahlik deems this provision to be 'far too general'.[14] In his view it is not enough merely to state that 'a *breach* of the *Convention*' is to be prosecuted and punished because '[o]ne can conceive of many different ways of violating the *[C]onvention*'.[15] Besides, leaving every detail

10 *1954 Convention*, art 28.

11 Some scholars believe that reference to 'whatever nationality' means that war crimes involving cultural property could be prosecuted anywhere on a theory of criminal universality. See, eg, Jiří Toman, *The Protection of Cultural Property in the Event of Armed Conflict: Commentary on the Convention for the Protection of Cultural Property in the Event of Armed Conflict and its Protocol, signed on 14 May 1954 in The Hague, and on other instruments of international law concerning such protection* (1996), 294; Cherif Bassiouni, 'Reflections on Criminal Jurisdiction in International Protection of Cultural Property' (1983) 10 *Syracuse Journal of International Law and Commerce* 281, 308-309, 315 ['Reflections']; James Nafziger, 'International Penal Aspects of Protecting Cultural Property' (1985) 19 *International Lawyer* 835, 846 ['International Penal Aspects']. But see Patrick Boylan, *Review of the Convention for the Protection of Cultural Property in the Event of Armed Conflict* (1993) , 93, para 9.9 (stressing that this is one of the most obvious weaknesses of Article 28 as its text fails to expressly refer to jurisdiction in relation to the geographical location where the offence is alleged to have taken place) [*Review*].

12 See, eg, Bassiouni, ibid 316; Toman, ibid 293.

13 Toman, ibid.

14 See, Stanislav Nahlik, 'International Law and the Protection of Cultural Property in Armed Conflict' (1976) 27 *Hastings Law Journal* 1069, 1083 ['International Law'].

15 Ibid.

concerning sanctions to state domain assures 'too great a diversity in the rules adopted by the various states',[16] and thereby a non-uniformity of interpretation in evaluating the seriousness of violations and with that the sanctions that are to be imposed.[17] Despite the shortcomings, Article 28 of the *1954 Convention* still provides a real possibility for enforcing sanctions for offences against cultural property and makes it clear that individuals cannot violate with impunity the obligations set forth in the *Convention*.[18]

C Protocol I Additional to the 1949 Geneva Conventions (Additional Protocol I)

Protocol I Additional to the 1949 Geneva Conventions (*Additional Protocol I*) requires the High Contracting Parties and the Parties to the conflict to repress grave breaches, and to take measures necessary to suppress all other breaches of the *1949 Geneva Conventions* or of the *Protocol*.[19] Grave breaches of *Additional Protocol I* are regarded as war crimes, entailing individual criminal responsibility.[20] Unlike the *1954 Convention*, which does not specify breaches that incur individual criminal responsibility, *Additional Protocol I*, in Article 85, does define a number of acts as grave breaches. As specified in its subparagraph (4)(d), one of these acts relates to attacks directed against cultural property.[21]

Article 85(4)(d) of *Additional Protocol I* stipulates that when committed wilfully and in violation of the *1949 Geneva Conventions* or *Additional Protocol I*, the following act must be qualified as a grave breach of the *Protocol* and thus be regarded as a war crime:

> making the clearly-recognized historic monuments, works of art or places of worship which constitute the cultural or spiritual heritage of peoples and to

---

16 Ibid 1084.

17 See, Stanislav Nahlik, 'Protection of Cultural Property' in UNESCO, *International Dimensions of Humanitarian Law* (1988) 210 ['Protection']. See also Nafziger, 'International Penal Aspects', above n 11, 838; Karen Detling, 'Eternal Silence: The Destruction of Cultural Property in Yugoslavia' (1993) 17 *Maryland Journal of International Law and Trade* 41, 73; David Meyer, 'The 1954 Hague Cultural Property Convention and its Emergence into Customary International Law' (1993) 11 *Boston University International Law Journal* 349, 357; Kifle Jote, *International Legal Protection of Cultural Heritage* (1994), 79.

18 See, eg, Nahlik, ibid; Toman, above n 11, 294; John Merryman, 'Two Ways of Thinking about Cultural Property' (1986) 80 *American Journal of International Law* 831, 842 ['Two Ways'].

19 *Additional Protocol I*, arts 85 and 86.

20 Ibid art 85(5).

21 *Additional Protocol I*, art 85(4)(d). Cultural property is also dealt with indirectly in Article 85(3)(f) which relates to the protective emblem. See Toman, above n 11, 393.

> which special protection has been given by special arrangement, for example, within the framework of a competent international organization, the object of attack, causing as a result extensive destruction thereof, where there is no evidence of the violation by the adverse Party of Article 53, sub-paragraph (b), and when such historic monuments, works of art and places of worship are not located in the immediate proximity of military objectives.[22]

This is a very complex and imprecise provision. It stipulates that in order to be regarded as a grave breach, the attack on the protected property must be deliberate and committed in violation of the *Geneva Conventions* or *Additional Protocol I*. Since the *Geneva Conventions* do not expressly cover cultural property, the violation is limited to Article 53 of *Protocol I*. As discussed, Article 53 governs the protection of historic monuments, works of art or places of worship which constitute the cultural or spiritual heritage of peoples. It is these objects to which Article 85(4)(d) refers. However, this Article adds a further requirement noting that these objects must also be under special protection which has been given by special arrangement, for example, within the framework of a competent international organisation. Yet neither this Article nor the remainder of the *Protocol* say anything more about 'special arrangement' or make any further reference to a 'competent international organization'.

Since UNESCO is an international organisation tasked with the protection of cultural property, reference to a 'competent international organization' could be interpreted as including this organisation. In that case the property that enjoys special protection by virtue of a special arrangement would be property which, in accordance with Article 8(6) of the *1954 Convention*, has entered into the International Register of Cultural Property under Special Protection, or property which consistent with Articles 11 and 27 of the *1999 Protocol to the 1954 Convention* has been included in the List of Cultural Property under Enhanced Protection, or property which has entered into the list/s provided for by the *World Heritage Convention*.[23] Consequently, as Toman observes, in defining this grave breach, Article 85(4)(d) goes beyond *Additional Protocol I* and its Article 53 as it also covers elements of the protection afforded by other international instruments.[24]

In addition to the specified requirements, for an act to be considered a grave breach of *Additional Protocol I* and to be regarded a war crime pursuant to Article 85(4)(d), the attack must also 'result' in extensive destruction of cultural objects or places of worship. This clearly deviates from the prohibition to 'direct' an attack against cultural property, as specified in Article 53(a) of *Additional Protocol I*. Moreover, these objects must not have been used in support of the

---

22 *Additional Protocol I*, art 85(4)(d).

23 See Toman, above n 11, 392.

24 Ibid 391-392.

military effort by the opposing party, as stipulated in Article 53(b), and they must not be situated in the immediate proximity of military objectives. It is when 'all' the requirements referred to in Article 85(4) and its sub-paragraph (d) are met that the act constitutes a war crime. High Contracting Parties have the obligation to repress this war crime, irrespective of where it has been committed and regardless of the nationality of the perpetrator, just as they have the obligation to do so in relation to other war crimes.[25]

Therefore, all three applicable instruments here contain provisions – Article 56 of the *1907 Regulations*, Article 28 of the *1954 Convention* and Article 85(4)(d) of *Additional Protocol I* – that envisage individual criminal responsibility for hostile acts directed against cultural property. Persons responsible for the commission of breaches of these instruments or for ordering the breaches to be committed can be brought to justice either at the national or the international level.

III Venues for Prosecution

Where criminal prosecution as a means for enforcing IHL is concerned, this law can be enforced through international, national and mixed (international-national) tribunals. Currently, individuals accused of violations of IHL can be tried by: (1) the permanent ICC, which on the basis of complementarity gives primacy to national jurisdictions; (2) tribunals established by special arrangements, set up under the powers of the United Nations Security Council, namely, the *ad hoc* international criminal tribunals, ICTY and ICTR, and *ad hoc* mixed tribunals, such as the Sierra Leone Tribunal and the Cambodian Tribunal; and (3) by national civilian or military courts or tribunals of the State where the alleged war crimes were committed under the *lex situs* rule, or the State of nationality of the person accused. With respect to national criminal prosecution, there is also a possibility and, indeed, the duty to try certain violations of IHL on the basis of universal jurisdiction, at least when concerned with crimes such as genocide and grave breaches of *Geneva Conventions* and *Additional Protocol I*, as well as the most serious violations of the *1999 Protocol to the 1954 Convention*.

In relation to the Old Bridge, even though its subject-matter jurisdiction includes cultural property-related crimes, the ICC does not have jurisdiction over this particular case because '[t]he Court has jurisdiction only with respect to crimes committed after the entry into force of [its] Statute'.[26] The *Statute of the ICC* entered into force on 1 July 2002, years after the destruction of the Bridge. With respect to the universal jurisdiction provisions of the *1999 Protocol*, the

25 See *Additional Protocol I*, art 86.

26 *Rome Statute of the International Criminal Court*, UN Diplomatic Conference of Plenipotentiaries on the Establishment of an International Criminal Court, UN Doc A/CONF 183/9 (17 July 1998) 2187 UNTS 3 (entered into force 1 July 2002), art 11 [*ICC Statute*], http://www.igc.org/icc/Rome/html.

Protocol does not apply to the Old Bridge either, for the same reasons of being adopted and entering into force well after the destruction of the Old Bridge took place.[27] But even if the *Protocol* had been in force and if Bosnia and Herzegovina was a contracting party, as a single act of destruction, the Old Bridge probably would not have fallen within the universal jurisdiction provisions. However, the destruction of the Bridge is still a breach of the original *1954 Convention*. Criminal proceedings would therefore depend on action by one of three parties: Bosnia and Herzegovina, because the alleged crime was committed in its territory; Croatia, if those responsible were Croatian nationals or under Croatian military control and discipline at the time; or the ICTY.

The expectation of the people who are most immediately affected, as well as of the broader international community is that those responsible are brought to justice. Claims that the destruction was carried out by the HVO and the CA and that the attack on the Bridge was not justified, and the demands to bring the perpetrators to justice have been voiced not only in Bosnia and Herzegovina[28] but also in Croatia,[29] and elsewhere.[30] However, neither Croatia nor the HVO acknowledged responsibility.

---

27 The *1999 Protocol* was adopted on 26 March 1999 and entered into force on 9 March 2004. See above n 8.

28 See, eg, Alija Kebo, 'A Two-Year Mourning Day', a letter of the editor, *Most*, No. 91, November/December 1995, http://w1.500.telia.com/~u50008760/91_2/most2_6.htm (Copy on file with author); Predrag Matvejević, 'The Bridge', *Most*, No. 91, November-December 1995, http://www.most.ba/002/062.htm; Lara Nettelfield and Sarah Wagner, 'Bosnia's Muslims still Cry out for Justice', *The Globe and Mail* (Toronto), Tuesday, 12 July 2005, http://theglobe.ca/servlet/story/RTGAM.20050712.wcomment0712/BNStory/ ; Human Rights Watch, 'Looking for Justice: The War Crimes Chamber in Bosnia and Herzegovina', *Human Rights Watch*, vol 18, No. 1(D), February 2006.

29 See, eg, Ivan Lovrenović, 'Svijet bez mosta – Mostar, devet godina poslije' ['The World without the Bridge – Mostar, Nine Years Later '] *Dani*, archives, No. 256, http://www.bhdani.com/arhiva/256/t25614.shtml; Rabia Ali and Lawrence Lifschultz, 'An Interview with Ivo Banac: The Last Days of Bosnia?' *Boston Review*, February 1994, http://bostonreview.mit.edu/BostonReview/BT19.1/banac.html [Banac Interview]; Vesna Pusić, 'Mostar – In the Croat Name', http://www.barnsdle.demon.co.uk/bosnia/vesna.html; 'War Truth Conference, Del Ponte: Tuđman's Transcripts Valuable Evidence', *Javno* (Croatia), 9 February 2007 (Croatian President Stjepan Mesić, who also participated in the conference, stressed that war crimes did not have justification: 'A Crime is a crime and not a single one should be swept under the rug').

30 See, eg, Message to President Franjo Tuđman from Mrs Leni Fischer, Chairperson of the Committee on Culture and Education, Parliamentary Assembly of the COE, of 10 November 1993, Committee on Culture and Education of Parliamentary Assembly of Council of Europe (COE), *Fourth Information Report*, doc 6999, 19 January 1994 [*Fourth COE Report*]. Letter from Daniel Cardon de Lichtbuer, Executive President of Europa Nostra to President Franjo Tuđman, of 8 December

A Croatia

Croatia rejected claims that it was involved in the Croat-Muslim conflict, in general,[31] and blamed the 'war-time conditions'[32] for the destruction of the Old Bridge, in particular. As discussed, the HVO claimed that the ABH had its positions near the Bridge, that the Bridge was used in clandestine transport of supplies, that it was neither sufficiently marked nor protected and thus that the Bridge was a legitimate military target and its destruction was not a war crime.

In relation to Croatia's alleged involvement in the destruction of the Old Bridge, despite an overwhelming amount of evidence on the subject there are many Croatians who insist that the Bridge was brought down by the Muslim side as an act aimed at depicting itself as a victim and obtaining the sympathy of the international community.[33] However, there are also those who adamantly disagree with this theory. Reportedly, in July 1998, an employee of the Zagreb-based Institute for the Protection of Monuments filed suit against one of the tank crew that destroyed the Old Bridge.[34] But there is no further information on this subject. Nor is there any information on whether any Croatian national or person under Croatian military control and discipline has ever been found responsible for the destruction of the Old Bridge by any Croatian tribunal.

B Bosnia and Herzegovina

Some steps towards bringing to justice those responsible for the destruction of the Old Bridge have been taken in Bosnia and Herzegovina. According to the *Fourth COE Information Report*, in 1993, the Mostar District Military

---

1993, *Fourth COE Report*, ibid; *Final Report of the United Nations Commission of Experts Established Pursuant to Security Council Resolution 780 (1992), Annex XI: Destruction of Cultural Property Report*, S/1994/674/Add.2 (Vol V) 28 December 1994 [*Final Report*].

31 See, eg, Letter from Professor Biserka Nagy, Advisor to President Tuđman to Leni Fischer, Chairperson of the Committee on Culture and Education, Parliamentary Assembly COE, 25 November 1993, *Fourth COE Report*, ibid [Letter from Professor Nagy].

32 Statement of President Tuđman, quoted in Letter from Baron Janko Vranyczany-Dobrinović, Ambassador of Croatia in Brussels, to Jonkheer Daniel Cardon de Lichtbuer, Executive President of Europa Nostra, 9 December 1993, *Fourth COE Report*, above n 30 [Baron Vranyczany-Dobrinović Letter].

33 See proceedings of 15 and 19 February 2007 in *The Prosecutor v Jadranko Prlić, Bruno Stojić, Slobodan Praljak, Milivoj Petković, Valentin Ćorić and Berislav Pušić*, Case No. IT-04-74-T [*Prlić* or *Prlić* case]. See also Ivica Mlivončić, 'Neretvanske obale samo će istina spojiti' ['Only the Truth will Connect the Neretva's Banks'], *Matica*, No 8-9, August-September 2004, 29-30.

34 Ephemera, a month-by-month wired news collection, 'Bridge Rebuilding', http://www.wired.com/news/meanwhile/0,1252,0-1998~7,00.html.

Court interrogated three HVO soldiers suspected of 'firing several tank projectiles which resulted in the collapse of the bridge'.[35] Consistent with a statement issued by the Court, the soldiers suspected of firing tank projectiles, 'acted on their own initiative, without orders from their commanding officers'.[36] The question of responsibility was not considered to have been answered at the time.[37] In 2001, it was reported that the Mostar Cantonal Court was conducting an investigation into the destruction of the Old Bridge. This Court made a similar statement to that by the Mostar Military District Court; that is, the investigation did not include commanding officers.[38] According to the statement made by the investigative Judge, the subject of the investigation was solely the tank crew suspected of firing grenades, without orders from their commanding officers, some of which hit the Old Bridge causing it to subsequently fall down.[39] However, this time, in accordance with the *Rules of the Road*,[40] the case was to be forwarded to the ICTY which could decide whether and at which level – the national or international – the case was to be prosecuted.

1 Rules of the Road

The possibility of arbitrary arrests and unfair trials was a key concern to the international community in the immediate post-conflict phase in Bosnia and Herzegovina. The *Rules of* the *Road* procedure, annexed to the *Rome Agreement*, was introduced to enable the ICTY to oversee prosecutions undertaken by the relevant authorities. The *Rome Agreement* was signed on 18 February 1996, between the Presidents of Bosnia and Herzegovina, Croatia and the Federal Republic of Yugoslavia. Under this agreement, the relevant authority was required to submit each case to the ICTY for approval to proceed to arrest and indict. Under the *Rules of the Road*,

35 *Fourth COE Report*, above n 30.

36 Zagreb Foreign Press Bureau Release, 22 December 1993, quoted in *Fourth COE Report*, ibid.

37 *Fourth COE Report*, ibid.

38 'Dovršava se istraga protiv trojice bivših pripadnika HVO-a: O rušiteljima Starog mosta odlučuje Haag' ['The Investigation into Three Ex-Members of the HVO is Coming to an End: The Hague Decides about the Destroyers of the Old Bridge'], *Večernji list*, 23 May 2001, http://www.hic.hr/hrvatski/vijesti/arhiv/latest/BiH_-_POLITIKA_23_5_2001.

39 Ibid.

40 The 'Rules of the Road' procedure was annexed to the *Rome Agreement*, which was signed on 18 February 1996, between Presidents Izetbegović, Tuđman and Milošević, www.ohr.int/ohr-dept/hr-rol/thedept/war-crime-tr/; http://www.cdsp.neu.edu.

> [p]ersons, other than those already indicted by the International Tribunal, may be arrested and detained for serious violations of international humanitarian law only pursuant to a previously issued order, warrant or indictment that has been reviewed and deemed consistent with international legal standards by the International Tribunal.[41]

The Rules of the Road Unit was established at the Office of the Prosecutor of the ICTY (OTP), tasked with reviewing and evaluating case files from Bosnia and Herzegovina on whether they should proceed.[42] The approval for prosecution at the domestic level was given for 'less serious' cases to be conducted in accordance with domestic laws, while the ICTY reserved for itself those cases where it had already issued a warrant or where it was conducting its own investigation. In total, the OTP reviewed 1,419 cases against 4,985 persons and gave approval for 848 persons to be arrested on war crimes charges. The Rules of the Road Unit was operational until 1 October 2004, when, due to the then scheduled closure of the ICTY,[43] the review of war crimes cases was taken over by the Prosecutor's Office of Bosnia and Herzegovina.

As a component of the ICTY's imminent closure, a specialised chamber – the War Crimes Chamber – was established within the State-level Court of Bosnia and Herzegovina to process 'highly sensitive' war crimes cases.[44] The cases found in the evaluation by the Prosecutor's Office of Bosnia and Herzegovina to be 'sensitive' are to be tried by the domestic courts under the jurisdiction of the Entities – cantonal courts in the Federation of Bosnia and Herzegovina and district courts in the Republika Srpska – and the Basic Court of the Brčko District.[45] According to the Prosecutor's Office of Bosnia and Herzegovina, there are more than 10,000 war crimes suspects on its list.[46] The

---

41 Ibid.

42 See ICTY Factsheet, 'Partnership and Transition between the ICTY and National Courts', http://www.un.org/icty/cases-e/factsheets/partnership-e.htm [para on 'Rules of the Road – Preventing Arbitrary Arrests in Bosnia and Herzegovina'].

43 See UN Security Council Resolution 1503 (2003) adopted by the Security Council at its 4817th meeting, on 28 August 2003, S/RES/1503 (2003).

44 The War Crimes Chamber of Bosnia and Herzegovina was formally established on 6 January 2005 and was inaugurated and began to function on 9 March 2005. For detailed information on the War Crimes Chamber, see, generally, BIRN, *In Pursuit of Justice: Guide to the War Crimes of the Court of BiH* (2006). See also OSCE Mission to Bosnia and Herzegovina, *War Crimes Trials before the Domestic Courts of Bosnia and Herzegovina: Progress and Obstacles*, March 2005, http://www.oscebih.org/documents/1407-eng.pdf.

45 BIRN, ibid 78.

46 Ibid. See also, Agence France-Presse, '12,000 Bosnians could be charged with war crimes: US official', *Dnevni Avaz*, Sarajevo, 14 June 2007; BBC Monitoring European, 'Bosnia announces further war crimes prosecutions', 29 November 2007

War Crimes Chamber will hear only a fraction of the cases – only the most serious cases – because it will have 'neither the resources nor the time to try all war crimes cases'.[47] An extremely high volume of remaining cases is expected to be tried by cantonal or district courts. According to some estimates, this may take decades.[48] Reportedly, courts in Bosnia and Herzegovina are swamped with a backlog of cases. At the beginning of 2006, cantonal and municipal courts in Bosnia and Herzegovina were reported to have 'over 1 m[illion] backlog cases, which is unprecedented in the history of local judiciary'.[49]

Research by this author indicates that there are no published cultural property-related war crimes cases that have been tried by courts in Bosnia and Herzegovina. There is no official public information as to the outcome of the investigation conducted by the Mostar Cantonal Court involving the three HVO soldiers who were suspected of firing projectiles that hit the Old Bridge following which the Bridge collapsed. Nevertheless, for many years there has been the possibility that the Old Bridge case could be dealt with at the international level, by the ICTY.

C The ICTY

The international efforts to bring to justice those responsible for violations of IHL began well before the end of the hostilities in Bosnia and Herzegovina. Determining that, such was the extent of the atrocities which had been committed in the territory of the former Yugoslavia, the situation constituted a threat to international peace and security, on 25 May 1993, acting under Chapter VII of the *UN Charter* powers to decide on measures necessary to maintain or restore international peace and security, the United Nations Security Council by its Resolution 827 (1993) established the ICTY.[50] The *Statute of the ICTY* was adopted by the same Resolution.[51] In relation to the particular circumstances of

(according to Milorad Barašin, deputy head of the War Crimes Department of the State Prosecutor's Office, Bosnia and Herzegovina, 'a total of 16,150 people' have so far been reported on suspicion of having committed war crimes during the 1992-1995 armed conflict in Bosnia and Herzegovina).

47 See 'Orientation Criteria for Sensitive Rules of the Road Cases', Office of the Bosnia and Herzegovina Prosecutor, 12 October 2004.

48 See, eg, OSCE Mission to Bosnia and Herzegovina, above n 44; 'Bosnian War Crimes Trials Halt as Local Courts Swamped with Backlog Cases', excerpt from report by Bosnian public broadcaster BHTV1 on 29 January 2006, BHTV1, Sarajevo, in Bosnian/Croatian/Serbian 1800 gmt 29 January 2006, BBC Worldwide Monitoring, Monday, 30 January 2006 ['Bosnian War Crimes Trials Halt'].

49 'Bosnian War Crimes Trials Halt' ibid.

50 See UN Security Council Resolution 827 (1993) of 25 May 1993, S/Res/827 (1993), para 2, http://www.un.org/icty/basic/statut/S-RES-827_93.htm.

51 Ibid.

the former Yugoslavia, the establishment of an international criminal tribunal and the prosecution of persons responsible for serious violations of IHL was an *ad hoc* measure by the Security Council aimed at 'put[ting] an end to such crimes and [at] bring[ing] to justice the persons who are responsible for them'.[52] At the same time, this was a measure that 'would contribute to the restoration and maintenance of peace'[53] and 'ensur[e] that such violations are halted and effectively redressed'.[54] Never before in the history of the United Nations has the Security Council responded to a threat to international peace and security by establishing an *ad hoc* international criminal tribunal. The circumstances created by the end of the Cold War – that is, the easing of tensions between East and West and the resultant improvement in cooperation amongst the permanent Security Council members, the so-called, Big Five – enabled the Council to take such a measure. The Council's opting for this measure can be seen as a confirmation of the exceptional gravity of the violations of IHL committed in the territory of the former Yugoslavia. Simultaneously, the Council's decision to take this particular measure is an affirmation of the inadequacy of addressing violations of such magnitude at the national level at the time.[55] Although the ICTY and national courts have concurrent jurisdiction over offences involving serious violations of IHL,[56] the ICTY has primacy over national courts as the latter are placed under an obligation to defer to the competence of the ICTY at any stage of the procedure.[57]

Consistent with the purpose of its founding resolution, the aim of the ICTY is to bring to justice persons allegedly responsible for serious violations of IHL, to render justice to the victims, to deter further crimes and to contrib-

52 Ibid Preamble para 5.

53 Ibid para 6.

54 Ibid para 7.

55 See Human Rights Watch, *Justice at Risk: War Crimes Trials in Croatia, Bosnia and Herzegovina, and Serbia and Montenegro*, Vol 16, No 7(D), October 2004, 5, http://hrw.org/reports/2004/icty1004/. See also Human Rights Watch, *War Crimes Trials in the Former Yugoslavia*, Vol 7, No 10, June 1995, http://www.hrw.org/reports/1995/Yugo.htm; OSCE Mission to Bosnia and Herzegovina, above n 44, 4 (2.3. Early Prosecutions of War Crimes in Bosnia and Herzegovina).

56 See *Statute of the International Criminal Tribunal for the Prosecution of Persons Responsible for Serious Violations of International Humanitarian Law Committed in the Territory of the Former Yugoslavia since 1991*, adopted by the UN Security Council Res 827, 25 May 1993, UN SCOR, 48th sess, 3217th mtg at 29 UN Doc S/827/1993, as amended by Res 1166, 13 May 1998 and by Res 1329, 30 November 2000, contained in UN Doc S/25704, Annex (1993), and attached to the 'Report of the Secretary-General Pursuant to Paragraph 2 of Security Council Resolution 808', art 9(1) [*ICTY Statute*]. See also *Report of the Secretary-General Pursuant to Paragraph 2 of Security Council Resolution 808 (1993)*, paras 41-42, UN Doc S/of 3 May 1993, 32 ILM 1159, para 64 [*Report of the Secretary-General*].

57 *ICTY Statute* art 9(2).

ute to the restoration of peace by holding accountable persons responsible for serious violations of IHL.[58] To achieve these aims, the ICTY has jurisdiction only over natural persons and not over legal persons. It has limited geographical and temporal jurisdiction. The former is restricted to the territory of the former Yugoslavia and the latter to serious violations of IHL committed since 1991. The Tribunal has the power to prosecute and try grave breaches of the *1949 Geneva Conventions*, violations of the laws or customs of war, genocide and crimes against humanity. The Tribunal's subject-matter jurisdiction includes violations of IHL involving cultural property. This chapter now turns to examination of the specific provisions of the *ICTY Statute* dealing with cultural property and their applicability to the Old Bridge case.

IV The ICTY's Approach to Cultural Property

A The ICTY Statute

1 Definition of Cultural Property

For the first time ever, cultural property is covered directly by a statute of an international criminal tribunal – the *ICTY Statute*. This is an unprecedented recognition of the significance of cultural property. However, the *ICTY Statute* does not explicitly use the term 'cultural property'. Its only provision, namely, Article 3(d), which covers cultural property directly, refers only to some components of what is considered to be cultural property within the meaning of the *1954 Convention*. The list of enumerated components of cultural property is very limited when compared to the expansive definition of cultural property given in Article 1 of the *1954 Convention*. Also, cultural property referred to in Article 3(d) of the *Statute* is not dealt with exclusively but, rather, is mixed with other property, such as institutions dedicated to religion, charity, education and science, which does not necessarily constitute cultural property.

Article 3(d) is not based exclusively on the *1954 Convention*, the specialist treaty protecting cultural property in armed conflict. Like its predecessor, the *IMT Charter*, the *ICTY Statute* echoes the language of the *1907 Regulations*. The reason for basing not only its sub-paragraph (d) but the whole Article 3 on the *1907 Regulations* is that when establishing the ICTY, the United Nations wanted the Tribunal to strictly adhere to the principle *nullum crimen sine lege*.[59] The *Report of the Secretary-General* concerning the establishment of the ICTY

58 Ibid Preamble. See also Fact Sheet on ICTY Proceedings, ICTY at a Glance, General Information, http://www.un.org/icty/cases-e/factsheets/generalinfo-e.htm [ICTY Fact Sheets].

59 See *Report of the Secretary-General*, above n 56, paras 34 and 35 (italics omitted in original; footnotes omitted).

does not specify which provisions of the *1907 Regulations* form the basis for Article 3 of the *ICTY Statute*.

As far as subparagraph (d) of this Article is concerned, protection is afforded to historic monuments and works of art and science, along with institutions dedicated to the arts, sciences, religion, charity and education. These objects are listed, either partly or in full, in Articles 27 and 56 of the *1907 Regulations*, as well as in Article 5 of *1907 Convention (IX)*. The term 'partly or in full' means that the scope of protection under these three articles is not the same. Article 27 of the *1907 Regulations* provides protection only to immovable property: 'buildings dedicated to religion, art, science, or charitable purposes, historic monuments, hospitals, and places where the sick and wounded are collected'.[60] Article 5 of *1907 Convention (IX)* also protects the following immovables: 'sacred edifices, buildings used for artistic, scientific, or charitable purposes, historic monuments, hospitals, and places where the sick or wounded are collected'.[61] Article 56 of the *1907 Regulations*, on the other hand, protects both immovable property ('institutions dedicated to religion, charity and education, the arts and sciences...and historic monuments') and movable property ('works of art and science').[62] Where immovable property is concerned, there is a difference between the scope of protection (with respect to the components of cultural property that are covered) of Article 56 and of Articles 27 and 5. Unlike Articles 27 and 5, Article 56 does not accord protection to 'hospitals, and places where the sick and/or wounded are collected'.

There is also a difference between the three Articles as to when they apply. Article 27 of the *1907 Regulations* is placed in Section II: Hostilities, Chapter I: Means of Injuring the Enemy, Sieges, and Bombardments, whereas Article 56 forms part of Section III: Military Authority over the Territory of the Hostile State. Article 5 of *1907 Convention (IX)* is included in Chapter II: General Provisions. Moreover, Article 27 of the *1907 Regulations* and Article 5 of *1907 Convention (IX)* include the exception of military necessity and the prohibition on the use of the protected property for military purposes, whereas there is no mention of these two elements in Article 56 of the *1907 Regulations*.

Since the *Report of the Secretary-General* does not specify which provisions of the *1907 Regulations* form the basis for Article 3(d) of the *Statute*, an examination of the IMT's approach and of the ICTY's approach to this question should be undertaken. The IMT acknowledged that the *1907 Regulations* in their totality formed part of customary international law. However, when discussing the applicable law, the IMT did not expressly refer to Article 27 of the *Regulations* either in relation to war crimes generally or when addressing the

60 *1907 Regulations*, art 27(1).

61 *1907 Convention (IX)*, art 5(1).

62 *1907 Regulations*, art 56.

offences involving cultural property specifically. Rather, the explicit reference was made to Article 56 of the *1907 Regulations*.[63]

The jurisprudence of the ICTY reveals an uneven approach to the question of the basis for Article 3(d) of the *ICTY Statute*. For instance, the Trial Chamber in *Jokić* refers to all of the above-mentioned Articles as the law applicable to cultural property but without specifying the basis for Article 3(d) of the *ICTY Statute*.[64] The Trial Chamber in *Strugar* held explicitly that Article 3(d) of the *Statute* is based on Article 27 of the *1907 Regulations*. The *Strugar* Trial Chamber's dealing with this question was very brief: 'Turning now to the crime under *Article 3(d)*, the Chamber notes that this provision *is based on Article 27 of the Hague Regulations*'.[65] It is regrettable that the *Strugar* Trial Chamber – the first ever to deal with immovable cultural property extensively – did not elaborate this finding fully.

Nevertheless, it is more likely that the scope of Article 3(d) coincides with that provided for in Article 56 than Article 27 of the *1907 Regulations*. Not only are the same objects enumerated in Article 56 of the *Regulations* as in Article 3(d) of the *ICTY Statute*, but also the acts that are listed as being prohibited – that is, 'seizure of, destruction or wilful damage done to' cultural and other objects – are identical. Article 27 does not make reference to 'seizure, destruction or damage'. Because it falls in the chapter of the *Regulations* which limits the means of warfare – Means of Injuring the Enemy, Sieges, and Bombardments – Article 27 imposes an obligation on the attacker to take 'all necessary steps… to spare, as far as possible' cultural property during 'sieges and bombardments', and also requires the possessor of the property enumerated therein to refrain from using such objects 'for military purposes'.[66] Moreover, 'hospitals, and places where the sick and wounded are collected', which are specifically referred to in Article 27 of the *1907 Regulations*, are not included in Article 3(d) of the *ICTY Statute*, just as they are not included in Article 56 of the *1907 Regulations*. Therefore, an identical wording of Article 56 of the *1907 Regulations* and Article 3(d) of the *ICTY Statute* makes it apparent that Article 3(d) is based on Article 56 and not on Article 27 of the *1907 Regulations*. However, this does not exclude the application of Article 27 or of other articles of the *1907 Regulations* relevant to cultural property.

---

63 See Trial of the Major War Criminals before the International Military Tribunal, Judgement, Nürnberg, 1 October 1946, Official Documents, vol I, 171 [*IMT* Judgement], War Crimes and Crimes against Humanity, (C) Pillage of Public and Private Property, para 1 and (F) The Law relating to War Crimes and Crimes against Humanity, para 3.

64 See *Jokić* Sentencing Judgement, para 47and nn 64 and 65.

65 *Prosecutor v Pavle Strugar*, Judgement, Trial Chamber II, 31 January 2005, Case No. IT-01-42-T, para 229 (emphasis added) [*Strugar* Trial Judgement].

66 *1907 Regulations*, art 27(1).

2 Crimes

The ICTY has competence *ratione materiae* over the following crimes: grave breaches of the *1949 Geneva Conventions*, spelt out in Article 2 of the *ICTY Statute*; violations of the laws or customs of war, provided for in Article 3 of the *Statute*; genocide, covered by Article 4 of the *Statute*, and; crimes against humanity, listed in Article 5 of the *Statute*. As discussed, only Article 3(d) makes direct reference to components of cultural property.

Since cultural property is also civilian property, in addition to the protection afforded by Article 3(d) of the *ICTY Statute*, it also enjoys the protection granted to civilian property. Several other provisions of Article 3 deal with civilian property generally, under the rubric of violations of the laws or customs of war, namely: Article 3(b) – wanton destruction of cities, towns or villages, or devastation not justified by military necessity; Article 3(c) – attack, or bombardment, by whatever means, of undefended towns, villages, dwellings, or buildings; and Article 3(e) – plunder of public or private property. Cultural property may also be protected by Article 2(d) – extensive destruction and appropriation of property, not justified by military necessity and carried out unlawfully and wantonly (a grave breach of the *1949 Geneva Conventions*). Cultural property also enjoys protection under Article 5(h) – persecutions on political, racial and religious grounds (a crime against humanity). Nevertheless, these Articles do not recognise the special status of cultural property. The protection given is the same as that provided for any other civilian object. In case of persecution it is the civilian population to which cultural property is attached that enjoys primary protection and not cultural property itself – cultural property plays only an auxiliary role here.[67]

This chapter now turns to an examination of the relevant provisions of the *ICTY Statute* dealing with cultural property. The chapter first considers provisions covering cultural property indirectly. The consideration is very brief, aimed only at highlighting the place assigned to cultural property in the *Statute*. These provisions otherwise will not be further addressed in this book. Attention will be focused solely on Article 3(d) of the *Statute*, which, as noted, in part deals with cultural property directly. Since this book focuses on immovable cultural property, provisions of the *Statute* dealing with movable cultural property will not be considered either.

---

67 For a detailed discussion on the scope for offences relating to the destruction of cultural property to be prosecuted under the *ICTY Statute*, see generally, Hirad Abtahi, 'The Protection of Cultural Property in Times of Armed Conflict: The Practice of the International Criminal Tribunal for the Former Yugoslavia' (2001) 14 *Harvard Human Rights Journal* 1.

(a) Provisions Dealing with Cultural Property Indirectly

With regard to jurisdiction *ratione materiae* of the ICTY, the majority of crimes are crimes against persons. Seven of eight offences punishable under Article 2 of the *Statute*, which are categorised as 'grave breaches of the *Geneva Conventions of 1949*', deal with crimes directed against persons. 'Extensive destruction and appropriation of property, not justified by military necessity and carried out unlawfully and wantonly'[68] (under sub-paragraph (d)) is the only grave breach of the *Geneva Conventions* included in Article 2 that relates to property.

In contrast to Article 2, Article 3 of the *Statute* is a property-related article. Four of its five provisions deal with property: 'wanton destruction of cities, towns or villages, or devastation not justified by military necessity';[69] 'attack, or bombardment, by whatever means, of undefended towns, villages, dwellings, or buildings';[70] 'seizure of, destruction or wilful damage done to institutions dedicated to religion, charity and education, the arts and science, historic monuments and works of art and science';[71] and 'plunder of public or private property'.[72]

Again, however, Article 5, covering crimes against humanity, is in its entirety a persons-related article. Likewise, Article 4, which covers genocide, does not include any direct reference to any property whatsoever. However, according to the jurisprudence of the ICTY, as well as that of the ICJ, unlike crimes against humanity (the crime of persecution to be more precise), acts directed against cultural property cannot amount to a crime of genocide.[73]

(b) Provisions Dealing with Cultural Property Directly – Article 3(d) of the ICTY Statute

Article 3(d) of the *ICTY Statute* protects historic monuments and works of art and science along with institutions dedicated to the arts, sciences, education, religion and charity. This Article states:

> The International Tribunal shall have the power to prosecute persons violating the laws or customs of war. Such violations shall include, but not be limited to:

68 *ICTY Statute*, art 2(d).

69 Ibid art 3(b).

70 Ibid art 3(c).

71 Ibid art 3(d).

72 Ibid art 3(e).

73 See, eg, *Prosecutor v Radislav Krstić*, Judgement, Trial Chamber I, 2 August 2001, Case No. IT-98-33-T, para 580 [*Krstić* Trial Judgement]; ICJ, *Application of the Genocide Convention*, para 344. http://www.icj-cij.org/cijwww/cdoket/cbhyjudgements/cbhy_cjudgment_20070226/.

...

(d) seizure of, destruction or wilful damage done to institutions dedicated to religion, charity and education, the arts and sciences, historic monuments and works of art and science.[74]

Article 3(d) accords protection to a limited number of categories of property. Only a few of the objects enumerated therein fall under the rubric of 'cultural property'. Notwithstanding this, Article 3(d) protects cultural property in its own right and does not require any link to a particular group of people. This article applies in both international and non-international armed conflict.[75]

(i) Prerequisites Common to All Article 3 Offences

The applicability of Article 3(d) of the *ICTY Statute* is subject to the fulfilment of several requirements common to all offences covered by Article 3 of the *Statute*. First of all, there must be an armed conflict at the time an offence is allegedly committed, and there must be a close nexus between an armed conflict and an alleged offence.[76] The Appeals Chamber in *Kunarac* held that an armed conflict 'need not have been causal to the commission of the crime, but the existence of an armed conflict must, at a minimum, have played a substantial part in the perpetrator's ability to commit it, his decision to commit it, the manner in which it was committed or the purpose for which it was committed'.[77] In addition to these two preliminary requirements, a further four, the so-called *Tadić* conditions must be met.

(ii) The Four *Tadić* Conditions relating to Article 3(d) of the *ICTY Statute*

The *Tadić* conditions require that:

---

74 *ICTY Statute*, art. 3(d).

75 See, eg, *Prosecutor v Duško Tadić aka 'Dule'*, Decision on the Defence Motion for Interlocutory Appeal on Jurisdiction, Appeals Chamber, 2 October 1995, Case No. IT-94-1-AR72 paras 86, 87, 94, 98, 127 [*Tadić* Jurisdiction Decision]; *Prosecutor v Furundžija*, Judgement, Trial Chamber II, 10 December 1998, Case No. IT-95-17/1-T, para 132 [*Furundžija* Trial Judgement]; *Strugar* Trial Judgement, para 216.

76 See, eg, *Tadić* Jurisdiction Decision, para 70; *Prosecutor v Mladen Naletilić aka 'Tuta' and Vinko Martinović aka 'Štela'*, Judgement, Trial Chamber, 31 March 2003, Case No. IT-98-34-T para 225 [*Naletilić* Trial Judgement or *Naletilić* case or *Naletilić*]; *Strugar* Trial Judgement, para 215.

77 *Prosecutor v Dragoljub Kunarac, Radomir Kovač and Zoran Vuković*, Judgement, Appeals Chamber, 12 June 2002, Case No. IT-96-23 & IT-96-23/1-A, para 58 [*Kunarac* Appeal Judgement].

(i) the violation must constitute an infringement of a rule of international humanitarian law;
(ii) the rule must be customary in nature or, if it belongs to treaty law, the required conditions must be met [...];
(iii) the violation must be 'serious', that is to say, it must constitute a breach of a rule protecting important values, and the breach must involve grave consequences for the victim [...];
(iv) the violation of the rule must entail, under customary or conventional law, the individual criminal responsibility of the person breaching the rule.[78]

Consistent with the first and second *Tadić* conditions, to be prosecutable under Article 3(d) of the *ICTY Statute*, the violation must constitute an infringement of a rule of IHL, and the rule must be customary in nature or, if it belongs to treaty law, the treaty must be binding on the parties at the time of the alleged offence and must not be in conflict with or derogating from peremptory norms of international law. The offence of destruction or wilful damage of cultural property covered by Article 3(d) of the *ICTY Statute* constitutes a breach of both customary and treaty IHL. As discussed, in armed conflict, cultural property is protected against destruction or wilful damage by Articles 27 and 56 of the *1907 Regulations*, the provisions that form part of customary IHL. These provisions are reflected in the *1954 Convention* the core provisions of which are also considered to be part of customary IHL.[79] Furthermore, the protection is accorded to cultural property by Article 52 of *Additional Protocol I* under the category of general protection of civilian objects. The principles embodied in this article are considered beyond doubt to be customary IHL.[80]

The Appeals Chamber in *Tadić* found that the customary rules relating to the protection of cultural property had developed to govern both international and non-international armed conflict.[81] Significantly, the *1954 Convention* expressly provides protection to cultural property in both types of armed con-

78 *Tadić* Jurisdiction Decision, para 94.

79 Ibid para 98; *Strugar* Trial Judgement, para 229.

80 See, eg, *Prosecutor v Pavle Strugar, Miodrag Jokić and Others*, Decision on Interlocutory Appeal, 22 November 2002, para 10, Case No. IT-01-42-AR72; *Prosecutor v Enver Hadžihasanović, Mehmed Alagić and Amir Kubura*, Decision on Interlocutory Appeal Challenging Jurisdiction in Relation to Command Responsibility, Appeals Chamber, 16 July 2003, Case No. IT-01-47-AR72, para 45 [*Hadžihasanović* Interlocutory Appeal Decision]; Jean-Marie Henckaerts and Louise Doswald-Beck (eds), *Customary International Humanitarian Law* (2005) vol I *Rules*, vol II *Practice*, Chapter 12: Cultural Property, 723 *et seq* [*Customary IHL*], vol. 1, 127-128.

81 *Tadić* Jurisdiction Decision, para 127. See also *Strugar* Trial Judgement, para 229.

flict.[82] Article 53 of *Additional Protocol I* and Article 16 of *Additional Protocol II* also protect cultural property in international and non-international armed conflict respectively. It follows that Article 3(d) of the *ICTY Statute* is a rule of IHL, which is treaty-based as well as custom-based and that, thus, the first two *Tadić* conditions are satisfied.

Under the third *Tadić* condition, the violation of IHL must be 'serious'. Namely, it must constitute a breach of a rule protecting important values, and the breach must involve grave consequences for the victim. As the Trial Chamber in *Strugar* observed, the very definition of cultural property points to the seriousness of the offence covered by Article 3(d) of the *ICTY Statute*, i.e., destruction or wilful damage to cultural property.[83] Article 1(a) of the *1954 Convention* expressly states that cultural property is property 'of great importance to the cultural heritage of every people'.[84] The victim of this offence is to be understood broadly as a 'people', rather than any particular individual. 'People' here is to be understood to be the people of whose cultural heritage the cultural property concerned is a constitutive part. Since 'each people makes its contribution to the culture of the world…damage to cultural property belonging to any people whatsoever means damage to the cultural heritage of all [hu]mankind'.[85] Accordingly, the notion of the victim in this context is even broader. It is ultimately 'all humankind' that is disinherited by the destruction of, or affected by the damage done to, cultural property. Consequently, the offence under Article 3(d) of the *Statute* is a very serious crime with ongoing effects. As held by the *Strugar* Trial Chamber, 'the offence can be said to involve grave consequences for the victim'.[86]

The reasoning in the *Jokić* Sentencing Judgement is illustrative of the 'seriousness' of the offence within the meaning of Article 3(d) of the *ICTY Statute*. The *Jokić* Trial Chamber noted that the destruction and damage to the Old Town of Dubrovnik were 'very serious crimes' with 'long-lasting consequences'.[87] Specifically, the crime of destruction or wilful damage done to institutions dedicated to religion, charity, education, and the arts and sciences, and to historic monuments and works of art and science 'represents a violation of *values especially protected by the international community*'.[88] The Trial Chamber held that the attack on the Old Town 'was an attack not only against the history and heritage of the region, but also against the cultural heritage of humankind'.[89]

82 See *1954 Convention*, arts 18(1) and 19(1).

83 See *Strugar* Trial Judgement, para 232.

84 *1954 Convention*, art 1(a).

85 Ibid Preamble para 2.

86 *Strugar* Trial Judgement, para 232.

87 *Jokić* Sentencing Judgement, para 45.

88 Ibid para 46 (emphasis added).

89 Ibid para 51.

Consequently, 'since it is a serious violation of international law to attack civilian buildings, *it is a crime of even greater seriousness to direct an attack on an especially protected site*'.[90] The *Jokić* Trial Chamber found that the 'unlawful attack on the Old Town [of Dubrovnik] must therefore be viewed as especially wrongful conduct'.[91] In view of the aforementioned, the offence under Article 3(d) of the *ICTY Statute* can be said to be a serious violation of IHL, which hence satisfies the third *Tadić* condition.

The fourth *Tadić* condition requires that the violation of the rule of IHL entails, under customary or treaty law, the individual criminal responsibility of the person breaching the rule concerned. Article 6 of the *IMT Charter* provided for individual criminal responsibility for war crimes.[92] As noted, the *IMT Charter* has been explicitly referred to by the UN Secretary-General as part of treaty IHL which has beyond doubt become part of customary IHL.[93] Article 28 of the *1954 Convention* also provides for individual criminal responsibility for breaches of rules concerning cultural property. This article stipulates that '[t]he High Contracting Parties undertake to take, within the framework of their ordinary criminal jurisdiction, all necessary steps to prosecute and impose penal or disciplinary sanctions upon those persons, of whatever nationality, who commit or order to be committed a breach of the Convention'.[94]

ICTY case law further confirms that Article 3(d) of the *ICTY Statute* entails individual criminal responsibility. A number of indictments charge the defendants with seizure, destruction or wilful damage done to objects enumerated in Article 3(d).[95] About one fifth of all ICTY cases deal with offences charged under Article 3(d) of the *ICTY Statute*.[96] Some of these cases have resulted in convictions for offences under Article 3(d).[97] Therefore, the fourth *Tadić* condition is also met.

---

90 Ibid para 53 (emphasis added).

91 Ibid.

92 See, eg, *Report of the Secretary-General*, above n 56, para 42; *Strugar* Trial Judgement, para 233.

93 *Report of the Secretary-General*, ibid para 35.

94 *1954 Convention*, art 28.

95 For a list of ICTY Indictments visit http://www.un.org/icty/cases/indictments-e.htm.

96 Some ICTY indictments initially included charges punishable under Article 3(d), but these were later dropped.

97 See 'Dubrovnik' cases involving charges related to cultural property: *Strugar* Trial Judgement (the accused General Strugar sentenced to eight years imprisonment); *Jokić* Sentencing Judgement (the accused Admiral Jokić pleaded guilty to six counts of violations of the laws or customs of war, and sentenced to seven years imprisonment).

(iii) Elements of the Crime of the Destruction or Wilful Damage of Cultural Property

When all the prerequisites common to all offences under Article 3 of the *ICTY Statute* are satisfied, additional elements must be met if an offence is to be charged under paragraph (d) of this Article specifically. Several ICTY cases have dealt with the definition of the crime under Article 3(d). As discussed, in *Blaškić* the Trial Chamber adopted the following definition:

> The damage or destruction must have been committed intentionally to institutions which may clearly be identified as dedicated to religion or education and which were not being used for military purposes at the time of the acts. In addition, the institutions must not have been in the immediate vicinity of military objectives.[98]

In *Naletilić*, the Trial Chamber rejected the holding in *Blaškić* that in order to be protected, the institutions must not have been located in the immediate vicinity of military objectives.[99] The Trial Chamber identified the following elements of the crime under Article 3(d) of the *ICTY Statute* with respect to destruction of institutions dedicated to religion: '(i) the general requirements of Article 3 of the *Statute* are fulfilled; (ii) the destruction regards an institution dedicated to religion; (iii) the property was not used for military purposes; (iv) the perpetrator acted with the intent to destroy the property'.[100]

The *Kordić* Trial Chamber observed that the offence under Article 3(d) overlaps to a certain extent with the offence of unlawful attacks on civilian objects.[101] However, the *Kordić* Trial Chamber stressed that 'the object of the offence within the meaning of Article 3(d) is more specific: the cultural heritage of a certain population'.[102] As far as acts against cultural heritage are concerned, the provision of Article 3(d) is *lex specialis* in the opinion of the Trial Chamber.[103] The Chamber further emphasised that, consistent with the custom codified in Article 27 of the *1907 Regulations*, protection will be lost if cultural property is used for military purposes.[104]

---

98 *Prosecutor v Tihomir Blaškić*, Judgement, Trial Chamber I, 3 March 2000, Case No. IT-95-14-T, para 185 [*Blaškić* Trial Judgement].

99 *Naletilić* Trial Judgement, para 604.

100 Ibid para 605.

101 *Prosecutor v Dario Kordić and Mario Čerkez*, Judgement, Trial Chamber III, 26 February 2001, Case No. IT-95-14/2-T, para 361 [*Kordić* Trial Judgement or *Kordić* case or Kordić].

102 Ibid.

103 Ibid.

104 Ibid para 362.

The Trial Chamber in *Strugar* observed that while both Article 4 of the *1954 Convention* and Article 53 of *Additional Protocol I* proscribe acts of hostility 'directed' against cultural property, Article 3(d) of the *ICTY Statute* criminalises explicitly only those acts which 'result' in damage to, or destruction of such property.[105] This is consistent with the wording of Article 56 of the *1907 Regulations*, with which Article 3(d) of the *Statute* is identical. In the *Strugar* Trial Chamber's view, a requisite element of the crime under Article 3(d) is therefore 'actual damage or destruction occurring as a result of an act directed against this property'.[106]

The *Strugar* Trial Chamber further underscores that cultural property loses protection where such property is used for military purposes.[107] To restate, with respect to the difference between the *Blaškić* and *Naletilić* Trial Chambers' holding regarding the use of the immediate surroundings of cultural property for military purposes, the *Strugar* Chamber held that 'the preferable view appears to be that it is the *use* of cultural property and not its location that determines whether and when the cultural property would lose its protection'.[108] This Chamber noted that, consistent with Article 27 of the *1907 Regulations*, referring to 'in sieges and bombardments', it is not because of the location of cultural property, but because of its use when such property loses its protection.[109] To strengthen its view, the *Strugar* Trial Chamber pointed to the *1999 Protocol* (to the *1954 Convention*). In accordance with Article 6(a)(i) of this *Protocol*, the protection of cultural property is waived 'when and for as long as that cultural property has, by its *function*, been made into a military objective'.[110] In relation to the *mens rea* element of the crime within the meaning of Article 3(d), the *Strugar* Trial Chamber noted that it was 'guided by the previous jurisprudence of the Tribunal that a perpetrator must act with a direct intent to damage or destroy the property in question'.[111] In view of the above, the *Strugar* Trial Chamber held that an act will fulfil the elements of the crime of destruction or wilful damage of cultural property, within the meaning of Article 3(d) of the *ICTY Statute* and insofar as that provision relates to cultural property, if:

(i) it has caused damage or destruction to property which constitutes the cultural or spiritual heritage of peoples;

---

105 *Strugar* Trial Judgement, para 308.

106 Ibid.

107 Ibid para 310.

108 Ibid (emphasis added).

109 Ibid fn 957.

110 *1999 Protocol*, art 6(a)(i) (emphasis added). Several other articles of the *1999 Protocol*, including Articles 12 and 13, dealing with the immunity of cultural property under enhanced protection, refer to the 'use' of cultural property for military purposes.

111 *Strugar* Trial Judgement, para 311.

(ii) the damaged or destroyed property was not used for military purposes at the time when the acts of hostility directed against these objects took place; and

(iii) the act was carried out with the intent to damage or destroy the property in question.[112]

3 Modes of Liability

Consistent with Article 6 of the *ICTY Statute*, the Tribunal has jurisdiction over natural persons. Persons responsible for crimes over which the ICTY has jurisdiction are individually responsible. Individual criminal responsibility is dealt with in Article 7 of the *Statute*. This Article envisages two forms of liability: individual criminal responsibility and superior or command responsibility. Drawn upon the precedents following WWII, Article 7 also contains provisions regarding the individual criminal responsibility of heads of States, government officials and persons acting in an official capacity.

(a) Individual Criminal Responsibility under Article 7(1) of the ICTY Statute

Pursuant to Article 7(1) of the *ICTY Statute*, all persons who participate in the planning, instigating, ordering or executing of a crime, or who aid and abet in the planning, preparation or execution of a crime falling under the jurisdiction of the ICTY contribute to the commission of the violation of IHL concerned and are, thus, individually responsible. In other words, individual criminal responsibility enshrined in Article 7(1) of the *ICTY Statute* goes beyond physically committing the crime.[113] In addition to responsibility for being the actual perpetrator of the *actus reus* of an offence, this mode of liability includes responsibility for offences committed by others, on the ground of 'ordering, planning, instigating or otherwise aiding and abetting in the planning, preparation, or execution of the crimes'.[114]

(b) Superior Responsibility under Article 7(3) of the ICTY Statute

Article 7(3) of the *ICTY Statute* provides that a superior may be held liable for crimes committed by a subordinate, on condition that the superior 'knew or had reason to know' that the subordinate was about to commit a crime or had done so and the superior 'failed to take the necessary and reasonable measures' to prevent the crime or to punish the perpetrators. This mode of liability is referred

---

112 Ibid para 312.

113 See *Prosecutor v Delalić et al* ('*Čelebići*'), Judgement, Trial Chamber II, 16 November 1998, Case No. IT-96-21-T, para 319 [*Čelebići* Trial Judgement].

114 See *Blaškić* Trial Judgement, para 265.

to as superior responsibility or command responsibility. Both terms are used here interchangeably. The principle of individual criminal responsibility for failure to prevent or to punish crimes committed by subordinates is an established principle of international customary law,[115] applicable to both international and non-international armed conflicts.[116] Superior responsibility comprises three essential elements as identified by the *Čelebići* Trial Chamber:

> (i) the existence of a superior-subordinate relationship;
> (ii) the superior knew or had reason to know that the criminal act was about to be or had been committed; and
> (iii) the superior failed to take the necessary and reasonable measures to prevent the criminal act or punish the perpetrator thereof.[117]

Not only military commanders but also civilian superiors are under the duty to prevent and punish, within the limits of their power. After all, to every superior position is attached a certain degree of responsibility, including responsibility for the failure to exercise control over subordinates. As held in *Krnojelac*:

> It cannot be overemphasized that where superior responsibility is concerned, an accused is not charged with the crimes of his subordinates, but with his failure to carry out his duty to exercise control.[118]

The case at hand raises the questions of whether the persons allegedly responsible for the destruction of the Old Bridge failed to take the necessary and reasonable measures to prevent the destruction of the Bridge, and whether those persons failed to punish the perpetrators. It also raises the question of responsibility under Article 7(1) of the *ICTY Statute*. However, before considering this question, it is necessary to examine whether the destruction of the Old Bridge amounts to a war crime within the meaning of the *ICTY Statute*. As noted, whereas the destruction of cultural property can amount to a crime under several articles of the *ICTY Statute*, only one article – Article 3(d) of the *Statute* – directly concerns cultural property. For present purposes, the following dis-

115 See, eg, *Prosecutor v Zejnil Delalić, Zdravko Mučić, aka 'Pavo', Hazim Delić, Esad Landžo, aka 'Zenga'*, Judgement, Appeals Chamber, 20 February 2001, Case No. IT-96-21-A, para 195 [*Čelebići* Appeal Judgement]; *Čelebići* Trial Judgement, para 343; *Strugar* Trial Judgement, para 357.

116 See, eg, *Hadžihasanović* Interlocutory Appeal Decision, para 31; *Strugar* Trial Judgement, para 357.

117 *Čelebići* Trial Judgement, para 346, followed in the *Naletilić* Trial Judgement, para 65.

118 *Prosecutor v Milorad Krnojelac*, Judgement, Appeals Chamber, 17 September 2003, Case No. IT-97-25-A, para 171 [*Krnojelac* Appeal Judgement].

cussion focuses solely on the applicability of Article 3(d) of the *ICTY Statute* to the destruction of the Old Bridge.

B Application of the ICTY Statute to the Old Bridge

For the act of the destruction of the Old Bridge, as with any other act, to amount to a war crime within the meaning of the *ICTY Statute* and to give rise to individual criminal responsibility, it is necessary to establish that the act is proscribed by the *Statute*, that there is evidence that the act has occurred and that someone is responsible.

1 Was the Destruction of the Old Bridge a Proscribed Act?

To amount to a crime under Article 3(d) of the *ICTY Statute*, destruction of cultural property must occur at the time an armed conflict existed and there must be a close nexus between the conflict and the alleged destruction. With respect to the first prerequisite, there is ample evidence that confirms the existence of armed conflict between the HVO forces and the ABH in the area of Mostar at the time of the attack on the Old Bridge and its final destruction on 9 November 1993. This is an adjudicated fact. In *Naletilić*, the Trial Chamber was 'satisfied that an armed conflict existed during the time relevant to the indictment, i.e., at least between 17 April 1993 and the end of February 1994'.[119] This Trial Chamber found that incidents between military formations of the HVO and of the ABH were taking place in Mostar around mid-April 1993. On 9 May 1993, large-scale hostilities broke out in this city. Single attacks went on during the summer and autumn of 1993 and ended only in late February 1994 as a consequence of the *Washington Agreement*.[120] As discussed, the absence of fighting between the HVO and the ABH on 8 and 9 November 1993 in the area of the Old Bridge does not affect the existence of armed conflict.

Since Article 3 of the *ICTY Statute* applies to both international and non-international armed conflicts, the applicability of Article 3(d) of the *Statute* is not dependent on the nature of the conflict in Mostar at the time of the destruction of the Old Bridge. The nature of the conflict is relevant only in relation to Article 2 of the *Statute* covering the grave breaches of the *1949 Geneva Conventions*. Nevertheless, an overwhelming amount of evidence relating to Croatia's involvement in this conflict – proving the international character of

119 *Naletilić* Trial Judgement, para 179.

120 Ibid fn 503.

the conflict – has been presented in several ICTY cases, including the *Naletilić* case,[121] the *Kordić* case,[122] the *Blaškić* case[123] and the ongoing *Prlić* case.[124]

With respect to the second prerequisite, a nexus between the crime and the armed conflict, it must be shown that the crime which was committed was closely related to the hostilities; that is, in the course, and as a consequence, of an armed conflict between the HVO and ABH. In other words, it must be proven that this conflict played a substantial part in the perpetrator's ability to commit this offence or decision to commit it, the manner in which it was committed or the purpose for which it was committed. Evidence suggests that the Old Bridge was destroyed by the HVO forces, which were a warring party in this conflict. The attack on the Bridge and its destruction occurred on 8 and 9 November 1993, in the course of the conflict. The destruction of the Bridge was not an incident unrelated to the conflict, but was directly related to the conflict. The Bridge was targeted on several occasions. The shelling was prolonged. The Bridge was destroyed by tank shells. The purpose of its destruction was, *inter alia*, to remove traces of the 'other'. Presumably, due to its Ottoman-era origins, the Bridge symbolised the 'otherness' in the HVO's view. Numerous reports and other evidence, including the HVO's own reports, indicate that the attack on the Bridge was a premeditated act. Therefore, the destruction of the Old Bridge satisfies the first two prerequisites under Article 3(d) of the *ICTY Statute*.

In addition to the above prerequisites, the four *Tadić* conditions must also be met: the violation must constitute an infringement of a rule of IHL; the rule must be customary in nature or if it belongs to treaty law, the treaty must be binding on parties to the conflict at the time the offence was allegedly committed; the violation must be serious; and the violation of the rule must entail, under customary or treaty law, individual criminal responsibility of the person breaching the rule. As discussed, the Old Bridge was a historic and architectural monument specifically protected under the relevant national cultural heritage laws. As such it also enjoyed protection of IHL accorded to cultural property. Under both treaty and customary IHL wilful destruction of cultural property, including monuments, not justified by military necessity is prohibited. As preservation of cultural property is of importance to all humankind, its destruction constitutes a breach of a rule protecting important values and has wide-ranging and long-lasting consequences for the victims. The 'victim' here is not one specific person, or one specific people, but it is a broader category.

121 Ibid paras 181-202.

122 *Kordić* Trial Judgement, paras 66-146.

123 *Blaškić* Trial Judgement, paras 75-123.

124 See, eg, testimony of Herbert Okun in *Prlić*, 4 April 2007 [Okun testimony]; testimony of Dr Ciril Ribičič in *Prlić*, 11 December 2007 [Ribičič testimony]; testimony of Marijan Biskić in *Prlić*, 5 March 2007 [Biskić testimony].

When destroying the Old Bridge, the HVO not only disinherited the Muslim population in Mostar, but also Croats, including the HVO members themselves, as well as others elsewhere, and undeniably future generations, as the Bridge belonged to everyone and to no one in particular, and was meant to remain in existence for many centuries. This Bridge was, as the Prosecution put it, 'an *international* landmark'.[125] It was a passage from here to there, 'built on the idea of a future'.[126] The Bridge was designed to last for one thousand years as some argue.[127] It was seen as 'one of the most beautiful bridges in the world whose construction show[ed] such invariable taste and such pleasing results'.[128] The Old Bridge was more than an object of striking beauty. It was a monument of great importance to the cultural heritage in the Balkans and to the cultural heritage of all humankind.[129] The response to its destruction at both the local and international level indicates the effect of the loss of the Bridge on people and certainly the seriousness of the crime.

The bombing of the Bridge is largely seen to be a symbolic act. The accused General Praljak and others accused in *Prlić* maintained that the HVO 'could have done it earlier if they had wanted to', thereby refuting the HVO's involvement in the destruction of the Bridge. Without a doubt, they could have destroyed the Bridge earlier. But they probably did it on 9 November 1993 as 'a way of breaking people's spirit'.[130] As Rose George observes, in Mostar 'the loss of the bridge means far more than a loss of stones'.[131] One woman said that she cried when her husband died and she cried when her children were killed in the conflict. But the day that she cried most 'was the day that the Old Bridge came down'.[132] With responses to the destruction of the Bridge like this one, it comes

125 *Prosecutor v Jadranko Prlić, Bruno Stojić, Slobodan Praljak, Milivoj Petković, Valentin Ćorić and Berislav Pušić*, Amended Indictment, 16 November 2005, Case No. IT-04-74-AU, para 116 (emphasis added) (Initial Indictment, 4 March 2004 (kept confidential until its unsealing on 2 April 2004)) [*Prlić* Indictment].

126 Slavenka Drakulić, 'Falling Down: a Mostar Bridge' (1993) 209 *The New Republic* 14(2).

127 See, Peter Slavin, 'In Bosnia, Restoring a Bridge to Multiethnic Unity; [*sic*] 1557 Old Bridge Fell 4 Years ago, a Casualty of War', *Pittsburgh Post-Gazette*, Monday, 16 February 1998, A-3.

128 Allan Little, 'Bridging the Bosnian Divide', BBC News, From Our Correspondent, was broadcast on Saturday, 24 July 2004 at 11.30 BST on BBC Radio 4 (quoting Rebecca West on how she saw the Old Bridge in 1936), http://newsvote.bbc.co.uk/mpapps/pagetools/print/news.bbc.co.uk/2/hi/programmes/fr.

129 See *1954 Convention*, Preamble, para 2.

130 Rose George, 'Story of Bridges', *Independent Sunday Review* 18 November 2001, http://www.rosegeorge.com/frameworks/generic/public_users/morearticles.asp?Articl [9].

131 Ibid.

132 Ibid. See also BBC Radio Program, 'Heritage: The Balkans', part 3/4, 29 August

as no surprise that East Mostar proclaimed 9 November a day of mourning.[133] 'When they destroy eternity, what has man become?'[134] is a question which has been asked. Of course, the four hundred or so years of the Bridge's existence is not an eternity. But the Bridge's exceptional qualities distinguished it from other objects and its destruction prompted strong worldwide reaction. Messages and statements made by UNESCO and other international bodies dealing with cultural property expressed the shock and anger of the international community in relation to the act of destruction of the Bridge and demanded that those responsible be brought to justice.[135] Consistent with applicable customary and treaty law, destruction of historic monuments, including the Old Bridge, entails individual criminal responsibility.

In addition to the two abovementioned prerequisites and the four *Tadić* conditions common to all offences under Article 3 of the *ICTY Statute*, an act must satisfy the three elements specifically required for the crime of destruction or wilful damage to cultural property within the meaning of Article 3(d) of the *ICTY Statute*: it must cause damage or destruction to cultural property; the damaged or destroyed cultural property must not have been used for military purposes at the time when the acts of hostility directed against such property took place; and the act must have been carried out with the intent to damage or destroy the property in question.[136]

As discussed, an overwhelming amount of evidence suggests that the Old Bridge was shelled for two consecutive days (on 8 and 9 November 1993) and was completely destroyed by the Croat tank fire on the second day of the shelling when it crumbled down into the Neretva. The very event of the destruction of the Bridge was filmed by several persons and the images of the destruction went around the world. The Bridge was rebuilt a decade after its destruction. The rebuilding was an international project which, *inter alia*, included recovering from the river stone blocks which had been part of the fallen original. These stone blocks reinforce the evidence that the destruction of the Bridge took place. Numerous persons were eyewitnesses to the shelling and the act of the destruction of the Bridge. They have claimed that the shelling came from the HVO side. The HVO's own reports point to their involvement in the destruction of the Old Bridge. It would follow from this that HVO shelling of the Old Bridge caused the destruction of the Old Bridge and that, therefore, the first element of the crime under Article 3(d) of the *Statute* would be satisfied.

2007 (Samir Gološ remembers the day when the Old Bridge fell down. He was in the hospital that day. The whole ward cried when the nurse told them the sad news about the Bridge. 'When the Bridge collapsed, it was like my whole life was collapsing, too', Gološ said).

133 See chapter three, n 179 and accompanying text.

134 George, above n 130.

135 See, eg, *Fourth COE Report*, above n 30; *Final Report*, above n 30.

136 See *Strugar* Trial Judgement, para 312.

In relation to the second element, the available sources indicate that the Bridge was not used for military purposes on 8 and 9 November 1993 and that even if the Bridge was so used for military purposes, such use could not pose any real danger to the HVO forces. Accordingly, the HVO was not entitled legitimately to attack the Bridge because the Bridge did not constitute a military objective. The HVO also put forward the claim that the vicinity of the Bridge was used for military purposes. Consistent with the findings of the *Strugar* Trial Chamber, 'the preferable view appears to be that it is the use of cultural property [itself] and not its location that determines whether and when the cultural property would lose its protection'.[137] Nevertheless, as with the Bridge itself, there is no evidence to suggest that its immediate vicinity was used for military purposes at the time or that any military objectives were located in the immediate vicinity of the Bridge at the time.

The evidence suggests that the attack on the Bridge was deliberate and militarily unnecessary. The Bridge was renowned for its unique cultural and historico-architectural significance. Also, its construction and colour made it visible from afar. The Bridge could not be mistaken for some other object and was not hit accidentally. It was shelled almost at point blank range in daylight for two days, with precision and determination to bring it down. This implies the perpetrators' direct intent to deliberately destroy this particular object of cultural property, which suggests that the third element of the crime of destruction or wilful damage of cultural property within the meaning of Article 3(d) of the *ICTY Statute* is also satisfied in relation to the destruction of the Old Bridge. Therefore, the destruction of the Old Bridge was a proscribed act within the meaning of the *ICTY Statute*.

2 Evidence of the Crime

This chapter now turns to the question of the evidence of the attack on the Old Bridge, the second requirement for an act to amount to a war crime and to give rise to individual criminal responsibility. According to various reports made by international bodies, as well as the accounts of eyewitnesses, the Old Bridge was targeted on several occasions prior to November 1993. Reportedly, the damage had been minor. According to the *Final Report of the UN Commission of Experts*, '[t]he initial objective, it would seem, had been to discourage people from using it'.[138] In contrast, the two-day shelling of the Old Bridge on 8 and 9 November 1993 was 'clearly aimed to destroy the [B]ridge'.[139]

137 Ibid para 310.

138 *Final Report,* above n 30, para III.A.4.

139 Ibid.

Reportedly, the destruction of the Old Bridge was carried out by tanks belonging to the Croat forces.[140] The witness Salčin claimed that he clearly saw with his own eyes a tank firing rounds at the Old Bridge from the Hum Hill, where the HVO had its positions.[141] The witness contended that he saw some 60 to 70 shells being fired by a tank at the Old Bridge on 8 November 1993.[142] He was at an observation post close to the Old Bridge at the time.[143] By the evening of 8 November, the Bridge was almost totally destroyed. The damage was so extensive that it seemed improbable that the Bridge would survive the night.[144] According to this witness, the Bridge crumbled the next morning, after six more tank rounds hit it.[145]

Another witness testifying in *Prlić*, Enes Delalić, filmed, from an apartment just a few hundred metres from the HVO positions, an HVO tank opening fire from the Stotina Hill, Hum, on the Old City of Mostar on 8 November 1993.[146] The shooting went on for almost the whole day, from about 10 am until about 5 pm. This witness observed the situation throughout the day, activating his camera from time to time. As he did so, he heard a news report on the radio that 'the HVO is firing on the Old Bridge'.[147] The witness concluded that this was the target of the tank located on Stotina which he was filming. According to the Prosecution in *Prlić*, the time indicator on witness Delalić's recording tallied with the time indicator on another recording, this one of the Old Bridge sustaining direct hits, a recording that was also shown in the Court.[148] The witness added that the shelling directed at the Old City continued the next morning until the Old Bridge was destroyed. He testified that the Bridge was destroyed at around 10.15 am on 9 November 1993[149] and that the falling of the Bridge into the water was followed by 'celebratory shooting' on the Croat side.[150]

Furthermore, the HVO's own documents indicate that the Old Bridge was targeted and destroyed by the HVO. According to the report by HVO commander Lasić of 8 November 1993 to the Main Staff of the HVO, it was an

140 Ibid para III.A.5. See also *Fourth COE Report*, above n 30, Contribution by Dr Colin Kaiser, para 69.

141 See testimony of Miro Salčin, the Prosecution witness in *Prlić*, 15 February 2007, T 14252, T 14211 [Salčin testimony].

142 Ibid T 14212.

143 Ibid T 14209.

144 Ibid T 14213.

145 Ibid T 14213-14214.

146 See testimony of Enes Delalić in *Prlić*, 17 May 2007, T 18677-18678 [Delalić testimony].

147 Ibid T 18678-18680.

148 Ibid T 18692-18693.

149 Ibid T 18699-18700.

150 Ibid T 18695.

HVO tank that fired shells in the direction of the Old City in which the Old Bridge was situated:

> from 8.10 in the morning, our tank was opening fire from Stotina during the whole day, and it fired 50 projectiles on Stari Grad [the Old City].[151]

In his report of 9 November 1993, again to the Main Staff, commander Lasić stated:

> In addition to fire from infantry weapons at around 10.00 hours our tank fired a few projectiles at a target which was determined earlier. At around 10.15 hours, our reconnaissance people from Hum reported the Stari Most [the Old Bridge], was torn down, but they could not say anything about the cause of its destruction.[152]

There is no evidence that the ABH launched any offensive on either 8 or 9 November 1993. According to the testimony of several witnesses in the *Prlić* case, the shelling of the bridges across the Neretva by the HVO did not stop on 9 November after the Old Bridge was destroyed.[153] Shortly after the Old Bridge fell, the Kamenica Bridge, which was located in the vicinity of the Old City, was destroyed. As one witness saw it, the shelling by the HVO 'continued, constantly hitting'[154] demonstrating their determination to destroy the Muslim side and take control of East Mostar.[155]

All in all, there is ample evidence of the attack on the Old Bridge by the HVO forces. During the attack, the Bridge was damaged wilfully and finally brought down. As discussed, under the *ICTY Statute* wilful damage and destruction of cultural property may amount to a war crime. War crimes incur individual criminal responsibility.

3 Who is Responsible for the Destruction of the Old Bridge?

The *ICTY Statute* has jurisdiction *ratione personae* 'over natural persons'.[156] As with any other international criminal tribunal, the personal jurisdiction of the ICTY is premised on the principle that crimes are committed by specific individuals and that 'individuals have international duties which transcend the

151 Ibid T 18696, Exhibit 0993.

152 Ibid T 18699, Exhibit No 0992.

153 Ibid T 18698.

154 Ibid T 18699.

155 Ibid.

156 *ICTY Statute* art 6.

national obligations of obedience imposed by individual states'.[157] These 'international duties' are abundantly obvious in the matter under consideration since cultural property has universal importance and since its destruction disinherits all humanity.

Reportedly, following the destruction of the Old Bridge, the District Military Prosecution in Mostar conducted a hasty investigation into the incident accusing the members of the HVO tank crew which fired the grenades at the Bridge.[158] According to the then military prosecutor, it was the 'HVO tank crew' (operating the 'HVO tank') that on 9 November 1993, at

> approximately 10am…independently and without following orders from their responsible commander…fired an undetermined number of shells at the Moslem forces and several hit the Stari Most [the Old Bridge] which collapsed at that moment.[159]

Allegedly, the HVO tank crew was paid for shelling the Old Bridge.[160] However, there is no information as to who so paid them. Nevertheless, on 23 November 1993, the prosecutor filed a request for an investigation, which the Military Court in Mostar and the investigative judge never managed to finish.[161] One commentator notes that '[t]he investigation sank into forgetfulness, and the public believed that General Slobodan Praljak [was] responsible for the destruction of the Stari Most [the Old Bridge]'.[162] Some information indicates that today it is impossible to hear the tank crew's version of the event because, allegedly, 'none of them are considered to be alive'.[163]

Since this book focuses on the response to the destruction of the Old Bridge at the international level, and specifically the ICTY's response, the allegation that General Praljak is responsible for the destruction of the Old Bridge is of greater interest here. The General was a senior officer of the HVO at the time, and the ICTY has focused on the high ranking officers accused of war

157 *Nuremberg International Military Tribunal, Trial of the Major War Criminals* (1947) 223.

158 *COE Fourth Report*, above n 30. See also Željko Rogošić, 'Shocking New Book on Mostar: Experts Claim: The Bridge was not Destroyed by HVO' *Nacional*, 23 February 2006, http://nacional.hr/hr/articles/view/23364 [14] (referring to the documents of the District Military Prosecution in Mostar of 22 November 1993).

159 Statement of the Military Prosecutor Mladen Jurišić in the Official Records of the District Military Prosecution in Mostar of 22 November 1993, quoted in Rogošić, ibid.

160 Rogošić, ibid (pointing to the amount of 30,000 DM but noting that this information was never verified during the investigation).

161 Ibid.

162 Ibid.

163 Ibid.

crimes falling under its jurisdiction. General Praljak has been widely blamed for the destruction of the Bridge ever since the destruction occurred. The General's alleged responsibility is not for being the actual perpetrator of the destruction of the Old Bridge but for the acts committed by others since he was Commander of the Main Staff, the military head of the HVO, at the time.

According to the *Prlić* Indictment, prior to this, from the early summer of 1991 (when he joined the CA) onwards, General Praljak held various positions and functions in Croatia and in HB,[164] including the position of Assistant Minister of Defence for Croatia and a member of Croatia's Council of National Defence,[165] and he served as the commander of the Main Staff of the HVO in HB from approximately 24 July 1993 to 9 November 1993.[166]

In March 2004, together with five other HB/HVO officials, namely, Jadranko Prlić, Bruno Stojić, Milivoj Petković, Valentin Ćorić and Berislav Pušić, General Praljak was indicted by the ICTY for war crimes committed during the Croat/Muslim armed conflict.[167] The Indictment includes twenty-six counts under which the six accused are charged with crimes against humanity, grave breaches of the *Geneva Conventions* and violations of the laws or customs of war.[168] Together with religious properties in East Mostar, the destruction of the Old Bridge is referred to in paragraph 116 of the *Prlić* Indictment. In its pertinent part, this paragraph states:

> On 9 November 1993, the Herceg-Bosna/HVO forces destroyed the Stari Most ('Old Bridge'), an international landmark that crossed the Neretva River between East and West Mostar.[169]

Allegations made in paragraph 116 (thus including the destruction of the Old Bridge) are dealt with in Count 21 of the Indictment: destruction or wilful damage done to institutions dedicated to religion or education, a violation of the laws or customs of war, punishable under Articles 3(d), 7(1) and 7(3) of the *ICTY Statute*. Allegations included in paragraph 116 of the Indictment are also referred to in: Count 1– persecutions on political, racial and religious grounds, a crime against humanity, punishable under Articles 5(h), 7(1) and 7(3) of the *ICTY Statute*; Count 19 – extensive destruction of property, not justified by military necessity and carried out unlawfully and wantonly, a grave breach of the *Geneva Conventions*, punishable under Articles 2(d), 7(1) and 7(3) of the *ICTY*

164 *Prlić* Indictment, paras 6-7.

165 Ibid para 6.

166 Ibid para 7.

167 The *Prlić* Initial Indictment of 4 March 2004 was kept confidential until its unsealing on 2 April 2004. The Indictment was amended on 17 November 2005.

168 *Prlić* Indictment, para 229.

169 Ibid.

Statute; Count 20 – wanton destruction of cities, towns or villages, or devastation not justified by military necessity, a violation of the laws or customs of war, punishable under Articles 3(b), 7(1) and 7(3) of the *ICTY Statute*; Count 24 – unlawful attack on civilians (Mostar), a violation of the laws or customs of war, as recognised under customary law and Article 51 of *Additional Protocol I* and Article 13 of *Additional Protocol II*, punishable under Articles 3, 7(1) and 7(3) of the *ICTY Statute*; Count 25 – unlawful infliction of terror on civilians (Mostar), a violation of the laws or customs of war, as recognised under customary law and Article 51 of *Additional Protocol I* and Article 13 of *Additional Protocol II*, punishable under Articles 3, 7(1) and 7(3) of the *ICTY Statute*; and Count 26 – cruel treatment (Mostar siege), a violation of the laws or customs of war, as recognised by Articles 3, 7(1) and 7(3) of the *ICTY Statute*.[170]

The *Prlić* Indictment alleges that the six accused, together with others, including Croatia's late President Tuđman (deceased, 10 December 1999),[171] were part of a joint criminal enterprise. This criminal enterprise allegedly sought 'to politically and militarily subjugate, permanently remove and ethnically cleanse Bosnian Muslims and other non-Croats who lived in areas on the territory of the Republic of Bosnia and Herzegovina which were claimed to be part of the Croatian Community (and later Republic) of Herceg-Bosna, and to join these areas as part of a "Greater Croatia"'[172] by criminal means, which, *inter alia*, included destruction of cultural property.[173] A territorial grab underlined this joint criminal enterprise: 'to establish a Croatian territory with the borders of the Croatian Banovina, a territorial entity that existed from 1939 to 1941'.[174] To realise the territorial ambition, the joint criminal enterprise was 'to engineer the political and ethnic map of these areas so that they would be Croat-dominated, both politically and demographically'.[175]

In accordance with paragraphs 218-228 of the *Prlić* Indictment, each of the accused is responsible for the crimes charged on the basis of individual criminal responsibility pursuant to Article 7(1) of the *ICTY Statute*, the joint criminal enterprise, also pursuant to Article 7(1) of the *Statute*, and superior responsibility, pursuant to Article 7(3) of the *ICTY Statute*. Allegedly, each of the accused 'planned, instigated, ordered, committed or otherwise aided and abetted' the crimes charged in the Indictment, pursuant to Article 7(1) of the *ICTY Statute*. Also, each accused, acting individually and in concert with or through other persons, knowingly participated in and contributed to the joint criminal enterprise, intending to further and accomplish the enterprise and its objectives. In

170 Ibid.

171 Ibid para 16.

172 Ibid para 15.

173 Ibid.

174 Ibid.

175 Ibid.

addition or in the alternative, to the extent that an accused was not a member of the joint criminal enterprise, the Indictment charges that he is criminally responsible for substantially aiding and abetting one or more members or perpetrators of the joint criminal enterprise, in the planning, preparation or execution of the crime, pursuant to Article 7(1) of the *ICTY Statute*.

Moreover, in addition or in the alternative, as to any crime charged in the Indictment which was not within the objective or an intended part of the joint criminal enterprise, such crime was the natural and foreseeable consequence of the joint criminal enterprise and of implementing or attempting to implement the enterprise. Allegedly, each accused was aware of the risk of such crime or its consequence and, despite this awareness, wilfully took that risk, in joining and/or continuing in the enterprise, and is therefore responsible for the crime as charged. Finally, the Indictment alleges that each of the accused is criminally responsible as a superior official or officer for the criminal acts or omissions of subordinates or other persons about or over whom he had effective *de jure* and/or *de facto* control, where he knew or had reason to know that such persons were about to commit or had committed such acts or omissions and failed to take necessary and reasonable measures to prevent such acts or omissions or punish such persons. The *Prlić* Indictment additionally asserted that '[n]one of the acts or omissions charged as crimes were justified by military necessity'.[176] With respect to acts, omissions or conduct charged in connection with the destruction of property, they 'were committed, omitted or carried out unlawfully and wantonly'.[177]

The *Prlić* trial commenced on 26 April 2006. This has been one of the largest ICTY trials, with joint proceedings against all six accused. The Prosecution completed its case on 24 January 2008. The Defence case commenced on 5 May 2008 and officially closed on 17 May 2010. The closing arguments took place between 7 February and 2 March 2011. The judgement is expected to be delivered in July 2012.

In relation to the accused General Praljak, the Prosecution alleged that in his various positions and functions, the General exercised *de jure* and/or *de facto* command and control over the HB/HVO armed forces.[178] According to paragraph 8 of the *Prlić* Indictment, the General 'exercised effective control and substantial influence over the Herceg-Bosna/HVO armed forces (including the operative zone commanders)' at times relevant to the Indictment.[179] He was responsible, *inter alia*, for the organisation, planning, preparation, training, discipline and operations of the HVO armed forces.[180] The General issued

176 Ibid para 238.

177 Ibid.

178 Ibid para 8.

179 Ibid.

180 Ibid.

organisational, strategic and combat orders. Also, he was responsible for ensuring that all HVO forces conducted themselves in accordance with the rules of IHL. In addition, the General had command authority over the HB/HVO civilian police, when they acted under or in coordination with the HB/HVO armed forces during times of armed conflict. According to the Prosecution, General Praljak was closely involved in all aspects of HB/HVO military planning and operations.[181] The Indictment stresses that while the Commander of the HVO Main Staff, the General 'was responsible for the activities and actions of [the HVO armed] forces in furtherance of the joint criminal enterprise and in connection with the crimes charged in this indictment'.[182] Regarding cultural property specifically, General Praljak allegedly,

> facilitated, supported, encouraged and participated in the joint criminal enterprise and crimes charged in [the *Prlić*] Indictment in planning, approving, preparing, supporting, ordering and/or directing military operations and actions during and as part of which cultural and religious property such as mosques were destroyed, and private property of Bosnian Muslims was looted, burned or destroyed, without justification or military necessity, and failing to prevent, stop, punish or redress such destruction and looting.[183]

Despite General Praljak's responsibility to ensure that the HVO armed forces conducted themselves in accordance with IHL, he participated in, facilitated, instigated, encouraged and condoned crimes and abuses against Bosnian Muslims by HVO forces, 'by failing to prevent and punish such crimes and by commending, rewarding, promoting or leaving in place HVO officers and soldiers who committed or played a role in such crimes'.[184] The case concerning the HVO officer who commanded the HVO forces involved in the killings at the Muslim village of Stupni Do, is one example. The attack occurred on 23 October 1993 while General Praljak was Commander of the HVO Main Staff. Apparently, there was no intention to punish the alleged crime. Rather, 'the what to do with the HVO officer' was part of a game: 'the international community was told that the HVO officer had been removed, when in fact, he simply changed his name, remained in essentially the same position and was never punished'.[185]

With respect to the Old Bridge, just as with all other charges, General Praljak denies any responsibility on his part. As discussed, he blames the Muslim side of the conflict for the destruction of the Bridge. The General claims that

181 Ibid.

182 Ibid para 17.3(a).

183 Ibid para 17.3(k).

184 Ibid para 17.3(n).

185 Ibid para 40.

he was not Commander of the HVO Main Staff on 9 November 1993 when the Bridge was destroyed. He maintains that the Bridge was destroyed when the power was 'in vacuum'; that is, during the two-day handover of duties to his successor, General Ante Roso. For instance, in 2002, General Praljak testified as Defence witness in *Naletilić*. During the cross-examination by the Prosecutor, Mr Kenneth Scott, General Praljak emphasised that he had already been relieved of his duties as Commander of the HVO Main Staff when the Old Bridge was destroyed:

> Q. When did you leave that position?
> …
> A. I handed over duty on the morning of the day when the [O]ld [B]ridge in Mostar was destroyed. Two days before that was the beginning of the takeover and assumption of duty.
> Q. …if the [O]ld [B]ridge was destroyed on approximately the 9th of November 1993, it was around that time that you ceased being the chief commander, correct?
> A. Not approximately but exactly. On the morning…on that morning, I signed with General Roso, who came after me, a paper on the taking over of duty. Two days before that, I was relieved of my duties as the main commander of the HVO. And for two days this handing over of duty took place. It lasted for two days. And at 9.00…or rather, 8.30 on that morning, I set out for Croatia.
> Q. And the person who took over top position was Ante Roso, is that correct?
> A. Correct.
> Q. He also came from the [CA]. A senior officer in the [CA], wasn't he?
> …
> A. Yes.[186]

Even if General Praljak was truly relieved of duties, he was still in Mostar on 8 November 1993. As discussed, the HVO shelled the Bridge from the morning until the evening on that day. Reports by the HVO commanders about the shelling were being issued. Besides, Mostar is a small city, and an action such as a day-long shelling of one target could hardly go unnoticed. This holds to an even greater extent considering the significance of the target in the case at hand. At the same time, the General was a very influential figure. His opinion mattered among the HVO soldiers.[187] There is no evidence whatsoever that he had done anything to stop the attack on the Bridge. Even if relieved of duties, the

---

186 Testimony of defence witness Slobodan Praljak in *Naletilić*, T 9322-9823, 2 April 2002, T 9531-9532 [Praljak testimony in *Naletilić*]. See also Rogošić, above n 158, para 15.

187 See Praljak testimony, ibid 4 April 2002, T 9511-9518; 5 April 2002, T 9610.

General remained an influential figure and a very senior officer. In *Naletilić*, in connection with 'aiding and abetting', the Trial Chamber held that

> the participation may happen before, during or after the commission of a crime. Aiding and abetting can also be committed through an omission as long as the omission had a significant effect on the commission of the crime and was accompanied by the necessary *mens rea*.[188]

General Praljak's presence in Mostar on 8 November 1993 does not in itself mean that he encouraged or supported the attack on the Old Bridge. There is no evidence to indicate that the General was present at the crime scene either. But his presence in Mostar as a Commander of the HVO Main Staff, as held by the *Naletilić* Trial Chamber, could 'be perceived as an important *indicium* for encouragement or support'.[189] Even if he was 'just' relieved of that duty, the General's presence, as a senior military and political figure, could not be perceived as insignificant in this regard. As such, he could have still made suggestions or given advice that would have had the potential of stopping the attack and averting its consequence, that is, the collapse of the Bridge the following day.

Contrary to General Praljak's claim that he was relieved of the duty of the military head of the HVO armed forces two days prior to the destruction of the Old Bridge, and that he was on his way to Croatia on the morning when the Bridge was destroyed, other sources indicate that he was still Commander of the Main Staff of the HVO at the time. For instance, the *Prlić* Indictment alleges that the General held this position '[f]rom approximately 24 July 1993 to 9 November 1993'.[190] In this period the General 'exercised *de jure* and/or *de facto* command and control over the Herceg-Bosna/HVO armed forces'.[191] He had 'effective control and substantial influence' over such forces 'including the operative zone commanders'.[192] To sum it up, General Praljak was 'closely involved in all aspects of Herceg-Bosna/HVO military planning and operations'.[193] Also, according to the British General, Sir Martin Garrod, who was in the European Community Monitoring Mission in Bosnia and Herzegovina during the Croat-Muslim conflict, and who was later appointed Chief of Staff of the European Union Administrator in Mostar,[194] the destruction of the Old Bridge took place at least one week before General Praljak's departure:

188 *Naletilić* Trial Judgement, para 63.

189 Ibid.

190 *Prlić* Indictment, para 7.

191 Ibid para 8.

192 Ibid.

193 Ibid.

194 See, eg, testimony of Sir Martin Garrod, the Prosecution witness in *Kordić*, 1

Q. Is it right, General, that on the 16th of November [1993], you recall a meeting between Philip Watkins and Slobodan Lovrenović, Boban's press advisor?

A. Yes. This was at a time when the Croatian…there were a lot of changes in the hierarchy of the Croatian Republic of Herceg-Bosna….

Q. And that same day [*16 November*] *did you learn of a change in the position of Praljak?*

A. Yes. General Slobodan Praljak, we heard that day, had been relieved by General Ante Roso. And I, at the time, assessed that *General Praljak's departure was due to* a…well, the lack of military success of the HVO, but also there were other recent factors which may well have played a part, such as Stupni Do, the loss of Vareš, and indeed *the destruction of the Stari Most, the Old Bridge in Mostar, which took place on the 9th of November, just one week before this changeover.*[195]

According to 'A Chronology' of events that occurred during the Croat-Muslim armed conflict, compiled by Bosnian and Herzegovinian Croats, it was on 12 November 1993 that General Roso was named as the new Chief of Main Staff of the HVO, replacing General Slobodan Praljak.[196] Accordingly, even if there was a two-day takeover, General Praljak could still be considered the military head of the HVO at the time of the attack on and the destruction of the Old Bridge. To the extent that this was the case, and the General was really on his way to Croatia at the time of the destruction of the Old Bridge in the morning on 9 November, the lack of geographical proximity might indicate the need for more *indicia* to prove his criminal responsibility, but it would not automatically absolve him from such responsibility. As held by the Trial Chamber in *Naletilić*, following the *Aleksovski* Trial Chamber, 'the more physically distant the superior was from the commission of the crime, the more additional *indicia* are necessary to prove that he knew of the crime'.[197] However, 'if the crimes were committed next to the superior's duty-station this suffices as an important *indicium* that the superior had knowledge of the crimes, even more if the crimes were repeatedly committed'.[198] So far, the General has not denied his presence in Mostar at least on 8 November, when the HVO shelled the Bridge for almost the whole day. Moreover, the Bridge was shelled on several occasions before that, which should be an indication of the General's knowledge of HVO forces

February 2000, T 13522-13523, [Garrod testimony in *Kordić*] and in *Naletilić*, 24 January 2002, T 8614- 8615 [Garrod testimony in *Naletilić*].

195 Garrod testimony in *Kordić*, ibid T 13522-13523 (emphasis added).

196 See Croats of Bosnia and Herzegovina, 'The Croat-Muslim War: A Chronology', http://www.hercegbosna.org/engleski/cromusl.html (Copy on file with author).

197 *Naletilić* Trial Judgement, para 72, referring to *Prosecutor v Zlatko Aleksovski*, Judgement, Trial Chamber I, 25 June 1999, Case No. IT-95-14/1-T, para 80.

198 Ibid.

committing acts of this type. Shelling was the subject of media reporting both internationally and locally. Furthermore, reports had been sent to the Main Staff of the HVO in connection with the shelling of the Old Bridge by the HVO forces. As noted, on 8 November 1993, at 1900 hours, the HVO district commander (Lasić) issued a report specifying that

> from 8.10 in the morning, [HVO] tank was opening fire from Stotina *during the whole day*, and it fired 50 projectiles on Stari Grad [the Old City].[199]

Consistent with the finding in *Čelebići*, this should have put the General on notice of the risk of cultural property-related offences and thus indicated the need for additional investigation in order to ascertain whether such crimes were committed or were about to be committed by his subordinates.[200] In addition to this, the HVO forces attacked and destroyed numerous other cultural objects in Mostar as well as in other municipalities. There is no information to indicate that anyone has ever been punished for such offences.

Notwithstanding this, if General Praljak was still considered Commander of the Main Staff of the HVO on 9 November 1993, even if he was physically distant from Mostar on that day, he could still be held responsible for the destruction of the Old Bridge. In that case, given various technological advances in the domain of communication, the General had the means and indeed the duty to acquire knowledge about the acts of his subordinates, specifically, the attack on the Bridge on 8 November 1993 and its destruction the following day by the HVO forces under his command positioned at Stotina Hill overlooking the Bridge.

(a) Superior Responsibility

To be held criminally responsible for crimes committed by his subordinates, the three elements relevant to the concept of superior responsibility must be satisfied: the existence of a superior-subordinate relationship between General Praljak and the HVO forces that attacked and destroyed the Old Bridge; General Praljak's knowledge about the crime at hand; and the General's failure to take the necessary and reasonable measures to prevent the crime or to punish the perpetrators.

The first requirement that there was the existence of a superior-subordinate relationship could be tested through 'effective command or control'. In other words, it should be determined whether General Praljak had 'the material ability to prevent and punish' the commission of the crime. 'Material ability' includes hierarchical and supervisory authority. The *Blaškić* Trial Chamber held

199 See Delalić testimony, above n 146, T 18695.

200 *Čelebići* Trial Judgement, para 383, affirmed on appeal, *Čelebići* Appeal Judgement, paras 222–241.

that this could be seen through the ability to make reports to the competent authorities so that appropriate measures could be taken.[201] The main issue in the matter under consideration is whether General Praljak was able to give orders and send reports to the authorities at the time of the attack on, and during the destruction of, the Old Bridge. The jurisprudence of the ICTR has distinguished cases where a person was able to give orders, but did not stand in the relationship of superior to those committing the offences, and did not exercise effective control over them.[202]

Assuming that a superior-subordinate relationship existed between General Praljak and the HVO forces that attacked and destroyed the Old Bridge, to be liable pursuant to Article 7(3) of the *ICTY Statute*, the General must have known or had reason to know about the attack on the Old Bridge. As discussed, the geographical and temporal circumstances enabled the General to acquire 'actual knowledge' about the attack on the Bridge on 8 November 1993. Also, various factors point to the likelihood that he had in his possession information, which, at least, would put him on notice of the risk of the destruction of the Old Bridge. According to the jurisprudence of the ICTY, the commander's position may indicate that he knew of the crime due to the chain of command established by him.[203] As the Commander of the Main Staff, General Praljak issued orders and both sent and received reports from his subordinates. There was a solid chain of command in the HVO structure.[204] In terms of hierarchy, he was its military head at the time. It would follow from this that the whole day shelling of the Bridge on 8 November 1993 and the report issued by the commander Lasić on the subject made General Praljak aware that the attack on the Old Bridge by the HVO forces occurred. This information was sufficient to put him on notice about the seriousness of the situation and the imminent destruction of the Bridge. Accordingly, the General needed to take steps to investigate to ascertain whether offences were being committed or were about to be committed by his subordinates.[205]

The third element of superior responsibility relates to the failure of the superior to take necessary and reasonable measures to prevent or punish the perpetrators. To the extent that General Praljak was in effective control, as a superior he was under a duty to exercise whatever ability he had to prevent and punish the commission of the crime of the destruction of the Old Bridge. He was also obligated to, *inter alia*, discipline the HVO forces.[206] Reportedly, there

201 *Blaškić* Trial Judgement, para 302.

202 See *Prosecutor v Jean de Dieu Kamuhanda*, Judgement, Trial Chamber, 22 January 2004, Case No ICTR-95-54A-T [*Kamuhanda* Trial Judgement].

203 See *Blaškić* Trial Judgement, para 332.

204 See *Prlić* Indictment.

205 *Čelebići* Appeal Judgement, para 236.

206 See *Prlić* Indictment, para 8.

was some investigation about the destruction of the Old Bridge.[207] As noted, the District Military Prosecution in Mostar conducted an investigation but rather hastily and the investigation took place about two weeks after the event. The investigation might have been conducted due to pressure caused by an extensive media reporting and due to a strong condemnation of this act by numerous international bodies, rather than because of a genuine desire to investigate the incident. That this investigation was not sufficiently serious indicates the fact that the case 'sank into forgetfulness'[208] as far as the HB/HVO authorities were concerned. The three suspects who were members of the HVO tank crew that allegedly shelled the Bridge on their own initiative, without orders having been issued by their commander, were never punished.[209]

Although the actual perpetrators have been identified, it is General Praljak who has been widely regarded as a person responsible for the loss of the Old Bridge. Allegedly, years after the event, even President Tuđman held him responsible.[210] General Praljak denies his responsibility. In a letter sent to President Tuđman, he asked 'why it was easier for everyone to proclaim [him] the destroyer even though [he] immediately and officially said that [he] had nothing to do with it'.[211] The General seems to be forgetting that he was a military commander, who was responsible for the training, discipline and compliance with IHL by the HVO forces over which he had command and control, and also substantial influence.[212] To restate the holding of the Trial Chamber in *Krnojelac*:

> where superior responsibility is concerned, an accused is not charged with the crimes of his subordinates, but with his failure to carry out his duty to exercise control.[213]

Should it be found that the superior-subordinate relationship between General Praljak and the perpetrators did not exist at the time, and that thus the argument of superior responsibility could not be sustained, there is still, at least according to the *Prlić* Indictment, the applicability of criminal responsibility under the joint criminal enterprise. In fact, the Indictment alleges all forms of joint criminal enterprise (form 1 to 3) for all six accused, two of which (form 1

---

207 See, eg, *COE Fourth Report*, above n 30; Salčin testimony, above n 141, T 14254-14255; Rogošić, above n 158, para 14.

208 Rogošić, ibid.

209 Ibid.

210 Ibid para 15.

211 Ibid (quoting General Praljak's letter sent to President Tuđman on 14 November 1997).

212 *Prlić* Indictment, para 8.

213 *Krnojelac* Appeal Judgement, para 171.

and form 3) would apply to the Old Bridge. But is this mode of liability the most adequate where the Old Bridge is concerned?

V Issues

A Invisibility of Cultural Property in the ICTY Statute

1 Primacy of Crimes against Persons

The ICTY has the competence to try alleged offenders for crimes enumerated in Articles 2-5 of its *Statute*, namely, grave breaches of the *1949 Geneva Conventions*, violations of the laws or customs of war, genocide, and crimes against humanity. Article 4, dealing with genocide, is in its entirety a persons-related article. Article 4 is based on Article II of the *Convention on the Prevention and Punishment of the Crime of Genocide* (*Genocide Convention*).[214] According to the ICTY jurisprudence,[215] as well as the ICJ jurisprudence,[216] the destruction of cultural property cannot amount to the crime of genocide. The ICTY's Trial Chamber in *Krstić* held that 'despite recent developments', the definition of acts of genocide is limited to those seeking the physical or biological destruction of a group.[217] The ICJ took a similar view in the case concerning the *Application of the Convention on the Prevention and Punishment of the Crime of Genocide (Bosnia and Herzegovina v Serbia and Montenegro*), finding that

> the destruction of historical, cultural and religious heritage cannot be considered to constitute the deliberate infliction of conditions of life calculated to bring about the physical destruction of the group. Although such destruction may be highly significant inasmuch as it is directed to the elimination of all traces of the cultural or religious presence of a group, and contrary to other legal norms, it does not fall within the categories of acts of genocide set out in Article II of the [Genocide] Convention.[218]

214 *Convention on the Prevention and Punishment of the Crime of Genocide*, adopted by the UN General Assembly, Resolution 260 A (III) 9 December 1948, art 2, 78 UNTS 277 (entered into force 12 January 1951), [*Genocide Convention*], http://fletcher.tufts.edu/multilaterals.html.

215 See, eg, *Prosecutor v Radislav Krstić*, Judgement, Trial Chamber I, 2 August 2001, Case No. IT-98-33-T, para 580.

216 See *Application of the Convention on the Prevention and Punishment of the Crime of Genocide (Bosnia and Herzegovina v Yugoslavia (Serbia and Montenegro))*, Merits, Judgement of 26 February 2007, ICJ Reports [2007], para 344 [*Application of the Genocide Convention*], http://www.icj-cij.org/cijwww/cdocket/cbhy/cbhyjudgemnts/cbhy_cjudgement_20070226.

217 *Krstić* Trial Judgement, para 580.

218 *Application of the Genocide Convention*, para 344.

Yet, as fashioned by Raphael Lemkin in 1944, the notion of genocide originally covered all forms of destruction of a group, including the destruction of cultural property.[219] The fact that in the end, cultural destruction was not included in the definition of genocide in the *Genocide Convention* does not mean that there is not a special case to be made that at least in this century intended obliteration of a targeted group's culture is a particularly heinous crime and that the definition of genocide should not be revisited.[220]

Article 2, covering the grave breaches, and Article 5, dealing with crimes against humanity, only partly encompass property-related acts. Of all grave breaches listed in subparagraphs (a)-(h) of Article 2, only one subparagraph ((d): extensive destruction and appropriation of property, not justified by military necessity and carried out unlawfully and wantonly) is property-related. Similarly, of all crimes listed in Article 5(a)-(i), only one crime ((h) persecutions) may be property-related. Neither Article 2(d) nor Article 5(h) specifically refers to cultural property. However, a review of the ICTY jurisprudence reveals that destruction of cultural property may amount to these crimes.[221] When Article 2(d) of the *Statute* is concerned, the protection to cultural property is provided indirectly, through that accorded to civilian property.

With respect to Article 5(h) of the *ICTY Statute*, the destruction of cultural property can amount to the crime of persecution.[222] But as with other crimes listed in Article 5, destruction of cultural property must be 'directed against any civilian population'.[223] Where the crime of persecution is concerned, there must also be a specific intent to discriminate against the civilian population concerned on political, racial and religious grounds. Thus, here too cultural property is protected indirectly, through the protection of the 'civilian popula-

219 See, eg, Raphael Lemkin, *Axis Rule in Occupied Europe* (1944) 79, 87-89; Report of the International Law Commission on the Work of its 48th Session, *Yearbook of the International Law Commission* (1996) vol. II, Part Two, 45-46.

220 For discussion of the need for a more expansive reading of the definition of genocide, see, eg, ICOMOS Sweden/Central Board of National Antiquities/ Swedish National Commission for UNESCO, *Information as an Instrument for Protection against War Damages to the Cultural Heritage. Report from a Seminar, June 1994* Stockholm, Svenska Unescoradets skriftserie, 4/1994 (1994) Stockholm: ICOMOS Sweden [*Information as an Instrument*]; András Riedlmayer, 'Killing Memory: The Targeting of Bosnia's Cultural Heritage', Testimony presented at a Hearing of the Commission on Security and Cooperation in Europe, US Congress, 4 April 1995, Community of Bosnia Foundation, http://www.haverford.edu/relg/sells/killing.html ['Killing Memory']; Colin Tatz, 'Genocide in Australia', AIATSIS Research Discussion Papers No. 8, Australian Institute of Aboriginal and Torres Strait Islander Studies (1999) 1, http://www.aiatsis.gov.au/rsrch_dp/genocide.htm; Bevan, above n 4.

221 See *Blaškić* Appeal Judgement, paras 144-149.

222 Ibid para 149.

223 *ICTY Statute*, art 5.

tion'. Given its universal value and the impact on all humanity when such property is destroyed or damaged, cultural property deserves more direct protection under 'crimes against humanity'.

In contrast to Articles 2, 4 and 5 of the *Statute*, Article 3 is predominantly a property-related article. Of the five violations listed in subparagraphs (a)-(e) all but one are property-related. None of the property-related crimes uses the term 'cultural property'. As discussed, only the crime under Article 3(d) directly refers to some components of cultural property. Yet, even here cultural property is not given a prominent place as such components are limited in numbers and are mixed with other types of property, which further adds to the invisibility of cultural property in the *ICTY Statute*.

Given the enormity of the scale of crimes against persons, it is understandable that the ICTY has jurisdiction over a number of such crimes. However, the former Yugoslavia had a rich cultural heritage, a great part of which was destroyed or heavily damaged during the 1990s conflicts. In certain areas, including Mostar, the extent of damage was horrific. The importance of cultural property and the extent of its destruction point to the need to give cultural property a more prominent place. This does not mean that crimes against cultural property should be considered equal to crimes against persons. The two are distinct although closely related categories. There is simply the need for a stronger emphasis on the direct rather than indirect protection of cultural property. Separation of cultural property from other property, for instance, in a separate subparagraph of an article could improve the 'visibility' of cultural property in the *Statute* and thereby enhance the significance of such property.

2 Cultural Property in the 'Hierarchy' of Crimes

There is no 'official' ranking of crimes in the *ICTY Statute*. This implies that although the destruction or damage to cultural property is criminalised explicitly only in Article 3(d) of the *ICTY Statute*, under 'violations of the laws or customs of war' – often referred to as 'war crimes' – and not under other crimes over which the ICTY has jurisdiction, such criminalisation should not minimise the seriousness of this particular crime. Still, it has been suggested that despite the absence of an 'official' ranking of crimes, some crimes are still more serious than others. The ICTR Trial Chamber in *Kambanda* held that 'genocide constitutes the *crime of crimes*' and that war crimes are 'considered as lesser crimes than genocide or crimes against humanity'.[224] The ICTY jurisprudence does not rank crimes in this way generally.[225]

224 *Prosecutor v Jean Kambanda*, Judgement, Trial Chamber, 4 September 1998, Case No. ICTR-97-23-S, paras 12-14, 16 (emphasis added) [*Kambanda* Trial Judgement]. See also *Prosecutor v Alfred Musema*, Judgement, Trial Chamber, 27 January 2000, paras 979-981 [*Musema* Trial Judgement].

225 See *Blaškić* Trial Judgement, paras 800-802.

Nevertheless, there are still some at the ICTY who consider war crimes as less serious than other crimes under the ICTY's jurisdiction. In accordance with the Joint Separate Opinion of Judge McDonald and Judge Vohran on the Appeal, in *Erdemović*, 'a punishable offence, if charged and proven as a crime against humanity, is more serious and should ordinarily entail a heavier penalty than if it were proceeded upon on the basis that it were a war crime'.[226] In the opinion of the ICTY Prosecutor, genocide is 'one of the greatest crimes you can imagine'. [227] The view that war crimes are less harmful than crimes against humanity is supported in scholarly writing. For instance, Allison Marston Danner argues that crimes against humanity should be considered more serious than war crimes[228] but because of its irreparably destructive consequences, it is genocide that is the most serious of all crimes.[229]

Thus, despite the absence of an 'official' ranking of crimes, some crimes are still considered more serious than others, with genocide on the top of the list. Yet, cultural property-related offences are directly referred to only under the rubric of 'war crimes', 'considered as lesser crimes than genocide or crimes against humanity'; they rank second with respect to crimes against humanity (as it is the civilian population concerned and not cultural property in its own right that is the primary subject of protection under the *Statute's* provision relevant to the crime of persecution); and, according to the jurisprudence of the ICTY, cultural property-related offences cannot amount to 'the crime of crimes'. But does the hierarchy of crimes really matter?

Apart from the obvious relevance to sentencing, the hierarchy of crimes impacts upon the 'degree' of importance of cultural property. The higher the 'ranking' of cultural property offences the higher the significance assigned to cultural property. With respect to genocide, consistent with Article 1 of the *Genocide Convention*, States are under duty not only to punish genocide but also to prevent it.[230] Prevention of cultural destruction is of great importance not only from the aspect of the preservation of cultural property but also when human life is concerned. As German poet Heinrich Heine warned, '[w]here books are burned in the end people will be burned, too'.[231] The ruling was along

---

226 *Prosecutor v Dražen Erdemović*, Judgement, Appeals Chamber, 7 October 1997, paras 20-21 (Joint Separate Opinion of Judge McDonald and Judge Vohran) [*Erdemović* Appeal Judgement], http://www.un.org/erdemovic/appeal/judgement/erd-asojmcd971007e.htm.

227 '10 Questions for Carla Del Ponte', *Time* Europe magazine, 21 August 2006, http://www.time.com/time/europe/magazine/article/0,13005,901060821-1226057,00.htm.

228 Ibid 475.

229 Ibid 482.

230 See *Genocide Convention*, art 1 (emphasis added). See also Article 8 of the *Genocide Convention* which amplifies the duty to prevent genocide. Ibid art 8.

231 Heinrich Heine, 1797-1856 (from his play 'Almansor' (1821) (Dort, wo man Bücher verbrennt, verbrennt man am Ende auch Menschen)).

these lines in the *Krstić* case, where the Trial Chamber held that attacks on cultural property 'may legitimately be considered as evidence of an intent to physically destroy the group'.[232] Although a case for a more expansive reading of the definition of genocide could be made in general, this book neither argues nor implies that the particular instance of the destruction of the Old Bridge amounts to the crime of genocide. The crime of genocide and the 'hierarchy' of crimes are mentioned here in general terms, only to demonstrate that cultural property has not been assigned as prominent a place at the ICTY as it is often thought should be the case, and to note that given a relatively modest ranking of the crime of the wilful damage and destruction of cultural property, the destruction of the Old Bridge in *Prlić et al*, as with any other complex case involving among other offences the destruction of a significant part of humanity's cultural heritage, might not get the attention it deserves.

3 Bypassing the 1954 Convention

(a) Definition of Cultural Property

The definition of cultural property in Article 3(d) of the *ICTY Statute* underscores two major dilemmas. The first regards the quandary as to which objects can be categorised as cultural property and the second points to the terminological difficulties.

(i) Which Objects Constitute Cultural Property?

Article 3(d) of the *ICTY Statute* is based on the *1907 Regulations* and not on the *1954 Convention*, the specialist treaty on the subject of cultural property protection in times of armed conflict. The wording of Article 3(d) most closely resembles that given in Article 56 of the *Regulations*. This is the only provision that directly refers to cultural property, or rather to some of its components. But even here, cultural property is not dealt with exclusively. Rather, it is mixed with other property, such as 'institutions dedicated to religion, charity and education', which are generally not considered cultural property.

Because Article 3 of the *ICTY Statute* is not exhaustive,[233] when sub-paragraph (d) of this Article is concerned, the ICTY can, among other instruments, apply the *1954 Convention* as a treaty that was binding on the parties to the conflicts in the former Yugoslavia. However, where cultural property-related charges are included in the ICTY Indictments under Article 3(d) of the *ICTY Statute*, the Prosecution does not make reference to the *1954 Convention*. It does not make reference to other applicable instruments either. It simply charges

232 *Krstić* Trial Judgement, para 580. This holding was endorsed by the ICJ. See *Application of the Genocide Convention*, para 344.

233 See *ICTY Statute*, art 3 ('such violations shall include, but not be limited to').

the accused, for instance, with 'destruction or wilful damage done to institutions dedicated to religion, charity and education, the arts and sciences, historic monuments and works of art and science', as a violation of the laws or customs of war, 'punishable under Article 3(d)'[234] of the *ICTY Statute*.

Some ICTY decisions do make reference to violations of the *1954 Convention*, as the treaty law binding upon the parties to the conflict. However, application of the relevant provisions of the *1954 Convention* has been somewhat puzzling.[235] Also, the *Convention* has been referred to mainly in passing and *Additional Protocol I* has been given primacy in the analysis of cultural property matters.[236] Yet Article 53 of *Additional Protocol I* is only an illustrative, shorter version of the cultural property matters that are dealt with more extensively in the *Convention*.

The main reason behind the confusion as to which objects are protected as cultural property under Article 3(d) of the *ICTY Statute* is that this Article is based on the outdated *1907 Regulations* with insufficient emphasis having been placed on the *1954 Convention*. The *ICTY Statute* was adopted at the end of the twentieth century whereas the *Regulations* were adopted at the beginning of that century. The *Convention* falls at the midpoint of these dates. Not only was the *Convention* the binding treaty at the time, but its core provisions became part of customary international law[237] by the time the *Statute* was adopted. The *Convention* should not have been overlooked in the *Statute* and more emphasis should have been placed on this instrument in the jurisprudence of the ICTY.

(ii) Terminology

Since Article 3(d) of the *ICTY Statute* is based on the *1907 Regulations*, which did not use the term 'cultural property', the *ICTY Statute* does not use this term either. A number of ICTY indictments charge the defendants with seizure, destruction or wilful damage to objects enumerated in Article 3(d) of the *Statute*.[238] The term 'cultural property' is almost absent from the indictments. With the exception of the 'Dubrovnik' cases, namely, the *Jokić* case and the *Strugar* case, the situation on the subject is not much better in the ICTY's decisions either.

234 See *Prosecutor v Pavle Strugar*, Third Amended Indictment, 10 December 2003, Case No. IT-01-42-PT, para 25.

235 See *Kordić* Trial Judgement, 360 (arguing that every educational institution constitutes immovable cultural property).

236 See *Kordić* Appeal Judgement, paras 89-91.

237 For a discussion of customary nature of the provisions of the *1954 Convention*, see generally Meyer, above n 17; *Customary IHL*, above n 80, vol. I, 127 *et seq*; vol. II, 723 *et seq*.

238 ICTY Indictments at, http://www.un.org/icty/cases/indictments-e.htm.

While the vast majority of property-related offences charged under Article 3(d) are not 'cultural' property-related within the meaning of Article 1 of the *1954 Convention*, there are still instances where the destruction of an object which actually *is* a cultural property object, is charged under the category of religious property instead of 'cultural' property. In the *Prlić* Indictment, the destruction of the Old Bridge of Mostar was charged in Count 21 as 'destruction or wilful damage done to *institutions dedicated to religion or education*',[239] as punishable under Article 3(d) of the *Statute*. Yet, the Old Bridge was neither an 'institution dedicated to religion' nor an 'institution dedicated to education'. Rather it was a secular object of cultural property, which was categorised as a public historico-architectural monument. In the Indictment, not only is there no mention of 'cultural property' in reference to the Old Bridge, but there is also a failure to mention the category of 'historic monuments' into which the Old Bridge clearly falls. Whereas the term 'cultural property' is absent from the *Statute*, the term 'historic monuments' is not – it is expressly referred to in Article 3(d).

Today, the terms 'cultural property' and 'cultural heritage', of which the former is a part, are widely in use. Since adequate terminology exists, things should be called by their proper name to avoid confusion. To this end, more reliance should be placed on the *1954 Convention* which introduced the term 'cultural property' into international law and defined the term.

(b) Acts that are Criminalised

Article 3(d) of the *ICTY Statute* criminalises 'seizure of, destruction or wilful damage done to'[240] objects which it enumerates. Only acts which result in actual 'seizure, destruction or damage' constitute the offence within the meaning of Article 3(d). In contrast, Article 4 of the *1954 Convention*, going much further, prohibits '*any act* of hostility *directed against* [cultural] property'.[241] Such an act need not result in destruction or damage of cultural property. Consistent with this Article, even a light shelling would put an object of cultural property in danger and would constitute a proscribed act. Thus, the prohibition in Article 4 of the *1954 Convention* provides for more extensive protection of cultural property than Article 3(d) of the *Statute*.

Still, as the fact that Article 3 uses the expression 'shall include, but not be limited to' means that this Article of the *ICTY Statute* not only covers violations of the *1907 Regulations* but can also include other violations of international law, thus including those envisaged in the *1954 Convention*, the ICTY is authorised to rely on the *1954 Convention* as the instrument binding on the parties to the

---

239 *Prlić* Indictment, para 229 (emphasis added).

240 *ICTY Statute*, art 3(d).

241 *1954 Convention*, art 4(1) (emphasis added).

conflict. Despite this possibility, the ICTY seems to be reluctant to expand the list of violations given in Article 3(d) of the *Statute*. For instance, in *Strugar*, which is considered the most important ICTY cultural property-related case to date, despite frequently referring to the *1954 Convention*, the Trial Chamber was of the view that as far as cultural property is concerned, actual damage and/or destruction of cultural property is the constitutive element of the offence under Article 3(d) of the *ICTY Statute*. In its reasoning, this Trial Chamber first noted the prohibition contained in Article 4 of the *1954 Convention* to 'direct' acts against cultural property, and then went on to say that the 'Statute explicitly criminalizes only those acts which *result in damage to, or destruction* of, such property'.[242] Accordingly, 'a requisite element of the crime [under Article 3(d) of the *Statute*] is *actual damage or destruction* occurring as a result of an act directed against this property'.[243]

Moreover, while the ICTY case law requires that 'the damaged or destroyed property was not used for military purposes at the time when the acts of hostility directed against these objects took place',[244] the use of cultural property for military purposes *per se* cannot amount to a crime under Article 3(d). In contrast, inasmuch as it prohibits any act of hostility directed against cultural property, Article 4 of the *1954 Convention* proscribes 'any *use* of [cultural] property and its immediate surroundings or of the appliances in use for its protection for purposes which are likely to expose it to destruction or damage in the event of armed conflict'.[245] The use of cultural property for military purposes may put such property in grave danger as under certain circumstances it may turn it into a legitimate military target, which, in turn, may lead to the destruction or damage to that property. Thus, the use of cultural property for military purposes may have consequences which are as fatal as acts of hostility directed against such property. The failure to criminalise the use of cultural property for military purposes in the *ICTY Statute* has allowed many who have misused cultural property to walk free. Under a hypothetical scenario in which the Old Bridge was used for military purposes and such use turned it into a legitimate military target, causing the attack and the destruction of it, no one could be held responsible within the meaning of Article 3(d) of the *ICTY Statute* because the *Statute* does not criminalise the 'use' of cultural property for military purposes.

242 *Strugar* Trial Judgement, para 308 (emphasis added).

243 Ibid (emphasis added).

244 Ibid para 312 (listing this requirement as one of the elements of the crime of destruction or wilful damage of cultural property under Article 3(d) of the *Statute*).

245 *1954 Convention*, art 4(1) (emphasis added).

B Cultural Property in Indictments and Decisions of the ICTY

1 The Non-Existence of Cases Relating Solely to Cultural Property

Despite the fact that the destruction of cultural property in the former Yugoslavia during the conflicts in the 1990s was widespread and systematic, no single case at the ICTY has dealt solely with cultural property. Instead, cultural property-related charges have tended to be lost in a much wider package of charges. Not even the *Jokić* case and the *Strugar* case (which are considered to be the most prominent ICTY cultural property cases) have focused solely on cultural property. Even here, 'destruction or wilful damage done to institutions dedicated to religion, charity, and education, the arts and sciences, historic monuments and works of art and science', a violation of the laws or customs of war, is one of several other charges.[246] Precisely, there were six counts in the Dubrovnik Indictment and cultural property charges were included in the last one.

There are many factors that make the multiplicity of charges in ICTY indictments understandable. The scale of various crimes committed during the 1990s Balkan conflicts in general, and the magnitude of crimes against persons, in particular, as well as limited resources, make it difficult to focus on one specific crime or on one type of crime. However, the scale of cultural property destruction and the wide-ranging and long-lasting consequences of it are among the reasons why cultural property deserves a more prominent place at the ICTY.

246 See *Jokić* Sentencing Judgement, paras 7-8 (referring to the Second Amended Indictment of 27 August 2003) and *Strugar* Trial Judgement, para 2 and fn 1 (referring to the Third Amended Indictment of 10 December 2003). Note that on 23 February 2001 the Initial Indictment charged together four persons, namely, Pavle Strugar, Miodrag Jokić, Vladimir Kovačević and Milan Zec for violations of the laws or customs of war committed by alleged attacks on Dubrovnik between 1 October and 31 December 1991. The charges against the fourth indictee were withdrawn in July 2001, and the cases against the remaining three were eventually separated. The *Kovačević* case was referred to Serbia. See Decision of the Trial Chamber on Referral of Case Pursuant to Rule *11bis*, 17 November 2006 and Decision of the Appeals Chamber on Appeal against the 17 November 2006 Decision on Referral under Rule *11bis*, 28 March 2007. The Second and Third Amended Indictments contained six counts all relating to violations of the laws or customs of war perpetrated on 6 December 1991.

C *The* Prlić et al *Case*

1 How Does the Old Bridge Rank in the Indictment?

(a) *Lost in the Ocean of Charges*

The *Prlić* Indictment contains twenty-six counts. The accused are charged for crimes against humanity, including persecution on political, racial and religious grounds, for grave breaches of the *1949 Geneva Conventions* and for violations of the laws and customs of war. Each of the twenty-six counts of the Indictment includes numerous allegations as specified in particular paragraphs of the Indictment relating to various municipalities. Paragraphs 43 to 217 cover eight municipalities, four of which are located in central Bosnia and Herzegovina and four in southwest Bosnia and Herzegovina. The Old Bridge is referred to in paragraph 116 of the Indictment which alleges that:

> On 9 November 1993, the Herceg-Bosna/HVO forces destroyed the Stari Most ('Old Bridge'), an international landmark that crossed the Neretva River between East and West Mostar.[247]

This is the only explicit reference to the Old Bridge in the Indictment. However, paragraph 116 does not deal with the Old Bridge exclusively as it also includes allegations relating to the destruction or damage to other property, notably religious property in East Mostar. Paragraph 229 of the Indictment, which enumerates various crimes under counts 1 to 26, does include allegations made in paragraph 116. In fact, paragraph 116 is referred to in several counts of the Indictment.[248] Despite these seemingly frequent references, the paragraph containing the allegations related to the Old Bridge must be searched for carefully as there are, as noted, references to numerous other paragraphs, each containing various other allegations.

(b) *Religious v Secular Cultural Property*

Paragraph 116 of the *Prlić* Indictment alleges that '[a]s part of and in the course of the East Mostar siege, the Herceg-Bosna/HVO forces deliberately destroyed or significantly damaged [a number of] *mosques or religious properties* in East Mostar'.[249] After specifying these properties, the Indictment then, in the same paragraph and under the same rubric of 'religious property', alleges the destruction of the Old Bridge although the Bridge was not a religious object but a

---

247 *Prlić* Indictment, para 116.

248 Ibid para 229 (Counts 1, 19, 20, 21, 24, 25, 26).

249 Ibid (emphasis added).

public, secular monument. This religious connotation further 'ethnicizes'[250] the Bridge which had been considered to belong to everyone and not to one particular community.

Religious connotations are amplified in the wording of Count 21 of the Indictment. This count charges the accused with 'destruction or wilful damage done to institutions dedicated to *religion or education*', the crime punishable under Article 3(d) of the *ICTY Statute*. It is not clear why the wording of this count did not extend to 'historic monuments' when Article 3(d) explicitly covers this category of cultural property. As noted, things should be called by their proper names, at least where adequate terminology exists. The Old Bridge easily fell into the category of historic monuments. Being charged under the rubric of 'institutions dedicated to religion or education' only adds to the invisibility of the Old Bridge as an object of 'cultural property' in the Indictment. As discussed, religious property (as well as institutions dedicated to education) is not necessarily cultural property. Mixing these two together lessens the distinctive character of cultural property.

Although it is often claimed that a considerable number of ICTY indictments have included cultural property charges, the fact is that where Article 3(d) of the *Statute* is concerned, with a few exceptions, the charges have been primarily focused on the destruction and damage to religious property. In most instances, there have been no details at all in the indictments as to whether those properties actually constituted cultural property (i.e., their age, historical, artistic or architectural importance, whether they have been protected by adequate national laws or simply regarded as objects of high importance to the cultural heritage). Similar arguments could be made in relation to the ICTY decisions. As in *Prlić*, charges in other indictments have often involved a number of municipalities and a number of religious objects. The absence of the necessary details makes it difficult to determine whether such objects could be considered cultural property. The inclusion of these details is not necessary for the purpose of bringing charges under Article 3(d) of the *ICTY Statute*. Still, even if they are absent from the indictments such details could be sought in the course of the proceedings. In that way the confusion as to what does and does not constitute cultural property could be reduced. Ultimately, this would lead to effective application of the *1954 Convention*, as well as the relevant provisions of the *Additional Protocols*.

2 The Mega Trial

An additional factor contributing to the slight nature of the charges related to the Old Bridge relates to the size of the *Prlić* case. As noted, this is one of the largest ICTY cases, involving six accused individuals in a joint trial on charges

---

250 Colin Kaiser, 'Crimes against Culture' *UNESCO Courier* Sept 2000, [8], http://web1.infotrac.galegroup.com/itw/infomark/109/511/ ['Crimes against Culture'].

for war crimes, grave breaches of the *1949 Geneva Conventions* and crimes against humanity, specified under twenty-six counts of the Indictment, stretching geographically over eight municipalities. Given that the charges related to the Old Bridge are only a drop in the ocean of charges overall, the majority of which are person-related charges, it is not likely that the destruction of the Bridge will get the attention it deserves.

The mega trials, including the case at hand, have been largely prompted by the ICTY's completion strategy.[251] While joint trials are in the general interest of judicial economy and have a number of other advantages, such as avoiding duplication of evidence, minimising the hardship of victims and witnesses who might otherwise be called to give the same evidence in numerous trials, and ensuring consistency of verdicts, they also raise many concerns ranging from the pure logistics of trying several defendants in the ICTY's limited courtroom space[252] to conflicts of interests among the accused and the associated problems of proper defence and fair trial.[253]

3 Liability

The *Prlić* Indictment charges all six accused individuals, *inter alia*, with the destruction of the Old Bridge.[254] The accused held different positions at the

---

251 See, eg, statements and written reports by the ICTY President and ICTY Prosecutor to the UN Security Council on the ICTY's completion strategy since the adoption of Security Council Resolution 1534 (March 2004), which requested the President and Prosecutor of both the ICTY and ICTR to provide the Council with assessments every six months in relation to their respective completion strategies, http://www.un.org/icty. See also Sean Murphy, 'Developments in International Criminal Law: Progress and Jurisprudence of the International Criminal Tribunal for the Former Yugoslavia' (1999) 93 *American Journal of International Law* 57, 79-80 (discussing the approach of the ICTY to joint trials generally); Janet Anderson, 'Nuremberg-Style Trial Planned for Bosnia's Worst Atrocity', The Institute for War and Peace Reporting (IWPR) Update No. 414, 9 July 2005, http://www.iwpr.net (discussing the pros and cons of the mega trials).

252 See Kelly Askin, 'Reflections on Some of the Most Significant Achievements of the ICTY' (2003) 37 *New England Law Review* 903, 907 ['Reflections'].

253 The issues of proper defence and fair trial have been repeatedly highlighted in *Prlić* by both the accused themselves and by their defence lawyers, especially by Michael Karnavas who represents Jadranko Prlić. See Daniel Barron, 'Yugoslav Tribunal Takes International Justice from Theory to Practice', IWPR's Tribunal Update No. 514 Part 1, 23 August 2007, http://www.iwpr.net (noting numerous objections raised by Michael Karnavas, including those relevant to fair trial). See also Jelena Pejić, 'Accountability for International Crimes: From Conjecture to Reality' (2002) 84 *International Review of the Red Cross* 13, 32 (stressing the importance of fair trial).

254 *Prlić* Indictment, para 229.

time relevant to the destruction of the Bridge, some in the civilian and others in the military sector of the HB/HVO: Jadranko Prlić was the Prime Minister of HB and, as the Prosecution alleges, 'had *de jure* and/or *de facto* power, effective control and/or substantial influence over the Herceg-Bosna/HVO government and military';[255] Bruno Stojić was head of the HVO Ministry of Defence, that is, 'that body's top political and management official, in charge of the Herceg-Bosna/HVO armed forces';[256] Slobodan Praljak was 'the military head of the Herceg-Bosna/HVO armed forces, with the title "Commander of the Main Staff"',[257] who, as the Prosecution alleges, 'exercised *de jure* and/or *de facto* command and control over the Herceg-Bosna/HVO armed forces [and] exercised effective control and substantial influence over [such] forces (including the operative zone commanders)';[258] Milivoj Petković was the deputy overall commander of the HB/HVO armed forces who exercised *de jure* and/or *de facto* command and control over the HB/HVO armed forces, and 'exercised effective control and substantial influence over [such] forces (including the operative zone commanders)';[259] Valentin Ćorić held the position of Chief of the Military Police Administration within the HVO Ministry of Defence[260] and had *de jure* and/or *de facto* command and control of the HVO Military Police, 'which regularly played important roles [*inter alia*] in combat and ethnic cleansing operations';[261] and Berislav Pušić was president of the commission to take charge of all HB/HVO prisons and detention facilities holding prisoners of war and detainees and was also a member of the HVO Commission for Exchange of Prisoners, and was, as the Prosecution alleges, 'an instrumental, high-level official in the Herceg-Bosna/HVO system concerning the detention, use, release, exchange, transfer and deportation of Bosnian Muslims'.[262]

Each of the accused is charged on the basis of Article 7(1) of the *Statute*, to be responsible for planning, instigating, ordering and/or committing the crimes charged in the Indictment, thereby including the destruction of the Old Bridge.[263] They are all also charged for the crimes pursuant to Article 7(3), on the basis of superior responsibility. Given the positions the accused held at the time, these modes of liability may be problematic as far as the Old Bridge is concerned at least in relation to the sixth accused, Berislav Pušić, whose area of responsibility was confined to matters related to prisoners of war and detainees.

---

255 Ibid para 3.

256 Ibid para 5.

257 Ibid para 7.

258 Ibid para 8.

259 Ibid para 10.

260 Ibid para 11.

261 Ibid para 12.

262 Ibid 14.

263 Ibid para 218.

Also, should the Court find that there was no superior-subordinate relationship between General Praljak and the HVO forces that attacked and destroyed the Bridge, the charges relating to superior responsibility pursuant to Article 7(3) of the *Statute* could be affected at least with respect to this accused.

(a) Joint Criminal Enterprise

In addition to criminal responsibility pursuant to Articles 7(1) and 7(3) of the *ICTY Statute*, the Prosecution alleges that the crimes charged in the *Prlić* Indictment were part of the joint criminal enterprise. According to the Indictment, four accused, that is, Prlić, Stojić, Praljak and Petković, are responsible, *inter alia*, for destruction of cultural property as part of the joint criminal enterprise.[264] The Indictment does not make reference to cultural property under the rubric of joint criminal enterprise in relation to the remaining two accused Ćorić and Pušić.

The Prosecution alleges all three forms of joint criminal enterprise in *Prlić*, two of which (specifically, form one and form three) cover, among other crimes, the destruction of the Old Bridge.[265] Form one of the joint criminal enterprise relates to the participatory acts or omission of the accused in the commission of crimes as members of or participants in the joint criminal enterprise, as well as aiding and abetting one or more members or perpetrators of the joint criminal enterprise, in the planning, preparation or execution of the crime, pursuant to Article 7(1) of the *Statute*. Form three of the joint criminal enterprise relates to any crime covered by the Indictment which was not within the objective or an intended part of the joint criminal enterprise but was the natural and foreseeable consequence of the joint criminal enterprise and of implementing or attempting to implement the enterprise.

The concept of a joint criminal enterprise is not expressly mentioned in the ICTY *Statute*. This form of criminal responsibility is a product of the jurisprudence of the ICTY. It allows courts to hold individuals criminally liable for group activities to which they have contributed in a criminally relevant way, extending criminal responsibility even to unforeseen consequences of such group activities, thereby enabling the prosecution and the court to extend criminal liability to high-level perpetrators that use subordinate persons for their criminal aims. Ever since the Appeals Chamber in *Tadić* held that joint criminal enterprise as a form of accomplice liability is well established in custom-

264 Ibid paras 17.1(u), 17.2(m), 17.3(k) and 17.4(h).

265 Ibid paras 221-227. Paras 224-226 of the *Prlić* Indictment cover form two of the joint criminal enterprise, which relates to the system of ill-treatment involving various detention facilities and deportation and transfer of Bosnian Muslims from areas claimed or controlled by the HVO at the time.

ary international law and implicitly contained in the *Statute*,[266] other Trial and Appeals Chamber decisions continue to follow this holding.[267]

Since the crimes committed in the former Yugoslavia during the 1990s conflicts were mostly of a systematic, large-scale and collective character, the advantages of the concept of joint criminal enterprise are obvious.[268] The concept is an especially useful tool in instances where there is not sufficient evidence to determine the existence of the superior-subordinate relationship and to pursue superior responsibility. However, there is much criticism of the concept of joint criminal enterprise, according to which it is claimed that it gives rise to conceptual confusion; it conflicts with some fundamental principles of criminal law, including the principle of culpability; and it invades the traditional ambit of superior responsibility liability.[269] It has been argued that, generally, the concept of joint criminal enterprise needs some tightening up. Form three of this concept has been particularly scrutinised. Its 'foreseeability' element is seen to be problematic as a penal law category of culpability and causation and thus to be in need of some qualification and greater precision.[270]

---

266 See *Prosecutor v Duško Tadić aka 'Dule'*, Judgement, Appeals Chamber, 15 July 1999, Case No. IT-94-1-A, para 220 [*Tadić* Appeal Judgement], and *ICTY Judicial Supplement* No. 6.

267 See, eg, *Milutinović et al*, Decision on Dragoljub Ojdanić's Motion Challenging Jurisdiction – Joint Criminal Enterprise, 2 May 2003, Case No. IT-99-37-AR72, *Judicial Supplement* No. 41; *Prosecutor v Milorad Krnojelac*, Decision on Form of Second Amended Indictment, Trial Chamber II, 11 May 2000, Case No. IT-97-25-PT; *Krnojelac* Appeal Judgement.

268 See, eg, Carla Del Ponte, 'Investigation and Prosecution of Large-Scale Crimes at the International Level: The Experience of the ICTY' (2006) 4 *Journal of International Criminal Justice* 539; Kai Hamdorf, 'The Concept of a Joint Criminal Enterprise and Domestic Modes of Liability for Parties to a Crime' (2007) 5 *Journal of International Criminal Justice* 208; Askin, 'Reflections', above n 252, 910-911.

269 See generally Allison Danner and Jenny Martinez, 'Guilty Associations: Joint Criminal Enterprise, Command Responsibility and the Development of International Criminal Law', International Law Workshop, University of California, Berkeley, Year 2004, Paper 3, http://repositories.cdlib.org/berkeley_ilw/fall2004/3. See also Harmen van der Wilt, 'Joint Criminal Enterprise: Possibilities and Limitations' (2007) 5 *Journal of International Criminal Justice* 91; Kai Ambos, 'Joint Criminal Enterprise and Command Responsibility' (2007) 5 *Journal of International Criminal Justice* 159; Jens David Ohlin, 'Three Conceptual Problems with the Doctrine of Joint Criminal Enterprise' (2007) 5 *Journal of International Criminal Justice* 69; Attila Bogdan, 'Individual Criminal Responsibility in the Execution of a "Joint Criminal Enterprise" in the Jurisprudence of the *ad hoc* International Tribunal for the Former Yugoslavia' (2006) 6 *International Criminal Law Review* 63.

270 See, eg, Antonio Cassese, 'The Proper Limits of Individual Responsibility under the Doctrine of Joint Criminal Enterprise' (2007) 5 *Journal of International Criminal Justice* 109 ['The Proper Limits'].

The scope of joint criminal enterprise is sweeping: it often spans several years and is capable of expanding into a wide geographical area; any member of the criminal enterprise may be found guilty of any crime committed within the scope of the joint criminal enterprise, in the case of forms one and two, and of any foreseeable crime outside the scope of the criminal enterprise in the case of form three. These attributes, or rather concerns, are also applicable to the *Prlić* case. The Prosecution alleges the participation of several individuals in the joint criminal enterprise, charging them, as noted, with all three forms for crimes committed over an extended period of time over a large territory. Such an extensive scope of the joint criminal enterprise may appear to be advantageous with respect to establishing criminal responsibility for the destruction of the Old Bridge. However, the expansive scope of the criminal enterprise, with too many charges and individuals included within it, conversely may weaken the charge relating to the destruction of the Bridge. Proof of personal participation in this particular crime would better establish proof of the criminality of the accused. In order words, this would highlight the principle of culpability and individualise the guilt.[271]

4 The Timing

More than ten years passed between the date of the destruction of the Old Bridge and the *Prlić* Indictment. The Bridge was destroyed on 9 November 1993 but it was not until 4 March 2004 that the Initial Indictment was confirmed. The Indictment was kept confidential until its unsealing on 2 April 2004 when it was made public.[272] The following year, on 16 November 2005, the Indictment was amended. The trial commenced on 26 April 2006. It should be noted that the ICTY Prosecution was required to complete all investigations and issue its last indictments by the end of 2004, which was the deadline accepted under the completion strategy. Thus, the *Prlić* Indictment was among the last of the indictments filed by the Prosecution.

---

271 See, eg, Danner and Martinez, above n 269, 38 (reminding of the limitations set in the IMT Judgement: 'criminal guilt is personal and…mass punishment should be avoided').

272 For discussion on the use of the ICTY's sealed indictments see, eg, Askin, 'Reflections', above n 252, 904-905; Ana Uzelac, 'Hague Prosecutors Rest Their Case', IWPR's Tribunal Update No. 387, 27 December 2004, http://www.iwpr.net (noting that the use of sealed indictments caused the first wave of criticism even within the OTP, and that ICTY ex-president Judge Antonio Cassese admitted he was 'very disturbed by the procedure' at the time and worried that the rights of the indictees could possibly be violated by the Tribunal); 'Use and Abuse of Sealed Indictment', IWPR's Tribunal Update No. 369, 30 July 2004, http://www.iwpr.net.

According to research, an investigation into the destruction of the Old Bridge was completed in 1994.[273] This highlights the slow pace of justice in this particular instance of the destruction of cultural property. Given the size of the *Prlić* case, i.e., the number of charges, geographical and temporal scope of crimes committed, number of the accused, number of documents (Prosecution exhibits: 4,914; Defence exhibits: Prlić: 1,619; Stojić: 1,032; Praljak: 1,047; Petković: 764; Ćorić: 422; Pušić: 63; Chamber exhibits: 15), number of witnesses (witnesses called by Prosecution: 145; Witnesses called by Defence: Prlić: 19; Stojić: 19; Praljak: 11; Petković: 11; Ćorić: 5; Pušić: 0) and large number of hours requested by the Prosecution and Defence for presenting their respective cases, *Prlić* was a lengthy (465 trial days), time-consuming trial. The appeal may take the case well up to the closure of the ICTY.

Delayed justice may to some extent prove to be denied justice for the destruction of the Old Bridge. The passage of time may alter perspectives. Although the destruction of the Bridge stirred passions on both sides, it should not be forgotten that the crime was committed almost two decades ago. Meanwhile, the 'new' Old Bridge, the replica of the original, has been built. Throughout the rebuilding process, people in Mostar refused to talk about the issues pertaining to justice with respect to the destruction of the Old Bridge. During research for this book, the author made numerous attempts to hear local opinion on the subject but with no success. The silence may have been due to the effects of the *Rules of the Road* obligations relating to the then on-going overall investigation in the *Prlić* case. But it could have also been due to selective amnesia, perhaps born out of fear that if they had spoken on the subject of responsibility for the destruction of the Bridge that would have somehow impacted negatively upon the rebuilding process, and the expected economic benefits, i.e., tourist dollars which were desperately needed in light of the complete economic collapse caused by the conflict.

Notwithstanding this, the truth remains somewhat elusive more than eighteen years after the destruction of the Bridge. The lapse of time may erode the memory of witnesses, which may impact upon the validity of evidence in the *Prlić* trial. Whereas some might not want to complicate the present reality with reminders of the pain and anger, others despite their goodwill might merely be unable to recall the relevant events with the necessary precision due to the lapse of time. On numerous occasions witnesses in *Prlić* have already highlighted the problem of not being able to recall events so many years *ex post facto*. The statement of the Prosecution witness Larry Forbes is illustrative of the problem:

273 See, eg, Jack Rosenberger, 'UN to Prosecute Culture Crimes' (1994) 82 *Art in America*, http://www.members.tripod.com/`UnconqueredBosnia/Cultur2.html [4] (noting in October 1994 that '[l]ed by Judge Richard A. Goldstone of South Africa, the UN war crimes tribunal recently completed an investigation of two test cases: Serbia's attempted destruction of the Croatian town of Dubrovnik and the Serb and Croat destruction of the Bosnian town of Mostar'); *Final Report*, above n 30, 28. For statistics about the *Prlić* case, see 'Case Information Sheet', at www.icty.org.

My memory's quite vague on it. It's been so long ago.[274]

Thus, justice might be perceived as coming late for the destruction of the Old Bridge, as well as for other crimes in the *Prlić* case. But again, as Professor Ruti Teitel argues, 'interest in the pursuit of justice does not necessarily wane with the passage of time'.[275] With the end of the last century there was a proliferation of calls for justice. Examples of various claims stretch back even to ancient injustices such as colonisation, the Inquisition, and the Crusades.[276] In any event, that there is perpetual interest in justice is confirmed in the international domain by the adoption of the *United Nations Convention on the Non-Applicability of Statutory Limitations to War Crimes and Crimes against Humanity*.[277] Nevertheless, this does not necessarily resolve tensions emanating from the ICTY's completion strategy.

D *Future Prospects*

1 The ICTY's Completion Strategy

(a) Time Pressure

(i) The Security Council Time Framework

The ICTY's completion strategy was established by the Security Council of the United Nations. It was endorsed by the President of the Security Council in 2002,[278] and one year later, on 28 August 2003, called on by Security Council Resolution 1503 (2003).[279] The completion strategy is intended to ensure a phased

274 Testimony of Larry Forbes in *Prlić*, T 21372 [Forbes testimony]. The problem of not being able to recall events properly is not confined to the *Prlić* case. Rather it is a wider issue, present in almost every other case. Still, the judges are aware of the problem and they do take it into consideration in weighing the evidence. See *Strugar* Trial Judgement, para 7.

275 Ruti Teitel, 'Transitional Justice Genealogy' (2003) 16 *Harvard Human Rights Journal* 69, 86.

276 Ibid. For the precedents for malicious destruction of immovable cultural treasures, such as the destruction of Carthage by the Romans, Cortez's razing of Aztec cities, the burning of the Library of Louvain, and the carpet bombings of Dresden and Tokyo, see, eg, Bevan, above n 4.

277 *Convention on the Non-Applicability of Statutory Limitations to War Crimes and Crimes Against Humanity* General Assembly Res. 2391, UN GAOR, 23rd Sess., Supp. No. 18, 40, UN Doc A/7218 (1968).

278 See the statement made by the President of the Security Council on 23 July 2002, S/PRST/2002/21.

279 See UN Security Council Resolution 1503 (2003), above n 43.

and coordinated completion of the ICTY's mission. Under this strategy, the ICTY is required to concentrate on the prosecution and trial of the most senior leaders suspected of being most responsible for crimes within the ICTY's jurisdiction and to refer other cases involving intermediate and lower rank accused to national courts.

With respect to The Hague aspect of the completion strategy, there are three phases. The first phase, which is already completed, regards investigations. The ICTY was required to take all possible measures to complete investigations by the end of 2004. The second and third phases regard the completion of trial activities at first instance and second instance respectively. To be precise, the ICTY was initially required to complete all trial activities at first instance by the end of 2008 and to complete all work in 2010.[280] As the time envisaged for phases two and three was running out, despite the possibility that phase two might continue into 2009, pressure to meet the deadlines was mounting in all cases, including the *Prlić* case.[281]

(ii) Effect on the Old Bridge

The pressure to complete the *Prlić* trial by the imposed deadlines resulted in time restrictions which have been a recurring feature of this trial since it began. Despite vehement protests by both the Prosecution and the Defence, the Trial Chamber slashed the time initially allowed for the Prosecution case and ordered that for their cross-examination of each witness, the Defence teams would each have one-sixth of the time used by the Prosecution for its examination-in-chief, unless they reached an agreement among themselves to divide the time otherwise. Both the Prosecution and Defence, as well as the accused themselves, have complained that the rush to complete the trial by the imposed deadlines impedes upon the right of fair trial.[282]

This race against time indicated that there might not be sufficient time to present and challenge properly the evidence regarding the Old Bridge. It

---

280 Ibid operative para 7. The subsequent Security Council Resolution 1534 (2004) of 26 March 2004 emphasises the importance of fully implementing the completion strategy as set out in resolution 1503 (2003). See UN Security Council Resolution 1534 (2004) adopted by the Security Council at its 4935th meeting, on 26 March 2004, S/RES/1534 (2004), operative para 3. These Resolutions also established the same completion strategy for the ICTR.

281 See Sense News Agency, 'Del Ponte Duels with Churkin in Security Council', 19 June 2007, http://www.sense-agency.com/en/stream.php?sta=3&pid=9866&kat=3.

282 See, eg, Barron, above n 253; Sense News Agency, 'Prlić: We Have already been Judged', The Hague, 16 April 2007, http://www.sense-agency.com/en/stream.php?sta=3&pid=9514&kat=3 (in his address to the Court, the accused Jadranko Prlić expressed his concern about the fairness of the trial). See also the *Prlić* case, T 21228 (the accused General Praljak complaining about the lack of time to conduct cross-examination properly).

had seemed that the Bridge would be dealt with quickly. Yet the case required extensive evidence, including expert witnesses. Due to time limitations as well as the size of the *Prlić* case, the Prosecution's evidence regarding the Bridge, as far as number of witnesses is concerned, was limited to just a few such witnesses. No expert witnesses were called to testify in the Prosecution's case in relation to the Bridge.[283] The Defence, on the other hand, seemed to be eager to present extensive evidence on the subject of the Bridge, including expert witnesses.[284] However, the accused General Praljak, who in addition to his defence counsel also examined and cross-examined witnesses, including on all matters relevant to the Old Bridge, complained about the lack of time to conduct this examination properly. This indicates that perhaps there was not sufficient time for the Old Bridge to be given the attention that it deserved.

VI Summary and Observations

The wilful destruction of cultural property is proscribed by IHL and may amount to a war crime incurring individual criminal responsibility. Such destruction is criminalised explicitly under the relevant provisions of the *ICTY Statute*. After a long silence, charges have finally been brought by the ICTY for the destruction of the Old Bridge. They are included among the array of other charges against the six accused in the *Prlić* case. Nevertheless, mere criminalisation of the destruction of cultural property or inclusion of cultural property-related charges in indictments does not in itself guarantee the prominent standing of cultural property. An examination of the *ICTY Statute*, indictments and decisions reveals some inadequacies in the treatment of cultural property. Contrary to what is often believed to be the case, cultural property is not ranked as highly as it should be at the ICTY. The *Statute* opts for somewhat dated law, whereas the Court although empowered to apply a more up-to-date specialist treaty puts more weight on other instruments which only briefly deal with cultural property. As a result, there is confusion as to the meaning of the term 'cultural property', as well as a missed opportunity to criminalise acts other than those resulting in the actual destruction or damage of cultural property. Also, despite

283 See hearing in *Prlić*, 17 May 2007, T 18734.-18735.

284 The expert witness Dr Slobodan Janković testified pursuant to the procedure in Rule 94*bis* of the *Rules of Procedure and Evidence* from 30 June 2008 through 1 July 2008, concerning the destruction of the Old Bridge. See Transcript in *Prlić* of 30 June-1 July 2008. See also Trial Chamber III Order of 25 May 2010 to admit evidence regarding the expert witness Slobodan Janković and expert witness Heinrich Pichler; Redacted Public Version Slobodan Praljak's Redacted Final Brief of 31 March 2011, 'Destruction of the Old Bridge, 9 November 1993', 107 *et seq* (General Praljak and his witnesses denied the HVO's responsibility for the destruction of the Old Bridge, repeating what this accused claimed throughout the Prosecution and Defence case).

the claim that there is no hierarchy of crimes and no primacy of crimes against persons over crimes against property, cultural property-related crimes appear to be rather subordinated in the *Statute*, as well as in indictments and decisions. Yet even in times of armed conflict human cultural needs matter and are indivisible from the need for physical survival.

Moreover, the Prosecution puts an emphasis on religious property. Given the extensive and widespread destruction of religious property such focus is understandable. But there is a misconception that because numerous places of worship are included in indictments under the charges pertaining to Article 3(d) of the *ICTY Statute*, many ICTY indictments and decisions deal with cultural property. While religious property enjoys protection under customary international law as well as treaty law, such property does not necessarily constitute 'cultural property'. Neither the indictments nor the ICTY's decisions provide details as to whether specific religious objects meet the conditions necessary for protection under the rubric of cultural property. As the Old Bridge demonstrates, there are also instances where cultural property otherwise devoid of religious significance is put under the rubric of religious property.

One should be realistic with respect to prosecution of cultural property-related crimes because such prosecution involves a number of difficulties.[285] Investigation of such crimes is time-consuming and costly. Many indictments that include charges pursuant to Article 3(d) of the *ICTY Statute* involve a number of objects and a number of locations, across different cities, towns, villages or regions. Proper investigation calls for the engagement of experts in various fields and adequately trained staff. The ICTY lacks this expertise. Besides, the Tribunal has experienced budgetary constraints and is under pressure to complete its work. As a result, no instances of the destruction of cultural property other than the 'Dubrovnik' cases have been dealt with closely. Still, even in these cases cultural property has not been dealt with exclusively. In other cases, too, charges under Article 3(d) of the *ICTY Statute* are included towards or at the very end of what is often a long list of charges.

In the *Prlić* Indictment the charges relevant to the Old Bridge are not easily identified. The pressure to meet the deadlines emanating from the ICTY's completion strategy has also resulted in the tendency to opt for the so-called joinders, which, in effect, as with the *Prlić* case, are the mega trials involving several accused individuals alleged to be responsible for a wide range of crimes, in terms of the number of crimes involved, their scale and the geographical context, as well as in terms of number of victims. The size of the *Prlić* case, where the charges relevant to the Old Bridge are difficult to spot, makes it unlikely that the Bridge will get adequate attention at the ICTY.

Also, preference for joint criminal enterprise as a mode of liability may not be as adequate a way to individualise the guilt as would be the concept of supe-

285 For discussion of various difficulties involved in prosecution of crimes under the ICTY's jurisdiction, see, eg, Del Ponte, above n 268; Barron, above n 253.

rior responsibility. In the case at hand, high expectations are attached to the individualisation of guilt. Finding exactly who is responsible for the destruction of the Old Bridge could play a significant role in the reconciliation of what is still perceived as the very much divided city of Mostar.

Finally, there is the problem of timing of ICTY indictments and trials. Sometimes justice which is achieved late is regarded as justice crippled or no justice at all as witnesses may have difficulty recalling the events years *ex post facto* or a destroyed object may be rebuilt by the time the trial commences, which may change the perspective on the crime committed, both problems in the *Prlić* case.

On the other hand, when juxtaposed against the reluctance to prosecute war crimes at the national level in general, and with virtual absence of cultural property-related cases before the national courts in particular, as well as with other challenges characteristic of the Balkan justice, such as a lack of expertise in handling war crimes cases, ethnic bias and inadequate witness protection, it must be stressed that the ICTY has played a significant role in enhancing the importance of the protection of cultural property. No other international tribunal in the history of humankind has dedicated more time and resources to crimes involving immovable cultural objects. Its historical antecedent, the IMT, albeit to a lesser degree, focused on movable cultural property.

Despite the practical difficulties, the Prosecution at the ICTY has made great effort concerning cultural property. Given the constraints mentioned and the magnitude of other crimes committed in the former Yugoslavia during the 1990s conflicts that it was required to investigate, the Prosecution work in the area of cultural property is, in fact, praiseworthy. A number of indictments have included cultural property-related charges. The high number of such indictments raises awareness and sends a clear message that unjustified attacks on cultural property will not be tolerated. The same could be said for the ICTY decisions dealing with cultural property. The ICTY's convictions warn military commanders to think twice before issuing orders to attack objects of cultural property.

It is difficult to evaluate how cultural property-related crimes have been ranked in respect to the gravity of such crimes and the penalties imposed because no person has been charged with or convicted solely for crimes involving cultural property. Notwithstanding this, convictions of persons found guilty, *inter alia*, of cultural property-related crimes send a message to the would-be destroyers of the cultural treasures of all humankind that there will be no impunity for such acts. While the ICTY could not and cannot completely prevent the destruction of cultural property, its deterrent effect has been felt already: since guilty verdicts and sentences for Admiral Jokić and General Strugar there have been no major incidents of destruction or wilful damage to cultural property in armed conflict. All in all, given the numerous hurdles it had to overcome, many beyond its control, and given a very modest set of precedents for guidance, the ICTY has made a tremendous step forward *vis-à-vis* enhancing the importance of respect for cultural property in times of armed conflict. There is, of course, much room for improvement in the area of justice for cultural property-related crimes, including the destruction of cultural property within the crime of genocide. But a long history of impunity has been broken and that is an invaluable step forward.

Chapter 7

Conclusion

The importance of cultural property transcends geographical and temporal boundaries. A high degree of universal interest in the preservation of cultural property is recognised in the international rules that have been devised to overcome various threats endangering the survival of such property. These rules are premised on the notion of the shared heritage of humankind and on the idea of intergenerational justice.

Despite the significance of cultural property and the existence of rules providing for its protection, such property has been the deliberate target of warfare. One of the reasons that cultural destruction continues from one armed conflict to another is impunity for blatant attacks against irreplaceable cultural treasures. States have been perennially reluctant to prosecute war crimes generally, let alone those involving cultural property.

It was not until the immediate aftermath of WWII that international law protecting cultural property was enforced through international criminal adjudication. However, the deterrent effect of the IMT has not been strongly felt as the deliberate destruction of cultural treasures has continued worldwide. In the more than one hundred armed conflicts that have occurred since 1945, damage to the cultural heritage of humankind has been incalculable.

Premeditated, vicious attacks on cultural property in the former Yugoslavia during armed conflicts in the 1990s are among more recent examples of the tragedies wrought on precious cultural objects. The Old Bridge of Mostar is emblematic of the fate of cultural property in armed conflict. Although it was devoid of military significance, this 427-year old monument of exceptional architectural and historic significance was targeted for two consecutive days at almost point blank range by the HVO tanks and wilfully destroyed.

Various excuses have been put forward to justify the attack, including that the Old Bridge was not a protected object within the meaning of IHL, that it was inadequately physically protected against the shelling, that it was not marked with a distinctive emblem and that both the Bridge and its immediate surroundings were used for military purposes, due to which it was thus a military necessity that it be destroyed.

Yet the Old Bridge did enjoy immunity under the relevant rules of IHL both as an object of cultural property and as a civilian object. While the Bridge was in need of additional physical protection, this still did not absolve the HVO from its obligation to respect it as an object of cultural property. Since the Bridge was an object of cultural property under general protection, the distinctive marking was not compulsory. With respect to the claim that the Bridge and its surroundings were used for military purposes, under IHL such a use does not automatically justify an attack. To be considered legitimate under IHL, an attack must be justified by military necessity.

However, the relevant law applicable to the destruction of the Old Bridge does not define military necessity. Nevertheless, it is universally accepted that in order to become a legitimate military target, an object must become a military objective. In addition to this requirement, a range of precautionary measures must be taken. The side under attack has an obligation to avoid locating military objectives within or near densely populated areas and to refrain from using cultural property for military purposes except in cases of military necessity. According to the jurisprudence of the ICTY an object of cultural property does not lose immunity because of its location. As for the use of the Bridge itself for military purposes, there is no evidence that there was fighting between the two opposing forces at the time. Even if the Bridge was used for military purposes there is no evidence that such a use was posing any significant threat to the HVO forces at the time.

The attack on the Old Bridge by the HVO forces and its subsequent destruction was not due to the lack of clarity of the relevant rules or the difficulty in identifying the Old Bridge. The Bridge was a well-known monument in the region both visually and culturally. The attack seems to have been premeditated and deliberate.

Notwithstanding this, the Old Bridge case exposes certain weaknesses in the applicable IHL regime. While the law envisages the exception of military necessity, it fails to define the concept. Although the definition of a military objective provided for in *Additional Protocol I* is taken to interpret the concept of military necessity, the problem is still not entirely removed as the definition of military objective does not deal with factors which may be critical to the survival of cultural property, such as specifying the level at which a decision to attack the cultural property is to be made, whether there should be warning prior to attack, and for how long an object of cultural property is to be considered a military objective.

Some of these matters are dealt with in the *1999 Protocol* to the *1954 Convention*. Article 6 of the *Protocol* specifies the circumstances under which a waiver on the basis of imperative military necessity may be invoked, including the duration of the waiver ('when and for as long as' an object of cultural property has, 'by its function' become a military objective and there is 'no feasible alternative available'),[1] the decision-making level for invoking imperative

1 *Protocol for the Protection of Cultural Property in the Event of Armed Conflict*, 26 March 1999, 38 ILM 769-82 (entered into force 9 March 2004), art 6(a) and (b)

military necessity ('an officer commanding a force the equivalent of a battalion in size or larger, or a force smaller in size where circumstances do not permit otherwise')[2] and the circumstances in which an effective advance warning in the case of attack must be given ('whenever circumstances permit').[3] Although this article substantially strengthens the protection of cultural property, its provisions still leave room for subjective interpretation. For instance, with respect to advance warning, the clause 'whenever circumstances permit' may easily be interpreted as 'never'. As to the definition of a military objective, it may not always be easy to determine whether the requirements envisaged in the definition of a military objective are present simultaneously. The situation is even harder if an attack is assessed *ex post facto*.

The need to apply ambiguous rules only adds to the problem of indeterminacy in the battlefield. The situation is particularly challenging in spatially restricted and densely populated urban areas. As military personnel may intermingle with civilians it may be difficult to distinguish between combatants and civilians and between military objectives and civilian objects. Ideally, the law that protects cultural property in armed conflict should not allow attacks on and/or the use of such property for military purposes under any circumstances. However, since the concept of military necessity is deeply ingrained in customary international law, it is very unlikely that such a ban will occur any time soon.

To ensure respect for cultural property, more attention should be given to international criminal adjudication for cultural property-related crimes. International criminal adjudication for these crimes has been one of the ways in which the international community has honoured its commitment with respect to cultural property. For the first time since Nürnberg, cultural property is being dealt with by an international criminal tribunal – the ICTY. However, as the examination of the ICTY's response to the destruction of the Old Bridge demonstrates, cultural property does not hold as prominent a place at the Tribunal as it should. A number of factors contribute to the 'invisibility' of cultural property at the Tribunal. The relevant provisions of the *ICTY Statute* are based on somewhat archaic norms of IHL. As a result, the *Statute* does not use the term 'cultural property'. It accords protection to a limited number of components of cultural property. These components are mixed with other types of property, which, in effect, undermines the special character of cultural property. Whereas any act directed against cultural property may endanger such property, the *Statute* criminalises only acts which result in actual damage or destruction.

The *Statute* is silent on the second component of the obligation to 'respect' cultural property in times of armed conflict, that is, the prohibition on the use

[*1999 Protocol*]. In relation to the *1954 Convention*, see *Convention for the Protection of Cultural Property in the Event of Armed Conflict*, 14 May 1954, 249 UNTS 240 (entered into force 7 August 1956), art 1(a) [*1954 Convention*].

2 *1999 Protocol*, ibid art 6(c).

3 Ibid art 6(d).

of cultural property and its surroundings for military purposes. Yet the use of cultural property for military purposes may seriously endanger cultural property. This problem is addressed in the *1999 Protocol*. Article 15(1)(b) of the *Protocol* criminalises the use of cultural property or its immediate surroundings in support of military action.[4] However, this is limited only to cultural property under enhanced protection – a new system of protection, the third under the *1954 Convention* regime. Even if the *Protocol* existed and was binding law at the time it would still not be applicable to the destruction of the Old Bridge because the Bridge enjoyed only 'general' protection within the meaning of the *1954 Convention*. Use for military purposes of cultural property under general protection could not be considered an offence within the meaning of Article 15(1)(b) of the *1999 Protocol*.

Moreover, although there is no 'official' hierarchy of crimes, some crimes are still deemed more serious than others. The destruction of cultural property is only directly referred to in Article 3(d) of the *ICTY Statute* as a violation of laws or customs of war. Crimes under Article 3 of the *Statute* are often referred to as war crimes. War crimes are generally considered to be crimes of a lesser seriousness than crimes against humanity and genocide. While the destruction of cultural property can constitute persecution, a crime against humanity, it cannot amount to a crime of genocide under the *Statute*. Where persecution is concerned, cultural property is protected indirectly, not because of its intrinsic value but because of its link with a civilian population against whom an attack is directed. This anthropocentric approach to cultural property, as the destruction of the Old Bridge demonstrates, to some extent 'ethnicizes' cultural property which is otherwise considered part of *shared* cultural heritage.

The situation is not much better in ICTY indictments and decisions. There are virtually no cases solely relating to cultural property. Due to an extensive destruction of religious property during the Balkan conflicts, the indictments put an emphasis on such property. Still, there is a misconception that because of a large number of indictments, including charges relating to the destruction of religious property, such property constitutes 'cultural' property. While the destruction of religious property is criminalised under the same article of the *ICTY Statute* as cultural property, religious property does not necessarily constitute cultural property.

However, in an assessment of the ICTY's approach to cultural property, problems underlying the prosecution of cultural property-related crimes must be taken into account. Given the overall scale of atrocities committed in the Balkans during the 1990s, the complexity of cases, the pressure to meet the imposed deadlines and the associated budgetary difficulties, the ICTY has made a significant contribution to ending impunity for wilful attacks on precious cultural treasures.

4 Ibid art 15(1)(b).

Notwithstanding this, a range of measures could be taken to increase the protection of cultural property in times of armed conflict. In future revisions of the IHL regime on the protection of cultural property, effort should be made to harmonise the definition of cultural property as between the relevant instruments of international law and to move towards a more precise definition of a military objective. Unambiguous definitions are essential in determining a legitimate military target. Criminalisation of the use for military purposes of any cultural property and not just cultural property under enhanced protection should also be considered. While the system of enhanced protection is reserved for select cultural property 'of the greatest importance for humanity'[5] and the system of special protection is confined to cultural property 'of very great importance',[6] a vast number of cultural objects are considered to be 'of great importance'[7] and as such are placed under general protection. Some of these cultural objects may be of an outstanding architectural, artistic or historical importance. Just because cultural objects, for various reasons, have not been placed under the system of enhanced or special protection does not necessarily mean that their loss is any less tragic. In addition, there is a need to relate targeted damage to cultural property to the extinction of a community and thus to rethink the current definition of genocide.

Furthermore, in future international prosecutions, closer attention should be given to cultural property-related charges. Also, more emphasis should be placed on the *1954 Convention*. This would significantly improve the standing of the specialist treaty and ultimately enhance the importance of cultural property protection. Since IHL is enforced not only at the international level but also, and in fact, primarily, at the national level, monitoring of domestic war crimes trials should be imperative in post-conflict societies which experience difficulties in the area of justice as is the case with Bosnia and Herzegovina.

A number of other peacetime as well as wartime measures should be taken to improve the prospects for survival of cultural property in armed conflict. Peacetime measures include vigorous educational campaigns on cultural property matters at all levels,[8] particularly the military level, as well as conflict prevention, extensive dissemination of knowledge on cultural property, military training, timely and adequate safeguarding measures, preventive UN/UNESCO authorised intervention in order to avert cultural disasters,

5 Ibid art 10(a).

6 *1954 Convention*, art 8(1).

7 Ibid art 1(a).

8 See, eg, ICOMOS Sweden/Central Board of National Antiquities/Swedish National Commission for UNESCO, *Information as an Instrument for Protection against War Damages to the Cultural Heritage. Report from a Seminar, June 1994* Stockholm, Svenska Unescoradets skriftserie, 4/1994 (1994) Stockholm: ICOMOS Sweden [*Information as an Instrument*]. For discussion of the role of education and training see also Lyndel Prott (ed), *Finishing the Interrupted Voyage* (2006).

and monitoring the implementation of the *1954 Convention* and its *Protocols*, with an emphasis on the involvement of civil society in such tasks, notably, the International Committee of the Blue Shield (ICBS) (comprising four expert organisations: the International Council on Archives (ICA), the International Council of Museums (ICOM), the International Council on Monuments and Sites (ICOMOS) and the International Federation of Library Associations and Institutions (IFLA)).

With respect to wartime measures, guarding cultural property by international forces should be a priority, particularly where objects of high cultural significance are concerned. Guarding by a third, neutral, party is particularly relevant to armed conflicts with ethnic connotations. Any UN peacekeeping force should include a unit of cultural property specialists. Given the perennial UN budgetary problems, such a unit might be considered a luxury by some. However, rebuilding and reconstructing cultural objects can be even more costly. The $15 million, four-year project of the rebuilding of the Old Bridge is a case in point. It should be noted that the repair of Mostar's historic fabric has cost much more.[9] Some steps with respect to the involvement of UN forces in the protection of cultural property have already been made. Guarding cultural objects in Kosovo by UNMIK (UN Interim Administration Mission in Kosovo) is one such example. Another example concerns the School for Peacekeeping Missions at Amersfoort Army Base, Netherlands, which provides training to military personnel that will serve abroad, under the flag of the UN or NATO. Part of this training relates to the significance of cultural property and its role in armed conflict.[10] An additional development concerns the signing of the agreement between UNESCO and Italy on the creation of a rapid deployment force, called 'cultural blue berets'. This force (initially to be composed entirely of Italians) is designed to reinforce UNESCO's ability to intervene quickly in emergency heritage situations.[11]

Each of these measures, as well as issues emanating from the application of IHL to the destruction of the Old Bridge, could be the subject of further research. The prospects for the effectiveness of the *1999 Protocol*, the likely approach to cultural property by the ICC, as well as the approach to cultural property by the Bosnia and Herzegovina War Crimes Chamber and other courts in the Balkans after the closure of the ICTY could in future also be explored.

Meanwhile, it remains to be seen how the ICTY will rule on the question of the destruction of the Old Bridge (in the *Prlić* case) and what effect the ruling will have on the city of Mostar and internationally. It is appropriate to be cau-

9 Koïchiro Matsuura, 'Why do we need the [O]ld [B]ridge at Mostar?' 6 July 2004, http://portal.unesco.org/en/ev.php.

10 See 'Instruction Cultural Awareness', http://odin.rug.nl/CB/CB_les.html.

11 See UNESCO Bureau of Public Information, 'UNESCO-Italy Agreement on Emergency Actions to Protect Heritage' Press Release No. 2004-97, 28 October 2004, http://portal.unesco.org/culture/en/ev.php.

tious in one's expectations, however. Given a long and complicated Indictment where the destruction of the Old Bridge figures almost as an afterthought, a byline in one paragraph (paragraph 116) after a long list of destroyed mosques,[12] and bearing in mind the time pressure emanating from the Tribunal's completion strategy, due to which all issues, including the Old Bridge, were and will be dealt with rather hurriedly, it is not likely that a judgement in *Prlić* will single out the question of the Bridge for special attention over all other charges in the Indictment.

It has been argued in this book that the Bridge did not constitute a military objective within the meaning of IHL and that its deliberate targeting and destruction represented a blatant disregard for the norms of IHL. The destruction of the Old Bridge has irreversible consequences. It has been predicted that this particular incident of cultural destruction 'will leave the strongest impression on the memory of…tragic war in Bosnia-Herzegovina'.[13]

Since 9 November 1993, '[t]here is no more Old Bridge'.[14] At around 10:15 am on that day, 'the painfully beautiful'[15] stone arch crumbled into the Neretva over which it had stood for 427 years. Whether the past embodied in other cultural objects will have a future greatly depends on how the present treats the past.

> Here, … the importance of sanctions against those who destroy cultural heritage. We must recognise that such attacks do not arise simply from 'the heat of the moment' but are calculated, pre-meditated and deliberate; in fact, they often form part of a strategy of hostility, especially in inter-ethnic conflicts. We must get to grips with these sobering realities. In facing them, we must not tire, we must not doubt the importance of our work, and we must not allow setbacks and disappointments to deter us [from protecting] the world's cultural heritage in all its rich diversity.[16]

12 See Frits Kalshoven, 'The Protection of Cultural Property in the Event of Armed Conflict within the Framework of International Humanitarian Law', (2005) 57 *Museum* 61, fn 18 and accompanying text ['The Protection of Cultural Property'].

13 Manfred Dinnes and Fuad Ćatović, *Hommage to Mostar* (1997) 7.

14 Ian Traynor, 'Shells Destroy Mostar Bridge' *Guardian* 19 November 1993, 10 (quoting spokeswoman for the UN Relief Agency).

15 *Prosecutor v Mladen Naletilić aka 'Tuta' and Vinko Martinović aka 'Štela'*, Judgement, Trial Chamber, 31 March 2003, Case No. IT-98-34-T. .

16 UNESCO, Address by Koïchiro Matsuura, Director-General of UNESCO at the Opening of the Fifth Meeting of the States Parties to the 1954 Hague Convention for the Protection of Cultural Property in the Event of Armed Conflict, DG/2001/115, UNESCO, 5 November 2001.

With the imminent closure of the ICTY and the jurisdiction of the ICC complementary to national criminal jurisdictions[17] strictly 'limited to the most serious crimes of concern to the international community as a whole',[18] it is a task for domestic courts, as it has always been, but long grossly neglected, to prosecute and try war crimes and to take this role seriously not only in relation to crimes against cultural property but any war crimes, in the successor States of the former Yugoslavia as everywhere. With regard to the destruction of the Old Bridge, irrespective of how this issue is to be resolved by the ICTY in the *Prlić* case, which deals with superior responsibility, the issue of individual responsibility in relation to the Bridge will remain unresolved until a proper investigation is conducted into the three HVO soldiers suspected of firing the projectiles that hit the Old Bridge[19] and the direct perpetrators of this crime are also brought to justice. Otherwise there will remain a sense of failure in achieving true closure for this event.

The Bosnia and Herzegovina War Crimes Chamber and the domestic courts of Bosnia and Herzegovina do have competence to try war crimes cases involving cultural property.[20] Now, they must demonstrate to the people of Bosnia and Herzegovina and to the entire international community that this State is willing to deal with war crimes in general and that the destruction of cultural property in particular is considered a grave offence. As long as the perpetrators of war crimes walk free their impunity insults both the most immediate victims of such crimes and the conscience of the whole of humanity. As Nobel Peace Prize winner Elie Wiesel has observed, '[t]he executioner always kills twice, the second time with silence'.[21] The Bosnia and Herzegovina War Crimes Chamber and the domestic courts of Bosnia and Herzegovina must break the silence with regard to 'the executioners' of the destruction of the Old Bridge.

---

17 See *Rome Statute of the International Criminal Court*, UN Diplomatic Conference of Plenipotentiaries on the Establishment of an International Criminal Court, UN Doc A/CONF 183/9 (17 July 1998) 2187 UNTS 3 (entered into force 1 July 2002) [*ICC Statute*], Preamble, para 10 ('the International Criminal Court established under this Statute shall be *complementary* to national criminal jurisdictions') (emphasis added).

18 Ibid art 5(1).

19 See chapter six, nn 158-163 and 209 and accompanying text.

20 See, eg, *Criminal Code of BH*; *Criminal Code of the Federation of BH*; BIRN, *In Pursuit of Justice: Guide to the War Crimes Chamber of the Court of BiH*, (2006); OSCE Mission to Bosnia and Herzegovina, *War Crimes Trials before the Domestic Courts of Bosnia and Herzegovina*, March 2005.

21 Nobel Peace Prize winner Elie Wiesel (quoted in Mounir Bouchenaki, Director, UNESCO World Heritage Centre, 'Breaking the Silence: Sites of Memory', *World Heritage Newsletter*, No. 23 (September/October 1999)), http://whc.unesco.org/news/23newsen.htm.

Cases

National Case Law

Bosnia and Herzegovina

The Destruction of Mosques in Banja Luka in 1993 Case

The Islamic Community in Bosnia and Herzegovina v The Republika Srpska, Decision on the Admissibility and Merits, Human Rights Chamber for Bosnia and Herzegovina, sitting in plenary session on 11 May 1999, delivered on 11 June 1999, Case No. CH/96/29, 11 May 1999, http://wwwuser.grdg.de/~ujvr/hrch/0000-0999/0029admmer.htm.

Canada

Case of the Vessel Marquis de Somereules, 1812 Stew. Adm.482.

Croatia

Perišić et al Case

District Court in Zadar, *The Public Prosecutor against Momčilo Perišić, Milić Potpara, Ilija Branković, Stojan Vučković, Nikola Germanac, Spasoje Čojić, Duško Gojković, Predrag Tasić, Željko Batinić, Saša Đurović, Senaid Grbo, Mile Rudić, Dragomir Jokić, Jovan Milivojević, Miroslav Bobić, Božo Perić, Aleksandar Lazarević, Mirko Marčeta and Nebojša Filipović*, Judgement of 24 April 1997, Case No. K. 74/96, unpublished.

France

Permanent Military Tribunal at Metz, *Lingenfelder* case, Judgement, 11 March 1947.

United States of America

Von Leeb (The High Command Trial) Case

Military Tribunal at Nürnberg, *The German High Command Trial, Trial of Wilhelm Von Leeb and Thirteen Others*, Judgement of 30 December 1947-28 October 1948, published in WCR, Vol. XII, 1949, 1.

Weizsaecker Case

Military Tribunal at Nürnberg, *Weizsaecker* case, Judgement, 14 April 1949.

International Case Law

International Court of Justice (ICJ)

Application of the Genocide Convention (Provisional Measures)

Application of the Convention on the Prevention and Punishment of the Crime of Genocide (Bosnia and Herzegovina v Yugoslavia (Serbia and Montenegro)), Request for the Indication of Provisional Measures, Order of 8 April 1993, ICJ Reports [1993] 3.

Application of the Genocide Convention (Preliminary Objections)

Application of the Convention on the Prevention and Punishment of the Crime of Genocide (Bosnia and Herzegovina v Yugoslavia (Serbia and Montenegro)), Preliminary Objections (Yugoslavia v Bosnia and Herzegovina), Judgement of 11 July 1996, ICJ Reports [1996] 595.

Application of the Genocide Convention (Merits)

Application of the Convention on the Prevention and Punishment of the Crime of Genocide (Bosnia and Herzegovina v Yugoslavia (Serbia and Montenegro), Merits, Judgement of 26 February 2007, ICJ Reports [2007], http://www.icj-cij.org/docket/files/.

Military and Paramilitary Activities in and against Nicaragua (Merits)

Military and Paramilitary Activities in and against Nicaragua (Nicaragua v United States of America), Merits, Judgement of 27 June 1986, ICJ Reports [1986] 14.

Nuclear Weapons

Legality of the Threat or Use of Nuclear Weapons, Advisory Opinion of 8 July 1996 [1996] ICJ Reports 66.

International Criminal Tribunal for Rwanda (ICTR)

Akayesu (ICTR-96-4)

Prosecutor v Akayesu, Case No. ICTR-96-4

Amended Indictment:
Prosecutor v Jean Paul Akayesu, Amended Indictment, 30 June 1997, Case No. ICTR-96-4-I.

Judgement:
Prosecutor v Jean Paul Akayesu, Judgement, Trial Chamber, 2 September 1998, Case No. ICTR-96-4-T.

Judgement on Appeal:
Prosecutor v Jean Paul Akayesu, Judgement, Appeals Chamber, 1 June 2001, Case No. ICTR-96-4-A.

Ntakirutinama (ICTR-96-10)

Prosecutor v Ntakirutinama et al, Case No. ICTR-96-10

Amended Indictment:
Prosecutor v Elizaphan Ntakirutinamal, Gerard Ntakirutinama, Obed Ruzindana and Charles Sikubwabo, Amended Indictment, 20 October 2000, Case No. ICTR-96-10-I.

Kambanda (ICTR-97-23-S)

Prosecutor v Jean Kambanda, Judgement, Trial Chamber, 4 September 1998, Case No. ICTR-97-23-S.

Kamuhanda (ICTR-99-54)

Prosecutor v Jean de Dien Kamuhanda, Judgement, Trial Chamber, 22 January 2004, Case No. ICTR-95-54A-T.

Kayishema (ICTR-95-1)

Prosecutor v Kayishema and Ruzindana, Case No. ICTR-95-1

First Amended Indictment:

Prosecutor v Clément Kayishema and Obed Ruzindana, Decision on the Motion Filed by the Prosecutor for Confirmation of the Trial Date and Submission of a Superseding Indictment, 10 April 1997, Case No. ICTR-95-1-I.

Judgement:

Prosecutor v Clément Kayishema and Obed Ruzindana, Judgement, Trial Chamber, 21 May 1999, Case No. ICTR-95-1-T.

Judgement on Appeal:

Prosecutor v Clément Kayishema and Obed Ruzindana, Judgement, Appeals Chamber, 1 June 2001, Case No. ICTR-95-1-A.

Musema (ICTR-96-13)

Prosecutor v Musema, Case No. ICTR-96-13

Judgement:

Prosecutor v Alfred Musema, Judgement, Trial Chamber, 27 January 2000, Case No. ICTR-96-13-I.

Judgement on Appeal:

Prosecutor v Alfred Musema, Judgement, Appeals Chamber, 16 November 2001, Case No. ICTR-96-13-A.

Nsabimana (ICTR-97-29)

Prosecutor v Nsabimana and Nteziryayo, Case No. ICTR-97-29

Indictment:

Prosecutor v Sylvan Nsabimana and Alphonse Nteziryayo, Indictment, 18 October 1997, Case No. ICTR-97-29-I.

Nyiramasuhuko (ICTR-97-21)

Prosecutor v Nyiramasuhuko and Ntahobali, Case No. ICTR-97-21

Indictment:

Prosecutor v Pauline Nyiramasuhuko and Arsène Shalom Ntahobali, Indictment, 26 May 1997, Case No. ICTR-97-21-I.

Rutaganda (ICTR-96-3)

Prosecutor v Rutaganda, Case No. ICTR-96-3

Judgement:

Prosecutor v Georges Anderson Nderubumwe Rutaganda, Judgement, Trial Chamber, 6 December 1999, Case No. ICTR-96-3-T.

Semanza (ICTR-97-20)

Prosecutor v Semanza, Case No. ICTR-97-20

Indictment:
Prosecutor v Laurent Semanza, Indictment, 21 October 1997, Case No. ICTR-97-20-I.

Judgement:
Prosecutor v Laurent Semanza, Judgement, Trial Chamber, 15 May 2003, Case No. ICTR-97-20-T.

International Criminal Tribunal for the Former Yugoslavia (ICTY)

Aleksovski (IT-95-14/1)

Prosecutor v Aleksovski, Case No. IT-95-14/1

(Initial Indictment, 10 November 1995)

Judgement:
Prosecutor v Zlatko Aleksovski, Judgement, Trial Chamber I, 25 June 1999, Case No. IT-95-14/1-T.

Judgement on Appeal:
Prosecutor v Zlatko Aleksovski, Judgement, Appeals Chamber, 24 March 2000, Case No. IT-95-14/1-A.

Blaškić (IT-95-14)

Prosecutor v Blaškić, Case No. IT-95-14

Decision on Defence Motion:
Prosecutor v Tihomir Blaškić, Decision on Defence Motion to Strike Portions of the Amended Indictment Alleging 'Failure to Punish' Liability, Trial Chamber, 4 April 1997, Case No. IT-95-14-PT.

Second Amended Indictment:
Prosecutor v Tihomir Blaškić, Second Amended Indictment, 25 April 1997, Case No. IT-95-14-AI.

Judgement:
Prosecutor v Tihomir Blaškić, Judgement, Trial Chamber I, 3 March 2000, Case No. IT-95-14-T.

Judgement on Appeal:
Prosecutor v Tihomir Blaškić, Judgement, Appeals Chamber, 29 July 2004, Case No. IT-95-14-A.

Brđanin (IT-99-36)

Prosecutor v Brđanin, Case No. IT-99-36

(Initial Indictment, 14 March 1999; Sixth Amended Indictment, 9 December 2004)

Judgement:
Prosecutor v Radoslav Brđanin, Judgement, Trial Chamber II, 1 September 2004, Case No. IT-99-36-T.

Delalić (IT-96-21)

Prosecutor v Delalić et al (*Prosecutor v Mučić et al*), Case No. IT-96-21

Initial Indictment:
Prosecutor v Zejnil Delalić, Zdravko Mučić, aka 'Pavo', Hazim Delić, Esad Landžo, aka 'Zenga' (*'Čelebići'*), Indictment, 21 March 1996, Case No. IT-96-21-I.

Judgement:
Prosecutor v Zejnil Delalić, Zdravko Mučić, aka 'Pavo', Hazim Delić, Esad Landžo, aka 'Zenga', Judgement, Trial Chamber II, 16 November 1998, Case No. IT-96-21-T.

Judgement on Appeal:
Prosecutor v Zejnil Delalić, Zdravko Mučić, aka 'Pavo', Hazim Delić, Esad Landžo, aka 'Zenga', Judgement, Appeals Chamber, 20 February 2001, Case No. IT-96-21-A.

Dokmanović (IT-95-13a)

Prosecutor v Dokmanović, Case No. IT-95-13a

Prosecutor v Slavko Dokmanović, Prosecutor's Response to the Trial Chamber's Request for a Brief on the use of cumulative criminal charges in relation to a proposed 'substantive' *ne bis in idem* principle in international criminal law, 21 July 1997, Case No. IT-95-13a-T.

(Second Amended Indictment, 2 December 1997)

Đukić (IT-96-20)

Prosecutor v Đukić, Case No. IT-96-20

Prosecutor v Đorđe Đukić, Indictment, 29 February 1996, Case No. IT-96-20-I.

Erdemović (IT-96-22)

Prosecutor v Erdemović, Case No. IT-96-22

(Indictment, 29 May 1996)

Sentencing Judgement:
Prosecutor v Dražen Erdemović, Sentencing Judgement, Trial Chamber I, 29 November 1996, Case No. IT-96-22-T.

Judgement on Appeal:
Prosecutor v Dražen Erdemović, Judgement, Appeals Chamber, 7 October 1997, Case No. IT-96-22-A.

Sentencing Judgement bis:
Prosecutor v Dražen Erdemović, Sentencing Judgement, Trial Chamber II, 5 March 1998, Case No. IT-96-22-Tbis.

Furundžija (IT-95-17/1)

Prosecutor v Furundžija, Case No. IT-95-17/1

(Initial Indictment, 10 November 1995; First Amended Indictment, 2 June 1998)

Judgement:
Prosecutor v Anto Furundžija, Judgement, Trial Chamber II, 10 December 1998, Case No. IT-95-17/1-T.

Judgement on Appeal:
Prosecutor v Anto Furundžija, Judgement, Appeals Chamber, 21 July 2000, Case No. IT-95-17/1-A.

Galić (IT-98-29)

Prosecutor v Galić, Case No. IT-98-29

Initial Indictment:
Prosecutor v Stanislav Galić and Dragomir Milošević, Initial Indictment, 26 March 1999, Case No. IT-98-29-I.

Judgement:
Prosecutor v Stanislav Galić, Judgement, Trial Chamber I, 5 December 2003, Case No. IT-98-29-T.

Hadžihasanović (IT-01-47)

Prosecutor v Hadžihasanović et al, Case No. IT-01-47

Initial Indictment:
Prosecutor v Enver Hadžihasanović, Mehmed Alagić and Amir Kubura, Initial Indictment, 13 July 2001 (kept confidential until its unsealing on 2 August 2001), Case No. IT-01-47.

Amended Indictment:
Prosecutor v Enver Hadžihasanović, Mehmed Alagić and Amir Kubura, Amended Indictment, 11 January 2002, Case No. IT-01-47-PT.

Decision on Joint Challenge to Jurisdiction:
Prosecutor v Enver Hadžihasanović, Mehmed Alagić and Amir Kubura, Decision on Joint Challenge to Jurisdiction, Trial Chamber II, 12 November 2002, Case No. IT-01-47-PT.

Decision on Command Responsibility:
Prosecutor v Hadžihasanović et al, Decision on Interlocutory Appeal Challenging Jurisdiction in Relation to Command Responsibility, Appeals Chamber, 16 July 2003, Case No. IT-01-47-AR72.

Judgement:
Prosecutor v Enver Hadžihasanović, Mehmed Alagić and Amir Kubura, Judgement, Trial Chamber II, 15 March 2006, Case No. IT-01-47.

Halilović (IT-01-48)

Prosecutor v Halilović, Case No. IT-01-48

(Initial Indictment, 12 September 2001 (kept confidential until its unsealing on 25 September 2001))

Judgement:
Prosecutor v Sefer Halilović, Judgement, Trial Chamber I, 16 November 2005, Case No. IT-01-48-T.

Judgement on Appeal:
Prosecutor v Sefer Halilović, Judgement, Appeals Chamber, 16 October 2007, Case No. IT-01-48-A.

Jelišić (IT-95-10)

Prosecutor v Jelišić, Case No. IT-95-10

Initial Indictment:
Prosecutor v Goran Jelišić aka Adolf and Ranko Cešić, Indictment, 21 July 1995, Case No. IT-95-10-I.

(First Amended Indictment, 12 May 1998; Second Amended Indictment, 19 October 1998)

Judgement:
Prosecutor v Goran Jelišić, Judgement, Trial Chamber I, 14 December 1999, Case No. IT-95-10-T.

Jokić, Miodrag (IT-01-42/1)

Prosecutor v Jokić, Case No. IT-01-42/1 ('*Dubrovnik*').

(Second Amended Indictment, 27 August 2003)

Sentencing Judgement:
Prosecutor v Miodrag Jokić, Sentencing Judgement, Trial Chamber I, 18 March 2004, Case No. IT-01-42/1-S.

Judgement on Sentencing Appeal:
Prosecutor v Miodrag Jokić, Judgement on Sentencing Appeal, Appeals Chamber, 30 August 2005, Case No. IT-01-42/1-SA.

Karadžić / Mladić (IT-95-5/18)

Prosecutor v Karadžić/ Mladić, Case Nos. IT-95-5/18

First Indictment:
Prosecutor v Radovan Karadžić, Indictment, 24 July 1995, Case No. IT-95-5-I.

Second Indictment:
Prosecutor v Ratko Mladić, Indictment, 16 November 1995, Case No. IT-95-18-I.

Review of the Indictments:
Prosecutor v Radovan Karadžić / Ratko Mladić, Review of the Indictments Pursuant to Rule 61 of the Rules of Procedure and Evidence, 11 July 1996, Cases No. IT-95-5-R61 and IT-95-18-R61.

Prosecutor v Radovan Karadžić, Amended Indictment, 31 May 2000, Case No. IT-95-5.

Prosecutor v Ratko Mladić, Amended Indictment, 11 October 2002, Case No. IT-95-18.

Kordić (IT-97-25)

Prosecutor v Kordić and Čerkez, Case No. IT-97-25

Initial Indictment:
Prosecutor v Dario Kordić, Tihofil aka Tihomir Blaškić, Mario Čerkez, Ivan aka Ivica Šantić, Pero Skopljak and Zlatko Aleksovski, Indictment, 10 November 1995, Case No. IT-95-14/2-I.

First Amended Indictment:
Prosecutor v Dario Kordić and Mario Čerkez, Amended Indictment, 30 September 1998, Case No. IT-95-14/2-AI.

Decision on the Joint Defence Motion:

Prosecutor v Dario Kordić and Mario Čerkez, Decision on the Joint Defence Motion to Dismiss the Amended Indictment for Lack of Jurisdiction Based on the Limited Jurisdictional Reach of Articles 2 and 3, 2 March 1999, Case No. IT-95-14/2-AI.

Judgement:

Prosecutor v Dario Kordić and Mario Čerkez, Judgement, Trial Chamber III, 26 February 2001, Case No. IT-95-14/2-T.

Judgement on Appeal:

Prosecutor v Dario Kordić and Mario Čerkez, Judgement, Appeals Chamber, 17 December 2004, Case No. IT-95-14/2-A.

Kovačević, Vladimir (IT-01-42/2)

Prosecutor v Vladimir Kovačević, Case No. IT-01-42/2 ('*Dubrovnik*')

(Second Amended Indictment, 17 October 2003)

Krnojelac (IT-97-25)

Prosecutor v Krnojelac, Case No. IT-97-25 ('Fo*ča*')

Initial Indictment:

Prosecutor v Milorad Krnojelac, aka 'Mićo', Indictment, 17 June 1997, Case No. IT-97-25-I.

(First Amended Indictment, 21 July 1999; Second Amended Indictment, 2 March 2000; Third Amended Indictment, 25 June 2001)

Judgement:

Prosecutor v Milorad Krnojelac, Judgement, Trial Chamber II, 15 March 2002, Case No. IT-97-25-T.

Judgement on Appeal:

Prosecutor v Milorad Krnojelac, Judgement, Appeals Chamber, 17 September 2003, Case No. IT-97-25-A.

Krstić (IT-98-33)

Prosecutor v Krstić, Case No. IT-98-33

Initial Indictment:

Prosecutor v Radislav Krstić, Indictment, 2 November 1998, Case No. IT-98-33-I.

(Amended Indictment, 27 October 1999)

Judgement:

Prosecutor v Radislav Krstić, Judgement, Trial Chamber I, 2 August 2001, Case No. IT-98-33-T.

Judgement on Appeal:
Prosecutor v Radislav Krstić, Judgement, Appeals Chamber, 19 April 2004, Case No. IT-98-33-A.

Kunarac (IT-96-23/2)

Prosecutor v Kunarac, Kovač and Vuković, Case No. IT-96-23/2 ('*Foča*')

Initial Indictment:
Prosecutor v Dragan Gagović, Gojko Janković, Janko Janjić, Radomir Kovač, Zoran Vuković, Dragan Zelenović, Dragoljub Kunarac, Radovan Stanković, Indictment, 26 June 1996, Case No. IT-96-23/2-I.

(Third Amended Indictment, 1 December 1999)

Judgement:
Prosecutor v Dragoljub Kunarac, Radomir Kovač and Zoran Vuković, Judgement, Trial Chamber II, 22 February 2001, Case Nos. IT-96-23-T and IT-96-23/1-T.

Kupreškić (IT-95-16)

Prosecutor v Kupreškić et al, Case No. IT-95-16

First Amended Indictment:
Prosecutor v Zoran Kupreškić, Mirjan Kupreškić, Vlatko Kupreškić, Drago Josipović, Dragan Papić, Vladimir Šantić aka 'Vlado', Amended Indictment, Trial Chamber II, 9 February 1998, Case No. IT-95-16-AI.

(Initial Indictment, 10 November 1995)

Judgement:
Prosecutor v Zoran Kupreškić, Mirjan Kupreškić, Vlatko Kupreškić, Drago Josipović, Dragan Papić, Vladimir Šantić aka 'Vlado', Judgement, Trial Chamber II, 14 January 2000, Case No. IT-95-16-T.

Kvočka (IT-98-30/1)

Prosecutor v Kvočka et al, Case No. IT-98-30/1

Amended Indictment:
Prosecutor v Miroslav Kvočka, Milojica Kos, Mladen Radić, Zoran Žigić, Amended Indictment, 26 October 2000, Case No. IT-98-30/1-AI.

Judgement:
Prosecutor v Miroslav Kvočka, Milojica Kos, Mladen Radić, Zoran Žigić, Dragoljub Prcać, Judgement, Trial Chamber I, 2 November 2001, Case No. IT-98-30/1-T.

Krajišnik (IT-00-39/40)

Prosecutor v Krajišnik, Case No. IT-00-39/40

(Consolidated Amended Indictment, 7 March 2002)

Judgement:
Prosecutor v Momčilo Krajišnik, Judgement, Trial Chamber I, 27 September 2006, Case No. IT-00-39/40-T.

Martić (IT-95-11)

Prosecutor v Martić, Case No. IT-95-11

Prosecutor v Milan Martić, Review of the Indictment Pursuant to Rule 61 of the Rules of Procedure and Evidence, Trial Chamber I, 8 March 1996, Case No. IT-95-11-R61.

(Initial Indictment, 25 July 1995; Amended Indictment, 18 December 2002; Second Amended Indictment, 9 December 2005)

Milošević (IT-02-54)

Prosecutor v Milošević, Case No. IT-02-54

Indictment:
Bosnia: Initial Indictment, 22 November 2001; Amended Indictment, 21 April 2004.

Kosovo: Initial Indictment, 24 May 1999; First Amended Indictment, 29 June 2001; Second Amended Indictment, 29 October 2001.

Croatia: Initial Indictment, 8 October 2001; First Amended Indictment, 23 October 2002; Second Amended Indictment, 28 July 2004.

Decision on Motion for Judgement of Acquittal:
Prosecutor v Slobodan Milošević, Decision on Motion for Judgement of Acquittal, Trial Chamber, 16 June 2004, Case No. IT-02-54-T.

Milutinović et al (IT-99-37)

Prosecutor v Milutinović et al, Case No. IT-99-37

Prosecutor v Milutinović et al, Decision on Dragoljub Ojdanić's Motion Challenging Jurisdiction – Joint Criminal Enterprise, 2 May 2003, Case No. IT-99-37-AR72.

Mrkšić (IT-95-13/1)

Prosecutor v Mrkšić et al, Case No. IT-95-13/1

Prosecutor v Mile Mrkšić, Miroslav Radić and Veselin Šljivčanin, Indictment, 26 October 1995, Case No. IT-95-13a-I.

Review of the Indictment:
Prosecutor v Mile Mrkšić, Miroslav Radić, Veselin Šljivčanin and Slavko Dokmanović, Review of the Indictment Pursuant to Rule 61 of the Rules of Procedure and Evidence, Trial Chamber I, 3 April 1996, Case No. IT-95-13-R61.

(Third Consolidated Amended Indictment, 15 November 2004)

Naletilić (IT-98-34)

Prosecutor v Naletilić and Martinović, Case No. IT-98-34

(Initial Indictment, 21 December 1998; Amended Indictment, 28 November 2000; Second Amended Indictment, 16 October 2001)

Judgement:
Prosecutor v Mladen Naletilić aka 'Tuta' and Vinko Martinović aka 'Štela', Judgement, Trial Chamber, 31 March 2003, Case No. IT-98-34-T.

Judgement on Appeal:
The Prosecutor v Mladen Naletilić aka 'Tuta' and Vinko Martinović aka 'Štela', Judgement, Appeals Chamber, 3 May 2006, Case No. IT-98-34-A.

Nikolić (IT-94-2)

Prosecutor v Nikolić, Case No. IT-94-2

Initial Indictment:
Prosecutor v Dragan Nikolić aka 'Jenki' Nikolić, Indictment, 4 November 1994, Case No. IT-94-2-I.

Review of the Indictment:
Prosecutor v Dragan Nikolić, Review of the Indictment Pursuant to Rule 61 of the Rules of Procedure and Evidence, Trial Chamber II, 20 October 1995, Case No. IT-94-2-R61.

(Third Amended Indictment, 31 October 2003)

Plavšić (IT-00-39 & 40/1)

Prosecutor v Plavšić, Case No. IT-00-39 & 40/1

(Initial Indictment, 7 April 2000; Amended Consolidated Indictment, 7 March 2002)

Judgement:
Prosecutor v Biljana Plavšić, Sentencing Judgement, Trial Chamber, 27 February 2003, Case No. IT-00-39&40/1-S.

Prlić (IT-04-74)

Prosecutor v Jadranko Prlić et al, Case No. IT-04-74

Prosecutor v Jadranko Prlić, Bruno Stojić, Slobodan Praljak, Milivoj Petković, Valentin Ćorić and Berislav Pušić, Amended Indictment, 17 November 2005, Case No. IT-04-74-AI.

(Initial Indictment, 4 March 2004 (kept confidential until its unsealing on 2 April 2004))

Rajić (IT-95-12)

Prosecutor v Rajić, Case No. IT-95-12

Initial Indictment:
Prosecutor v Ivica Rajić aka Viktor Andrić, Indictment, 23 August 1995, Case No. IT-95-12-I.

Review of the Indictment:
Prosecutor v Ivica Rajić aka Viktor Andrić, Review of the Indictment Pursuant to Rule 61 of the Rules of Procedure and Evidence, 13 September 1996, Case No. IT-95-12-R61.

(Amended Indictment, 14 January 2004)

Stakić (IT-97-24)

Prosecutor v Stakić, Case No. IT-97-24

(Fourth Amended Indictment, 10 April 2002)

Judgement:
Prosecutor v Milomir Stakić, Judgement, Trial Chamber II, 31 July 2003, Case No. IT-97-24-T.

Strugar (IT-01-42)

Prosecutor v Strugar, Case No. IT-01-42 ('*Dubrovnik*')

Initial Indictment:

Prosecutor v Pavle Strugar, Miodrag Jokić, Milan Zec and Vladimir Kovačević, Indictment, 22 February 2001 (unsealed 2 October 2001), Case No. IT-01-42-I.

(Amended Indictment, 31 March 2003, Second Amended Indictment, 17 October 2003)

Third Amended Indictment:
Prosecutor v Pavle Strugar, Third Amended Indictment, 10 December 2003, Case No. IT-01-42-PT.

Decision on Defence Motion for Acquittal:
Prosecutor v Pavle Strugar, Decision on Defence Motion Requesting Judgement of Acquittal Pursuant to Rule 98 *BIS*, Trial Chamber II, 21 June 2004, Case No. IT-01-42-T.

Judgement:
Prosecutor v Pavle Strugar, Judgement, Trial Chamber II, 31 January 2005, Case No. IT-01-42-T.

Tadić (IT-94-1)

Prosecutor v Tadić, Case No. IT-94-1

Interlocutory Appeal:
Prosecutor v Duško Tadić aka 'Dule', Decision on the Defence Motion for Interlocutory Appeal on Jurisdiction, Appeals Chamber, 2 October 1995, Case No. IT-94-1-AR72 ('Jurisdiction Decision').

Second Amended Indictment:
Prosecutor v Duško Tadić aka 'Dule' and Goran Borovnica, Second Amended Indictment, 14 December 1995, Case No. IT-94-1-I.

(Initial Indictment, 13 February 1995; First Amended Indictment, 1 September 1995)

Prosecutor's Pre-Trial Brief:
Prosecutor v Duško Tadić aka 'Dule', Prosecutor's Pre-Trial Brief, 10 April 1996, Case No. IT-94-1-T.

Response to Prosecutor's Pre-Trial Brief:
Prosecutor v Duško Tadić aka 'Dule', Response of the Defence to the Prosecutor's Pre-Trial Brief, 23 April 1996, Case No. IT-94-1-T.

Judgement:
Prosecutor v Duško Tadić aka 'Dule', Judgement, Trial Chamber II, 7 May 1997, Case No. IT-94-1-T.

Judgement on Appeal:
Prosecutor v Duško Tadić aka 'Dule', Judgement, Appeals Chamber, 15 July 1999, Case No. IT-94-1-A.

Vasiljević (IT-98-32)

Prosecutor v Vasiljević, Case No. IT-98-32

(Initial Indictment, 26 October 1998; Amended Indictment, 20 July 2001)

Judgement:

Prosecutor v Mitar Vasiljević, Judgement, Trial Chamber II, 29 November 2002, Case No. IT-98-32-T.

International Military Tribunal For Germany (IMT Nürnberg)

Case of the Major War Criminals

Indictment:

Trial of the Major War Criminals before the International Military Tribunal, Indictment, Nuremberg, 20 November 1945, Official Documents, Vol. I, 27.

Judgement:

Trial of the Major War Criminals before the International Military Tribunal, Judgement, Nuremberg, 1 October 1946, Official Documents, Vol. I, 171.

International Military Tribunal for the Far East (IMT Tokyo)

International Military Tribunal for the Far East, established by a Special Proclamation by the Supreme Commander for the Allied Powers at Tokyo, 19 January 1946, TIAS No. 1589, 4 Bevans 20.

Case of the Major War Criminals

Indictment:

Trial of the Major War Criminals before the International Military Tribunal, Indictment, Tokyo, 29 April 1946.

Judgement:

Trial of the Major War Criminals before the International Military Tribunal, Judgement, Tokyo, 4-12 November 1948.

Toyoda Case

US v Soemu Toyoda, Judgement of 6 September 1949.

Legal Instruments

National Legislation

Bosnia and Herzegovina

The Law (Statute) on the Protection and Use of Cultural-Historical and Natural Heritage of Bosnia and Herzegovina (Official Gazette, SR BH, No. 20/85 and 12/87), http://www.spomenici-sa.ba/eng/heritage/legal_base.html.

The Book of Regulations for the Assets of Cultural-Historical and Natural Heritage Categorization as well as a Categorization Procedure (Legal Code SR BH, No. 29/86).

The Book of Regulations for the Protected Cultural-Historical and Natural Heritage Goods, Register Managing (Legal Code SR BH, No. 1/87).

Decree with Force of Law on Deferral upon Request by the International Tribunal, 10 April 1995, published in Službeni list Republike Bosne i Hercegovine (Official Gazette of the Republic of Bosnia and Herzegovina), No. 12/95, 10 April 1995, 317-323.

The Law of the Republika Srpska on Cultural Assets (Official Gazette, RS 11/95).

Amnesty Law No. 155 (1996), 12 June 1996, published in Službene Novine Federacije Bosne i Hercegovine (Official Gazette of the Federation of Bosnia and Herzegovina), No. 9/96, 30 June 1996, 287 ff.

Criminal Code of the Republic of Bosnia and Herzegovina, adopted by Bosnia and Herzegovina Parliamentary Assembly and published in the Official Gazette of Bosnia and Herzegovina No. 37/03, entered into force 1 March 2003, correction, Official Gazette of Bosnia and Herzegovina No. 32/03. High Representative Decision Enacting the Law on Amendments to the Criminal Code of Bosnia and Herzegovina, Official Gazette of Bosnia and Herzegovina No. 54/04 – Law on Amendments to the Criminal Code of Bosnia and Herzegovina, Official Gazette of Bosnia and Herzegovina No. 61/04 – Amendments to the Criminal Code of Bosnia and Herzegovina, Official Gazette of Bosnia and Herzegovina No. 30/05 are not included in the Consolidated Version of the Criminal Code of Bosnia and Herzegovina, December 2006.

Criminal Code of the Federation of Bosnia and Herzegovina, Official Gazette of the Federation of Bosnia and Herzegovina No. 36/03, entered into force 1 August 2003.

(On the day of entering into force of this Code, Criminal Code of the Federation of Bosnia and Herzegovina No. 327, adopted by the House of Representatives of the Parliament of the Federation of Bosnia and Herzegovina on 29 July 1998 and by the House of Peoples of the Federation of Bosnia and Herzegovina on 17 July 1998, published in Službene Novine Federacije Bosne i Hercegovine (Official Gazette of the Federation of Bosnia and Herzegovina), No. 43/98, 20 November 1998, 1649-1733, and Nos. 2/99, 15/99, 29/00 and 59/02, ceased to apply.)

Law on Amnesty of the Federation of Bosnia and Herzegovina, published in Službene Novine Federacije Bosne i Hercegovine (Official Gazette of the Federation of Bosnia and Herzegovina), No. 48/1999.

The Law of Library Field (Legal Code of Canton Sarajevo, No. 4/99).

Law No. 02-736/96 on Amnesty of the Republika Srpska, 19 June 1996, published in Službeni glasnik Republike Srpske (Official Gazette of the Republika Srpska), No. 17/1999, 15 July 1999, 355.

Criminal Code of the Republika Srpska, 22 June 2000, published in Službeni glasnik Republike Srpske (Official Gazette of the Republika Srpska), No. 22/2000, 31 July 2000, 513-560.

The Book of Regulation for the Technical Protection and other Conditions, Protection Measures, Library Maintenance and Property Use (Legal Code, Federation of BH, No. 26/00).

The Law of Museum Work (Legal Code, Canton Sarajevo, No. 2/00).

Republic of Bosnia and Herzegovina, Wartime Presidency of the Mostar Municipality, *Decision about proclaiming 10 November 1993 a Day of Mourning in the Mostar Municipality*, 9 November 1993, published in *Most*, No. 108-109 November - December 1998, http://www.most.ba/01920/006.htm.

Cambodia

Law on the Establishment of Extraordinary Chambers in the Courts of Cambodia for the Prosecutions of Crimes Committed during the Period of Democratic Kampuchea, as adopted by the National Assembly on 2 January 2001, approved by the Senate on 15 January 2001 and promulgated on 10 August 2001 (Law on the Khmer Rouge Trial (2001)).

Croatia

Constitution, 22 December 1990, published in Narodne novine (Official Gazette), No. 56, 22 December 1990, 1236-1247.

Code of Criminal Procedure, 1993, published in Narodne novine (Official Gazette), No. 34, 21 May 1993.

Defence Law, 1993, published in Narodne novine (Official Gazette), No. 74, 6 August 1993, Narodne novine (Official Gazette), No. 57, 12 July 1996, and Narodne novine (Official Gazette), No. 31, 6 March 1998.

Law on Military Service, 1995, published in Narodne novine (Official Gazette), No. 32, 26 April 1996.

Constitutional Law on the Cooperation of the Republic of Croatia with the International Criminal Tribunal, 19 April 1996, published in Narodne novine (Official Gazette), No. 32, 26 April 1996.

Law on General Amnesty, 20 September 1996, published in Narodne novine (Official Gazette), No. 80, 27 September 1996.

Criminal Code, 19 September 1997, published in Narodne novine (Official Gazette), No. 110, 21 October 1997, 3461-3516, entered into force 1 January 1998, Narodne novine (Official Gazette), No. 27, 27 February 1998, correction concerning derogations from Article 204, paras 1 and 2, in Narodne novine (Official Gazette), No. 50, 17 May 2000.

SFRJ (Socialist Federal Republic of Yugoslavia – The Former Yugoslavia)

Criminal Code of Socialist Federal Republic of Yugoslavia, adopted by the SFRJ Assembly at the session of the Federal Council held on 28 September 1976, declared by a decree of the President of the Republic on 28 September 1976, published in the Official Gazette SFRJ No. 44 of 8 October 1976, a correction was made in the Official Gazette SFRJ No. 36 of 15 July 1977, took effect on 1 July 1977.

International Instruments

Treaties

Convention (II) with respect to the Laws and Customs of War on Land, The Hague, 29 July 1899, 32 Stat. 1803, Treaty Series 403 (entered into force 4 September 1900).

Regulations concerning the Laws and Customs of War on Land, annexed to *Convention (II) with respect to the Laws and Customs of War on Land*, The Hague, 29 July 1899 (entered into force 4 September 1900).

Convention (IV) respecting the Laws and Customs of War on Land, The Hague, 18 October 1907, 36 Stat 2277 (entered into force 26 January 1910).

Regulations concerning the Laws and Customs of War on Land, annexed to *Convention (IV) respecting the Laws and Customs of War on Land*, The Hague, 18 October 1907 (entered into force 26 January 1910).

Hague Convention (IX) concerning Bombardment by Naval Forces in Times of War, The Hague, 18 October 1907, 36 Stat 2351 (entered into force 26 January 1910).

Treaty of Peace with Germany, signed at Versailles, 28 June 1919, 2 Bevans 43, (1919) 11 Marthens Nouveau Recueil (ser. 3) 323 *(Treaty of Versailles)*.

Treaty Providing for the Renunciation of War as an Instrument of National Policy, 27 August 1928, 46 Stat. (1929) 2343, 2346, TS No. 796, 94 LNTS 57, 63 (*Kellogg-Briand Pact*).

The Athens Charter for the Restoration of Historic Monuments, adopted at the First International Congress of Architects and Technicians of Historic Monuments, Athens 1931.

Treaty on the Protection of Artistic and Scientific Institutions and Historic Monuments, Washington, D.C., 15 April 1935, 49 Stat 3267 TS 899, 167 LNTS 289, *(Roerich Pact)*, http://fletcher.tufts.edu/multi/www.roerich.html.

Agreement between the Government of the United States of America, the Provisional Government of the French Republic, the Government of the United Kingdom of Great Britain and Northern Ireland and the Government of the Union of Soviet Socialist Republics for the Prosecution and Punishment of the Major War Criminals of the European Axis, London, 8 August 1945, 59 Stat.1544, EAS No. 427, 82 UNTS 279.

Charter of the International Tribunal for Germany, concluded by the Government of the United States of America, the Provisional Government of the French Republic, the Government of the United Kingdom of Great Britain and Northern Ireland, and the Government of the Union of Soviet Socialist Republics, acting in the interests of all the United Nations and by their representatives duly authorized thereto, annexed to the *London Agreement*, London, 8 August 1945, 58 Stat. 1544, EAS No. 427, 82 UNTS 280.

Charter of the United Nations, adopted by the Conference on International Organisations, San Francisco, 26 June 1945, 59 Stat. 1031, TS 993, 3 Bevans 1153 (entered into force 24 October 1945).

UNESCO Constitution, signed 16 November 1945 (entered into force 4 November 1946), http://portal.unesco.org/en/ev.php.

Convention on the Prevention and Punishment of the Crime of Genocide, adopted by the UN General Assembly, Res. 260 A (III), 9 December 1948, 78 UNTS 277 (entered into force 12 January 1951), http://fletcher.tufts.edu.multilaterals.html.

Convention (I) for the Amelioration of the Condition of the Wounded and Sick in Armed Forces in the Field, signed at Geneva, 12 August 1949, 75 UNTS 31 (entered into force 21 October 1950).

Convention (II) for the Amelioration of the Condition of the Wounded, Sick and Shipwrecked Members of Armed Forces at Sea, signed at Geneva, 12 August 1949, 75 UNTS 84 (entered into force 21 October 1950).

Convention (III) Relative to the Treatment of Prisoners of War, signed at Geneva, 12 August 1949, 75 UNTS 135 (entered into force 21 October 1950).

Convention (IV) Relative to the Protection of Civilian Persons in Time of War, signed at Geneva, 12 August 1949, 75 UNTS 287 (entered into force 21 October 1950).

Treaty of Peace Signed between the Allied Powers and Japan, San Francisco, 8 September 1951.

Convention on the Settlement of Matters Arising out of the War and the Occupation (with Annex), Bonn, 26 May 1952, also known as the Transference Treaty, as amended by Schedule IV to the Protocol on the Termination of the Occupation Régime in the Federal Republic of Germany, Paris, 23 October 1954.

European Cultural Convention, opened for signature 19 December 1954, 218 UNTS 139 (entered into force 5 May 1955), http://fletcher.tufts.edu/multi/www/bh312.html.

Convention for the Protection of Cultural Property in the Event of Armed Conflict, opened for signature 14 May 1954, 249 UNTS 215 (entered into force 7 August 1956).

Regulations for the Execution of the Convention for the Protection of Cultural Property in the Event of Armed Conflict, 14 May 1954 (annexed to the *Convention for the Protection of Cultural Property in the Event of Armed Conflict*, opened for signature 14 May 1954, 249 UNTS 215 (entered into force 7 August 1956)).

Protocol for the Protection of Cultural Property in the Event of Armed Conflict, opened for signature 14 May 1954, 249 UNTS 358 (entered into force 7 August 1956).

Final Act of the Intergovernmental Conference on the Protection of Cultural Property in the Event of Armed Conflict, The Hague, 14 May 1954, 1037 UNTS 151.

Second Protocol to the Hague Convention of 1954 for the Protection of Cultural Property in the Event of Armed Conflict, opened for signature 26 March 1999, 38 ILM 769 (entered into force 9 March 2004).

International Convention on the Elimination of All Forms of Racial Discrimination, adopted by the UN General Assembly, Res. 2106 A (XX), 21 December 1965.

International Covenant on Civil and Political Rights, adopted by the UN General Assembly, Res. 2200 A (XXI), 16 December 1966 (entered into force 23 March 1976).

International Covenant on Economic, Social and Cultural Rights, adopted by the UN General Assembly, Res. 2200 A (XXI), 16 December 1966 (entered into force 3 January 1976).

Convention on the Non-Applicability of Statutory Limitations to War Crimes and Crimes against Humanity, adopted by the UN General Assembly, Res. 2391 (XXIII), 26 November 1968, UN GAOR, 23rd Session, Supp., No. 18, 40, UN Doc. A/7218 (1968).

Convention on the Law of Treaties, Vienna, 23 May 1969, 1155 UNTS 331.

Convention on the Means of Prohibiting and Preventing the Illicit Import, Export and Transfer of Ownership of Cultural Property, adopted by the 16th Session of the UNESCO General Conference, Paris, 14 November 1970, opened for signature 14 November 1970, 832 UNTS 231, reprinted in 10 ILM 289 (1971) (entered into force 24 April 1972).

Convention concerning the Protection of the World Cultural and Natural Heritage, opened for signature 16 November 1972, UN Doc. A/CONF.48/PC/11/Add 3.15 (1972), 1037 UNTS 151 (entered into force 17 December 1975).

European Convention on the Non-Applicability of Statutory Limitations to Crimes against Humanity and War Crimes, Strasbourg, 25 January 1974.

Protocol Additional to the Geneva Conventions of 12 August 1949, and relating to the Protection of Victims of International Armed Conflict, Geneva, 8 June 1977, 1125 UNTS 3 (entered into force 7 December 1978) (*Protocol I*).

Protocol Additional to the Geneva Conventions of 12 August 1949, and relating to the Protection of Victims of Non-International Armed Conflict, Geneva, 8 June 1977, 1125 UNTS 609 (entered into force 7 December 1978) (*Protocol II*).

Convention for the Protection of the Architectural Heritage of Europe (1985), http://fletcher.tufts.edu/multi/texts/BH872.txt.

European Convention on Offences Relating to Cultural Property, opened for signature 23 June 1985, 25 ILM 44, http://fletcher.tufts.edu/multi/www.bh863.html.

Convention concerning Indigenous and Tribal Peoples in Independent Countries, ILO Convention No. 169, adopted by the ILO General Conference, Geneva, 27 June 1989.

Statute of the International Criminal Tribunal for the Prosecution of Persons Responsible for Serious Violations of International Humanitarian Law Committed in the Territory of the Former Yugoslavia since 1991, adopted by the UN Security Council, Resolution 827 (1993) of 25 May 1993, UN SCOR, 48th Session, 3217th Meeting, UN Doc. S/RES/827 (1993), as amended by Resolution 1166 (1998) adopted 13 May 1998 by the Security Council at its 3878th Meeting, UN Doc. S/RES/1166 (1998), Resolution 1329 (2000) adopted 30 November 2000 by the Security Council at its 4240th Meeting, UN Doc. S/RES/1329 (2000), and by Resolution 1411 (2002) adopted by the Security Council at its 4535th Meeting on 17 May 2002, UN Doc. S/RES/1411 (2002). The Statute is contained in UN Doc. S/25704, Annex 1. (1993) and attached to the 'Report of the Secretary-General Pursuant to Paragraph 2 of Security Council Resolution 808 (1993)'.

Statute of the International Criminal Tribunal for the Prosecution of Persons Responsible for Genocide and Other Serious Violations of International Humanitarian Law in the Territory of Rwanda and Rwandan Citizens Responsible for Genocide and other such Violations Committed in the Territory of Neighbouring States between 1 January 1994 and 31 December 1994, adopted by the UN Security Council, Resolution 955 (1994) of 8 November 1994, UN Doc. S/RES/955 (1994) as amended by Resolution 1165 (1998) of 30 April 1998, UN Doc. S/RES/1165 (1998), and by Resolution 1329 (2000) of 30 November 2000, UN Doc. S/RES/1329 (2000).

UNIDROIT Convention on Stolen or Illegally Exported Cultural Objects, opened for signature 24 June 1995, 34 ILM 1322 (entered into force 1 July 1998), http://www.unidroit.org/english/conventions/c-cult.htm.

General Framework Agreement for Peace in Bosnia and Herzegovina, initialed in Dayton, 21 November 1995, signed in Paris, 14 December 1995 (*Dayton Peace Agreement*), http://www.ohr.int/.

Annex 8 of the General Framework Agreement for Peace in Bosnia and Herzegovina, Agreement between the Republic of Bosnia and Herzegovina, the Federation of Bosnia and Herzegovina and the Republika Srpska on Commission to Preserve National Monuments, http://www.usip.org/library/pa/bosnia/dayton_annex8.html.

Agreement signed by Presidents Izetbegović, Milošević and Tuđman, Rome, Italy, 18 February 1996. Rome communiqué, section 5 on 'Cooperation on War Crimes and Respect for Human Rights' (Rules of the Road), The Bosnian Institute, Bosnia Report, February-March 1996, http://www.bosnia.org.uk/bosrep/febmar96/rome.cfm.

Agreement on Normalisation of Relations between the Republic of Croatia and the Federal Republic of Yugoslavia, Belgrade, 23 August 1996.

Statute of the International Criminal Court, adopted by the UN Diplomatic Conference of Plenipotentiaries on the Establishment of an International Criminal Court, Rome, 17 July 1998, UN Doc. A/CONF.183/9 opened for signature 17 July 1998, 2187 UNTS 3 (entered into force 1 July 2002), http://www.igc.org/icc/Rome/html.

Agreement between the United Nations and the Government of Sierra Leone on the Establishment of a Special Court for Sierra Leone, Freetown, 16 January 2002, annexed to Letter dated 6 March 2002 from the UN Secretary-General to the President of the UN Security Council, UN Doc. S/2002/264, 8 March 2002, 17.

Statute of the Special Court for Sierra Leone, annexed to the 2002 *Agreement on the Special Court for Sierra Leone*, Freetown, 16 January 2002, annexed to Letter dated 6 March 2002 from the UN Secretary-General to the President of the UN Security Council, UN Doc. S/2002/246, 8 March 2002, 29.

Convention for the Safeguarding of the Intangible Cultural Heritage, 17 October 2003, http://www.unesco.org/culture/laws/2003/html.

Resolutions

Resolutions Adopted by the UN Security Council

Resolution on the Political Settlement of the Situation in Yugoslavia, SC Res. 740 (1992) of 7 February 1992, UN Doc. S/RES/740 (1992).

Resolution on Establishment of the United Nations Protection Force, SC Res. 743 (1992) of 21 February 1992, UN Doc. S/RES/743 (1992).

Resolution on Political Conditions in Bosnia and Herzegovina, SC Res. 752 (1992) of 15 May 1992, UN Doc. S/RES/752 (1992).

Resolution on Enlargement of the Mandate and the Strength of the UN Protection Force and Humanitarian Assistance to Bosnia and Herzegovina, SC Res. 758 (1992) of 8 June 1992, UN Doc. S/RES/758 (1992).

Resolution on Deployment of Additional Elements of the United Nations Protection Force in Bosnia and Herzegovina, SC Res. 761 (1992) of 29 June 1992, UN Doc. S/RES/761 (1992).

Resolution on Violations of Humanitarian Law in the Territory of the Former Yugoslavia and in Bosnia and Herzegovina, SC Res. 771 (1992) of 13 August 1992, UN Doc. S/RES/771 (1992).

Resolution on Enlargement of the Mandate of the UN Protection Force, SC Res. 776 (1992) of 14 September 1992, UN Doc. S/RES/776 (1992).

Resolution on Establishment of the Commission of Experts to Examine and Analyse the Information submitted pursuant to Security Council Resolution 771 (1992) on the Situation in the Former Yugoslavia, SC Res. 780 (1992) of 6 October 1992, UN Doc. S/RES/780 (1992).

Resolution Demanding That All Forms of Interference from Outside Bosnia and Herzegovina Cease Immediately, SC Res. 787 (1992) of 16 November 1992, UN Doc. S/RES/787 (1992).

Resolution Supporting Initiative of the European Council to Dispatch a Fact-Finding Mission to Bosnia and Herzegovina, SC Res. 798 (1992) of 18 December 1992, UN Doc. S/RES/798 (1992).

Resolution on Establishment of an International Tribunal for the Prosecution of Persons Responsible for Violations of International Humanitarian Law Committed in the Territory of the Former Yugoslavia since 1991, SC Res. 808 (1993) of 22 February 1993, UN SCOR, 48th Session, 3175th Meeting, UN Doc S/RES/808 (1993).

Resolution on Treatment of Certain Towns and Surroundings in Bosnia and Herzegovina, SC Res. 824 (1993) of 6 May 1993, UN Doc. S/RES/824 (1993).

Resolution on Establishment of the International Tribunal for Prosecution of Persons Responsible for Serious Violations of International Humanitarian Law Committed in the Territory of the Former Yugoslavia since 1991, SC Res. 827 (1993) of 25 May 1993, UN Doc. S/RES/827 (1993).

Resolution on Adoption of the Statute of the International Criminal Tribunal for the Former Yugoslavia, SC Res. 827 (1993) of 25 May 1993, UN SCOR, 48th Session, UN Doc. S/RES/827 (1993).

Resolution Requesting the Secretary-General To Establish a Commission of Experts To Examine Violations of International Humanitarian Law Committed in Rwanda, SC Res. 935 (1994) of 1 July 1994, UN Doc. S/RES/935 (1994).

Resolution on Establishment of an International Tribunal for Rwanda and Adoption of the Statute of the Tribunal, SC Res. 955 (1994) of 8 November 1994, UN Doc. S/RES/955 (1994).

Resolution on Establishment of a Rapid-Reaction Force within the UN Protection Force (UNPROFOR), SC Res. 998 (1995) of 16 June 1995, UN Doc. S/RES/998 (1995).

Resolution on Implementation of the Peace Agreement for Bosnia and Herzegovina and Transfer of Authority from the UN Protection Force (UNPROFOR) to the Multinational Implementation Force (IFOR), SC Res. 1031 (1995) of 15 December 1995, UN Doc. S/RES/1031.

Resolution on the Situation in Kosovo, Yugoslavia, SC Res. 1199 (1998) of 23 September 1998, UN Doc. S/RES/1199 (1998).

Resolution on the Deployment of International Civil and Security Presences in Kosovo, SC Res. 1244 (1999) of 10 June 1999, UN Doc. S/RES/1244 (1999).

Resolution on Establishment of a Multinational Peace Force in East Timor, SC Res. 1264 (1999) of 15 September 1999, UN Doc. S/RES/1264 (1999).

Resolution on Establishing a Special Court in Sierra Leone, SC Res. 1315 (2000) of 14 August 2000, UN Doc. S/RES/1315 (2000).

Resolution on Authorizing a Multinational Stabilization Force (SFOR) To Continue Its Mandate for a Further Period of 12 Months, SC Res. 1491 (2003) of 11 July 2003, UN Doc. S/RES1491 (2003).

Resolution on ICTY's Completion Strategy, SC Res.1503 (2003) of 28 August 2003, 4817th Meeting, UN Doc. S/RES/1503 (2003).

Resolution on the Importance of Fully Implementing the Completion Strategy As Set Out in SC Res. 1503 (2003), SC Res. 1534 (2004) of 26 March 2004, 4935th Meeting, UN Doc. S/RES/1534 (2004).

Resolutions Adopted by the UN General Assembly

Resolution 3 (I) on Extradition and Punishment of War Criminals, 13 February 1946, adopted without a vote.

Resolution 95 (I) on Affirmation of the Principles of International Law Recognized by the Charter of the Nürnberg Tribunal, 11 December 1946, adopted without a vote.

Resolution 177(II) on Formulation of the Principles Recognized in the Charter of the Nürnberg Tribunal and in the Judgement of the Tribunal, 21 November 1947.

Resolution 217 A (III) on International Bill of Human Rights: A Universal Declaration on Human Rights, 10 December 1948, UN doc A/71 (1948).

Resolution 260 A (III) on Prevention and Punishment of the Crime of Genocide, 9 December 1948.

Resolution 2200 A (XXI) on International Covenant on Economic, Social and Cultural Rights, International Covenant on Civil and Political Rights and Optional Protocol to the International Covenant on Civil and Political Rights, 16 December 1966, adopted without a vote (entered into force 3 January 1967).

Resolution 2338 (XXII) on Question of the Punishment of War Criminals and of Persons Who Have Committed Crimes against Humanity, 18 December 1967.

Resolution 2391 (XXIII) on the Convention on the Non-Applicability of Statutory Limitations to War Crimes and Crimes against Humanity, 26 November 1968.

Resolution 2675 on Basic Principles for the Protection of Civilian Populations in Armed Conflicts, adopted during the 25th Session of the General Assembly, on 9 December 1970, http://www.un.org/documents/resga.htm.

Resolution 47/80 on 'Ethnic Cleansing' and Racial Hatred, 16 December 1992, adopted without a vote.

Resolution 48/15 on the Return or Restitution of Cultural Property to the Countries of Origin, UN GAOR 47th Plenary Meeting, UN Doc. A/RES/48/15 (1993).

Resolution 48/30 on United Nations Decade of International Law, 9 December 1993, adopted without a vote.

Resolutions Adopted by ECOSOC

Resolution 1158 (XLI) on Question of Punishment of War Criminals and of Persons Who Have Committed Crimes against Humanity, 5 August 1966.

Resolution 3 (XXI) on Question of Punishment of War Criminals and of Persons Who Have Committed Crimes against Humanity, 9 April 1965.

Resolution 1988/47 on Prosecution and Punishment of all War Criminals and Persons Who Have Committed Crimes against Humanity, 8 March 1988, adopted without a vote.

Resolutions Adopted by other International Organisations

Council of Europe (Parliamentary Assembly Recommendations)

Cultural Situation in the Former Yugoslavia, No. 1239 of 14 April 1994.

The Implementation of the Dayton Agreements for Peace in Bosnia and Herzegovina, No. 1297 of 25 April 1996.

ICOMOS General Assembly

Resolutions of the International Symposium on the Conservation of Smaller Historic Towns (1975), http://www.getty.edu/conservation/research_resources/charters/charters/charter 23.html.

Other Instruments

Instructions for the Government of Armies of the United States in the Field, prepared by Francis Lieber, promulgated as General Order No. 100 by President Abraham Lincoln, Washington D.C., 24 April 1863 (*Lieber Code*), Adjutant General's Office, 1863, Washington 1898: Government Printing Office.

Project of an International Declaration concerning the Laws and Customs of War, Brussels, 27 August 1874.

The Laws of War on Land, adopted by the Institute of International Law, Oxford, 9 September 1880.

The Laws of Naval War Governing the Relations between Belligerents, adopted by the Institute of International Law, Oxford, 9 August 1913.

Report of the Commission on Responsibility (Report submitted to the Preliminary Conference of Versailles by the Commission on Responsibility of the Authors of the War and on Enforcement of Penalties), Versailles, 29 March 1919.

Rules concerning the Control of Wireless Telegraphy in Time of War and Air Warfare, Part II, drafted by a Commission of Jurists, The Hague, December 1922-February 1923 (*Hague Rules of Air Warfare*).

Declaration concerning Atrocities, made at the Moscow Conference, signed by the United States of America, the United Kingdom of Great Britain and Northern Ireland, the Union of Soviet Socialist Republics and China, Moscow, 30 October 1943.

Allied Control Council Law No. 10: Punishment of Persons Guilty of War Crimes, Crimes against Peace and against Humanity, enacted by the Allied Control Council of Germany, composed of the United Kingdom of Great Britain and Northern Ireland, France, the United States of America and the Union of Soviet Socialist Republics, Berlin, 20 December 1945.

Charter of the International Military Tribunal for the Far East, approved by an Executive Order, General Douglas MacArthur, Supreme Commander for the Allied Powers in Japan, Tokyo, 19 January 1946, amended on 26 April 1946.

American Declaration on the Rights and Duties of Man, adopted by the Ninth International Conference of American States, Res. XXX, Bogotá, 2 May 1948.

Universal Declaration on Human Rights, adopted by the UN General Assembly, Res. 217 A (III), 10 December 1948.

Principles of International Law Recognized in the Charter of the Nuremberg Tribunal and in the Judgement of the Tribunal, adopted by the International Law Commission, UN Doc. A/1316, New York, 5 June-29 July 1950.

Draft Code of Offences against the Peace and Security of Mankind, adopted by the International Law Commission, reprinted in Report of the International Law Commission on the work of its sixth session, UN Doc. A/2693, 1954.

International Charter for the Conservation and Restoration of Monuments and Sites, approved 31 May 1964 (ICOMOS) at the International Congress of Architects and Technicians of Historic Monuments, held in Venice from 25 to 31 May 1964, (*Venice Charter 1964*), http://www.icomos.org/docs/venice_charter.html.

UNESCO, *Recommendation concerning the Protection, at National Level, of the Cultural and Natural Heritage*, General Conference of UNESCO, Paris, 17th Session, October 17-18 November 1972, UNESCO Doc 17 C/107, 15 November 1972.

UNESCO, Documents, 5 C/PRG/6, Annex I and 7 C/PRG/7, Annex I.

UNESCO, Document CLT-97/WS/12, August 1997.

Declaration on the Elimination of All Forms of Intolerance and of Discrimination Based on Religion or Belief, adopted by the UN General Assembly, Res. 36/55, 25 November 1981.

Declaration of Dresden (1982), ICOMOS Symposium held in Dresden from 15-19 November 1982 on the subject of the 'Reconstruction of Monuments Destroyed by War', http://www.icomos.org/docs/dresden.html and. http://www.getty.edu/conservation/research_resources/charters/charter34.html.

Statement on Respect for Humanitarian Principles, signed by the Presidents of the Six Republics of the Former Yugoslavia, The Hague, 5 November 1991.

Draft Code of Crimes against the Peace and Security of Mankind, adopted by the International Law Commission, reprinted in Report of the International Law Commission on the work of its forty-third session, 29 April-19 July 1991, UN Doc. A/46/10, 1991.

Memorandum of Understanding on the Application of International Humanitarian Law between Croatia and the Socialist Federal Republic of Yugoslavia, Geneva, 27 November 1991.

Addendum to the Memorandum of Understanding of 27 November 1991 between Croatia and the Federal Republic of Yugoslavia, Geneva, 23 May 1992.

Agreement between Representatives of Mr Alija Izetbegović (President of the Republic of Bosnia and Herzegovina and President of the Party of Democratic Action), Representatives of Mr Radovan Karadžić (President of the Serbian Democratic Party), and Representatives of Mr Miljenko Brkić (President of the Croatian Democratic Community), Geneva, 22 May 1992.

Agreement No. 2 between Representatives of Mr Alija Izetbegović (President of the Republic of Bosnia and Herzegovina and President of the Party of Democratic Action), Representatives of Mr Radovan Karadžić (President of the Serbian Democratic Party), and Representative of Mr Miljenko Brkić (President of the Croatian Democratic Community) on the implementation of the Agreement of 22 May 1992, Geneva, 23 May 1992.

Agreement No. 3 between Representatives of Mr Alija Izetbegović (President of the Republic of Bosnia and Herzegovina and President of the Party of Democratic Action), Representative of Mr Radovan Karadžić (President of the Serbian Democratic Party), and Representative of Mr Miljenko Brkić (President of the Croatian Democratic Community) on the ICRC Plan of Action, Geneva, 6 June 1992.

UNESCO Executive Board, *Review of the application of the Convention for the Protection of Cultural Property in the Event of Armed Conflict* (The Hague, 14 May 1954), Item 5.5.3 of the provisional agenda, 140th Session, 140 EX/26, Paris, 11 September 1992, UNESCO Archives, 2 October 1992.

Joint Declaration by President Dobrica Ćosić of the Federal Republic of Yugoslavia and President Franjo Tuđman of the Republic of Croatia, Geneva, 30 September 1992, annexed to Report of the UN Secretary-General on the International Conference on the Former Yugoslavia, UN Doc. S/24795, 11 November 1992, Annex II.

Joint Declaration by President Dobrica Ćosić of the Federal Republic of Yugoslavia and President Franjo Tuđman of the Republic of Croatia, Geneva, 20 October 1992, annexed to Report of the UN Secretary-General on the International Conference on the Former Yugoslavia, UN Doc. S/24795, 11 November 1992, Annex VI.

Programme of Action on Humanitarian Issues agreed between the Co-chairmen of the London International Conference and the Parties to the conflict in Bosnia and Herzegovina, London, 27 August 1992, annexed to Report by the Special Rapporteur of the UN Commission on Human Rights on the situation of human rights in the territory of the former Yugoslavia, UN Doc. E/CN.4/1993/50, 10 February 1993, Annex III.

Recommendation on the Tragic Situation of Civilians in Bosnia and Herzegovina, adopted at the invitation of the International Committee of the Red Cross and signed by Representatives of Mr Alija Izetbegović (President of the Republic of Bosnia and Herzegovina and President of the Party of Democratic Action), Representative of Mr Radovan Karadžić (President of the Serbian Democratic Party), and Representative of Mr Mate Boban (President of the Croatian Democratic Community), Geneva, 1 October 1992.

Agreement among the Parties to Halt the Conflict in Bosnia and Herzegovina, signed by the representatives of the Hrvatsko Vijeće Obrane (Croatian Defence Council (HVO)) and the Army of Bosnia and Herzegovina (ABH), Kiseljak, 9 June 1993.

Franco-German Declaration on the War in Bosnia and Herzegovina, 61st French-German Consultations, Beaune, 2 June 1993.

Republic of Bosnia and Herzegovina, Wartime Presidency of Mostar Municipality, *Decision on Proclaiming 10 November 1993 a Mourning Day in the Mostar Municipality*, 9 November 1993, published in *Most*, No. 108–109 November–December 1998, http://www.most.ba/01920/006.htm.

Declaration of the World Heritage Committee on the Destruction of Cultural Heritage of Bosnia and Herzegovina, mtg in Cartagena, Colombia, 6-11 December 1993, *World Heritage Newsletter* vol II, No. 6, 11 December 1993.

Resolution on Information As an Instrument for Protection against War Damages to the Cultural Heritage, an expert meeting convened by the Swedish Central Board of National Antiquities, the Swedish National Commission for UNESCO and ICOMOS Sweden, 10 June 1994, http://www.unesco.org/culture/laws/sweden/html_eng/page1.shtml.

Draft Statute for an International Criminal Court, adopted by the International Law Commission, reprinted in *Report of the International Law Commission on the Work of Its 46th Session*, 2 May-22 July 1994, UN Doc. A/49/10, 1994.

UNESCO, *Convention concerning the Protection of the World Cultural and Natural Heritage*, World Heritage Committee, 18th Session, Phuket, Thailand, 12-17 December 1994, Information Note: International Register of Cultural Property under Special Protection Coordination of Implementation of Conventions Protecting the Cultural Heritage WHC-94/CONF.003/INF, 16 November 1995.

'Rules of the Road' procedure annexed to the *Rome Agreement*, signed on 18 February 1996, between Presidents Alija Izetbegović (Bosnia and Herzegovina), Franjo Tuđman (Croatia) and Slobodan Milošević (Serbia and Montenegro), http://www.ohr.int/ohr-dept/hr-rol/thedept/war-crime-tr/, http://www.cdsp.neu.edu.

Draft Code of Crimes against the Peace and Security of Mankind, adopted by the International Law Commission, reprinted in report of the International Law Commission on the work of its 48th Session, 6 May-26 July 1996, UN Doc. A/51/10, 1996.

NATO, 'Partnership for Peace (PfP)' Conference on Cultural Heritage Protection in Wartime and in State of Emergency, 18-21 June 1996, Cracow, Poland, Final Communiqué, 21 June 1996, http://www.icomos.org/blue_shield/krakowna.html.

Draft Provisions for the Revision of the 1954 Hague Convention and Commentary from the UNESCO Secretariat, Paris, October 1997, UNESCO Doc. CLT-97/CONF.208/2.

UNESCO, *Declaration on Responsibility of Present Generations towards Future Generations* (1997), http://www.unesco.org/culture/.

Diplomatic Conference on the Draft Second Protocol to the 1954 Hague Convention, 'Final Act of the Diplomatic Conference', HC/1999/8, Meetings of forum 15-26 March 1999, The Hague, adopted 26 March 1999, http://unescodoc.unesco.org.

International Committee of the Blue Shield (ICBS), 'Appeal for the Protection of the Cultural Heritage in Yugoslavia' 19 April 1999, http://www.aam-us.org/aamicomstatement.htm.

Observance by United Nations Forces of International Humanitarian Law, Secretary-General's Bulletin, UN Secretariat, UN Doc. ST/SGB/1999/13, 6 August 1999.

Charter of Fundamental Rights of the European Union, signed and proclaimed by the European Parliament, the Council and the Commission of the European Union, Nice, 7 December 2000.

International Register of Cultural Property under Special Protection, UNESCO Doc. CLT/CIH/MCO/2008/PI/46, 2000, http://unesdoc.unesco.org/images/0015/001585/158587eb.pdf.

Rules of Procedure and Evidence of the International Criminal Tribunal for the Former Yugoslavia, The Hague, 11 February 1994, Rev. 18, as amended 14 July 2000.

United Nations Millennium Declaration, adopted by the UN Millennium Summit, New York, 6–8 December 2000, endorsed by the UN General Assembly, Res. 55/2, 8 September 2000.

Regulation on the Establishment of Panels with Exclusive Jurisdiction over Serious Criminal Offences, UN Doc. UNTAET/REG/2000/15, Dili, 6 June 2000.

Draft Articles on Responsibility of States for Internationally Wrongful Acts, adopted by the International Law Commission, reprinted in Report of the International Law Commission on the work of its 53rd Session, 23 April-1 June and 2 July-10 August 2001, UN Doc. A/56/10, 2001.

Rules of Procedure and Evidence of the International Criminal Tribunal for Rwanda, Arusha, 29 June 1995, as amended on 31 May 2001.

Universal Declaration on Cultural Diversity, adopted by 31st UNESCO General Conference, Paris, 2 November 2001, UNESCO Press No. 2001-120-5, http://www.unesco.org/bpi/eng/unsecopress/2001/01-120e.shtml.

Finalized Draft Text of the Elements of Crimes, adopted by the 23rd meeting of the Preparatory Commission for the International Criminal Court, New York, 30 June 2000, *Report of the Preparatory Commission for the International Criminal Court*, UN Doc. PCNICC/2000/INF/3/Add.2, Addendum, 6 July 2000, as adopted by the Assembly of States Parties, First Session, 3-10 September 2002, *Official Records of the Assembly of States Parties to the Rome Statute of the ICC*, UN Doc. ICC-ASP/1/3, 25 September 2002, and ICC-ASP/1/3/Corr.1, 31 October 2002.

Finalised Draft Text of the Rules of Procedure and Evidence, adopted by the 23rd Meeting of the Preparatory Commission for the International Criminal Court, New York, 30 June 2000, *Report of the Preparatory Commission for the International Criminal Court*, UN Doc. PCNICC/2000/1/Add.1, Addendum, Part I, 2 November 2000, as adopted by the Assembly of States Parties, First Session, 3-10 September 2002, *Official Records of the Assembly of States Parties to the Rome Statute of the ICC*, UN Doc. ICC-ASP/1/3, 25 September 2002, and ICC-ASP/1/3/Corr.1, 31 October 2002.

United Nations Security Council, 4833rd Meeting, Wednesday, 24 September 2003, 9 am, Agenda: 'Justice and the Rule of Law: the United Nations Role', S/PV.4833.

Declaration concerning the Intentional Destruction of Cultural Heritage, elaborated pursuant to Resolution 31C/26, 31st Session UNESCO General Conference, October-November 2001, adopted unanimously by the 32nd Session of the UNESCO General Conference, September-October 2003, 32 C/25, Paris, 17 October 2003.

Yamato Declaration on Integrated Approaches for Safeguarding Tangible and Intangible Cultural Heritage, adopted at International Conference on the Safeguarding of Tangible and Intangible Cultural Heritage, 20-23 October 2004, Nara, Japan, http://portal.unesco.org/culture/en/ev.phpURL.

Final Conclusions of Asian Meeting on Cultural Property Protection in Armed Conflict, Phnom Penh, December 2004, Regional Expert Meeting on 'The Protection of Cultural Property in the Event of Armed Conflict', Phnom Penh, 6-8 December 2004.

Select Bibliography

Books

Abtahi, Hirad and Gideon Boas (eds), *The Dynamics of International Criminal Justice* (2006) Dordrecht/Boston/London: Martinus Nijhoff Publishers.

Ackerman, John and Eugene O'Sullivan, *Practice and Procedure of the International Criminal Tribunal for the Former Yugoslavia* (2000) The Hague/London/Boston: Kluwer Law International.

Amann, Diane Marie, 'Assessing International Criminal Adjudication of Human Rights Atrocities' in International Third World Legal Studies Association (INTWORLSA), *Third World Legal Studies – 2000-2003* (2003) Valparaiso: The International Third World Legal Studies Association and The Valparaiso University School of Law, 169.

Arendt, Hannah, *Eichmann in Jerusalem: A Report on the Banality of Evil* (1964) New York: Viking Press.

Aristotle, *Nicomachean Ethics* (Roger Crisp trans, 2000 ed) New York: Cambridge University Press.

Armaly, Maha et al, 'Economics of Investing in Heritage: Historic Centre of Split' in Ismail Serageldin et al (eds), *Historic Cities and Sacred Sites: Cultural Roots for Urban Futures* (2001) World Bank Publications, 165.

Askerud, Pernille and Étienne Clément, *Preventing the Illicit Traffic in Cultural Property: A Resource Handbook for the Implementation of the 1970 UNESCO Convention* (1997) Paris: UNESCO, http:////unescdoc.unesco.org/images/0011/001187/118783eo.pdf.

Attila Hoare, Marko, *How Bosnia Armed* (2004) London: Saqi Books in association with The Bosnian Institute.

Baier, Annette, 'For the Sake of Future Generations' in J. Regan (ed), *Earthbound: New Introductory Essays in Environmental Ethics* (1984) 214.

Ball, Howard, *Prosecuting War Crimes and Genocide* (1999) Kansas: University Press of Kansas.

Barakat, Sultan, et al, 'Challenges and Dilemmas Facing the Reconstruction of War-Damaged Cultural Heritage: The Case Study of Počitelj, Bosnia-Herzegovina' in Robert Layton et al (eds), *Destruction and Conservation of Cultural Heritage* (2001) London/New York: Routledge, 169.

Barthel, Diane, *Historic Preservation: Collective Memory and Historical Identity* (1996) New Brunswick, New Jersey: Rutger University Press.

Bassiouni, Cherif, *Crimes against Humanity in International Criminal Law* (2nd ed, 1999), The Hague: Kluwer Law International.

Bassiouni, Cherif (ed), *Post-Conflict Justice* (2002) Ardsley, New York: Transnational Publishers.

Bassiouni, Cherif, 'Accountability for Violations of International Humanitarian law' in Cherif Bassiouni (ed), *Post-Conflict Justice* (2002) Ardsley, New York: Transnational Publishers, 3.

Bassiouni, Cherif, 'The United Nations Commissions of Experts Established pursuant to Security Council Resolution 780 (1992) to Investigate Violations of International Humanitarian Law in the Former Yugoslavia' in Cherif Bassiouni (ed), *Post-Conflict Justice* (2002) Ardsley, New York: Transnational Publishers, 429.

Bassiouni, Cherif, 'The Permanent International Criminal Court' in Mark Lattimer and Philippe Sands (eds), *Justice for Crimes against Humanity* (2003) Oxford: Hart Publishing, 173.

Bassiouni, Cherif and Peter Manikas, *The Law of the International Criminal Tribunal for the Former Yugoslavia* (1996) Irvington/Hudson/New York: Transnational Publishers.

Bator, Paul, *The International Trade in Art* (2nd ed, 1996) Chicago/London: University of Chicago Press.

Belamarić, Joško, 'Croatian Monuments as Targets, 1991/92' in Pamela Vandiver et al (eds), *Materials Issues in Art and Archaeology III* (1992) Pittsburgh, Pennsylvania: Materials Research Society, 127.

Benarie, Michael and James Druzik, 'Catastrophes and Entropy of Cultural Properties' in Pamela Vandiver et al (eds), *Materials Issues in Art and Archaeology III* (1992) Pittsburgh, Pennsylvania: Materials Research Society, 17.

Best, Geoffrey, *Humanity in Warfare: The Modern History of the International Law of Armed Conflict* (1980) London: Weidenfeld & Nicholson.

Bevan, Robert, *The Destruction of Memory: Architecture at War* (2006) Reaktion Books.

Bianca, Stefano, 'Resources for Sustaining Cultural Identity' in Ismail Serageldin et al (eds), *Historic Cities and Sacred Sites: Cultural Roots for Urban Futures* (2001) World Bank Publications, 18.

BIRN, *In Pursuit of Justice: Guide to the War Crimes Chamber of the Court of BiH* (2006) Sarajevo: Balkanske Istraživačke Mreže, www.birn.eu.com.

Black, Cyril and Richard Falk (eds), *The Future of the International Legal Order* (1971) Princeton: Princeton University Press.

Bogdanović, Bogdan, *Grad i smrt* (*City and Death*) (1994) Beograd: Beogradski krug (Belgrade: Belgrade Circle).

Boylan, Patrick, *Review of the Convention for the Protection of Cultural Property in the Event of Armed Conflict (The Hague Convention of 1954)* (1993) Paris: UNESCO Publishing.

Brooks, Thom (ed), *The Global Justice Reader* (2008) Maleden/Oxford/Carlton: Blackwell Publishing.

Brown, Jack, *Provenance Bibliography* (2007) Art Institute of Chicago.

Broz, Svetlana, *Dobri ljudi u vremenu zla: Sudionici i svjedoci* (*Good People in an Evil Time: Participants and Witnesses*) (1999) Banja Luka: Media Centar Prelom.

Chamberlain, Kevin, *War and Cultural Heritage: An Analysis of the Hague Convention for the Protection of Cultural Property in the Event of Armed Conflict* (first published 2004, 2nd ed, 2005) Leicester, Great Britain: Institute of Art and Law.

Charlesworth, Esther, *Architects without Frontiers: War, Reconstruction and Design Responsibility* (2006) Oxford: Architectural Press.

Cigar, Norman, *Genocide in Bosnia: The Policy of 'Ethnic Cleansing'* (1995) Texas A&M University Press.

Clausewitz, Von, *On War* (J.J. Graham trans of extracts from original Vom Kreige of 1832, Penguin Classics ed, 1908, 1968 ed) London: Penguin Books.

Coles, Harry and Albert Weinberg, *United States Army in World War II, Special Studies, Civil Affairs: Soldiers Become Governors* (1992) Washington DC: Centre of Military History, http://www.armymil/cmh-pg/books/wwii/civaff/.

Corzo, Miguel, 'The Hague Convention of 1954: History, Significance and Compliance' in Pamela Vandiver *et al* (eds), *Materials Issues in Art and Archaeology III* (1992) Pittsburgh, Pennsylvania: Materials Research Society, 5.

Čelebi, Evlija, *Putopis* (*Book of Travel*) (1996 ed) Sarajevo: Sarajevo Publishing.

Darraby, Jessica, *Artifact and Architecture Law* (2006) Thomson West.

Delissen, Astrid and Gerard Tanja (eds), *Essays in Honour of Frits Kalshoven* (1991) Dordrecht/Boston/London: Martinus Nijhoff Publishers.

Detter, Ingrid, *The Law of War* (first published 1987, reprinted 1989, 2nd ed, 2000) Cambridge, UK: Cambridge University Press.

Dinnes, Manfred and Fuad Ćatović, *Hommage to Mostar* (1997) Mostar: Slovo Printing and Publishing Company.

DuBoff, Leonard (ed), *Art Law: Domestic and International* (1975) South Hackensack, N.J.: Rothman & Co.

DuBoff, Leonard and Christie King, *Deskbook of Art Law Looseleaf* (1993) Oceana Publications.

DuBoff, Leonard and Sally Holt Caplan, *The Deskbook of Art Law* (2nd ed, 1996).

DuBoff, Leonard and Christie King, *Art Law in a Nutshell* (4th ed, 2006) West Publishing Corporation.

Eide, Asbjørn, Catarina Krause and Allan Rosas (eds), *Economic, Social and Cultural Rights* (1995) Dordrecht/Boston/London: Martinus Nijhoff Publishers.

Emerick, Keith, 'Use, Value and Significance in Heritage Management' in Robert Layton et al (eds), *Destruction and Conservation of Cultural Property* (2001) London/New York: Routledge, 276.

Falk, Richard, *A Study of Future Worlds* (1975) New York: The Free Press.

Ferencz, Benjamin, 'From Nuremberg to Rome: A Personal Account' in Mark Lattimer and Philippe Sands (eds), *Justice for Crimes against Humanity* (2001) Oxford: Hart Publishing, 31.

Fiedler, Wilfried and Stefan Turner, *Bibliography on the Law of the International Protection of Cultural Property/Bibliographie zum Recht des Internationalen Kulturgüterschutzes* (2003) Berlin: De Gruyter Recht.

Fitz Gibbon, Kate, *Who Owns the Past? Cultural Policy, Cultural Property, and the Law* (2005) Piscataway, NJ: Rutgers University Press.

Fleck, Dieter (ed), *The Handbook of Humanitarian Law in Armed Conflict* (1995) New York: Oxford University Press.

Gardam, Judith (ed), *Humanitarian Law* (1999) Aldershot, England: Darmouth Publishing Company.

Geertz, C., *The Interpretation of Cultures* (1973).

Gerstenblith, Barbara, *Art, Cultural Heritage, and the Law: Cases and Materials* (2004) Carolina Academic Press.

Gillman, Derek, *The Idea of Cultural Heritage* (2006) Institute of Art and Law, UK.

Gopal, Sarvepalli (ed), *Anatomy of a Confrontation* (1991).

Graham, Brian and Peter Howard (eds), *The Ashgate Research Companion to Heritage and Identity* (2008) Aldershot: Ashgate.

Greenfield, Jeanette, *The Return of Cultural Treasures* (first published 1989, 3rd ed, 2007) Cambridge: Cambridge University Press.

Greenwood, Christopher, 'Customary Law Status of the 1977 Geneva Protocols' in Astrid Delissen and Gerard Tanja (eds), *Essays in Honor of Frits Kalshoven* (1991) Dordrecht/Boston/London: Martinus Nijhoff Publishers, 93.

Hamber, Brandon, 'Remembering to Forget: Issues to Consider when Establishing Structures for Dealing with the Past', in Brandon Hamber (ed), *Past Imperfect: Dealing with the Past in Northern Ireland and Societies in Transition* (1998) Derry/Londonderry: University of Ulster, 56.

Hannah, Lawrence, 'The Partnership for Mostar' in Ismail Serageldin et al (eds), *Historic Cities and Sacred Sites: Cultural Roots for Urban Futures* (2001) World Bank Publications, 385.

Handler, Richard, 'Who Owns the Past?: History, Cultural Property, and the Logic of Possessive Individualism' in Brett Williams (ed), *The Politics of Culture* (1991) 63.

Henckaerts, Jean-Marie and Louise Doswald-Beck (eds), *Customary International Humanitarian Law: Volume I Rules*, (2005) Cambridge: Cambridge University Press.

Henckaerts, Jean-Marie and Louise Doswald-Beck (eds), *Customary International Humanitarian Law: Volume II Practice* (2005) Cambridge: Cambridge University Press.

Hensel, Howard (ed), *Law of Armed Conflict* Global Interdisciplinary Studies Series (2007) Aldershot: Ashgate.

Herbert, David (ed), *Heritage, Tourism and Society* (1995) London/New York: Mansell.

Hladík, Jan, 'The Review Process of the 1954 Hague Convention for the Protection of Cultural Property in the Event of Armed Conflict and Its Impact on International Humanitarian Law' in *Yearbook of International Humanitarian Law* vol. 1, 1998 (1998) The Hague: T.M.C. Asser Press, 313.

Hladík, Jan, 'The Control System under The Hague Convention for the Protection of Cultural Property in the Event of Armed Conflict 1954 and Its Second Protocol' in the *Yearbook of International Humanitarian Law* vol. 4, 2001 (2004) The Hague: T.M.C. Asser Press, 419.

Hladík, Jan, 'The Main Activities of the UNESCO Secretariat Related to the Implementation of the Second Protocol to the Hague Convention of 1954' in Paul Meerts (ed), *Culture and International Law* (2008) 155.

Hoffman, Barbara (ed), *Art and Cultural Heritage: Law, Policy, and Practice* (2006) Cambridge/New York: Cambridge University Press.

Holtorf, Cornelius, 'Is the Past a Non-Renewable Resource?' in Robert Layton et al (eds), *Destruction and Conservation of Cultural Property* (2001) London/New York: Routledge 286-297.

Houdek, Frank, 'Protection of Cultural Property and Archaeological Resources' in *A Collection of Bibliographical and Research Resources* (1984) Oceana.

Hulme, Karen, *War Torn Environment: Interpreting the Legal Threshold* (2004) Dordrecht/Boston/London: Martinus Nijhoff Publishers.

Human Rights Watch, *Genocide, War Crimes and Crimes against Humanity: Topical Digests of the Case Law of the International Criminal Tribunal for Rwanda and the International Criminal Tribunal for the Former Yugoslavia* (2004) New York: Human Rights Watch, http://hrw.org/reports/2004/ij.

Hutt, Sherry and Lawyers' Committee for Cultural Heritage Preservation, *Yearbook of Cultural Property Law* (2006) Left Coast Press.

IBA, *Protecting Cultural Heritage*, online book, http://www.ibaculturalheritage.com/english/.

Ignatieff, Michael, *Empire Lite: Nation-Building in Bosnia, Kosovo and Afghanistan* (2003) London: Vintage.

Institute of Art and Law, *Cultural Heritage Statutes* (2nd ed, 2004), Institute of Art and Law, UK.

International Council on Monuments and Sites (ICOMOS), *Heritage at Risk: ICOMOS World Report 2000 on Monuments and Sites in Danger* (2000) München: K·G·Saur.

International Military Tribunal for the Far East (1946) Tokyo, 3 May 1946 – 4 November 1948 (308 vols), (typed transcripts) Tokyo: Japan.

Jote, Kifle, *International Legal Protection of Cultural Heritage* (1994) Stockholm: Juristförlaget.

Joyner, Christopher (ed), *The United Nations and International Law* (1997) Cambridge: Cambridge University Press.

Kalshoven, Frits, *Constraints on the Waging of War* (1987) Geneva: International Committee of the Red Cross.

Kalshoven, Frits, 'Introduction' in Frits Kalshoven (ed), *The Centennial of the First International Peace Conference* (2000) 1.

Kaufman, Roy, *Art Law Handbook* (2000) Aspen Law and Business.

Kila, Joris, 'Utilizing Military Cultural Experts in Times of War and Peace: An Introduction Cultural Property Protection within the Military, Experiences in Theatre, Different Perceptions of Culture and Practical Problems' in Paul Meerts (ed), *Culture and International Law* (2008) The Hague: Hague Academic Press, 183.

King Thomas, *Cultural Resources Laws and Practice: An Introductory Guide* (2004) AltaMira Press.

Knuth, Rebecca, *Burning Books and Leveling Libraries: Extremist Violence and Cultural Destruction* (2006) Greenwood Publishing Group.

Koscević, Želimir, 'Monuments as Targets' in Pamela Vandiver et al (eds), *Materials Issues in Art and Archaeology III* (1992) Pittsburgh, Pennsylvania: Materials Research Society.

Laban Hinton, Alexander, 'The Dark Side of Modernity: Toward an Anthropology of Genocide' in Alexander Laban Hinton (ed), *Annihilating Difference: The Anthropology of Genocide* (2002) The University of California Press, http://www.ucpress.edu/books/pages/9412/9412.ch01.html.

Lattimer, Mark and Philippe Sands (eds), *Justice for Crimes against Humanity* (2003) Oxford: Hart Publishing.

Layton, Robert et al (eds), *Destruction and Conservation of Cultural Property* (2001) London/New York: Routledge.

Lemkin, Raphaël, *Axis Rule in Occupied Europe: Laws of Occupation, Analysis of Government, Proposals for Redress* (1944) Washington: Carnegie Endowment for International Peace (Chapter IX 'Genocide' 1.Genocide A New Term and New Conception for Destruction of Nations' 79).

Lewis, Geoffrey, 'The Return of Cultural Property' *The Royal Society of Arts Proceedings* (1981) 435.

Logan, William, 'Cultural Diversity, Heritage and Human Rights' in Brian Graham and Peter Howard (eds), *The Ashgate Research Companion to Heritage and Identity* (2008) Aldershot: Ashgate, 439.

Lowenthal, David, *Possessed by the Past: The Heritage Crusade and the Spoils of History* (1996) New York: The Free Press.

Madex, Diane (ed), *All about Old Buildings: The Whole Preservation Catalog* (1985) Washington: The Preservation Press.

Mahić, Mirsad, Mustafa Šoše and Hakija Klarić, *Neretva i njene obale u Mostaru* (*The Neretva and its Banks in Mostar*) (2007) Mostar: Solvej.

Mandal, D., *Ayodhya: Archaeology after Demolition* (1993).

Marke, Julius (ed), *A Catalogue of the Law Collection at New York University: With Selected Annotations* (1999) Union, New Jersey: The Law Book Exchange, Ltd.

Martin, Daniel, 'Art Law: A Selected Bibliography' in *Art, Artifact and Architecture Law* (2006) Thomson West.

McClean, Daniel (ed), *The Trials of Art* (2007) Ridinghouse Editions.

McCormack, Timothy and Gerry Simpson (eds), *The Law of War Crimes: National and International Approaches* (1997) The Hague: Kluwer Law International.

McCormack, Timothy, 'Their Atrocities and Our Misdemeanours: The Reticence of States to Try Their "Own Nationals" for International Crimes' in Mark Lattimer and Philippe Sands (eds), *Justice for Crimes against Humanity* (2003) Oxford: Hart Publishing, 107.

McDonald, Gabrielle Kirk and Olivia Swaak-Goldman (eds), *Substantive and Procedural Aspects of International Criminal Law: The Experience of International and National Courts* (1999) The Hague/London/Boston: Kluwer Law International, BRILL.

McDowell, Sara, 'Heritage, Memory and Identity' in Brian Graham and Peter Howard (eds), *The Ashgate Research Companion to Heritage and Identity* (2008) Aldershot: Ashgate, 37.

McLean, George, *Civil Society and Social Reconstruction* (1997) Washington, DC: The Council for Research in Values and Philosophy.

McMahan, Jeff, 'Future Generations' in Ted Honderich (ed), *The Oxford Companion to Philosophy* (1995) Oxford/New York: Oxford University Press, 302.

Meerts, Paul (ed), *Culture and International Law* (2008) The Hague: Hague Academic Press.

Merryman, John, *Thinking about the Elgin Marbles: Critical Essays on Cultural Property, Art and Law* (2000) The Hague/London/Boston: Kluwer Law International.

Merryman, John, *Imperialism, Art and Restitution* (2006) Cambridge/New York/Melbourne/Madrid/Cape Town/Singapore: Cambridge University Press.

Merryman, John, Albert Elsen and Stephen Urice, *Law, Ethics and the Visual Arts* (2nd ed 1987, 5th ed, 2007) The Hague/London/Boston: Kluwer Law International.

Messenger, Phyllis (ed), *The Ethics of Collecting Cultural Property: Whose Culture? Whose Property?* (first published 1989, 2nd ed, 1999) Albuquerque: University of New Mexico Press.

Micewski, Edwin and Gerhard Sladek (eds), *Protection of Cultural Property in the Event of Armed Conflict – A Challenge in Peace Support Operations*, Series of the Austrian Society for the Protection of Cultural Property (2002) Vienna: Austrian Military Printing Press.

Morris, Virginia and Michael Scharf, *An Insider's Guide to the International Criminal Tribunal for the Former Yugoslavia: A Documentary History and Analysis* vol 1 and 2 (1995) Irvington-on-Hudson, New York: Transnational Publishers.

Mostarlija, *Luciferov pohod na Mostar* (*Devil's Campaign on Mostar*) (1998) Mostar: Biblioteka 'Svjedočanstva' Društvene Djelatnosti Općine Stari Grad Mostar.

Mullins, C., *The Leipzig Trials* (1921).

Murphy, David, *Plunder and Preservation: Cultural Property Law and Practice in the People's Republic of China* (1995) Hong Kong/Oxford/New York: Oxford University Press.

Nahlik, Stanislaw, 'Convention for the Protection of Cultural Property in the Event of Armed Conflict, The Hague, 1954: General and Special Protection' in Istituto internazionale di diritto umanitario, *La protezione internazionale dei beni culturali/ The International Protection of Cultural Property/ La protection internationale des biens culturels* (1986) Rome: Fondazione Europea Dragan, 87.

Nahlik, Stanislaw, 'Protection of Cultural Property' in UNESCO, *International Dimensions of Humanitarian Law* (1988) Paris/Geneva/Dordrecht: UNESCO – Henry Dunant Institute – Martinus Nijhoff Publishers, 203.

Nieć, Halina, 'Casting the Foundation for the Implementation of Cultural Rights' in UNESCO, *Cultural Rights and Wrongs* (1998) Paris/London: UNESCO Publishing and Institute of Art and Law, 176.

Oeter, Stefan, 'Means and Methods of Combat' in Dieter Fleck (ed), *The Handbook of Humanitarian Law in Armed Conflict* (1995) New York: Oxford University Press, 105.

O'Keefe, Patrick, *Law and the Cultural Heritage: Volume 2. Creation, Preservation and Destruction* (1997) LexisNexis Butterworths.

O'Keefe, Patrick, *Trade in Antiquities: Reducing Destruction and Theft* (1997) Paris: UNESCO.

O'Keefe, Roger, *The Protection of Cultural Property in Armed Conflict* (2006) Cambridge: Cambridge University Press.

Olusanya, Olaoluwa (ed), *Rethinking International Criminal Law: The Substantive Part* (2007) Europa Law Publishing.

Parks, Hays, 'Protection of Cultural Property from the Effects of War' in *The Law of Cultural Property and Natural Heritage* (1998) Evanson, Illinois: Kalos Kapp Press, 3.1.

Pašić, Amir, *The Old Bridge (Stari Most) in Mostar* (1995) Istanbul: Research Centre for Islamic History, Art and Culture.

Partsch, Karl Joseph, 'Protection of Cultural Property' in Dieter Fleck (ed), *The Handbook of Humanitarian Law in Armed Conflict* (1995) New York: Oxford University Press, 377.

Patridge, E. (ed), *Responsibilities to Future Generations* (1981).

Paust, Jordan et al, *International Criminal Law: Cases and Materials* (1996) Durham, North Carolina: Carolina Academic Press.

Peacock, Sir Alan (ed), *Does the Past Have a Future?: The Political Economy of Heritage* (1998) London: The Institute of Economic Affairs.

Pettman, Ralph, *Reason, Culture, Religion: The Metaphysics of World Politics (Culture and Religion in International Relations)* (2004) New York: Palgrave MacMillan.

Petrovic, Jadranka, 'Cultural Context of Peace Operations' in Jessica Howard and Bruce Oswald (eds), *The Rule of Law on Peace Operations* (2002) The Hague/London/New York: Kluwer Law International, 213.

Pictet, J.S., *The Geneva Conventions of 12 August 1949* (4 vols) (1952-1960) Geneva: ICRC.

Piloud, Claude et al, *Commentary on the Additional Protocols* (1987).

Porterfield, Todd, *The Allure of Empire: Art in the Service of French Imperialism 1798-1836* (1998) New Jersey: Princeton University Press.

Prott, Lyndel and Patrick O'Keefe, *Law and the Cultural Heritage* vol. 1 *Discovery and Excavation* (1984) Abingdon, Oxon: Professional Books.

Prott, Lyndel, 'Commentary: 1954 Hague Convention for the Protection of Cultural Property in the Event of Armed Conflict' in Ronzitti, N., *The Law of Naval Warfare* (1988) Dordrecht: Martinus Nijhoff Publishers, 582.

Prott, Lyndel and Patrick O'Keefe, *Law and the Cultural Heritage* vol. 3: *Movement* (1989) Butterworth's.

Prott, Lyndel, *Commentary on the UNIDROIT Convention* (1997) Leicester: Institute of Art and Law.

Prott, Lyndel, 'Understanding One Another on Cultural Rights' in UNESCO, *Cultural Rights and Wrongs* (1998) Paris/London: UNESCO Publishing and Institute of Art and Law, 161.

Prott, Lyndel (ed), *Finishing the Interrupted Voyage* (2006) Institute of Art and Law, UK.

Ratner, Steven and Jason Abrams, *Accountability for Human Rights Atrocities in International Law* (2001) Oxford: Oxford University Press.

Riedlmayer, András, 'From the Ashes: The Past and Future of Bosnia's Cultural Heritage' in Shatzmiller, Maya (ed), *Islam and Bosnia: Conflict Resolution and Foreign Policy in Multiethnic States* (2002) Montreal & Kingston/London/Ithaca: McGill Queen's University Press, 98.

Roberts, Adam and Richard Guelff (eds), *Documents on the Laws of War* (first published 1982, 3rd ed, 2000), Oxford: Oxford University Press. http://www.icrc.org/ihl.nsf.

Rogers, A.P.V., *Law on the Battlefield* (first published 1996, revised ed, 2004) Manchester/New York: Manchester University Press.

Rothfield, Lawrence, *Antiquities under Siege – Cultural Heritage Protection after the Iraq War* (2008) Lanham/New York/Toronto/Plymouth, UK: Rowman & Littlefield Publishers.

Sadat, Leila, *The International Criminal Court and the Transformation of International Justice: Justice for the New Millennium* (2002) Ardsley/New York: Transnational Publishers.

Sandoz, Yves *et al* (eds), *Commentary on the Additional Protocols I and II of 9 June 1977* (1987) Geneva: Martinus Nijhoff Publishers.

Schabas, William, *An Introduction to the International Criminal Court* (2001) Cambridge: Cambridge University Press.

Scharf, Michael, *Balkan Justice: The Story behind the First International War Crimes Trial since Nuremberg* (1997) Durham, NC: North Carolina Academic Press.

Scharf, Michael and Nigel Rodley, 'International Law Principles on Accountability' in Cherif Bassiouni (ed), *Post-Conflict Justice* (2002) Ardsley, New York: Transnational Publishers, 89.

Sells, Michael, *The Bridge Betrayed: Religion and Genocide in Bosnia* (1996) Berkeley: University of California Press.

Serageldin, Ismail et al (eds), *Historic Cities and Sacred Sites: Cultural Roots for Urban Futures* (2001) World Bank Publications.

Serageldin, Ismail and Ephin Shluger, 'Introduction' in Ismail Serageldin et al (eds), *Historic Cities and Sacred Sites: Cultural Roots for Urban Futures* (2001) World Bank Publications, xi.

Sharma, Ram Sharan, 'The Ayodhya Issue' in Robert Layton et al (eds), *Destruction and Conservation of Cultural Property* (2001) London/New York: Routledge, 127.

Shatzmiller, Maya (ed), *Islam and Bosnia: Conflict Resolution and Foreign Policy in Multiethnic States* (2002) Montreal & Kingston/London/Ithaca: McGill Queen's University Press.

Shaw, Malcolm, *International Law* (4th ed, 1997) Cambridge, United Kingdom: The Press Syndicate of the University of Cambridge.

Shelley, P.B., *A Defence of Poetry* (1904).

Shirer, William, *The Rise and Fall of the Third Reich* (1960) London: Seker & Warburg.

Silber, Laura and Alan Little, *Yugoslavia: Death of a Nation* (1997) New York: Penguin Books.

Silverman, Helaine and D. Fairchild Ruggles, *Cultural Heritage and Human Rights* (2007) Springer Science and Business Media.

Singh, Kishore, 'UNESCO and Cultural Rights' in UNESCO, *Cultural Rights and Wrongs* (1998) Paris/London: UNESCO Publishing and Institute of Art and Law, 146.

Solioz, Christophe and Tobias Vogel (eds), *Dayton and Beyond: Perspectives on the Future of Bosnia and Herzegovina* (2005) Baden-Baden: Die Deutsche Bibliothek.

Spennemann, Dirk and David Look (eds), *Disaster Management Programs for Historic Sites* (1998) San Francisco, California: US National Park Service/ San Francisco, California: Western Chapter of the Association for Preservation Technology/ Albury, Australia: The Johnstone Centre, Charles Sturt University.

Steiner, Henry and Philip Alston, *International Human Rights in Context: Law, Politics, Morals* (2nd ed, 2000), New York: Oxford University Press.

Sunga, Lyal, *The Emerging System of International Criminal Law: Developments in Codification and Implementation* (1997) The Hague: Kluwer Law International.

Šulc, Branka, 'The Protection of Croatia's Cultural Heritage during War 1991-1995' in Robert Layton et al (eds), *Destruction and Conservation of Cultural Property* (2001) London/New York: Routledge, 157.

Taylor, Telford, *The Anatomy of the Nuremberg Trials: A Personal Memoir* (1992) New York: Alfred A. Knopf.

Teitel, Ruti, *Transitional Justice* (2000) New York: Oxford University Press.

Toman, Jiří, *The Protection of Cultural Property in the Event of Armed Conflict: Commentary on the Convention for the Protection of Cultural Property in the Event of Armed Conflict and its Protocol, signed on 14 May 1954 in The Hague, and on other Instruments of International Law concerning such Protection* (1996) Hants / Paris: Dartmouth Publishing Company/UNESCO Publishing.

Toman, Jiří, 'The Control System under the 1954 Hague Convention and its 1999 Second Protocol' in Paul Meerts (ed), *Culture and International Law* (2008) 121.

Tremmel, Joerg (ed), *Handbook of Intergenerational Justice* (2006) Cheltenham, UK: Edward Elgar Publishing Limited.

Treue, Wilhelm, *Art Plunder: The Fate of Works of Art in War and Unrest* (1961).

Trial of the Major War Criminals before the International Military Tribunal, Nuremberg, 14 November 1945 - 1 October 1946, Nuremberg (1947) – 42 volumes (1947) Nuremberg.

Tsang, Louise, *Legal Protection of Cultural Property: A Selective Resource Guide* (2007) LLRX.com, http://www.llrx.com/features/culturalproperty.htm.

Tubb, Kathryn (ed), *Antiquities, Trade or Betrayed: Legal Ethical and Conservation Issues* (1995) London: Archetype Publications.

Tunbridge, J.E. and G.J. Ashworth, *Dissonant Heritage: The Management of the Past as a Resource in Conflict* (1996) Chichester/New York/Brisbane/Toronto/Singapore: John Wiley & Sons.

Tunbridge, John, 'Plural and Multicultural Heritages' in Brian Graham and Peter Howard (eds), *The Ashgate Research Companion to Heritage and Identity* (2008) Aldershot: Ashgate, 299.

Tutorow, Norman (ed), *War Crimes, War Criminals and War Crime Trials: An Annotated Bibliography and Source Book* (1986) New York: Greenwood Press.

UNESCO, *The Protection of Movable Cultural Property. Compendium of Legislative Texts* (2 vols) (1984) Paris: UNESCO.

UNESCO, *Conventions and Recommendations of UNESCO concerning the Protection of the Cultural Heritage* (revised ed, 1985) Paris: UNESCO.

UNESCO, *International Dimensions of Humanitarian Law* (1988) Paris/Geneva/Dordrecht: UNESCO – Henry Dunant Institute – Martinus Nijhoff Publishers.

UNESCO, *Memory of the World: Lost Memory – Libraries and Archives Destroyed in the Twentieth Century* (1996) Paris: UNESCO Publishing.

UNESCO, *Cultural Rights and Wrongs* (1998) Paris/London: UNESCO Publishing and Institute of Art and Law.

United Nations, *The Blue Helmets. A Review of United Nations Peacekeeping* (2nd ed, 1990) New York: United Nations.

Vandiver, Pamela et al (eds), *Materials Issues in Art and Archaeology III* (1992) Pittsburgh, Pennsylvania: Materials Research Society.

Vierri, Pietro, *Dictionary of the International Law of Armed Conflict* (1992) ICRC.

Von Hirsh, Andrew et al (eds), *Restorative Justice and Criminal Justice: Competing or Reconcilable Paradigms?* (2003) Oxford: Hart Publishing.

Vrdoljak, Ana, 'Self-Determination and Cultural Rights' in Francesco Francioni and Martin Scheinn (eds), *Cultural Human Rights* (2008) Martinus Nijhoff Online, http://www.nijhoffonline.nl.ezproxy.lib.monash.edu.au/view_pdf?page=1&id=nij978.

Walzer, Michael, *Just and Unjust Wars* (4th ed, 2006) New York: Basic Books.

Wedgwood, Ruth, 'National Courts and the Prosecution of War Crimes' in Gabrielle Kirk McDonald and Olivia Swaak-Goldman (eds), *Substantive and Procedural Aspects of International Criminal Law: The Experience of International and National Courts* (1999) The Hague/London/Boston: Kluwer Law International, BRILL.

Weiss, Edith Brown, *In Fairness to Future Generations: International Law, Common Patrimony, and Intergenerational Equity* (1989) Tokyo: United Nations University.

Williams, Harold, 'Historic Cities: The Sense of Place, Sacred and Secular' in Ismail Serageldin et al (eds), *Historic Cities and Sacred Sites: Cultural Roots for Urban Futures* (2001) World Bank Publications, 401.

Williams, Sharon, *The International and National Protection of Movable Cultural Property: A Comparative Study* (1978) Dobbs Ferry, New York: Oceana Publications.

Wolfrum, Rüdiger, 'Enforcement of International Humanitarian Law' in Dieter Fleck (ed), *The Handbook of Humanitarian Law in Armed Conflict* (1995) New York: Oxford University Press, 517.

Wollen, Peter, *Raiding the Icebox: Reflections on Twentieth-Century Culture* (1993) London/New York: Verso.

Woodward, S., *Balkan Tragedy: Chaos and Dissolution after the Cold War* (1995) Washington, DC: Brookings Institution.

Woudenberg van, Nout, 'Second Protocol to the 1954 Hague Convention – Dutch Involvement' in Paul Meerts (ed), *Culture and International Law* (2008), 167.

Woudenberg van, Nout and Liesbeth Lijnzaad (eds), *Protecting Cultural Property in Armed Conflict: An Insight into the 1999 Second Protocol to the Hague Convention of 1954 for the Protection of Cultural Property in the Event of Armed Conflict* (2010) Leiden/Boston: Martinus Nijhoff Publishers.

Yarwood, John, *Rebuilding Mostar: Urban Reconstruction in a War Zone* (1999) Liverpool, England: Liverpool University Press.

Young, Alison, *Judging the Image: Art, Value, Law* (2004) London/New York: Routledge.

Journal Articles

Abtahi, Hirad, 'The Protection of Cultural Property in Times of Armed Conflict: The Practice of the International Criminal Tribunal for the Former Yugoslavia' (2001) 14 *Harvard Human Rights Journal* 1.

Adams, Nicholas, 'Architecture as the Target' (1993) 52 *Journal of the Society of Architectural Historians* 389.

Akhavan, Payam, 'Justice in The Hague, Peace in the Former Yugoslavia? A Commentary on the United Nations War Crimes Tribunal' (1998) 20 *Human Rights Quarterly* 737.

Aldana-Pindell, Raquel, 'In Vindication of Justiciable Victims' Rights to Truth and Justice for State-Sponsored Crimes' (2002) 35 *Vanderbilt Journal of Transnational Law* 1399.

Ambos, Kai, 'Establishing an International Criminal Court and an International Criminal Code – Observations from an International Criminal Law Viewpoint' (1996) 7 *European Journal of International Law* 519.

Ambos, Kai, 'Joint Criminal Enterprise and Command Responsibility' (2007) 5 *Journal of International Criminal Justice* 159.

Askin, Kelly, 'Reflections on some of the most Significant Achievements of the ICTY' (2003) 37 *New England Law Review* 903.

Bassiouni, Cherif, 'Reflections on Criminal Jurisdiction in International Protection of Cultural Property' (1983) 10 *Syracuse Journal of International Law and Commerce* 281.

Bassiouni, Cherif, 'The United Nations Commission of Experts Established Pursuant to Security Council Resolution 780 (1992)' (1994) 88 *American Journal of International Law* 784.

Bassiouni, Cherif, 'Former Yugoslavia: Investigating Violations of International Humanitarian Law and Establishing an International Criminal Tribunal' (1995) 18 *Fordham International Law Journal* 1191.

Bassiouni, Cherif, 'From Versailles to Rwanda in Seventy-Five Years: The Need to Establish a Permanent International Criminal Court' (1997) 10 *Harvard Human Rights Journal* 11.

Bassiouni, Cherif, 'Combating Impunity for International Crimes' (2000) 71 *University of Colorado Law Review* 409.

Bator, Paul, 'An Essay on the International Trade in Art' (1982) 34 *Stanford Law Review* 275.

Bhat, Ishwara, 'Protection of Cultural Property under International Humanitarian Law: Some Emerging Trends' (2001) 4 *ISIL Year Book of International Humanitarian and Refugee Law*, http://www.worldlii.org/int/journals/ISILBIHRL/2001/4.html.

Blake, Janet, 'On Defining the Cultural Heritage' (2000) 49 *International and Comparative Law Quarterly* 61.

Bogdan, Attila, 'Individual Criminal Responsibility in the Execution of a "Joint Criminal Enterprise" in the Jurisprudence of the *ad hoc* International Tribunal for the Former Yugoslavia' (2006) 6 *International Criminal Law Review* 63.

Bogdanos, Matthew, 'The Casualties of War: The Truth about the Iraq Museum' (2005) 109 *American Journal of Archaeology* 477.

Borodkin, Lisa, 'The Economics of Antiquities Looting and a Proposed Legal Alternative' (1995) 95 *Columbia Law Review* 377.

Byron, Christine, 'Armed Conflicts: International or Non-International?' (2001) 6 *Journal of Conflict and Security Law* 63.

Carnahan, Burrus, 'Lincoln, Lieber and the Laws of War: The Origins and Limits of the Principle of Military Necessity' (1998) 92 *American Journal of International Law* 213.

Caruthers, Claudia, 'International Cultural Property: Another Tragedy of the Commons' (1998) 7 *Pacific Rim Law and Policy Journal* 143.

Cassese, Antonio, 'On the Current Trends towards Criminal Prosecution and Punishment of Breaches of International Humanitarian Law' (1998) 9 *European Journal of International Law* 1.

Cassese, Antonio, 'The Proper Limits of Individual Responsibility under the Doctrine of Joint Criminal Enterprise' (2007) 5 *Journal of International Criminal Justice* 109.

Chadha, Neeru, 'Protection of Cultural Property during Armed Conflict: Recent Developments' (2001) 12 *ISIL Year Book of International Humanitarian and Refugee Law*, http://www.worldlii.org/int/journals/ISILBIHRL/2001/12.html.

Chamberlain, Kevin, 'The Protection of Cultural Property in Armed Conflict' (2003) 8 (2) *Art Antiquity and Law* 209.

Charney, Jonathan, 'The Impact on the International Legal System of the Growth of International Courts and Tribunals' (1999) 31 *New York University Journal of International Law and Politics* 697.

Clément, Étienne, 'Some Recent Practical Experiences in the Implementation of the 1954 Hague Convention' (1994) 3 *International Journal of Cultural Property* 11.

Colwell-Chanthaphonh, Chip and John Piper, 'War and Cultural Property: The 1954 Hague Convention and the Status of US Ratification' (2001) 10 *International Journal of Cultural Property* 217.

Corey, Ian, 'The Fine Line between Policy and Custom: *Prosecutor v Tadić* and the Customary International Law of Internal Armed Conflict' (2000) 166 *Military Law Review* 145.

Cowan, Henry, 'Cities in Conflict' (2007) 50 *Architectural Science Review* 1.

Danner, Allison, 'Constructing a Hierarchy of Crimes in International Criminal Law Sentencing' (2001) 87 *Virginia Law Review* 415.

Danner, Allison and Jenny Martinez, 'Guilty Associations: Joint Criminal Enterprise, Command Responsibility and the Development of International Criminal Law' (2004) Paper 3, International Law Workshop (University of California, Berkeley) (forthcoming *California Law Review* January 2005), http://repositories.cdlib.org/berkeley_ilw/fall2004/3.

Del Ponte, Carla, 'Investigation and Prosecution of Large-Scale Crimes at the International Level' (2006) 4 *Journal of International Criminal Justice* 539.

Desch, Thomas, 'The Second Protocol to the 1954 Hague Convention for the Protection of Cultural Property in the Event of Armed Conflict' (1999) 2 *Yearbook of International Humanitarian Law* 63.

Detling, Karen, 'Eternal Silence: The Destruction of Cultural Property in Yugoslavia' (1993) 17 *The Maryland Journal of International Law & Trade* 41.

Dodds, Jerrilynn, 'Bridge over the Neretva' (1998) 51 *Archaeology* 1.

Doyle, Michael, 'Liberalism and World Politics' (1986) 80 *American Political Science Review* 1151.

Drakulić, Slavenka, 'Falling Down: a Mostar Bridge' (1993) 14(2) *The New Republic* 209.

Eagen, Sarah, 'Preserving Cultural Property: Our Public Duty: A Look at How and Why We Must Create International Laws that Support International Actions' (2001) 13 *Pace International Law Review* 407.

Elsen, Albert, 'Introduction: Why Do We Care about Art?' (1976) 27 *Hastings Law Journal* 951.

Ewins, Tristan, 'Multiculturalism and the False Lure of Moral and Cultural Relativism', 19 September 2002, *Online Journal*, http://www.onlinejournal.com.

Fechner, Frank, 'The Fundamental Aims of Cultural Property Law' (1998) 7 *International Journal of Cultural Property* 376.

Fenrick, William, 'Humanitarian Law and Criminal Trials' (1997) 7 *Transnational Law and Contemporary Problems* 23.

Fenrick, William, 'The Application of the Geneva Conventions by the International Criminal Tribunal for the Former Yugoslavia' (30 June 1999) No. 834 *International Review of the Red Cross* 317.

Forbes, Stephanie, 'Securing the Future of Our Past: Current Efforts to Protect Cultural Property' (1996) 9 *Transnational Lawyer* 235.

Francioni, Francesco and Federico Lenzerini, 'The Destruction of the Buddhas of Bamiyan and International Law' (2003) 14 *European Journal of International Law* 619.

Frid, Alexander, 'The Common Heritage Doctrine and the Treatment of Cultural Property: History, Theory, and Practice' (1998) *University of California Undergraduate Research Journal* 1.

Frigo, Manlio, 'Cultural Property v Cultural Heritage: A "Battle of Concepts" in International Law?' (2004) 86 *International Review of the Red Cross* 367.

Gallant, Kenneth, 'Jurisdiction to Adjudicate and Jurisdiction to Prescribe in International Criminal Courts' (2003) 4 *Villanova Law Review* 763.

Gardam, Judith, 'Proportionality and Force in International Law' (1993) 87 *American Journal of International Law* 391.

Gattini, Andrea, 'Restitution by Russia of Works of Art Removed from German Territory at the End of the Second World War' (1996) 7 *European Journal of International Law* 67.

Gersenblith, Patty, 'Identity and Cultural Property' (1995) 75 *Boston University Law Review* 559.

Greppi, Edoardo, 'The Evolution of Individual Criminal Responsibility under International Law' (1999) No 835 *International Review of the Red Cross* 531.

Grodach, Carl, 'Reconstituting Identity and History in Post-War Mostar, Bosnia and Herzegovina', (2002) 6 *City* 61.

Hamber, Brandon, 'Living with the Legacy of Impunity: Lessons for South Africa about Truth, Justice and Crime in Brazil' (1997) 13 *Latin American Report* 4.

Hamdorf, Kai, 'The Concept of a Joint Criminal Enterprise and Domestic Modes of Liability for Parties to a Crime' (2007) 5 *Journal of International Criminal Justice* 208.

Hamilton, Marci, 'Four Questions about Art' (1994) 13 *Cardozo Arts and Entertainment* 119.

Harding, Sarah, 'Value, Obligation and Cultural Heritage' (1999) 31 *Arizona State Law Journal* 291.

Haunton, Marion, 'Peacekeeping, Occupation and Cultural Property' (1993) 4 *Humanitäres Völkerrecht – Informations – Schriften* (Bonn, German Red Cross) 199.

Hazan, P., 'The Revolution by the ICTY: The Concept of Justice in Wartime' (2004) 2 *Journal of International Criminal Justice* 533.

Henckaerts, Jean-Marie, 'New Rules for the Protection of Cultural Property in Armed Conflict' (1999) 81 *International Review of the Red Cross* 593-620, reproduced in María Teresa Dutli, *Protection of Cultural Property in the Event of Armed Conflict: Report on the Meeting of Experts (Geneva, 5-6 October 2000)* (February 2002) Geneva: International Committee of the Red Cross (ICRC) Advisory Service on International Humanitarian Law, 27.

Henckaerts, Jean-Marie, 'The Significance of the Second Protocol to the 1954 Hague Convention for the Protection of Cultural Property in the Event of Armed Conflict' (1999) No. 835 *International Review of the Red Cross* 593.

Hladík, Jan, 'Information on the Implementation of the Convention for the Protection of Cultural Property in the Event of Armed Conflict (The Hague) 1954-1995 Reports' (1997) 6 *International Journal of Cultural Property* 417.

Hladík, Jan, 'The Third Meeting of the High Contracting Parties to the Hague Convention for the Protection of Cultural Property in the Event of Armed Conflict of 1954 (Paris, November 13, 1997)' (1998) 7 *International Journal of Cultural Property* 268.

Hladík, Jan, 'The 1954 Hague Convention for the Protection of Cultural Property in the Event of Armed Conflict and the Notion of Military Necessity' (1999) 81 *International Review of the Red Cross* 621.

Hladík, Jan, 'Diplomatic Conference on the Second Protocol to the Hague Convention for the Protection of Cultural Property in the Event of Armed Conflict, The Hague, Netherlands (March 15-26, 1999)' (1999) 8 *International Journal of Cultural Property* 526.

Hladík, Jan, 'Second Partnership for Peace Workshop on the Protection of Cultural Property, Klagenfurt, Austria (4-7 October 1999)' (2000) 9 *International Journal of Cultural Property* 164.

Hladík, Jan, 'Reporting System under the 1954 Convention for the Protection of Cultural Property in the Event of Armed Conflict' (2000) 82 *International Review of the Red Cross* 1001.

Hladík, Jan, 'The NATO/PfP Seminar "Protection of Cultural Property in the Event of Armed Conflict – A Challenge in Peace Support Operations" Bregenz, Austria (24-28 September 2001)' (2002) 11 *International Journal of Cultural Property* 166.

Hladík, Jan, 'Marking of Cultural Property with the Distinctive Emblem of the 1954 Hague Convention for the Protection of Cultural Property in the Event of Armed Conflict' (2004) 86 *International Review of the Red Cross* 379.

Hladík, Jan, 'The UNESCO Declaration concerning the Intentional Destruction of Cultural Heritage' (2004) 9 *Art Antiquity and Law* 215.

Jacovides, Andrew, 'International Tribunals: Do They Really Work for Small States?' (2001) 34 *New York University Journal of International Law and Politics* 253.

Jochnick, Chris af and Roger Normand, 'The Legitimation of Violence: A Critical History of the Laws of War' (1994) 35 *Harvard International Law Journal* 49.

Jonas, Stacie, 'The Ripple Effect of the Pinochet Case' Global Policy Forum (2004) 11 (3) *Human Rights Brief* 36.

Jorda, C., 'The Major Hurdles and Accomplishments of the ICTY' (2004) 2 *Journal of International Criminal Justice* 572.

Kalshoven, Frits, 'The Undertaking to Respect and Ensure Respect in All Circumstance: From Tiny Seed to Ripening Fruit' (1999) 2 *Yearbook of International Humanitarian Law* 3.

Kalshoven, Frits, 'The Protection of Cultural Property in the Event of Armed Conflict' (2005) 57 *Museum International* 61.

Karlen, P.H., 'What is Art?: A Sketch for a Legal Definition' (1978) 94 *Law Quarterly Review* 383.

Kastenberg, Joshua, 'The Legal Regime for Protecting Cultural Property during Armed Conflict' (1997) 42 *The Air Force Law Review* 277.

Kingsbury, Benedict, 'Foreword: Is the Proliferation of International Courts and Tribunals a Systemic Problem? (1999) 31 *New York University Journal of International Law and Politics* 679.

Lachs, Manfred, 'The Defences of Culture' (1985) 37 *Museum* 167.

Lemkin, Raphaël, 'Genocide' (April 1946) 15 (2) *American Scholar* 227.

Lippman, Matthew, 'The Other Nuremberg: American Prosecutions of Nazi War Criminals in Occupied Germany' (1992) 3 *Indiana International and Comparative Law Review* 1.

Lippman, Matthew, 'Art and Ideology in the Third Reich: The Protection of Cultural Property and the Humanitarian Law of War' (1998) 17 *Dickinson Journal of International Law* 1.

Manhart, Cristian, 'UNESCO's Mandate and Recent Activities for the Rehabilitation of Afghanistan's Cultural Heritage' (2004) 86 *International Review of the Red Cross* 401.

Mastalir, Roger, 'A Proposal for Protecting the "Cultural" and "Property" Aspects of Cultural Property under International Law' (1993) 16 *Fordham International Law Journal* 1033.

Matyk, Stephen, 'The Restitution of Cultural Objects and the Question of Giving Direct Effect to the Protocol to the Hague Convention for the Protection of Cultural Property in the Event of Armed Conflict 1954' (2000) 9 *International Journal of Cultural Property* 341.

McAuliffe deGuzman, Margaret, 'The Road from Rome: The Developing Law of Crimes against Humanity' (2000) 22 *Human Rights Quarterly* 335.

McDonald Kirk, Gabrielle, 'Problems, Obstacles and Achievements of the ICTY' (2004) 2 *Journal of International Criminal Justice* 558.

Meharg, Sarah, 'Identicide and Cultural Cannibalism: Warfare's Appetite for Symbolic Place', (2001) 33 *Peace Research Journal* 89.

Meron, Theodor, 'The Continuing Role of Custom in the Formation of International Humanitarian Law' (1996) 90 *American Journal of International Law* 238.

Meron, Theodor, 'The Protection of Cultural Property in the Event of Armed Conflict within the Case-Law of the International Criminal Tribunal for the Former Yugoslavia' (2005) 57 *Museum International* 41.

Merryman, John, 'International Art Law: From Cultural Nationalism to a Common Cultural Heritage' (1983) 15 *New York University Journal of International Law and Politics* 757.

Merryman, John, 'Two Ways of Thinking about Cultural Property' (1986) 80 *American Journal of International Law* 831.

Merryman, John, 'The Public Interest in Cultural Property' (1989) 77 *California Law Review* 339.

Merryman, John, 'The UNIDROIT Convention: Three Significant Departures from the Urtext' (1996) 5 *International Journal of Cultural Property* 1.

Merryman, John, 'The Free International Movement of Cultural Property' (1998) 31 *New York University Journal of International Law and Politics* 1.

Meyer, David, 'The 1954 Hague Cultural Property Convention and its Emergence into Customary International Law' (1993) 11 *Boston University International Law Journal* 349.

Mose, Gregory, 'The Destruction of Churches and Mosques in Bosnia-Herzegovina: Seeking a Rights-Based Approach to the Protection of Religious Cultural Property' (1996) 3 *Buffalo Journal of International Law* 180.

Moustakas, John, 'Group Rights in Cultural Property: Justifying Strict Inalienability' (1989) 74 *Cornell Law Review* 1179.

Müller, Markus, 'Cultural Heritage Protection: Legitimacy, Property, and Functionalism' (1998) 7 *International Journal of Cultural Property* 395.

Mundis, Daryl, 'New Mechanisms for the Enforcement of International Humanitarian Law' (2001) 95 *American Journal of International Law* 934.

Murphy, Sean, 'Progress and Jurisprudence of the International Criminal Tribunal for the Former Yugoslavia' (1999) 93 *American Journal of International Law* 57.

Myerowitz, Elissa, 'Protecting Cultural Property during a Time of War: Why Russia Should Return Nazi-Looted Art?' (1997) 20 *Fordham International Law Journal* 1961.

Nafziger, James, 'UNESCO-Centered Management of International Conflict over Cultural Property' (1976) 27 *Hastings Law Journal* 1051.

Nafziger, James, 'Comments on the Relevance of Law and Culture to Cultural Property Law' (1983) 10 *Syracuse Journal of International Law and Commerce* 323.

Nafziger, James, 'International Penal Aspects of Protecting Cultural Property' (1985) 19 *International Lawyer* 835.

Nafziger, James, 'Protection of Cultural Property and Archaeological Resources: A Comprehensive Bibliography of Law-Related Materials' (1990) 22 *Case Western Reserve Journal of International Law* 1.

Nahlik, Stanislaw, 'Des crimes contre les biens culturels' (1959) 29 *Annuaire de l'Association des auditeurs et anciens auditeurs de l'Académie de droit international de La Haye* 14.

Nahlik, Stanislaw, 'On Some Deficiencies of The Hague Convention of 1954 on the Protection of Cultural Property in the Event of Armed Conflict' (1974) 44 *Annuaire de l'A.A.A.* 100.

Nahlik, Stanislaw, 'International Law and the Protection of Cultural Property in Armed Conflict' (1976) 27 *Hastings Law Journal* 1069.

Nieć, Halina, 'Legislative Models of Protection of Cultural Property' (1976) 27 *Hastings Law Journal* 1089.

Niec, Halina, 'The "Human Dimension" of the Protection of Cultural Property in the Event of Armed Conflict' (1993) 4 *Humanitäres Völkerrecht – Informations – Schriften* (Bonn, German Red Cross) 204.

Parks, William, 'Command Responsibility for War Crimes' (1973) 62 *Military Law Review* 1.

Ohlin, Jens, 'Three Conceptual Problems with the Doctrine of Joint Criminal Enterprise' (2007) 5 *Journal of International Criminal Justice* 69.

O'Keefe, Patrick, 'The First Protocol to the Hague Convention Fifty Years on' (2004) 9 *Art Antiquity and Law* 99.

O'Keefe, Roger, 'The Meaning of "Cultural Property" under the 1954 Hague Convention' (1999) XLVI *Netherlands International Law Review* 26.

O'Keefe, Roger, 'Protection of Cultural Property under International Criminal Law' (2010) 11 *Melbourne Journal of International Law* 339.

Osiel, Mark, 'Obeying Orders: Atrocity, Military Discipline, and the Law of War' (1998) 86 *California Law Review* 939.

Oyer, Harvey, 'The 1954 Hague Convention' (1999) 23 *Columbia-VLA Journal of Law and the Arts* 49.

Özkan, Suha, 'The Destruction of Stari Most' (1994) 14 *Development Network* 5.

Patt, Jodi, 'The Need to Revamp Current Domestic Protection for Cultural Property' (2002) 96 *Northwestern University Law Review* 1207.

Paust, Jordan, 'Applicability of International Criminal Laws to Events in the Former Yugoslavia' (1994) 9 *American Journal of International Law* 499.

Pejić, Jelena, 'Accountability for International Crimes: From Conjecture to Reality' (2002) 84 *International Review of the Red Cross* 13.

Phelan, Marilyn, 'The UNIDROIT Convention on Stolen or Illegally Exported Cultural Objects Confirm Separate Property Status for Cultural Treasures' (Symposium: Reclamation of Cultural Property on the International Front: Is Home Where the Art Is?) (1998) 5 *Villanova Sports and Entertainment Law Journal* 31.

Phelan, Marilyn, 'Cultural Property' (2000) 34 *International Lawyer* 697.

Peskin, Victor, 'International Justice and Domestic Rebuilding' (2000) *The Journal of Humanitarian Assistance*, 3.

Pillai, Shivanii and Hyder Gulam, 'Protecting Cultural Property' (2004) 78 *Law Institute Journal* 66.

Piper John and Chip Colwell-Chanthaph, 'War and Cultural Property: The 1954 Hague Convention and the Status of U.S. Ratification' (2001) 10 *International Journal of Cultural Property* 217.

Pocar, Fausto, 'The Proliferation of International Criminal Courts and Tribunals' (2004) 2 *Journal of International Criminal Justice* 304.

Powles, S., 'Joint Criminal Enterprise' (2004) 2 *Journal of International Criminal Justice* 606.

Prott, Lyndel, 'International Control of Illicit Movement of the Cultural Heritage: The 1970 UNESCO Convention and Some Possible Alternatives' (1983) 10 *Syracuse Journal of International Law and Commerce* 333.

Prott, Lyndel, 'Problems of Private International Law for the Protection of the Cultural Heritage' (1989) 217 *Recueil des cours* 215.

Prott, Lyndel and Patrick O'Keefe, '"Cultural Heritage" or "Cultural Property"?' (1992) 1 *International Journal of Cultural Property* 307.

Prott, Lyndel, 'The Protocol to the Convention for the Protection of Cultural Property in the Event of Armed Conflict (The Hague Convention) 1954' (1993) 4 *Humanitäres Völkerrecht – Informations – Schriften* (Bonn, German Red Cross) 191.

Prott, Lyndel and Jan Hladík, 'The Fourth Meeting of the High Contracting Parties to the Hague Convention for the Protection of Cultural Property in the Event of Armed Conflict, 1954, Paris, France (November 18, 1999)' (2000) 9 *International Journal of Cultural Property* 172.

Prott, Lyndel, 'The International Movement of Cultural Objects' (2005) 12 *International Journal of Cultural Property* 225.

Romano, Cesare, 'The Proliferation of International Judicial Bodies: The Pieces of the Puzzle' (1999) 31 *New York University Journal of International Law and Politics* 709.

Rosenberg, Jack, 'UN to Prosecute Culture Crimes' (1994) 82 *Art in America* 2.

Rosenne, Shabtai, 'The Jurisdiction of the International Criminal Court' (1999) 2 *Yearbook of International Humanitarian Law* 119.

Roussin, Lucille, 'Cultural Heritage and Identity' (2003) 11 *Cardozo Journal of International and Comparative Law* 707.

Sagoff, Mark, 'We Have Met the Enemy and He Is Us or Conflict and Contradiction in Environmental Law' (1982) 12 *Environmental Law* 283.

Sax, Joseph, 'Heritage Preservation as a Public Duty: The Abbe Gregoire and the Origins of an Idea' (1990) 88 *Michigan Law Review* 1142.

Schmitt, Michael, 'Targeting and Humanitarian Law: Current Issues' (2004) 34 *Israel Yearbook on Human Rights* 59.

Seršić, Maja, 'Protection of Cultural Property in Time of Armed Conflict' (1996) 27 *Netherlands Yearbook of International Law* 3.

Simpson, Graeme, 'Reconstruction and Reconciliation' (1997) 7 *Development in Practice* 475.

Stephens, Dale and Mike Lewis, 'The Law of Armed Conflict – A Contemporary Critique' (2005) 6 *Melbourne Journal of International Law* 55.

Stewart, James, 'Towards a Single Definition of Armed Conflict in International Humanitarian Law: A Critique of Internationalized Armed Conflict' (2003) 85 *International Review of the Red Cross* 313.

Symonides, Janusz, 'Towards the Amelioration of the Protection of Cultural Property in Times of Armed Conflict: Recent UNESCO Initiatives concerning the 1954 Hague Convention' (1997) 2 *Human Person and International Law*, Bruylant, Bruxelles, 1533.

Šljivić, Ana, 'Why Do You Think It's Yours? An Exposition of the Jurisprudence Underlying the Debate between Cultural Nationalism and Cultural Internationalism' (1998) 31 *George Washington Journal of International Law and Economics* 393.

Teitel, Ruti, 'Transitional Justice Genealogy' (2003) 16 *Harvard Human Rights Journal* 69.

Teitel, Ruti, 'Transitional Justice in a New Era' (2003) 26 *Fordham International Law Journal* 893.

The Human Rights Centre and the International Human Rights Law Clinic, University of California, Berkeley, and the Centre for Human Rights, University of Sarajevo, Report: 'Justice, Accountability and Social Reconstruction: An Interview Study of Bosnia Judges and Prosecutors' (2000) 18 *Berkeley Journal of International Law* 102.

Thomason, Douglas, 'Rolling Back History: The United Nations General Assembly and the Right to Cultural Property' (1990) 22 *Case Western Reserve Journal of International Law* 47.

Toman, Jiří, 'The Hague Convention – A Decisive Step Taken by the International Community' (2005) No. 228 *Museum International* 7.

Vernon, Catherine, 'Common Cultural Property: The Search for Rights of Protective Intervention' (1994) 26 *Case Western Reserve Journal of International Law*, 435.

Wangkeo, Kanchana, 'Monumental Challenges: The Lawfulness of Destroying Cultural Heritage during Peacetime' (2003) 28 *Yale Journal of International Law* 183.

Warbrick, Colin, Elena Martin Salgado and Nicholas Goodwin, 'The Pinochet Cases in the United Kingdom' (1999) 2 *Yearbook of International Humanitarian Law* 91.

Van der Wilt, Harmen, 'Joint Criminal Enterprise: Possibilities and Limitations' (2007) 5 *Journal of International Criminal Justice* 91.

Yarwood, John, 'Cultural Warfare' (2003) 8 *Art Antiquity and Law* 191.

Zgonjanin, Sanja, 'The Prosecution of War Crimes for the Destruction of Libraries and Archives during Times of Armed Conflict' (2005) 40 *Libraries and Culture* 128.

Military Manuals

Instructions on the Implementation of the International Law of War in the Armed Forces of the Republic of Bosnia and Herzegovina, Official Gazette of ABH, No. 2/92, 5 December 1992.

Compendium 'Law of Armed Conflicts – Commanders' Manual, Republic of Croatia, Ministry of Defence, 1992.

Rules of Conduct for Soldiers, Republic of Croatia, Ministry of Defence, 1992.

Instructions 'Basic Rules of International Humanitarian Law Applicable in Armed Conflicts', Republic of Croatia, Ministry of Defence, 1993.

Newspaper/Magazine Articles

Associated Press, 'Ethnic Strife Destroys Mostar's Symbol of Diversity' *The San Francisco Chronicle* (San Francisco), 10 November 1993, A10 1993 WL 6434487, http://web2westlaw.com/result/text.wl?RecreatePath=Search/default.wl&RS-WLW2.6.

Associated Press and New York Times News Service, 'Mortar Fire Kills Nine Sarajevo Schoolchildren' *San Diego Union-Tribune* (San Diego), 10 November 1993, A17 1993 WL 11765221, http://web2.westlaw.com/result/text.wl.

Bajruši, Robert, 'Slobodan Praljak under ICTY Investigation' *Nacional* (Croatia) 26 April 2001, http://www.nacional.hr.htm/284052.en.htm.

'Balkans: Trying War Criminals "Precondition for Reconciliation" Says Conference', *Kronos International* 9 February 2007, http://www.adki.com/index_2Level_Englich.php?cat=Politics&loid=8.385105538&par=0.

Bevan, Robert, 'Heritage Caught in the Crossfire' *The Australian* (Sydney), 24 March 2006, http://www.theaustralian.news.com.au/common/story_page/0,5744,18580641%2555E16947,00.html.

Block, Robert, 'Croatian Death Squad Talks Tough around the Pool Table' *The Independent* (London), 6 September 1993.

Boylan, Patrick, 'We Need Greater Punishment for Cultural Property Crimes' *The Art Newspaper* (London), No 162, October 2005, http://www.theartnewspaper.com.

'Closing in – International Justice' *The Economist* (London) 27 October 2007, http://listserv.buffalo.edu/archives/justwatch-l.html.

Edwards, Steven, 'PM Backs UN's Right to Invade: Five-Point Plan Would Enable World Body to "Intervene Much Faster in Situations like Darfur"' *National Post* (Canada), 23 September 2004.

George, Rose, 'Story of Bridges' *Independent on Sunday Review*, 18 November 2001, http://www.rosegeorge.com/frameworks/generic/public_users/morearticles.asp?Articl.

Harris, Lucian, 'US Snipers on Samarra's Spiral Minaret', *The Art Newspaper* (London), 25 February 2005, http://www.theartnewspaper.com/news/article.asp?idart=11727.

HIC News, 'Dovršava se istraga protiv trojice bivših pripadnika HVO-a: O rušiteljima Starog mosta odlučuje Haag' ('An Investigation into Three Ex-Members of the HVO Is Coming to an End: The Hague Decides about the Destroyers of the Old Bridge') *H, Večernji list* (Croatia), 23 May 2001, 13, http://www.hic.hr/hrvatski/vijesti/arhiv/latest/BiH_-_POLITIKA_23_5_2001.

HINA, 'Praljak: Nije bilo dogovora sa Srbima oko Mostara' (Praljak: There was no Deal with the Serbs about Mostar'), *Klik Magazin* (Croatia), 16 March 2004, http://www.klik.hr/naslovnica/politika/20020430002029.html.

Hooper, John, 'UNESCO's "Blue Berets" to Rescue Cultural Treasures' *The Guardian* (UK), 28 October 2004, http://www.guardian.co.uk/international/story/0,,1337570,00.html.

Ignatieff, Michael, 'When a Bridge Is Not a Bridge' *The New York Times* (New York), 27 October 2002, http://www.nytimes.com/2002/10/27/magazine/27MOSTAR.html.

Koïchiro Matsuura, 'Why We Need the Old Bridge at Mostar' *International Herald Tribune* 20 July 2004.

Lippman, Peter, 'Bridge Can't Heal Bosnia Divisions' *The Seattle Times* (Seattle), Editorials and Opinion, 23 July 2004, http://listserv.buffalo.edu/archives/justwatch-l.html.

Liptak, Adam, 'When Letter of the Law Does Not Spell "Clarity"' *The New York Times* (New York), 1 May 2002, http://www.nytimes.com/2002/05/01/international/middleeast/01LAW.html.

Malić, Gordan, 'Herceg Camp' *Feral Tribune* (Split, Croatia), 29 April 1996, http://free.freespeech.org/ex-yupress/feral/feral31.html.

Mlivončić, Ivica, 'Neretvanske obale samo će istina spojiti' ('Only the Truth Will Connect the Neretva's Banks') *Matica* (Croatia), No 8–9 2004.

Nettelfield, Lara and Sarah Wagner, 'Bosnia's Muslims Still Cry out for Justice' *The Globe and Mail* (Toronto), 12 July 2005.

'Over 80 People Sentenced over Kosovo March Violence so far – UNMIK' *Koha Ditore* (Priština), 3 October 2004, 1, 3.

Pomfret, John, 'A Bridge Becomes a Wedge as Span Crumbles, Unity Dreams Die' *The Seattle Times* (Seattle) 30 August 1993, A3 1993 WL 6014999, http://web2westlaw.com/.

Rogošić, Željko, 'A Shocking New Book on Mostar: Experts Claim: The Bridge Was Not Destroyed by the HVO' *Nacional* (Croatia), 23 February 2006, http://nacional.hr/hr/articles/view/23364.

Schwartz, Amy, 'Is It Wrong to Weep for Buildings?' *Washington Post* (Washington), 19 May 1994, 17.

Sudetić, Chuck, 'Croatians Destroy Historic Ottoman Bridge in Bosnia' *New York Times* (New York), 9 November 1993, http://www.members.tripod.com/~UnconqueredBosnia/Mostar3.html.

TANJUG, 'Tuđman's Stenographs Confirm Joint Criminal Enterprise' *Tanjug*, 4 October 2004, http://www.tfeagle.army.mil/tfeno/Feature_Story.asp?Article=81820.

'The Hague Prepares New Accusations against Herzegovinian Croats' *Glas Srpski* (Banja Luka, Bosnia and Herzegovina), 30 December 1998, posted to Justwatch Discussion List by Frank Tiggelaar, 31 December 1998, http://listserv.buffalo.edu/archives/justwatch-l.html.

Tjednik, Interview with General Slobodan Praljak, 'People Are Guilty, Not Blaškić or Kordić' *Tjednik* (Zagreb, Croatia), 9 May 1997, http://free.freespeech.org/ex-Yupress/tjednik/tjednik1.html.

Tjednik, Interview with Stjepan Mesić, the last chairman of the former Yugoslavia Presidency and the current President of Croatia, 'Division of Bosnia was Tuđman's Only Option', *Tjednik* (Zagreb, Croatia), 16 May 1997, translated on 21 February 2001, http://www.cdsp.neu.edu/info/students/marko/tjednik/tjednik2.html.

Traynor, Ian, 'Shells Destroy Mostar Bridge' *Guardian* (UK), 19 November 1993, 10.

Wald, Patricia, 'UN Should Stay the Course in The Hague' *The Korea Herald* (Korea), 10 November 2007, http://listserv.buffalo.edu/archives/justwatch-l.html.

War Truth Conference, 'Del Ponte: Tuđman's Transcripts Valuable Evidence', *Javno* (Croatia) 9 February 2007, http://www.javno.com/en/croatia/clanak.php?id=19703.

Williams, Carol, 'Destruction of Landmark Mostar Span Felt Deeply – Warring Foes United in Grief' *The Seattle Times* (Seattle), 14 November 1993, A3 1993 WL 6027206, http://web2.westlaw.com/.

Yuenger, James, 'Crossing into History War Brings Down a Bridge that Spanned Centuries and Linked Memories' *Chicago Tribune* (Chicago), 25 November 1993.

Press Releases

Agence France Presse, 'Croat General Shows No Regret for Shelling of Mostar Bridge', 23 July 2004, http://listserv.buffalo.edu/archives/justwatch-l.html.

Deutsche Presse-Agentur, 'US Ambassador for War Crimes Issues Visits Bosnia' 13 June 2007, http://listserv.buffalo.edu/archives/justwatch-l.html.

HINA Croatian News Agency, '13 000 People Suspected of Committing War Crimes in Bosnia, Public Prosecutor Says', 1 June 2006, http://listserv.buffalo.edu/archives/justwatch-l.html.

ICTY, 'Address by Carla Del Ponte, Prosecutor of the International Criminal Tribunal for the Former Yugoslavia to the Security Council 13 June 2005' (Press Release, Office of the Prosecutor, The Hague, 13 June 2005, CDP/MOW/977-e), http://www.un.org/icty/.

ICTY, 'Statement by Judge Theodor Meron, President, International Criminal Tribunal for the Former Yugoslavia, to the Security Council 13 June 2005' (Press Release, President, The Hague, 13 June 2005, TM/MOW/976e), http://www.un.org/icty/latest/index.htm.

ICTY, 'President Pocar Updates Security Council on Tribunal's Mission and Completion Strategy' (Press Release, The Hague, 7 May 2006, LM/MOW/1084e), <http://www.un.org/icty/pressreal/2006/p1084-e.htm>.

ICTY, 'Prosecutor Del Ponte's Address before the Security Council' (Press Release, The Hague, 18 June 2007, OK/MOW/1166e), http://www.un.org/icty/pressreal/2007/pr1166e.htm.

ICTY Referral Bench, 'Vladimir Kovačević Case Referred to Serbia' (Press Release, The Hague, 17 November 2006, CVO/MOW/1127e), http://www.un.org/icty/pressreal/2006/p1127-e.htm.

International Committee of the Red Cross, 'Cultural Property: Respect for People's Dignity Includes Respect for their Culture' (Press Release 04/11, 13 February 2004), http://www.icrc.org/web/eng/siteengo.nsf/html/5W5JU9.

International Criminal Court, 'The Office of the Prosecutor of the International Criminal Court Opens its First Investigation' (Press Release, 23 June 2004), http://www.icc-cpi.int/pressrelease_details&id=26&1=en.html.

Security Council, 'Security Council Stresses Importance, Urgency of Restoring Rule of Law in Post-Conflict Societies – Presidential Statement Follows Day-Long Debate', Security Council 5052nd Meeting (AM & PM) (Press Release, SC/8209, 6 October 2004).

Sense News Agency, 'Ljubičić and Rajić Opposed to BH Trial' 20 September 2005, http://www.sense-agency.com/portal/english/index.php?sta=3&pid=6970.

Sense News Agency, 'Del Ponte Duels with Churkin in Security Council', ICTY, The Hague, 19 June 2007, http://www.sense-agency.com/en/sream.php?sta=3&pid=9866&kat=3.

UNESCO Bureau of Public Information, 'UNESCO-Italy Agreement on Emergency Actions to Protect Heritage' (Press Release No. 2004-97, 28 October 2004).

United Nations in Vienna, 'Security Council Briefed on Establishment of War Crimes Chamber within State Court of Bosnia and Herzegovina', SC/7888 (Press Release, 9 October 2003), http://www.unis.unvienna.org/unis/pressrels/2003/sc7888.html.

UN News Service, 'UNESCO and Italy Sign Pact to Handle Heritage Emergencies' (Press Release, 29 October 2004), http://www.un.org/news.

UN News Service, 'UN Conference Seeks 40 Million to Restore Cultural Heritage Sites in Kosovo' (Press Release, 13 May 2005), http://www.un.org/news.

UN News Service, 'General Assembly Hears Appeals by Tribunal Judges to "Keep Doors Open" until All War Criminals in Rwanda, Balkans Are Brought to Justice', (Press Release, 10 October 2006) http://www.un.org/news.

Reports

American Commission for the Protection and Salvage of Artistic and Historic Monuments in War Areas, *Report 48* (1946), Staff Orders issued by the Commander-in-Chief of the Allied Forces, General Eisenhower on 29 December 1943.

Balkan Investigative Reporting Network (BIRN) Justice Reports (available at www.birn.eu.com):

- Ahmetašević, Nidžara and Mirna Mekić, 'The Future of War Crimes Trials' BIRN Justice Report, 18 November 2006.
- Ahmetašević, Nidžara, 'Between Truth and Politics', BIRN Justice Report, 29 June 2006.
- Ahmetašević, Nidžara, 'Criminal Code Confusion Casts Doubt on War Crimes Justice' BIRN Justice Report, 7 July 2006.
- BIRN, 'Hunger Strikers Call for Law Harmonisation', BIRN Justice Report, 5 January 2007.
- BIRN, 'Hunger Strikers Call for Harmonization' BIRN Justice Report, 9 January 2007.
- BIRN, 'Bosnian Minister Urges War Crimes Law Reform' BIRN Justice Report, 24 September 2007.
- Jelačić, Nerma, 'If Truth Commissions Are to Do Any Good, their Relationship to Existing Courts Must Be Sorted out First', BIRN Justice Report, 31 August 2006.
- Mekić, Mirna, 'Indictees "on Hunger Strike"', BIRN Justice Report, 9 January 2007.

Boylan, Patrick, 'The Legal Background to Protection of Cultural Heritage', Expert Report 5, http://ww.unseco.org/webworld/archives/sro_citra/ER5.html.

Council of Europe, Parliamentary Assembly, Committee on Culture and Education Reports (COE Reports) (available at http://assembly.coe.int):

- *Information Reports on the Destruction by War of the Cultural Heritage in Croatia and Bosnia and Herzegovina*:
  - *First Information Report*, Doc 6756, 2 February 1993.

  - *Second Information Report*, Doc 6869, 17 July 1993.
  - *Third Information Report*, Doc 6904, 20 September 1993.
  - *Fourth Information Report*, Doc 6999, 19 January 1994.
  - *Fifth Information Report*, Doc 7070, 12 April 1994.
  - *Seventh Information Report*, Doc 7308, 15 May 1995.
  - *Eighth Information Report*, Doc 7341, 28 June 1995.
- *Report on Looted Jewish Cultural Property*, Doc 8563, 6 October 1999 (Rapporteur: Mr Emanuelis Zingeris, Lithuania, European Democratic Group)

Dutli, María Teresa, *Protection of Cultural Property in the Event of Armed Conflict: Report on the Meeting of Experts (Geneva, 5-6 October 2000)* (February 2002) Geneva: International Committee of the Red Cross (ICRC) Advisory Service on International Humanitarian Law.

Final Report of the United Nations Commission of Experts Established Pursuant to Security Council Resolution 780 (1992), Annex XI: Destruction of Cultural Property Report, Annex XI.A. The Battle of Dubrovnik and the Law of Armed Conflict, S/1994/674/Add.2 (Vol. V) 28 December 1994.

Herscher, Andrew and Andras Riedlmayer, 'The Destruction and Reconstruction of Architectural Heritage in Kosovo: A Post-War Report' (October-December 2000) No. 19/20 *Bosnia Report*, http://www.bosnia.org.uk/bosrep/report_format.cfm.

Herscher, Andrew and András Riedlmayer, 'The Destruction of Cultural Heritage in Kosovo, 1998-1999: A Post-War Survey' (2001) Kosovo Cultural Heritage Project, Cambridge, Massachusetts USA., Report presented as Prosecution evidence in the *Milošević* case, ICTY.

Human Rights Watch Reports (available at http://hrw.org/reports/):
- 'War Crimes Trials in the Former Yugoslavia' June 1995, vol. 7, No. 10, *Human Rights Watch*.
- 'Chile – When Tyrants Tremble: The Pinochet Case' October 1999, vol. 11, No., 1(B), *Human Rights Watch*.
- 'International Justice', World Report 2001, *Human Rights Watch*.
- Dicker, Richard and Elise Keppler, 'Beyond The Hague: The Challenges of International Justice', World Report 2004, *Human Rights Watch*.
- 'Justice at Risk: War Crimes Trials in Croatia, Bosnia and Herzegovina, and Serbia and Montenegro', October 2004, *Human Rights Watch*.
- 'Looking for Justice: The War Crimes Chamber in Bosnia and Herzegovina', 8 February 2006, vol. 18, No. 1(D), *Human Rights Watch*.

Institute for Protection of Cultural Monuments, 'War Damage and Destruction Inflicted on the Culture, Monuments, Sites and Historical Centres in Croatia', Preliminary Report, Zagreb, Ministry of Education, Culture and Sports, 2 April 1992.

Institute for Protection of Cultural Monuments, 'War Damage on Cultural Heritage in Croatia: Damage and Destruction in May and June 1992', Zagreb, Ministry of Education, Culture and Sports.

Institute for War and Peace Reporting (IWPR) (available at http://www.iwpr.net/):

- Alić, Aida, Aida Šunje and Hugh Griffiths, 'Courting Controversy in Bosnia' IWPR's Balkan Crisis Report, No. 562, 27 June 2005.
- Anderson, Janet, 'Nuremberg-Style Trial Planned for Bosnia's Worst Atrocity', IWPR's Tribunal Update No. 414, 9 July 2005.
- Barron, Daniel, 'Yugoslav Tribunal Takes International Justice from Theory to Practice', IWPR's Tribunal Update, No. 514 Part 1, 23 August 2007.
- Boyle, Katherine, 'Bosnia: A House Divided' IWPR's Tribunal Update No. 484, 12 January 2007.
- Bullough, Oliver, 'Transcripts Suggest Croatia Conspired to Break up Bosnia' IWPR's Tribunal Update No. 524, 2 November 2007.
- Clifford, Lisa and Caroline Tosh, 'Prosecution and Defence Lawyers Object to Interventions by Judges', IWPR's Tribunal Update No. 494, 23 March 2007.
- Glassborow, Katy, 'Making Justice Matter – War Crimes Courts Invest in Outreach Programmes to Better Communicate their Work to Victims and their Communities', IWPR's Tribunal Update No. 487, 2 February 2007.
- Džidić, Denis, 'Tribunal Urged to Continue Beyond 2010 – Experts Say Local Courts Not Robust Enough to Try Defendants as High-Profile as Karadžić and Mladić', IWPR's Tribunal Update No. 520, 5 October 2007.
- Griffiths, Hugh, 'Bosnia: War Crimes Trials Lottery' IWPR's Balkan Crisis Report, 4 March 2005.
- Ivanišević, Bogdan, 'Hague Claims Flawed', IWPR's Tribunal Update No. 379, 30 October 2004.
- IWPR, 'Use and Abuse of Sealed Indictment' IWPR's Tribunal Update No. 369, 30 July 2004,
- IWPR Special Report, 'The Hague Tribunal and Balkan Reconciliation', IWPR's Tribunal Update, No. 462, 21 July 2006.
- Jungvirth, Goran, 'Strugar Jailed for Dubrovnik Attack', IWPR's Tribunal Update No. 392, 5 February 2005.
- Matvejević, Predrag, 'Old Bridges, Old Values' IWPR, War Report Issue, 23 December 1993.
- Sadović, Meridijana, 'Thousands Suspected of Crimes in Bosnia' IWPR's Tribunal Update No. 516, 7 September 2007.
- Tosh, Caroline, 'Can a Fast Trial Be a Fair Trial?', IWPR's Tribunal Update No. 488, 12 February 2007.
- Uzelac, Ana, 'Hague Prosecutors Rest their Case', IWPR's Tribunal Update No. 387, 27 December 2004.

International Centre for Transitional Justice, 'Serbia and Montenegro: Selected Developments in Transitional Justice', October 2004, http://www.ictj.org/.

International Centre for Transitional Justice, 'Bosnia and Herzegovina: Selected Developments in Transitional Justice', October 2004, http://www.ictj.org/.

International Commission on Intervention and State Sovereignty (ICISS), 'The Responsibility to Protect', Report, December 2001, http://www.dfait-maeci.gc.ca/iciss-ciise/report2-en.asp.

OSCE Mission to Bosnia and Herzegovina, Human Rights Department, 'War Crimes Trials before the Domestic Courts of Bosnia and Herzegovina: Progress and Obstacles', March 2005, http://www.oscebih.org/documents/1407-eng.pdf.

Perry Valery, 'ECMI Civil Society Project in Bosnia and Herzegovina: Annex 8 of the General Framework Agreement for Peace and the Role of the Preservation of National Monuments in Successful Peace Implementation' Workshop 2: Implementation, Professionalism and Community Involvement, Banja Luka, Bosnia and Herzegovina, 12 April 2002, European Centre for Minority Issues (ECMI) Report # 29, July 2002, http://www.ecmi.de.

Public International Law and Policy Group, The Balkan Institute, 'Bringing War Criminal to Justice' 1997, www.nesl.edu/center/pubs/warcrim1.htm.

'Report of the International Law Commission on the Work of its 48th Session', *Yearbook of the International Law Commission* (1996) vol. 2, Part 2, 45.

Riedlmayer, András, 'Destruction of Cultural Heritage in Bosnia-Herzegovina, 1992-1996: A Post-War Survey of Selected Municipalities', 2002, Cambridge, Massachusetts, USA, Report presented as Prosecution evidence at the ICTY in the *Milošević* case.

UNESCO *Reports on the Implementation of the 1954 Hague Convention for the Protection of Cultural Property in the Event of Armed Conflict*, received by the Director-General in 1962, 1965-1966, 1969-1970, 1977-1978, 1984, 1989, 1995 and 1998–2004, and published in UNESCO Documents (available at http://portal.unesco.org/culture/en/ev.php):

- CA/RBC/1/3 and Add. 1-6, SHC/MD/1 dated 19 May 1967
- SHC/MD/6 dated 30 April 1970
- CC/MD/41 of July 1979
- CLT/MD/3 of December 1984
- CC/MD/11 of December 1989
- CLT-95/WS/13 of December 1995
- CLT-2005/WS/6, 2005.

UNESCO, 'Protection of Cultural Property in the Event of Armed Conflict, Proceedings of Thursday, 18 March 1999 (on Chapter 4 provisions of the Draft Second Protocol (HC/1999/1/rev1) concerning jurisdiction and responsibility), http://www.unesco.org/culture/legalprotection/war/html_eng/precis18.shtml.

UNESCO, Diplomatic Conference on a Draft Second Protocol to the 1954 Hague Convention for the Protection of Cultural Property in the Event of Armed Conflict 15–26 March 1999, Daily Proceedings of the Diplomatic Conference, Summary Report of the Diplomatic Conference, http://www.unesco.org/culture/legalprotection/war/html_eng/report.shtml.

UNESCO, Diplomatic Conference on the Second Protocol to the Hague Convention for the Protection of Cultural Property in the Event of Armed Conflict (The Hague, 15–26 March 1999), Summary Report, Paris, June 1999, http://unescodoc.unesco.org/images/0013/001332/133243e0/pdf.

UNESCO, Fourth Meeting of the High Contracting Parties to the Convention for the Protection of Cultural Property in the Event of Armed Conflict (The Hague, 1954), UNESCO Headquarters, Paris, 18 November 1999, *Final Report*, CLT-99/CONF.206/4, Paris, December 1999.

UNESCO, Fifth Meeting of the High Contracting Parties to the Convention for the Protection of Cultural Property in the Event of Armed Conflict (The Hague, 1954), UNESCO Headquarters, Paris, 5 November 2001, *Final Report*, CLT-01/CONF/204/4, Paris, 26 November 2001.

UNESCO, *National Implementation of the Penal Provisions of Chapter 4 of the Second Protocol of 26 March 1999 to the Hague Convention of 1954 for the Protection of Cultural Property in the Event of Armed Conflict*, Report prepared by Dr Roger O'Keefe, University of Cambridge, UNESCO Doc. CLT/CIH/MCO/2002/PI/H/1, Paris, 29 March 2002.

UNESCO, *In Focus: Inauguration of Mostar Bridge*, http://portal.unesco.org/en/ev.php.

United Nations, *Report of the Secretary-General Pursuant to Paragraph 2 of Security Council Resolution 808 (1993)*, UN Doc. S/25704 of 3 May 1993, 32 ILM 1159.

United Nations, Economic and Social Council, *Civil and Political Rights, including the Questions of: Independence of the Judiciary, Administration of Justice, Impunity – The Right to Restitution, Compensation and Rehabilitation for Victims of Gross Violations of Human Rights and Fundamental Freedoms*, Final Report of the Special Rapporteur, Cherif Bassiouni, submitted in accordance with Commission Resolution 1999/33, UN ECOSOC, Commission on Human Rights, 56th session, Item 11 (d) of the provisional agenda, E/CN.4/2000/62 of 18 January 2000.

United Nations, *Prevention of Armed Conflict*, Report of the Secretary-General, General Assembly 55th session, Report of the Secretary-General on the work of the Organization, A/55/985, S/2001/574, 7 June 2001.

United Nations, Economic and Social Council, *The Right to a Remedy and Reparation for Victims of Violations of International Human Rights and Humanitarian Law*, Report of the Chairperson-Rapporteur, Ambassador Alejandro Salinas (Chile), on the consultative meeting on the draft Basic principles and guidelines on the right to a remedy and reparation for victims of violations of international human rights and humanitarian law, UN ECOSOC, Commission on Human Rights, 59th session, Item 11 of the provisional agenda (Civil and Political Rights), E/CN.4/2003/63 of 27 December 2002.

United States Institute of Peace, Special Report, *Lawless Rule versus Rule of Law in the Balkans*, December 2002, http://www.usip.org/pubs/specialreports/sr97.html.

United Nations, High Panel on Threats, Challenges and Change, *A More Secure World: Our Shared Responsibility*, 2 December 2004, http://www.un.org/secureworld.

Other Materials

Address by HE Nagendra Singh, Judge at the International Court of Justice, at the celebration of the thirtieth anniversary of the Hague Convention, in UNESCO, *Information on the Implementation of the Convention for the Protection of Cultural Property in the Event of Armed Conflict, The Hague, 1984 Reports*, UNESCO Doc. CLT/MD/3, Paris, December 1984, 15.

Ali, Rabia, and Lawrence Lifschultz, Interview with Ivo Banac, 'The Last Days of Bosnia?' *Boston Review*, February 1994, http://bostonreview.mit.edu/BostonReview/BR19.1/banac.html.

BBC Monitoring International Reports, 'Bosnian Courts Said to Need around 100 Years to Try All War Crimes', Sunday, 12 August 2007 (source: Independent TV Hayat, Sarajevo, in Bosnian/Croatian/Serbian 1700 gmt 9 August 2007, excerpt from report by Bosnia Independent TV Hayat of 9 August), http://listserv.buffalo.edu/archives/justwatch-l.html.

Behram, Alija, 'The World is Destroyed: Criminals Have Destroyed the Old Bridge' *Most* 91(2) November/December 1995, http://www.most.ba/002/050.htm.

Belanov, Mirjana, 'The Mostar Bridge – Conservation Issue', December 1995, http://www.gen-eng.florence.it/stari,ost/10_contr/belanov/belanov01.htm.

Bogdanović, Bogdan, 'Može li grad bez svog mosta, može li most bez svog grada?' ('Can the City be without Its Bridge; Can the Bridge be without Its City?'), *Most*, No. 139, June 2001, http://wl.500.telia.com~u5000875/50/010.htm.

Bos, Adrian, 'The Importance of the 1899, 1907 and 1999 Hague Conferences for the Legal Protection of Cultural Property in the Event of Armed Conflict' December 2005, No. 228 *Museum International* 32.

Bouchenaki, Mounir, 'Breaking the Silence: Sites of Memory' The World Heritage Newsletter, No. 23 (September/October 1999), http://whc.unesco.org/news/23newsen.htm.

Boylan, Patrick, 'The Heritage Dimension in Late 20th Century Culture', Research Paper for the Council of Europe's Task Force on Culture and Development, 1994-95, 13 February 1997, http://www.city.ac.uk/artspol/heritage.html.

Boylan, Patrick, 'Protecting the World's Cultural Heritage in Times of Armed Conflict' (Paper tabled at the symposium in the absence of the author, 1998), http://kafka.uvic.ca/~maltwood/tmr/boylan.html.

Boylan, Patrick, 'Come Hell or High Water' *Source* UNESCO No. 117 November 1999, 10, http://www.unesco.org/sources.

Boylan, Patrick, 'Major New Treaty on Protecting Cultural Property in Times of Armed Conflict Adopted in The Hague, 26 March 1999' *Museum Security Network*, http://www.museum-security.org/boylan.html.

Boylan, Patrick, 'Comparison of Definitions of Cultural Property in Different International Instruments', City University London, http://web.city.ac.uk/artspol/cult-def.html.

Brittain, Victoria, 'Property: Wanton Destruction', *Crimes of War Project*, http://www.crimesofwar.org/thebook/property-wanton.html

Brljavac, Bedrudin, 'Bosnia: Between Ethnic-Nationalism and Europeanization', *TransConflict*, 17 January 2012.

Bugnion, François, 'The Origins and Development of the Legal Protection of Cultural Property in the Event of Armed Conflict', 11 October 2004, http://www.icrc.org/Web/eng/siteengo.nsf/htmlall/65SHTJ.

Burgess, Peter, 'Law and Cultural Identity' Arena Working Paper, WP 97/14, http://www.arena.uio.no/publications/wp97_14.htm.

Burke-White, William, 'The Domestic Influence of International Criminal Tribunals: The International Criminal Tribunal for the Former Yugoslavia and the Creation of the State Court of Bosnia & Herzegovina', 22 October 2007, University of Pennsylvania Law School, Paper 185, http://1sr.nellco.org/upenn/wps/papers/185.

Burnham, Bonnie, 'Architectural Heritage: The Paradox of its Current State of Risk' (World Monuments Watch) 1998 International Cultural Society, 149 (Copy on file with author).

Carnegie Endowment for International Peace, *A Symposium on Destruction and Rebuilding of Architectural Treasures in Bosnia and Herzegovina*, Washington, Monday, 2 May 1994, 8:30 am – 1:00 pm, http://www.kakarigi.net/manu/carnegie.htm.

Centar za mir i multietničku saradnju (Centre for Peace and Multicultural Cooperation) Mostar, 'Mostar Urbicid 1992–1995' ('Mostar Urbicide 1992–1995'), http://www.centarzamir.org.ba/index.html.

Cleere, Henry, 'Preserving our Common Heritage: the 1972 World Heritage Convention', http://www.icomos.org/usicomos/sympoo/cleere.htm.

Coalition for International Justice (CIJ), 'Expert Testifies that Systematic Destruction of Bosnia's Non-Serb Cultural Heritage Largely Took Place in 1992', 23 May 2005.

Coward, Martin, 'Community as Heterogeneous Ensemble: Mostar and Multiculturalism' (Paper prepared for ISA Annual Convention, Chicago 21–24 February 2001, Panel SB05: Methodological Options, Political Consequences (Saturday 24 February, 2001, 10.30am)), http://www.isanet.org/archive/coward.html.

DeSaussure, Hamilton, 'Military Objectives' in *Crimes of War Project*, http://www.crimesofwar.org/thebook/military-objective.html.

Docker, John, 'Raphael Lemkin's History of Genocide and Colonialism', Paper for United States Holocaust Memorial Museum, Centre for Advanced Holocaust Studies, Washington DC, 26 February 2004, http://www.ushmm.org/conscience/events/colonialism/colonialism.php.

Dworkin, Anthony, 'The Trials of Global Justice' Global Policy Forum, 15 June 2005, http://globalpolicy.igc.org/intljustice/icc/2005/0615transitional.htm.

Đikić, Ivica, 'ABC of Croatian Crimes in Bosnia-Herzegovina' (January–May 2001) No. 21/22 *Bosnia Report*, http://www.bosnia.org.uk/news_body.cfm?newsid=1617.

'Bridge Rebuilding', *Ephemera*, 30 July 1998, http://www.wired.com/news/meanwhile/0,1252,0-1998~7,00.html.

European Commission, European Research in Action, 'Endangered Heritage' (printed in Belgium) (Copy on file with author).

Extraordinary Chambers in the Courts of Cambodia, Legal Documents, http://www.ecc.gov.kh/english/documents.

Feral Tribune, 'Historical Transcript: Tuđman on Ethnic Cleansing' *Transitions Online* (Prague), posted on TOL Wire on 17 July 2003, http://www.tol.cz/look/wire/article.tpl?IdLanguage=1&IdPublication=10&NrIssue=733.

Fischer, Horst, 'Principle of Proportionality' in *Crimes of War Project*, http://crimesofwar.org/thebook/proportion-principle.html.

General Engineering, 'The Old Bridge Project, Bridge Description, Part III, 2.3.7. The Destruction Event', http://www.gen-eng.florence.it/starimost/01_intro/descr/des01c.htm.

'Genocide in Bosnia-Herzegovina', A Hearing before the Commission on Security and Cooperation in Europe, Washington, DC, 4 April 1995, http://www.fas.org/irp/congress/1995_hr/genocideinbosnia.html.

Getty Conservation Institute, 'Cultural Heritage and International Law: A Conversation with Lyndel Prott', *Conservation*, The Getty Conservation Institute Newsletter, 16(2), Summer 2001, http://web1getty.edu/.

Global Policy Forum, 'Justice Unfettered? Internationalizing Justice in the Human Rights Era' July 2006, http://www.globalpolicy.org/intljustice/general/2006/0706unfettered.htm.

Global Policy Forum, 'Special Court for Sierra Leone', http://www.globalpolicy.org/intljustice/sierraindx.htm.

Gutman, Roy and Daoud Kuttab, 'Indiscriminate Attack' in *Crimes of War Project*, http://www.crimesofwar.org/thebook/indiscriminate-attack.html.

Guttman, Cynthia, 'Kosovo: Burned Books and Blasted Shrines', Interview with András Riedlmayer, Aga Khan Program Bibliographer at Harvard's Fine Art Library, UNESCO *Courier*, September 2000, http://www.unesco.org/courier/2000_09/uk/signe.htm.

Hampson, Françoise, 'Military Necessity' in *Crimes of War Project*, http://www.crimesofwar.org/thebook/military-necessity.html.

Handwerk, Brian, 'Iraq War Threatens Ancient Treasures' *National Geographic News*, 21 March 2003, http://news.nationalgeographic.com/news/2003/03/0319_030319_iraqiantiquities.html.

'Heritage – The Balkans', presenter: Malcolm Billings, producer: Brigid O'Hara, (episodes 1–4:Wednesday, 15 August 2007, 9.05–9.30am; Wednesday, 22 August 2007, 9.05–9.30am; Wednesday, 29 August 2007, 9.05–9.30am; and Wednesday, 5 September 2007, 9.05–9.30am) BBC Network Radio.

Herscher, Andrew, 'Remembering and Rebuilding in Bosnia' (1998) 5 *Transitions*, http://www.omri.cz/publications/transition/Index.html.

Humo, Džemal, 'Prlić's Shot at Hayreddin – Diary from Hell' *Most*, January-February 1996, http://wl500.telia.com/~u50008760/2122/2122_056.htm.

Humo, Džemal, 'Prlićev pucanj u Hajrudina' (Prlić's Shot at Hayreddin') *Most*, No. 110-111, February, 1999, 4, http://ww1.500.telia.com/~u50008760/2122/2122_056.htm.

Humphreys, Stephen, 'The Destruction of Cultural Memory' (2001 Presidential Address), *Middle East Studies Association Bulletin*, Summer 2002, http://w3fp.arizona.edu/mesassoc/bulletin/Pres%20Addresses/humphreys.htm.

ICOMOS Sweden/Central Board of National Antiquities/Swedish National Commission for UNESCO, *Information As an Instrument for Protection against War Damages to the Cultural Heritage. Report from a Seminar, June 1994* Stockholm, Svenska Unescoradets skriftserie, 4/1994 (1994) Stockholm: ICOMOS Sweden.

ICRC Advisory Service on International Humanitarian Law, 'Practical Advice for the Protection of Cultural Property in the Event of Armed Conflict', http://www.icrc.org.

ICRC, 'National Implementation of International Humanitarian Law: Protection of Cultural Property', http://www.icrc.org/Web/eng/siteengo.nsf.

ICRC, 'Protection of Cultural Property in Armed Conflict: A Collection of Basic Rules Disseminated during the Kosovo Conflict' 30 September 2001, No. 843 *International Review of the Red Cross* 862.

ICRC, 'The Origins of the Legal Protection of Cultural Property in the Event of Armed Conflict under Treaty-Based and Customary International Humanitarian Law', meeting to mark the 50th anniversary of the Hague Convention of 1954 Cairo, 14 February 2004, http://www.icrc.org/Web/eng/siteengo.nsf/html/5XUAR6.

ICTY Outreach Programme, 'View from The Hague: Heritage Destruction' Balkan, 24 March 2004, 6, http://www.un.org/icty/bhs/outreach/arcticles/eng/article-040324e.htm.

ICTY Factsheet, 'Partnership and Transition between the ICTY and National Courts', http://www.un.org/icty/cases-e/factsheets/partnership-e.htm.

Integrated Coastal Management, Bosnia-Herzegovina – ICM Country Profile, http://www.globaloceans.org/country/bosniaherzegovina.html.

International Criminal Court, Situations and Cases, http://www.icc-cpi.int/cases.html.

International Criminal Tribunal for the Former Yugoslavia, 'Bringing Justice to the Former Yugoslavia: The Tribunal's Five Core Achievements', http://www.un.org/icty/glance/index.htm.

IRIN In-Depth, 'Justice for a Lawless World? Rights and Reconciliation in a New Era of International Law: Justice Unfettered? Internationalising Justice in the Human Rights Era' July 2006, http://www.irinnews/org/webspecials/RightsAnd reconciliation/default.asp.

IRIN News, 'The Price of Healing' 4 August 2006, http://listserv.buffalo.edu/archives/justwatch-l.html.

Kaiser, Colin, 'Crimes against Culture' *UNESCO Courier* September 2000, 41.

Kebo, Alija, 'A Letter of the Editor: A Two-Year Day of Mourning' *Most* 91(2) November/December 1995, http://www.most.ba/002/006.htm.

Lawrence, Karen, 'International Dimensions of Genocide' London School of Economics and Political Science, 1996, http://www.veritnet.com/karen/genocide.html.

Lazarus Kgalema, 'Symbols of Hope: Monuments as Symbols of Remembrance and Peace in the Process of Reconciliation', Research paper written for the Centre for the Study of Violence and Reconciliation, October 1999, http://www.csvr.orgza/papers/papkgal1.htm.

Lemkin, Raphaël, 'Acts Constituting a General (Transnational) Danger Considered as Offences against the Law of Nations', Additional explications to the Special Report presented to the 5th Conference for the Unification of Penal Law in Madrid (14–20 October 1933), http://www.preventgenocide.org/lemkin/madrid1933-english.htm.

Levin, Jeffrey, 'Cultural Heritage under Fire', *Conservation at the Getty*, Newsletter 7.1 Winter 1992, http://www.getty.edu/conservation/publications/ewsletters/7_1/cultural.html.

Little, Alan, 'Bridging the Bosnian Divide' BBC News, From Our Own Correspondent, Saturday, 24 July 2004 at 11.30 BST on BBC Radio 4, http://news.bbc.co.uk/go/pr/fr//2hl/programmes/from_our_own_correspondent/3919839.stm.

Lovrenović, Ivan, 'Svijet bez mosta – Mostar, devet godina poslije' ('The World without the Bridge – Mostar, Nine Years Later') *Dani* (Bosnia and Herzegovina), Archives, No. 256, http://www.bhdani.com/arhiva/256/t25614.shtml.

Maass, Peter, 'Cultural Property and Historical Monuments' in *Crimes of War Project*, http://www.crimesofwar.org/thebook/cultural_property-histor.html.

Malić, Gordan, 'Herzeg-Lager' *Bosnia Report*, Issue 15, April-June 1996.

Matsuura, Koïchiro, Director-General of UNESCO at the Opening of the Fifth Meeting of the States Parties to the 1954 Hague Convention for the Protection of Cultural Property in the Event of Armed Conflict, DG/2001/115, UNESCO, 5 November 2001.

Matsuura, Koïchiro, 'Why We Need the [O]ld [B]ridge at Mostar?', 6 July 2004, http://portal.unesco.org/en/ev.php.

Matvejević, Predrag, 'The Bridge', *Most*, No. 91, November–December 1995, http://www.most.ba/002/062.htm.

Meron, Theodor, 'Customary Law' in *Crimes of War Project*, http://www.crimesofwar.org/thebook/customary-law.html.

Merryman, John, 'Cultural Property, International Trade, and Human Rights' in *Occasional Papers in Intellectual Property*, New York, NY, Benjamin Cardozo School of Law, Yeshiva University, No. 9, 2000, http://www.cardozo.yu.edu/news_events/papers/9.pdf.

'Mostar Bridge', Video, ABC, 7 October 2003, 9.20 pm (Copy on file with author).

'Mostar: The Old Bridge', Video, SBS, Tuesday, 24 July 2001, 8.00-8.30 pm (Copy on file with author).

'Mostar 2004' – Official website on the Re-Inauguration of the Old Bridge and the Old City of Mostar, http://www.mostar2004.ba/.

'Mostar Restores Its Ancient Bridge, but Hangs on to Ethnic Politics', Feature Service: World, 7 February 2004, 7:41:00 am, http://www.chn.ir/english/eshownews.asp?no=1886.

Nafziger, James, 'Protection of Cultural Heritage in Time of War and Its Aftermath', *International Foundation for Art Research* (IFAR), http://www.ifar.org/heritage.htm.

O'Connell, Mary, 'Occupation Failures and the Legality of Armed Conflict: The Case of Iraqi Cultural Property' Ohio State University Moritz College of Law Working Paper Series (2004) Paper 6, http://law.bepress.com/osulwps/moritzlaw/art6.

Oručević, Safet, Letter to the Mostar Citizens (by the City Mayor) about the reconstruction of the Old Bridge, 'The Oldest and the Youngest' *Most*, No. 91 (2) November/December 1995, http://www.most.ba/002/010.htm.

Pašić, Amir, 'Culture, Identity, and Security: An Overview', Project on World Security Rockefeller Brothers Fund, 1998.

Pašić, Amir, 'Mostar in Bosnia and Herzegovina', Mostar 2004 Workshop, Introductory Remarks, http://www.mostar2004-ircica.org/files/95/95lecture2.html.

Petrovic, Jadranka, 'Cultural Property Protection in International Law' (Paper presented at the National Postgraduate Law Students Conference 2002, Melbourne Law School, The University of Melbourne, 28–30 June 2002, Sunday 30 June 2002) (unpublished, copy on file with author).

Petrovic, Jadranka, 'The Destruction of Cultural Property as a War Crime' (2007) (unpublished manuscript, on file with author).

Petrovic, Jadranka, 'The World Heritage List Sites and Other Cultural Property at the ICTY' (2007) (unpublished manuscript, on file with author).

Piliso-Seroke, Joyce and Puleng LenkaBula, 'Cultural Genocide, Identity and Nation Building in Post-Apartheid South Africa' (2001) Institute for Justice and Reconciliation (paper), http://www.ijr.org.za/papers/seroke.html.

Polimac, A., 'Some New Data about the Old Bridge' *Most* 1977, 14.

'Prevent Crimes against Culture' The World Heritage Newsletter, 30 May-June 2001, http://www.unesco.org/opi2/afghan-crisis/.

Radio-Most, Interview with Safer Halilović, in Sarajevo, and Slobodan Praljak, in Zagreb, on who is responsible for Croat-Muslim armed conflict in Bosnia and Herzegovina, 28 February, 1999, 13:45 (Transcript on file with author).

Rado, Gabby, 'Legitimate Military Targets' in *Crimes of War Project*, http://www.crimesofwar.org/thebook/legit-military-target.html.

Radović, Darko, 'War in Yugoslavia and the Right to the City' (paper), http://www.arbld.unimelb.edu.au/envjust/papers/.

Ratner, Steven, 'Categories of War Crimes' in *Crimes of War Project*, http://www.crimesofwar.org/thebok/war-crimes-categories.html.

Ratner, Steven, 'International v Internal Armed Conflict' in *Crimes of War Project*, http://www.crimesofwar.org/thebook/intl-vs-internal.html.

Ravn, Bente, 'Bridge over Troubled Waters' first published in SFOR *Informer* # 11 May 1997, http://www.nato.int/sfor/engineers/mostarbridge/intoduction/introduc.htm.

Records of the Conference Convened by the United Nations, Educational, Scientific and Cultural Organization, Held at The Hague from 21 April to 14 May 1954, (1961) Government of the Netherlands, The Hague, Staatsdrukkerijen Uitgevrijbedrijf.

'Re-Inauguration of the Old Bridge of Mostar', video, July 2004, combined TV Networks (Copy on file with author).

Riedlmayer, András, 'Killing Memory: The Targeting of Bosnia's Cultural Heritage', Testimony presented at a Hearing of the Commission on Security and Cooperation in Europe, US Congress, 4 April 1995, Community of Bosnia Foundation, http://www.haverford.edu.relg/sells/killing.html.

Riedlmayer, András, 'Erasing the Past: The Destruction of Libraries and Archives in Bosnia-Herzegovina' (July 1995) *Middle East Studies Association Bulletin*, http://fparizona.edu/mesassoc/Buletin/bosni.htm.

Rosenberg, Jack, 'UN to Prosecute Culture Crimes' (1994) 82 *Art in America*, http://www.members.tripod.com/UnconqueredBosnia/Cultur2.html.

Schmitt, Michael, 'Rethinking the Geneva Conventions' 30 January 2003 in *Crimes of War Project*, http://www.crimesofwar.org/expert/genevaConventions/gc-schmitt.html.

Schmitt, Michael, 'The Law of Belligerent Occupation' in *Crimes of War Project*, 15 April 2003, http://www.crimesofwar.org/expert/.

School for Peacekeeping Mission at Amersfort Army Base (Prins Bernhardkazerne), 'Instruction Cultural Awareness', http://odin.let.rug.nl/CB/CBe_les.html.

Shearer, Ivan, 'Rules of Conduct during Humanitarian Interventions', http://www.unc.edu/depts/diplomat/archives_roll/2001_07_09/hum_intervention/hum.

Shimmon, Ross, 'The Blue Shield: the Cultural Red Cross?' World Library and Information Congress: 69th IFLA General Conference and Council Satellite Meeting, 31 July-1 August 2003, http://www.ifla.org/blueshield.htm.

Society for the Protection of Ancient Buildings (SPAB), 'The SPAB Manifesto: The Principals of the Society for the Protection of Ancient Buildings as Set Forth upon its Foundation (1877)', http://www.getty.edu/conservation/research_resources/charters/charter00.html.

Statement by the Board of AAM/ICOM on the Destruction of Cultural Property in Yugoslavia, 10 December 1991, http://ww.aam-us.org/aamicomstatement.htm.

Stone, Alby, 'The Perilous Bridge' *At the Edge*, No 1, 1996, http://www.indigogroup.co.uk/edge/pbridge.htm.

Symposium: 'The Scope of Genocide Research', University of Tokyo, Komaba Campus, 13 December 2003.

Tatz, Colin, 'Genocide in Australia', AIATSIS Research Discussion Papers No. 8, Australian Institute of Aboriginal and Torres Strait Islander Studies (1999), http://www.aiatsis.gov.au/rsrch_dp/genocide.htm.

Taylor, Laurie, 'The Limits of Bridge Building' BBC Radio 4 – Thinking Allowed, 27 November 2002, http://www.bbc.co.uk/radio04/factual/thinkingallowed_20021127.shtml.

The United Kingdom Parliament, Select Committee on Culture, Media and Sport, Appendices to the Minutes of Evidence, Appendix 11, 'Memorandum Submitted by the European Association of Archaeologists', http://www.publications.parliament.uk/pa/cm199900/cmselect/cmcumeds/371/371ap1.

Theissen, Gunnar, 'Supporting Justice, Co-existence and Reconciliation after Armed Conflict: Strategies for Dealing with the Past', http://www.berghof-handbook.net.

Tsang, Louise, 'Legal Protection of Cultural Property: A Selective Resource Guide', http://www.llrx.com/features/culturalproperty.htm.

UN & Conflict Monitor, 'A Digest of News and Documents Focusing on the UN's Role in Conflict Prevention, Management and Resolution, Peacekeeping, Peacebuilding and Peacemaking' *UN & Conflict Monitor* Issue 9, Autumn 2000, http://www.brad.ac.uk/acad/confres/monitor/UNmonitor9.pdf.

UN Secretary-General's Message to the World Culture Open (delivered by Mr Maurice Strong, Special Advisor and Personal Envoy of the Secretary-General), New York, 10 September 2004, http://www.un.org/apps/sg/.

UN General Assembly, Social, Humanitarian and Cultural Committee (Third Committee), Topic Area One: Genocide, Topic Area Two: Preservation and Protection of Culture, Harvard World MUN, Bello Horizonte 2002.

UNESCO, Address by Mr Federico Mayor, Director-General of the United Nations Educational, Scientific and Cultural Organisation (UNESCO) at the opening of the Diplomatic Conference on the draft Second Protocol to the Convention for the Protection of Cultural Property in the Event of Armed Conflict, DG/99/9, The Hague, 15 March 1999.

UNESCO, Address by Mr Koïchiro Matsuura, Director-General of the United Nations Educational, Scientific and Cultural Organisation (UNESCO), at the Opening of the Fifth Meeting of the States Parties to the 1954 Hague Convention for the Protection of Cultural Property in the Event of Armed Conflict, DG/2001/115, UNESCO, 5 November 2001.

UNESCO, 'Preface to the Inserts on The Second Protocol to the Hague Convention of 1954 for the Protection of Cultural Property in the Event of Armed Conflict1999', http://www.unesco.org.

UNESCO, 'Stari Most, Old Bridge of Mostar', 2003, UNESCO, http://portal.unesco.org/culture/en/ev.php.

UNESCO, 'Rebuilding of Stari Most (Old Bridge) and the Rehabilitation of the Old Town of Mostar', http://www.unesco.org/opi2/starimost.htm.

UNESCO Culture Sector, 'Bosnia Cultural Heritage: A Bridge to a Shared Future', the International Conference of Ministers on Culture of South-Eastern Europe and Italy in Mostar (Bosnia and Herzegovina), 19 July 2004, adopted 'Mostar Declaration', Joint declaration of the Ministers responsible for culture in South-East Europe and Italy concerning the enhancement of cultural heritage for the stabilisation and the sustainable development of the region, Mostar (Bosnia and Herzegovina), 19 July 2004; and Action Plan for the Implementation of the Mostar Declaration, 19 July 2004, http://portal.unesco.org/culture/en/ev.php.

UNESCO, Culture of Peace Program (1998), http://www.peace.ca/unesco.htm.

UNESCO Culture Sector, 'UNESCO and Cultural Heritage: UNESCO's Action', http://portal.unesco.org/culture/en/ev.php.

UNESCO, World Heritage, 'Old Bridge Area of the Old City of Mostar', 2006 New Inscriptions, http://whc.unesco.org/en/list/946.

UNESCO, 'Protect Cultural Property in the Event of Armed Conflict', Information Kit, 2008, UNESCO Doc. CLT/CIH/MCO/2008/PI/69/REV., http://portal.unesco.org/en/ev.php.

Vasić, M., 'About the Building of the Old Bridge of Mostar' *Balcanica* 1977, VII.

Verrengia, Joseph, 'Wiping out a Cultural Heritage is a Kind of Cultural Genocide', *The Associated Press,* 13 March 2003, http://aanf.org/midwest/mar2003/wiping_out.htm.

Wenzel, Marian, 'Cultural Preservation and the Dayton Accord', *Bosnia Report*, The Bosnian Institute, Issue 14, February-March 1996, http://www.bosnia.org.uk/bosrep/febmar96/culture.cfm.

'Who Owns Culture? War and Cultural Property', National Arts Journalism Program, 58, http://www.WhoOwnsCulture/058-071War&CulturalProperty.pdf.

Woodard, Colin, 'Stillborn' *Bulletin of the Atomic Scientists* vol 56, Issue 4, Saturday, 1 July 2000, 7/1/00 Bull. Atom. Scientists 1719 2000 WL 1049 163, http://web2.westlaw.com.

World Monuments Watch, 'Countering Cultural Terrorism: A Response to the Destruction in Afghanistan', http://www.wmf.org/html/programs/Afghanistan.html.

Websites

http://fletcher.tuft.edu/multi/cultural.html.

http://fletcher.tufts.edu/multi/warfare.html.

http://listserv.buffalo.edu/archives/justwatch-1.html.

http://mapa.fit.ba/mgm/MapaGradaMostara.swf.

http://nuremberg.law.harvard.edu/php/docs_swi.php?DI=I&text=overview.

http://portal.unesco.org/en/ev.php.

http://whc.unesco.org/.

http://www.crimesofwar.org/thebook/.

http://www.culturalheritagelaw.org/.

http://www.ets.uwe.ac.uk/genocide/.

http://www.european-heritage.net/sdx/herein/.

http://www.globalpolicy.org/intljustice/general/.

http://www.ial.uk.com.

http://www.icc-cij.org.

http://www.icc-cpi.int/Menus/ICC/Situations+and+Cases/.

http://www.iccrom.org.

http://www.icj-cij.org.

http://www.icrc.org.

http://www.icrc.org/ihl.nsf/WebFULL?OpenView.

http://www.international.icomos.org/home.htm.

http://www.mazal.org/Default.htm.

http://www.nizkor.org/hweb/people/.

http://www.2.rgu.ac.uk/schools.mcrg/stdoc.htm.

http://www.unesco.org.

http://www.un.org.

http://www.un.org/ictr.

http://www.un.org/icty.

http://www.yale.edu/lawweb/avalon/imt/imt.htm#proc.

http://www.yale.edu/lawweb/avalon/lawofwar/hague02.htm.

Index

D

E

F

G

H

I

J

K

L

M

Q

R

S

T

U